SOUTH ASIAN FILMSCAPES

SOUTH ASIAN FILMSCAPES

Transregional Encounters

EDITED BY

ELORA HALIM CHOWDHURY

ESHA NIYOGI DE

UNIVERSITY OF WASHINGTON PRESS

Seattle

Composed in Minion Pro, typeface designed by Robert Slimbach

24 23 22 21 20 5 4 3 2 1

Printed and bound in the United States of America

UNIVERSITY OF WASHINGTON PRESS
uwapress.uw.edu

LIBRARY OF CONGRESS CATALOGING-IN-PUBLICATION DATA
LC record available at https://lccn.loc.gov/2020013711
LC ebook record available at https://lccn.loc.gov/2020013712

ISBN 978-0-295-74784-2 (hardcover), ISBN 978-0-295-74785-9 (paperback),
ISBN 978-0-295-74786-6 (ebook)

COVER PHOTOGRAPH: *Meherjaan* (dir. Rubaiyat Hossain, 2011). Image courtesy of Rubaiyat Hossain.

The paper used in this publication is acid free and meets the minimum requirements of American National Standard for Information Sciences—Permanence of Paper for Printed Library Materials, ANSI Z39.48–1984.∞

Elora dedicates this book to her mother, Shamsun Nahar Chowdhury, whose stories about love, intimacy, community, and loss inspired her to pursue nondominant knowledges about 1971 and gender justice.

Esha dedicates this book to the memory of her grandfather, Jnananjan Niyogi, friend to impoverished Muslims in British Calcutta and Freedom Fighter.

CONTENTS

ACKNOWLEDGMENTS

This volume, the inaugural publication of the South Asian Regional Media Scholars Network (SARMSNet), has been inspired by a series of stimulating conferences and discussions held across Pakistan, India, and Bangladesh.

The editors and cofounders of SARMSNet wish to thank the American Institute of Pakistan Studies and the then president of AIPS, Kamran Asdar Ali, for their generous support in organizing the SARMSNet conference at the Lahore University of Management Sciences in Pakistan.

Esha is deeply thankful to colleagues Ali Khan at LUMS and Abhijit Roy and Madhuja Mukherjee at Jadavpur University for co-organizing conferences, in Lahore and Kolkata respectively, and for coimagining with her what "transregional cinema" means on these grounds. For Elora's intellectual comradeship, Esha's gratitude is immeasurable—for jointly envisioning and founding SARMSNet, and for carrying forward our cross-border vision with so much courage and solidarity. As always, Suranjan has been her partner and supporter through the thick and thin of these cross-border endeavors.

Elora is grateful for the transregional conversations and friendships that spawned both SARMSNet and this volume. In particular, she is grateful to Esha for her keen convictions and steadfast commitments to intellectual and political inquiry. She is forever in debt to the cross-generational, cross-national, and cross-historical exchanges and relationships enabled and envisioned in the pages of this book.

The Regional Fulbright Scholars Program both funded Esha's transregional scholarship and helped her cross borders in South Asia. Esha extends thanks for all their help and guidance to Catherine Johnston Matto in Washington, DC, Zulfikar Ali Bhutto in Islamabad, Shevanti Narayan in Kolkata, and Shaheen Khan in Dhaka.

Elora and Esha are deeply appreciative of Larin McLaughlin, our brilliant editor at the University of Washington Press, who believed in and nurtured this project. Tremendous gratitude to Hanni Jalil, assistant editor, for shepherding the authors through the various stages of publication. It has been an absolute joy to work with the University of Washington Press team.

Shilpi Suneja, Emma Stoskopf Ehrlich, and Riva Pearson provided meticulous and diligent editorial support. Warm appreciation to them for making the manuscript submission process so smooth and efficient. The College of Liberal Arts Deans Office at University of Massachusetts Boston funded travel and research for the book, and the authors are grateful for their generous support.

SOUTH ASIAN FILMSCAPES

INTRODUCTION

TRANSREGIONAL ARCHIVES, CINEMATIC ENCOUNTERS

Filmscapes across South Asia

ELORA HALIM CHOWDHURY AND ESHA NIYOGI DE

IF ONE STUDIES THE HISTORIES OF INDUSTRIAL AND INDEPENDENT cinemas in South Asia, an intertwining of South Asian histories and their mutual cultural influences becomes apparent. These histories illuminate how film cultures that presuppose geopolitical and social boundaries are at the same time porous and hybrid. Cinematic portrayals and their material contexts encode, on the one hand, the effects of the massive geopolitical rifts born in postcolonial South Asia of religious, linguistic, and ethnic conflicts—the primary ones being the India-Pakistan Partition (1947) and the Bangladesh Liberation War (1971). Practices and policies of cinema in the nation-states (India, Pakistan, and Bangladesh) likewise reinforce prevailing hierarchies of identity and belonging. On the other hand, the combined histories of cinema and sociality in the South Asian region are replete with cross-fertilization, the effects of which lingered on well past the Partition of India and Pakistan and the birth of Bangladesh.

This edited volume is born of a collaborative effort to excavate the complex politics and poetics of bordered identity and of crossing. While a number of the chapters reveal ways in which fixed notions of national identity have been destabilized by the cross-border mobility of filmed arts and practitioners, several others interrogate how filmic politics intersect with discourses around nationalism, sexuality and gender, religion, and language. Overall, we attempt a fluid and interconnected approach to studying these multiple histories and encounters that conjures South Asia as a geographic and political entity in the region and globally, through a cinematic imagination. Spread evenly across the subcontinent, the historical and theoretical perspectives collected in this volume call upon us to rethink the southern region per se—both in terms of filmic geographies and, more generally, as a field of knowledge production. Not only does our volume illuminate the *necessity of reaching into archives* hitherto unexplored or even unrecognized as sources of knowledge about cinemas and the region; beyond this, we essay methods of regional inquiry that pivot on *a multiplicity of historical perspectives and affects.* These perspectives encounter, complement, and inflect one another. While encounters between historical perspectives and formations are portrayed or implied within the texts studied by individual authors, they are also implicit across the chapters. This book stages a rare scholarly colloquy between frames of reference spread across India, Pakistan, and Bangladesh. Our introduction provides that account.

TRANSREGIONAL ARCHIVES: FILMSCAPES ACROSS SOUTH ASIA

Film archives constitute what Nasreen Rehman calls a "multisensory" historical lens (see chapter 5 in this volume). These archives contain multiple affective insights into the connected histories of a border-riddled region such as South Asia, because the cinema is susceptible to opposite trends of boundary formation and of rupture. To begin with, infrastructures of production and exhibition tend to be restricted by national and global regimes of finance and of knowledge. Furthermore, the aesthetic form of the narrative moving image replete with shooting and editing mechanisms guides the viewer's "directionality of observation" (Fuhrmann 2017, 253). The camera could tutor the viewer in ways of looking at the other and distinguishing the same (Kaplan 1993), just as it could "literalize" the boundaries of space (Rosen 2006, 5). Plot lines likewise could control the meaning of human movement across space, aiding in the framing and suturing of bodies and destinations such that the timelines of propriety, civility, and historical agency are defined.

Yet as a "collaborative medium" (Cook 2012, 252) of producing knowledge in multiple sensory forms, the cinema also is open to competing social and political claims staked by the makers, financiers, and target audiences. The form could well be deployed to exceed or to transgress division and hierarchy as well as to critique cognitive categories, be they regional, statist, or global. Thus, cinematic archives contain contradictory insights on sociality and personhood. These insights are immanent in the processes of shooting, editing, and weaving in of stories with myriad voices and speech forms. In this vein, plot weaving and storytelling themselves could acquire what Walter Benjamin (1968, 84, 88) calls the "full corporeality . . . [of] social process" through the ways in which they inflect voices and languages of the many other storytellers who remain nameless and unheard. All in all, cinematic archives not only reinforce teleology but also imply an "'equal rights' perspective on temporality" (Fuhrmann 2017, 256). Delving into selected archives of the cinema in South Asia, the studies in the volume uncover complex spatiotemporalities—bounded, hybrid, and dissident.

Part 1, "Nations and Regional Margins," focuses on films navigating borders and differences internal to the nation-states of Bangladesh, Pakistan, and India. Examining homogenous national formations of language, geography, religion, and gender, some authors delineate how film cultures marginalize or subsume nonnormative identities and regional peripheries. Glen Hill and Kabita Chakma illuminate the exoticization of the indigenous non-Bengali and the Chittagong Hill region in Bangladeshi cinema, whereas Amit Ranjan discusses how an assimilation of religious difference goes hand in hand with the suppression of cultural inequities in Bollywood representations of the patriotic Sikh hero. Authors also delve into archives of independent and experimental-mainstream cinema to explore how margins of national, religious, sexual, and labor structures are performed on screen, fragmenting binary categories. Fahmidul Haq examines alternative figurations of Islam and Bengaliness while Chakma and Hill delineate the poetics of Fourth filmmaking in the Chittagong Hill Tracts. For his part, Kamran Asdar Ali excavates queer desires (same-sex, incestuous) that irrupt into Pakistani representations of bourgeois nationalist family values. Nasreen Rehman's study of an ambivalent politics of female labor and patriarchal hierarchy complements Ali's exploration of experimental Urdu cinema in Pakistan.

Part 2, "Transregional Crossings," turns the lens to filmic histories of porosity and cross-fertilization on the subcontinent and beyond. The chapters by Madhuja Mukherjee and Lotte Hoek are contrapuntal to studies of dominant and alternative national trends in part 1 insofar as they delve into forgotten archives of film practice connecting lives and professions between statist hierarchies. Mukherjee studies how pre-Partition exhibition culture interlinked cities such as Calcutta and Lahore, whereas Hoek uncovers hidden records of Urdu filmmaking in Dhaka. Illuminating the porosity of aesthetic and production practices in regional-language Indian films (post-independence), Hariprasad Athanickal demonstrates that mainstream cinemas cross-fertilize films by parallel authors in South India. Gwendolyn Kirk and Esha Niyogi De follow the mobility of Pakistani genres (Punjabi and Urdu), artists, and resources on and beyond the subcontinent. Their studies demonstrate that locations elsewhere provide both aesthetic grounds (Kirk, Niyogi De) and infrastructures (Niyogi De) for unsettling statist/linguistic dominance (Kirk) and censorship (Niyogi De) in Pakistan. Examining Pakistani New Cinema, Zebunnisa Hamid situates the practice at the intersection of a post-9/11 Pakistani state, the international war on terror, and shifts in local media culture.

Part 3, "Fractured Geographies, South Connectivities," inflects the emphasis on cinematic and regional porosity in earlier chapters by focusing on border-war and trauma films produced in South Asia. Turning to archives both of narrative cinema and of documentaries, authors in this part examine works portraying the vicissitudes of the Bangladesh Liberation War (Akhter, Junaid), postwar trauma (Chowdhury), and state violence in India (Kurian). Considering Bangladesh Liberation War cinema in a comparative light, both Fahmida Akhter and Naadir Junaid interconnect archives of Third Cinema and liberation struggles across regions of the global South. On their part, Alka Kurian and Elora Halim Chowdhury position South Asian trauma films in relation to archives of the women-of-color South located within the global North. While both Akhter and Chowdhury note the gendered inflections in nationalist trauma films, Chowdhury demonstrates that feminist national cinema in Bangladesh stages encounters between different South Asian perspectives.

The parts of this volume work together to situate questions of identity, difference, and conflict at the transregional crossroads of subcontinental and global histories of cinema and social politics. Our *transregional* approach to South Asian film cultures attempts to move beyond the typical "spatial containers" (Harootunian 2012, 7) of area studies. Historically, these containers have included static geographical boundaries (defining remote world regions and nations during the Cold War era) and "permanent ethnocultural determinations" of identities (found in post–Berlin Wall area studies) (Harootunian 2012, 7). Our notion of the transregional rides the crest of a recent imperative to transform area and identity studies into an analytic for "comparative and global contexts of regional experience" (Bentley 2005, 1). Moreover, we clarify the *trans* in our regional approach in at least two ways. On the one hand, we take transregional to signify *heterogeneous cinematic movements*. These encompass aesthetic, material, and critical processes moving both *across* borders (statist, subnational) within the South Asian region and also *beyond* the historical space of the subcontinent to interrelate with other regions of the global South. On the other hand, we assume that a transregional approach to postcolonial South Asia necessarily accounts for *binary mobility*, that is, the process of *moving to* a one-sided destination that excludes other sides and perspectives (a telling example is the high-caste Sikh man's destination of patriotic heroism in Hindu-centric Bollywood cinema, post-Pogrom; see chapter 3). As such, our transregional framework extends the critical insights on global mobility and border conflict offered by transnational studies.[1] By underscoring regional archives hitherto unexplored or unrecognized in global spaces, we eschew the emphases on global North migrations and ethnicities customary to transnational cultural and cinema studies (see, e.g., Naficy 2001; White 2015). We attempt also to think beyond transnational comparative approaches that enclose subcontinental cinema within a Bollywood/Hollywood framework and, by implication, a south/north dichotomy (see, e.g., Kaur and Sinha 2005). Instead, we focus on south-south cinematic relations that at once unsettle the nation-state as a rigid formation and point to the processes of its formation and ruptures.

In this vein, our volume shines light on South Asia as a web of *filmscapes*, understood as sets of "perspectival . . . landscapes" (Appadurai 1990, 296) made, experienced, navigated, transformed, and challenged by agents. This notion permits us to explore how perspectival landscapes unfold both on and off the screen, conditioned as much by geopolitical and financial formations as by affective and theoretical legacies. While each chapter investigates a specific cultural landscape, combined, the studies in this book engage in an interdisciplinary encounter of perspectival approaches to multisensory cinematic archives. While film historians explore archives against and with the grain (Hoek, Haq, Hill and Chakma, Hamid) or plumb the archeology of cinema and society (Mukherjee), cultural and linguistic anthropologists read the corporeality of plots, dialogue, and speech forms as "allegories" (Marcus 1995, 109) that disturb institutional orders (Asdar Ali, Kirk, Chowdhury). Scholars of cinematic practice relate sensory forms onscreen to sociologies of production and infrastructure (Rehman, Athanickal, Niyogi De), whereas political historians emphasize filmic responses to conflict or oppression (Ranjan, Akhtar, Kurian).

The authors collected here certainly draw on prevalent paradigms of South Asian cinema studies that theorize nationalism and regionality (Vasudevan 2000; Dadi 2016; Srinivas 2015); the ambiguities of cultural and religious identity formation (Raju 2015); or the contradictions of statist capital and heterogeneous flows (Gazdar 1997; Khan and Ahmad 2016). Yet both individually and collectively, the chapters of this book substantially extend the current field of South Asian inquiry by speaking to the knowledge gaps bred in and about the subcontinent through historical rifts and global conditions. As we discuss in the next section, this volume as a whole arose from encounters between historical perspectives and affect. These encounters illuminate the conflicted landscape our book traverses in relation to the histories of South Asia, both as a geopolitical formation and as a field of knowledge production.

BACKSTORIES: HISTORIES, BORDERS, ENCOUNTERS

This book is the first publication by the South Asian Regional Media Scholars Network (SARMSNet), an alliance set up by the coeditors of this volume to enable joint research and cross-regional dialogues on film and media in relation to geopolitics across South Asia. The idea of the network was born from conversations in the course of a regional (multicountry) Fulbright fellowship that had taken Esha Niyogi De to India, Pakistan, and Bangladesh in 2013–14, for the study of border-crossing women-made cinemas. It has since blossomed through a series of conferences held in the subcontinent, as well as through scholarly interactions in virtual space, sponsored by the American Institute of Pakistan Studies and universities in Pakistan and India (detailed below). The support for cross-regional and comparative research on South Asia by these major funding institutions of the United States (Fulbright, AIPS) stems no doubt from the recent "mobility turn" (Mielke and Hornidge 2017, 3) in the notions of area and identity described in the previous section. Yet the backstory of SARMSNet demonstrates how institutional perspectives on both area research and area policing, held by global/national interest groups, shift as individual agents and perspectival landscapes encounter one another.

As she spoke to scholars at her Fulbright host institutions and elsewhere in India, Pakistan, and Bangladesh, Esha Niyogi De was repeatedly struck by a number of shared concerns and hopes about the study of filmic and historical connectivities across South Asia. On one side, scholars expressed regret about their ignorance of films and cultural archives in neighboring countries, especially in India with regard to popular Pakistani and Bangladeshi cinemas. This point was reiterated by Indian film studies faculty at Jadavpur University, including Moinak Biswas and Madhuja Mukherjee (author of chapter 7). On another side, scholars across these countries were extremely eager to converse about intertwined cultural and familial linkages at the same time as they confronted the political challenge of cross-border exchange across a fractured subcontinent. As described by Abhijit Roy from Jadavpur University in India, interactions are urgently needed between the few "liberal-secular efforts (by academics, artists . . .) strewn" across the "conflicting states" of the subcontinent to counteract "outfits who are against 'any kind' of relations" in this region. Likewise, Ali Khan, from Lahore University of Management Sciences in Pakistan, called on "academics . . . to find innovative ways to promote a shared vision and understanding of . . . history, tradition and culture" across South Asia. Ali Khan and Abhijit Roy (jointly with Madhuja Mukherjee) were later to lead the efforts in co-organizing SARMSNet conferences at their own universities (in 2016 and 2018, respectively). Immediately after her Fulbright travels, Esha Niyogi De was joined by Elora Halim Chowdhury from University of Massachusetts Boston in cofounding SARMSNet as a transnational initiative. This scholarly alliance was especially meaningful for De and Chowdhury because they speak to each other from a *dui Bangla* / two Bengals perspective. Both share the linguistic heritage of Bengal, one of two regions of the subcontinent fractured by the Partition of 1947.

The hopes and concerns about transregional collaborations voiced by like-minded scholars, narrated above, responded eloquently to the academic and personal inclinations that had motivated Esha Niyogi De's idea of a region-encompassing Fulbright project in the first place. The project had been inspired as much by De's comparative interests in border-crossing cinema and gender (see chapter 8) as through her family's histories of multiple belongings and border breaches. She had grown up in West Bengal, India, hearing from family elders nostalgic pre-Partition stories of her maternal grandmother as a young girl in the early twentieth century swimming in the rivers and roaming the mango groves of a village in Faridpur (then in East Bengal, now Bangladesh) and of her father's cousins thriving in the cosmopolitan bustle of 1930s Lahore, where her father's uncle had been a college principal. Still, one family legend superseded these nostalgic tales of lost or impossible connections. This legend articulated anew with such contemporary conditions as India's swing toward Hindu right nationalism, together with extremist violence, hand in hand with Islamophobia on a global scale. She had often heard of how her paternal grandfather's endeavors for the economic uplift of the historically underprivileged Muslim slum dwellers of Rajabajar, Kolkata (notorious in its day for gang activity) had been reciprocated with valiant dedication in the face of Partition violence; when the Partition riots broke out, the slum dwellers De's grandfather used to help rallied around his family home and vocational training center, set in the middle of the slum, and fought for his life over days against fellow Muslims coming in from other neighborhoods. Over the years, this family story had come to embody for Esha Niyogi De those peculiarly subcontinental cultures of connectivity and conflict that presuppose borders (both within and across state divides) at the same time as they are hybrid in commitment and in voice. The story of her grandfather and his underprivileged Muslim friends motivated her to begin exploring cross-communal filmic histories in reference to a bordered subcontinent.

The conferences we have held, or attempted (more soon on this), since the inception of SARMSNet have not only revealed myriad hopes for border crossing and connective understanding. They have reinforced both the realities of geopolitical policing by the nation-states and, hand in hand, the gaps and erasures in mutual knowledge that can come in the way of trusting alliances. We begin to account for our present-day experiences of borders in the subcontinent by turning to Ayesha Jalal's observation about the division of India and Pakistan, globally conditioned as it was by British colonization. In Jalal's words, "Partition is not just an event that occurred in 1947 . . . as the founding myth of the postcolonial nation-states of India, Pakistan, and Bangladesh. . . . [It] is a way of seeing and being that separates what were once historically indivisible people"; the "innumerable slippages, elisions, and contestations in narratives" about nations and divides are daily, often violently, reenacted in the countries (Star Weekend 2017). That being noted, we also need a different frame to understand the vicissitudes coming down from the second partition of the subcontinent, that is, the Bangladesh war of 1971. In the words of Dina Siddiqi, this second partition or Liberation War "displaced and reconstituted older meanings of Partition . . . [by brutally exposing] the irresolution . . . in the meaning of Pakistan [of the question of] Bengal's Muslims" (Siddiqi 2017). This need to reframe and rethink the divides within the subcontinent, in a new era of regional/global hierarchies, was demonstrated by the divergent experiences of traversing borders by different historically located members of our SARMSNet collective.

Kamran Asdar Ali (author of chapter 2), for example, was "heartbroken" upon being denied a visa to India because he was a person of Pakistani descent. Although now a dual citizen located at a US institution and applying under a US passport, Asdar Ali shared the fate of the many other persons of Pakistani descent who are being blocked today by an Indian state dominated by the Hindu Right concurrent with global Islamophobia. To put the issue in context, let us note that, similarly situated as a US citizen of Indian descent, Esha Niyogi De has been granted multiple visas to Pakistan. Indian citizens Abhijit Roy and Madhuja Mukherjee were, however, denied visas to Pakistan when they sought to attend the SARMSNet workshop at Lahore. To return to Kamran Asdar Ali's experience, having been both a participant and an active supporter of our network meeting at Lahore (as the then president of the American Institute of Pakistan), Asdar Ali was coming to India to participate in the next workshop, scheduled to be held at Jadavpur University in 2018. The memories that flooded to his mind upon denial of access to India are best told in Kamran Asdar Ali's own words:

> Kolkata is the city of my childhood. . . . This is where my maternal grandfather went to college from 1918 to 1922. He then taught at University of Murshidabad and then Calcutta [now Kolkata], where he was the warden of Carmichael Hall [the Muslim students hostel]. My mother grew up there. I was speaking to her yesterday, and she was saying how the Muslim students initiated the violence in 1946 and that her father was threatened and had to leave for Delhi. Later, he was to work in Delhi in the Department of Education. Moreover, my paternal aunt was with the Communist Party of India in the 1960s and headed the Tram Workers Union in Calcutta. . . . We would visit her every year on our way to Gaya, Bihar (to visit my grandmother) and I fondly remember the Durga Puja festivities. New Market is where all our clothes were bought; we went on our annual pilgrimage to the Calcutta Zoo and Victoria Memorial; and I saw *Guide*, *Pyar Mohabat*, *Padosan*, and later *Do Rastey* and *Aradhana* in the cinema halls of Calcutta (Kolkata).

Not unlike Esha Niyogi De's family memories from pre-Partition India, Kamran Asdar Ali's familial and personal memories of post-Partition interactions with India as a Pakistani intermingle longings with a quest for interstitial dissidence and hybridity. Yet if Indians and Pakistanis share a nostalgia and concord about their histories and belonging, the same cannot be said about Bangladeshis and Pakistanis. As already noted, there is need for a different frame to understand the lasting legacies of the second partition of the subcontinent. This was demonstrated by Elora Halim Chowdhury's experiences of crossing borders, meaningfully engaging in interpersonal dialogue with individuals across the war-torn countries, and exploring the possibilities of reconciliation and healing at a personal as well as scholarly level (see chapter 15).

Raised in postwar Bangladesh in the context of a family and community with strong anticolonial and nationalist political leanings, Chowdhury's generation grew up under the dual shadow of the ubiquitous and defining narrative of the Liberation War yet with limited understanding of how the same war was understood and remembered in Pakistan. It is not a stretch to say that many of her generation grew up cultivating a heavy dose of outrage and hatred toward those they had come to define as their former oppressors. Even today as a scholar-teacher in the field of South Asian Studies, Chowdhury finds it limiting to discuss among colleagues and students the conflicted legacies of the two partitions, not least because of the knowledge gaps that still hinder trust. Thus, when she traveled to Pakistan for the first time in her life to participate in the second SARMSNet conference in Lahore (2016), Elora Halim Chowdhury's emotions were riding high.

Our intellectual inclination to forge regional connections and conviviality had already been thwarted by state politics at the cusp of the inaugural conference to the series, which had been planned to take place on the campus of Dhaka University in January 2016. Over thirty scholars across South Asia and beyond were to gather over three days to share their research and to collaborate on the creation of the South Asian Media Scholars Network (later renamed South Asian Regional Media Scholars Network). But barely two weeks before the conference was set to start, the vice-chancellor and the Syndicate Committee of Dhaka University suspended all academic exchange with Pakistan, thereby making it impossible for the Pakistani scholars to participate in the conference. Relations between the two countries had been rife with tension following the verdicts of the Bangladesh War Crimes Tribunals and the executions of war criminals who had collaborated with the Pakistani Army in 1971, toward whom the Pakistani state was sympathetic. The University of Dhaka stressed that all intellectual relationships with Pakistan would be severed until Pakistan apologized for the 1971 genocide. Because the impetus for the conference was to foster cross-border conversations and to launch the South Asian Regional Media Scholars Network for collaborative research, Chowdhury and her co-organizers (including De) decided, with heavy hearts, that without their Pakistani colleagues, this vision would be compromised. The financial, emotional, and intellectual losses of this cancellation were grave and deeply felt by participants from near and far, many of whom had already bought tickets and made myriad travel arrangements.

While we were all crushed by Dhaka University's bewildering stance to stop fostering scholarly exchange between Bangladeshi and Pakistani thinkers, the cancellation catalyzed a robust email exchange. Many participants came together in virtual space. Naeem Mohaiemen, PhD candidate at

Columbia University and scholar of Bangladesh, voiced the urgent need for bridges among activist scholars, with view to a "deeper understanding of the complex and evolving scenario of academic freedoms, and the linked impact on state policy [in Pakistan and worldwide]." Another thoughtful email came from a Pakistani scholar: "Personally, I would not be at all upset or offended if the conference were to go ahead in the absence of Pakistani scholars. Whilst I understand you all have good reasons to be critical of the policy (and broader reactionary nationalist discourse in Bangladesh), as a Pakistani, I find it very difficult to criticize the decisions of the Bangladeshi government/State on this matter." He offered suggestions for SARMSNet to move forward:

> Thinking constructively about my own context, it would be useful to know what you think should be done by Pakistani academics to facilitate academic exchange between Pakistan and Bangladesh. Some of the onus must surely fall on us and some considerable part of what is to be done surely has to comprise addressing the historic silence of the Pakistani state about its crimes during the genocide of 71. At [the scholar's own institution], many of us try to do what we can in our teaching and research but as you know, dominant views of the past in contemporary Pakistan are utterly divorced from the sordid truth. *Transregional Filmscapes: Histories, Borders, Encounters* inaugurates our bridge of scholarship—excavating the geopolitical and affective divides described here, talking across and against them.

Given this tumultuous start to SARMSNet, Elora Halim Chowdhury was disappointed but not surprised when the Pakistan Consulate in New York informed her that her visa application was being scrutinized by the Pakistan Inter-Services Intelligence (ISI). Thankfully, however, high-level negotiations between the host institution faculty in Lahore and the Pakistani UN representative in New York resulted in a visa stamp mere hours before she was to board the flight to Lahore and just in time to arrive for the conference. In this instance, our efforts of solidarity, stemming from regional histories of mutuality and conviviality, had disrupted state control in small but not insignificant ways.

Chowdhury's presentation at the Lahore University of Management Sciences (LUMS) in the conference "Cinema and Transnationalism in Pakistan and South Asia: Regional Histories" invoked anxiety for her, given the historical and political weight of the topic and the venue—a country she had long learned to associate with the pillage and devastation of her own. Her paper, titled "Ethical Encounters: Friendship, Reckoning and Healing in Contemporary Films about the Bangladesh Liberation War," was an exploration of friendship, love, and intimacy across cultures as modes for enacting social responsibility and care for the other. Deploying a transnational feminist analysis, she examined films by Bangladeshi feminist directors Shameem Akhtar and Rubaiyat Hossain, *Meherjaan* (2011) and *Daughters of History* (1999), with women of color theories of friendship politics to further a discussion of solidarity among women.

Through an investigation of the conflictual yet cooperative alliance between Lalarukh, a Pakistani researcher working on war crimes enacted by Pakistani military on Bengalis in 1971, and Monika, her Bengali activist friend whose family survived the war's devastation, she reflected on the idea of dissident friendship and argued that relationships between individuals of heterogeneous backgrounds with discrepant power positions in society can elicit a deeper understanding of human connection. Similarly, the love between a Bengali woman and a Pakistani soldier amid the war in Meherjaan questioned nationalist narratives of war and engendered lesser known and diverse understandings of women's complex and varied relationships to war. In addition, the rejection and embracing of "war babies," as featured in both these films as well as Munsur Ali's *Shongram 1971* (2015), raised questions of healing and agency. Exploring contested relations—between women, women and the nation, state and citizenship—she discussed whether such conflicted alliances are inevitably crushed within dominant patriarchal colonial relations or whether they can cause a change in self-and-other perception. She further explored whether this process trumps, or is trumped by, other competing loyalties women might have, to family, community, or nation. The responses at and beyond the conference will stay with her as precious and heartfelt engagements between individuals of war-torn countries in the region, interactions that are rare yet full of promise.

The question of loss was complicated by a Pakistani scholar who shared with Chowdhury late into that night her father's story of being posted in Dhaka as an engineer during the war. Prior to the war, when the army was warning West Pakistani civilians to leave for the western wing, this man chose to remain in the East and ended up providing shelter to his Bengali neighbors. The horrors he witnessed in those months have remained with him throughout his entire life. She also shared stories of "war widows" in West Pakistan, whose husbands—Bengali men—left to join the resistance and never returned. The stories of loss Chowdhury heard from Pakistani colleagues were tinged with the loss of separation and the absence of space for reflection. On the other hand, the meaning of loss was inflected by the joy of liberation in the stories of 1971 often found narrated in fiction and film from Bangladesh. In a poignant statement, in Shameem Akhtar's film *Daughters of History*, Monika challenges Lalarukh about their differing positions toward the war by posing the question "Separation or liberation?"

A jarring response came from the younger cohort of scholars and attendees. One stands out in particular. A younger scholar revealed that her father was a journalist and activist who still had ties in Bangladesh. Following Chowdhury's presentation, she called and asked him, "What were you doing in 1971? Were you on the streets marching and protesting?" Her father responded, "We did not know what was going on in East Pakistan. What could we have done?" It is noteworthy that during Chowdhury's brief time in Pakistan, Mir Quasem Ali, the convicted war criminal, was executed in Bangladesh. She woke up on the morning of September 5 on the campus of LUMS to read the headlines in the national daily *Dawn* condemning the execution.

Another experience in Pakistan, which occurred beyond the parameter of the academic conference, is noteworthy and reflective of the conflicted terrain SARMSNet and this volume traverse in relation to borders and histories in the subcontinent. Professor Salima Hashmi, artist, activist, and daughter of the late revolutionary poet Faiz Ahmed Faiz, generously invited Esha Niyogi De to her house, which was also where Faiz had lived. During the course of the evening, she pointed to an armchair in the parlor and said, "That's the chair on which my father sat utterly devastated upon his return from Dhaka in 1974. He could not believe that his Bengali friends there—who were like his brothers—would no longer speak to him with the same warmth." She was referring to the criticism Faiz encountered from some of his contemporaries in Bangladesh about the actions of the Pakistan state and the less than vigorous resistance of Pakistani intellectuals. Professor Hashmi talked about the censorship of the media at the time and how it was like the entire western wing of the country was "under a blackout." More recently, Salima Hashmi has been anointed by the prime minister of Bangladesh as a Friend of Bangladesh on behalf of her father's contributions to the Bengali resistance. She recalled those days in 1971 and the lives lost—young men in Pakistan who went into the war without even knowing what they were fighting against. She is currently editing the memoir of one such fighter. We narrate these personal stories as a way to understand how we might rethink and reframe the divides within South Asia in our present era of regional/transnational hierarchies, silences, and erasures.

KNOWING SOUTH ASIA? TRANSREGIONAL INQUIRY

This takes us to the larger question of how the South Asian region has been framed and theorized in the global context. While the regional histories underlying the personal experiences described above are taken up from different angles by the chapters of this volume, our combined exploration of the subcontinent as an interrelated filmscape challenges the hierarchies within the field of South Asian studies in Euro-American academies. To get there, we must briefly consider the genealogy of knowledge production in the field of South Asian studies.

As noted, not unlike other area studies of the global South, South Asian studies carries a history of "spatial containers" (Harootunian 2012, 7) conditioned by both geopolitical and institutional politics in the global North. It is useful in our post-9/11 world to recall these categorical containers, because the stratification of the subcontinent within this academic field intersects today with a worldwide xenophobia classifying desirable and questionable identities. Born in the post–World War United States, South Asian studies carries an Orientalist history that led to the privileged institutionalization from within of Indian and Hindu-centric studies (Dirks 2004, 345–49). Since the premise for classifying South Asia and its people was the idea of religion-centric "civilizations," Indian and Pakistani, Hindu and Muslim scholarship often got divided, with Pakistan coming to be grouped with Middle Eastern and Islamic civilizational studies despite the fact that there are many more Muslims in South Asia (Dirks 2004, 361) than in West Asia and North Africa (the region institutionally and geostrategically classified as the Middle East). These categories hide not only the rich Islamic history indigenous to South Asia but also the syncretic routes of regional Islam through diverse linguistic cultures, such as its routes through the Bengal delta, now Bangladesh (Van Schendel 2009, 1–46).

As the field of South Asian studies itself has flourished it has, in more recent years, been restratified according to fresh global hierarchies. The post–Berlin Wall trend of self-contained identity studies accompanied by euphoria about global capitalist democratization (especially in the US academy), for example, further elevated Indian identity while giving it a homogeneous standing for ethnic proficiency in global progress (often technological; Harootunian 2012, 13). Today, these institutional stratifications adapt to Islamophobia. Pakistan studies as a field and as an institution to be funded is prone to be contained in a "security studies/Islamic threat paradigm" (Kermani, Farruki, and Asdar Ali, 2015) such that explorations of popular culture or film history find little disciplinary room. Bangladesh studies, on the other hand, is constituted as a "central laboratory for the developmentalist genre . . . [classified under] notions of disaster and impoverishment" (Mookherjee 2006, 77) as well as health and disease risks. As such, from within the institutional frameworks of US and European academies, India-based formulations take the lead in making the field of South Asian studies recognizable as an academic area.

Willem van Schendel (2002, 650) draws on Neferti Tadiar to note that the recognition of an area as a flourishing academic field depends on it being not simply "an object of inquiry" based on preexisting forms of knowing, but in itself a "geography of knowing": it must be constituted as a geography that provokes "a theoretical problematique . . . an 'area' offering new sets of questions and methodologies." The field of South Asian studies indeed has matured into a sophisticated ground for critical theory. Not only has it fallen in step with developments in Euro-American theory, but it has also talked back. It has sought to "provincialize" progressive Western modernity—the "politically modern position . . . [of a] future that 'will be'" (Chakrabarty 2000, 251)—and to illuminate alternative temporalities. The Subaltern School, in particular, has taken an exemplary role in laying out a problematic of academic inquiry that offers field-orienting debates "about the nature of modernity, the failure of the Enlightenment, the violence of the state . . . [and] the politics of culture" (Dirks 2004, 371). Important as they are, these critical developments in the field by and large reference the history of Hindu-dominant Indian nationalism and concomitant formations of the nation-state and global connectivity. Thus, the theoretical problematic offered by South Asian studies—and determined by the history of the field in northern academies—has come to be spatiotemporally contained and limited. A core endeavor behind our SARMSNet Collective is to trouble this epistemic determination. We seek, instead, a transregional space for "reciprocal" (Dirks 2004, 379) academic and political inquiry into cinematic histories. As noted at the outset of this introduction, our volume has taken reciprocity to mean encounters between both historical perspectives and paradigms of inquiry—encounters that mutually complement and inflect one another.

Our collective book suggests two preliminary premises for approaching the subcontinent—and other such regions of the global South—as a heterogeneous geography of filmic knowledge. First, our volume presupposes that a *comparative historical encounter* between film archives spread across South Asia will shine light on translocal linkage *and* difference. Lotte Hoek delineates a way of excavating regional connectivities (of imagination and resource) from vertical film archives (chapter 7), whereas Amit Ranjan demonstrates how situated and interdisciplinary readings of well-explored archives (such as Bollywood) in relation to different internecine conflicts could act as touchstones through which submerged forms of postcolonial violence can be assessed (chapter 3). Locating border-crossing Indian cinema in Pakistani film cultures, chapters 2, 8, and 10, by Kamran Asdar Ali, Esha Niyogi De, and Gwendolyn Kirk, respectively, come together in offering an analytical perspective on the historical incommensurability underlying regional intersections of culture, language, and the market. These studies explore how figurations of sexuality, womanhood, and the heteropatriarchal family grow relatively unstable or even transgressive as images and plots travel from a more normative and coherent Hindi screen to mainstream Pakistani screens—contrary to a widespread perception that Pakistani films are pale copies of Indian originals. The authors conclude that the relationships of industrial film forms with national projects and with state governance historically differ between India and Pakistan.

Second, our collective research underscores the necessity of a transregional *encounter between methods* of opening South Asian archives of cinema and society, and reading the historical nuances. Noteworthy in this vein are the analyses of Bangladesh Liberation War / Muktijuddho films. Rather than presupposing the postcolonial critique of the Enlightenment and its "failure" (Dirks 2004, 371)—an assumption widespread in Indian studies—the Muktijuddho film scholars assembled here valorize the politically modern temporality of human rights activism. These authors take a "cosmopolitan" approach that is central to Bangladesh trauma studies: an analytic characterized by what Nayanika Mookherjee (2011) describes as "intertextuality and intercitationality." Elora Halim Chowdhury argues for an intertextual "conversation" of Bangladeshi feminist struggle with women of color advocacy in the United States (chapter 15). Her point of theorizing feminist cinema in Bangladesh in relation to an African American feminist framework of abjection and recuperation (Hartman 2008) is to carve out a transnational common ground of political recognition, eschewing a parochial national historical perspective. On his part, Naadir Junaid aligns Bangladeshi political film with the new cinema movements of protest sprouting across France, Germany, Brazil, Argentina, and India (chapter 14). Such intercitational approaches as these look to overcome hierarchies of knowledge, and challenge historical oblivion, by forging a collective southern space—a space, as described by Fahmida Akhter, for voicing a "plea for justice on the part of subjugated people worldwide" (chapter 12). Our book juxtaposes such cosmopolitan readings of political cinema as these, anchored in temporalities of activist identity and revolutionary advocacy, with a postcolonial study such as Hariprasad Athanickal's, which plumbs regional senses of belonging that permeate authorial identities in parallel cinema.

All in all, the chapters of this book speak to one another and they speak together. Combined, they sketch something of a new problematic for South Asian studies of films and their material cultures. Our regionally nuanced framework pivots on encounters among a multiplicity of historical perspectives, of affect, and of methodological choices in opening and reading affective legacies of postcolonial suffering and agency. Indeed, this volume is the first of its kind in its geographical and historical breadth and depth. The chapters of this book do emphasize transregional connectivity between subcontinental cinemas and societies. At the same time, they reveal the urgency of *crossing* regional histories and methodological perspectives such that we interrogate knowledge gaps and boundaries on both fronts. It seems to us that a problematic such as this—premised on crossings and encounters—is helpful for studying not only South Asia but other regions of the global South torn asunder by neo/colonial processes yet immanently entwined.

NOTE

1 See, for example, Naficy (2001). For transnational theory of borders and cross-border solidarity, see Mohanty (2003).

REFERENCES

Appadurai, Arjun. 1990. "Disjuncture and Difference in the Global Cultural Economy." *Theory, Culture, Society* 7. http://tcs.sagepub.com.

Benjamin, Walter. 1968. "The Storyteller: Reflections on the Works of Nikolai Leskov." In *Illuminations: Essays and Reflections*, edited by Hannah Arendt, translated by Harry Zohn, 83–110.New York: Schocken Books.

Bentley, Jerry H. 2005. "Regional Histories, Global Processes, Cross-Cultural Interactions." In *Interactions: Transregional Perspectives on World History*, edited by Jerry H. Bentley, Renate Bridenthal, and Anand A. Yang, 1–13. Honolulu: University of Hawai'i Press.

Chakrabarty, Dipesh. 2000. *Provincializing Europe: Postcolonial Thought and Historical Difference*. Princeton, NJ: Princeton University Press.

Cook, Pam. 2012. "No Fixed Address: The Woman's Picture from *Outrage* to *Blue Steel*." In *Gender Meets Genre in Postwar Cinemas*, edited by Christine Gledhill, 29–40. Chicago: University of Illinois Press.

Dadi, Iftikhar. 2016. "Modernity and Its Vernacular Remainders in Pakistani Cinema." In *Film and Social Change in Pakistan*, edited by Ali Khan and Ali Nobil Ahmad, 77–100. Karachi: Oxford University Press.

Dirks, Nicholas B. 2004. "South Asian Studies Futures Past." In *The Politics of Knowledge: Area Studies and the Disciplines*, edited by David Szanton, 341–85. Berkeley: University of California Press.

Fuhrmann, Arnika. 2017. "*This Area Is [NOT] under Quarantine*: Rethinking Southeast/Asia through Studies of the Cinema." In *Area Studies at the Crossroads: Knowledge Production after the Mobility Turn*, edited by Katja Mielke and Anna Katharina Hornidge, 251–68. New York: Palgrave Macmillan.

Gazdar, Mushtaq. 1997. *Pakistan Cinema, 1947–1997*. Karachi: Oxford University Press.

Haroontunian, Harry. 2012. "'Memories of Underdevelopment' after Area Studies." *Positions: East Asia Cultures Critique* 20, no. 1 (Winter): 7–35.

Hartman, Saidiya. 2008. "Venus in Two Acts." *Small Axe* 12, no. 2: 1–14.

Kaplan, E. Ann. 1993. *Looking for the Other: Feminism, Film, and the Imperial Gaze*. New York: Routledge.

Kaur, Raminder, and Ajay J. Sinha. 2005. *Bollyworld: Popular Indian Cinema through a Transnational Lens*. New Delhi: Sage Publications.

Kermani, Sheema, Asif Farruki, and Kamran Asdar Ali, eds. 2015. *Gender, Politics, and Performance in South Asia*. Karachi: Oxford University Press.

Khan, Ali, and Ali Nobil Ahmad, eds. 2016. *Cinema and Society: Film and Social Change in Pakistan*. Karachi: Oxford University Press.

Marcus, George E. 1995. "Ethnography in/of the World System: The Emergence of Multi-sited Ethnography." *Annual Review of Anthropology* 24: 95–117.

Mielke, Katja, and Anna Katharian Hornidge. 2017. "Knowledge Production, Area Studies and the Mobility Turn." In *Area Studies at the Crossroads: Knowledge Production after the Mobility Turn*, edited by Katja Mielke and Anna Katharian Hornidge. New York: Palgrave Macmillan.

Mohanty, Chandra Talpade. 2003. *Feminism without Borders: Decolonizing Theory, Practicing Solidarity*. Durham: Duke University Press.

Mookherjee, Nayanika. 2006. "Muktir Gaan: The Raped Woman and Migrant Identities of the Bangladesh War." In *Gender, Conflict, and Migration*, edited by Navnita Chadha Behara, 72–96. New Delhi: Sage Publications.

———. 2011. "Never Again: Aesthetics of 'Genocidal' Cosmopolitanism and the Bangladesh War Museum." Special issue, "The Aesthetics of Nations: Anthropological and Historical Approaches," edited by Nayanika Mookherjee and Christopher Pinney. *Journal of the Royal Anthropological Institute* 17, suppl. 1: 71–91.

Naficy, Hamid. 2001. *An Accented Cinema: Exilic and Diasporic Filmmaking*. Princeton, NJ: Princeton University Press.

Raju, Zakir Hossain. 2015. *Bangladesh Cinema and National Identity: In Search of the Modern?* London: Routledge.

Rosen, Philip. 2006. "Border Times and Geopolitical Frames: The Martin Walsh Memorial Lecture 2006." *Revue Canadienne d'études cinématographiques / Canadian Journal of Film Studies* 15, no. 2: 2–19.

Siddiqi, Dina M. 2017. "Ghosts of 1947." *Daily Star*, August 26, 2017.

Srinivas, S. V. 2015. "Region in Focus." *Bioscope* 6, no. 2: vii–ix.

Star Weekend. 2017. "Separating a Once Historically Indivisible People: In Conversation with Ayesha Jalal." *Daily Star*, August 26, 2017.

van Schendel, Willem. 2002. "Geographies of Knowing, Geographies of Ignorance: Jumping Scale in Southeast Asia." *Environment and Planning D: Society and Space* 20: 647–68.

———. 2009. *A History of Bangladesh*. Cambridge: Cambridge University Press.

Vasudevan, Ravi S. 2000. "The Politics of Cultural Address in a 'Transitional Cinema': A Case Study of Indian Popular Cinema." In *Reinventing Film Studies*, edited by Christine Gledhill and Linda Williams, 130–64. London: Arnold.

White, Patricia. 2015. *Women's Cinema, World Cinema: Projecting Contemporary Feminisms*. Durham: Duke University Press.

PART I

NATIONS AND REGIONAL MARGINS

1 NATIONAL IDENTITY AND CINEMATIC REPRESENTATION

Independent Films in Bangladesh

FAHMIDUL HAQ

STUART HALL (1999, 38) CLAIMS THAT "THE NATION-STATE WAS never simply a political entity. It was always also a symbolic formation—a 'system of representation'—which produces an 'idea' of the nation as an 'imagined community.'" If the nation is indeed an "imagined community," as described by Benedict Anderson (2001), or an "artificial construct," as claimed by Gayatri Spivak (1990), then the very existence of the nation depends on the continuous and repetitive construction of "nation-ness" through artistic, cultural, and literary means. Modern forms of representational culture, such as cinema, play an increasingly vital role in identity construction and reinforcement and therefore in the symbolic formation of the nation.

Bangladeshi filmmakers, especially independent and art house filmmakers, use cinema as a vehicle to tackle questions of national identity.[1] For the most part, these films have reproduced dominant discourses of identity and nationalism. In this chapter I analyze how independent filmmakers from Bangladesh have represented national identity in their films. First, I explore three approaches to Bengali-Muslim identity. These include "Bengaliness," "Muslimness," and "popular religion." Next, I outline the history of Bangladeshi independent filmmaking from the 1950s to now. Finally, I analyze how independent art filmmakers have portrayed these identities in their cinematic texts by looking at the works of leading Bangladeshi contemporary filmmakers Tanvir Mokammel (*A River Named Modhumoti*, 1995, and *A Tree without Roots*, 2001), Morshedul Islam (*Dollhouse*, 2006, and *Rain*, 2000) and Tareque Masud (*The Clay Bird*, 2002). For each director, I selected at least one film that deals with the Bangladesh Liberation War and religion.

IDENTITY QUESTIONS

In mainstream discourses about identity in Bangladesh, only two approaches are continuously addressed: Bengali nationalism and Bangladeshi nationalism, or "Bengaliness" and "Bangladeshiness." Both approaches are essentialist in nature, one emphasizing ethnic identity and the other religious identity. Therefore, throughout this chapter, I refer to these two approaches as "Bengaliness" and "Muslimness.'

In discussing Bengaliness, Willem van Schendel (2009, 202) says, "From the 1950s to the 1970s, the delta's [Bangladesh is often called the Bengal Delta] vernacular elite had imagined Bangladesh as the homeland of Bengalis who had been denied justice under Pakistan. To them the Bengali nation stood for much more than a linguistic community [hence subsequently they formed a nation-state through the Liberation War]."

On the other hand, van Schendel explains the narrative of Bangladeshiness as originating from the movement for Pakistan during the Partition of India and then later during the 1971 Liberation War.[2] He states that the Bangladeshi nation was the ultimate manifestation of the delta's Muslim-Bengali identity, which matured during the British and Pakistan periods. The 1947 Partition of India and Pakistan into three districts based on religious majorities was necessary for 1971 liberation of Bangladesh (then East Pakistan) from Pakistan (then West Pakistan) (203).

Van Schendel identifies the emergence of Bangladeshiness with the 1975 collapse of control of the state by the Awami League, the liberal democratic party that led the Liberation War. During this period, a new narrative of the nation developed in order to justify the military regime of Ziaur Rahman (1977–81), who came to prominence after assuming power as the chief of the army after the 1975 military coup and the assassination of Sheikh Mujib. Zia dissolved the Parliament and instituted a state of emergency under martial law. He became president after the resignation of President Abu Sadat Mohammad Sayem, with a promise of reform and democratic elections. It was Ziaur Rahman's political move to bring back the predominance of Muslim identity from 1947 to counter the predominance of Bengali identity that had its origins in the late 1960s and was established through victory against Pakistan in 1971. In creating a distinction between Bengalis and Bangladeshis, the religious dimensions of the identities are accentuated, making Bangladeshiness essentially Muslim (van Schendel 2009, 202). Historian Badruddin Umar (1974) reinforces this and argues that Bangladeshi nationalism is nothing but communalism based on religion, intended to incite strife between Hindu and Muslim communities. It is in fact a revival of the two-nation theory in a new and far more deceptive garb.[3]

For me, Bengaliness is an ethnolinguistic identity of the nation that emerged in the Middle Ages in Bengal through Bengali literature and culture and reached its peak in the 1960s in the autonomy movement against the central West Pakistan government following the Bengali language movement in 1952, leading to the birth of the nation in 1971.[4] Muslimness is a religious identity that was first evident in nineteenth-century Bengal. Later, Muslimness as a religious identity was converted into the Pakistan movement in 1910–50 in British India. It was revived in the post-1975 Bangladesh period.

During British colonialism, the Hindu community in India held much of the power allowed by the British, leaving Bengali Muslims behind. The British took power in India from the Muslim rulers in 1757. Indian Hindus eventually became closer to the British, and got into the British-implemented education system, which allowed them to get clerical jobs in the colonial capital of Kolkata and other towns. Earlier, under the land reform policy initiated by British rulers, a class of landlords had emerged who were predominantly Hindus and were assigned to collect land revenues from peasants who were predominantly Muslims. Muslims took a long time to get into the British education system. In the early 1920s, after the late emergence of a middle class, Muslims looked for a separate identity. Bengali Muslims were pioneers of the idea of establishing a separate state named Pakistan during the Partition of India in 1947. After Partition, however, due to the economic and cultural discrimination enacted through the centralization of power in West Pakistan, the same Bengali Muslims wanted to be free from Pakistan.

If Pakistan was created by the allegiance to Muslimness, then Bangladesh independence was born from a Bengaliness approach to national identity. In contemporary, post-independence Bangladesh, both identities are at play in the political, state, and public spheres. Two major political parties control the narrative around these two conflicting identities; the conflict has extended to street fighting between activists of the two major political parties. If Bengaliness represents a secular-modern and ethnolinguistic identity, Muslimness can be identified as a nonsecular and rigid religious identity. Generally the Awami League (AL), along with some small left parties, represents Bengaliness, and the Bangladesh Nationalist Party (BNP), along with some small Islamic parties, represents Muslimness. The AL and BNP alternated between holding power and assuming the position of main opposition in the post-independence period, and most of the time these two parties (or broadly, two approaches to identity) were in conflict.

It must be noted that in Bangladesh, Islam has not been a monolithic force. It has evolved throughout the country's history. In its early phase, before the conquest of Bengal by Turkish Muslims in 1204, Sufi Islam—an Iranian form of liberal Islam that we will call *popular Islam*—came to Bengal and impacted the popular psyche of Bengal Muslims. After the Islamic reformist movement in the nineteenth century, many Bengal Muslims began to feel an affinity with the "original" Islam of Saudi Arabia, which we will call *scholastic Islam*. Finally, there was growth in the political sphere of what can be called *political Islam*. The Muslim League before and after the birth of Pakistan and Jamat-E-Islami and some other minor Islamic parties before and after the birth of Bangladesh all practice political Islam.

In this context, in addition to Bengaliness and Muslimness, I propose a third kind of syncretic identity, which I term *popular religion*. Buddhist Tantricism, Islamic Sufism, and Hindu Vaishnavism—all liberal streams of major religions—gave birth to several popular religious practices in Bengal, cumulatively known as the Baul Cult. Liberal humanist philosophy, esoteric yogic practices, and syncretic religious beliefs are some of the basic principles and practices of the popular religions. In the Middle Ages in Bengal, popular religion was once a mainstream identity, but after the arrival of Muslim jingoism in the nineteenth century, this form of religious interpretation became less visible in Bengal society. What is called popular religion in Bangladesh is sometimes also called "minor religious sects," "subreligions" (Chaterjee 2005), or "obscure religious cults" (Dasgupta 1976) and is sometimes also framed as "mysticism." These religions are often seen as being in opposition to the orthodoxy of mainstream religions. Sudhir Chaterjee (2005, 19–20) mentioned as many as 102 subreligions found in late eighteenth-century Bengal. These subreligions evolved by negating the orthodoxy of Brahmanism and Islamism.

INDEPENDENT FILMS IN BANGLADESH

Bangladesh is a cinephile country with a substantial film culture and a modest commercial film industry producing more than fifty films every year. The Bangladeshi film industry was established in the 1950s, although there were a few instances of filmmaking before then. The first Bengali-language feature film, *Mukh o mukhosh* (The face and the mask), was completed in 1956 after two years of shooting, and it was a huge success. Before that, only

Pakistani, Indian, and Hollywood films played in Bangladesh (East Pakistan at the time), because producers and distributers did not believe locals were capable of making quality films (Waheed 2005). The film industry was stable in the 1960s and 1970s but declined in 1980s and 1990s. Some external factors are responsible for this decline. The introduction of VCRs in the 1980s and satellite television in 1990s can be identified as the main external forces that reduced audiences in the theaters. The industry was internally weak, thus it suffered a lot from the advent of new technologies. In the first two decades of the new millennium, the industry has declined even further; however, recently there have been signs that the industry is being revived, in part due to major contributions from the independent sector.

The independent film movement began in Bangladesh in the 1980s. Since then, there has been steady growth of independent film culture, although the length, format, and characteristics of independent cinema have changed over time. Now independent auteurs are regarded as the most reputable filmmakers in the country as well as the leading art house filmmakers. Along with five to ten independent feature films, independent documentaries are also produced annually in Bangladesh. Though these films are often not popular with audiences due to their relatively complex form and content, they do win awards on the international film festival circuit and have become the backbone of national cinema in Bangladesh, introducing actors, directors, and cinematographers to the wider industry.

According to film critic Roger Ebert, an independent movie is “a film made outside the traditional Hollywood studio system, often with unconventional financing, and it’s made because it expresses the director’s personal vision rather than someone’s notion of box-office success” (quoted in Levy 1999, 3). In the context of Bangladesh, independent films are made outside of the control of the Bangladesh Film Development Corporation (BFDC), the only government-established studio. Though the production and distribution systems of independent films operate outside the mainstream cinema, the content and form of these films are often conventional, suggesting that they are not in fact alternative in the accepted meaning of the term. As Bangladesh’s independent film movement was emerging, filmmakers worked to develop Bangladeshi independent cinema as a Western-style art cinema as well as to normalize textual patterns of Euro-American classics as standard film language for Bangladeshi cinema (Raju 2015). Thus, most of the films are made in the classical narrative style set by Hollywood, and the subjects are either about the Liberation War of 1971 or contemporary social problems.

The history of Bangladesh independent cinema can be discussed in three stages: early short art films (1984–92), the films of transformation (1993–99), and contemporary global (2000 onward) (Raju 2015; Haq and Balraj 2013). In the 1980s a new kind of film developed. These were short in length, self-financed by the directors, shot outside of the studio system, distributed independently, and exhibited outside of the cine-theaters. In that sense, *Agami* (Toward, 1984) by Morshedul Islam was the first independent film since it was the first out-of-studio and self-financed film made in Bangladesh. This was immediately followed by *Holliya* (Wanted, 1984) by Tanvir Mokammel. This trend of filmmaking continued until the mid-1990s.

According to Tareque Masud (personal interview, February 11, 2007), the earlier short-film movement created two major streams of independent filmmaking in Bangladesh: one based on nationalist and melodramatic cliché (*Agami*) and the other based on experimental film influenced by Sergei Eisenstein and Dziga Vertov (*Holliya*). Several short films made in the late 1980s broadly followed these two streams. However, some earlier independent films were *Aborton* (The cycle, 1988) by Abu Sayeed, *Adam surat* (Inner strength, 1989) by Tareque Masud, *Protyabartan* (The return, 1986) by Mostafa Kamal, and *Chakki* (The ring, 1986) by Enayet Karim Babul. There was an ideological aspect to this filmmaking since these movies possessed a secular, anticommunal ideology, inherited from the Liberation War of 1971, married to a leftist political ideal. However, despite being left-leaning and secular, their films continued to have a nationalist approach. The dominant leftist politics of the 1960s, along with the sense of modernity and Marxism of the filmmakers, were localized in the ideology of Bengaliness.

In the second phase, feature-length fictional films replaced short-fiction films in the independent sector. Morshedul Islam made *Suchona* (The beginning, 1988, 62 minutes), again within the nationalist discourse of the Liberation War. Tanvir Mokammel's *Nadir naam Madhumoti* (A river named Madhumoti, 1995, 120 minutes) also explored nationalist discourses. The next film by Morshedul Islam was *Chaka* (The wheel, 1993, 65 minutes), based on the play of the same name by the eminent playwright Selim Al Deen, which tells the story of the struggle of two bullock cart drivers to bury an unidentified body. *Chaka* not only won awards in international festivals but was also the first Bangladeshi feature film to be distributed by a European company. The next film of Tanvir Mokammel, *Chitra nadir pare* (In the Bank of Chitra, 1999, 114 minutes), dealt more broadly with the historical background to the Liberation War—the Partition of India/Bengal in 1947.

At the same time, Tareque and Catherine Masud made a full-length documentary *Muktir gaan* (Song of freedom, 1995, 78 minutes). The documentary used footage of the Liberation War shot by an American filmmaker, Lear Levin. The Masuds assembled this footage and combined it with other archival clips from different parts of the world to make the film, which was successfully revived in 1995.

In the mid-1990s, independent filmmakers tried to overcome their limitations by attempting to reach a wider audience. These films suffered from low budgets, a 16 mm format, and their short length; they could not reach a wide audience because their short length and incompatible celluloid format prevented theatrical release. Morshedul Islam successfully made *Dukhai* (1997) and *Dipu Number Two* (1996) within the mainstream production and distribution system. *Dipu Number Two* got a government grant and attracted substantial revenue from mainstream theaters.

Independent film gradually matured, both in content and form. This is especially true for post-2000 films. In content, the filmmakers chose different issues with much greater diversity of subject matter, especially those new to digital filmmaking, who were trying to make subjective and social films rather than adhering to the old paradigm. Though most independent filmmaking follows classical narrative form, the experiments with film language in films like *Shankhonad* (2004) by Abu Sayeed, *Aha!* (2007) by Enamul Karim Nirjhar, *Under Construction* (2015) by Rubayiat Hossain, and *Doob* (2017) by Mostofa Sarwar Farooki are appreciated by critics who value their formal innovation. However, contemporary films, even those in a classical narrative style, are technically more modern: the editing is smarter, camera movement is consistent with the situation, and the quality of the sound and picture markedly improved.

Despite the fact that it is an established movement, the greatest setback for independent film remains its limited distribution. Films tend to be released in only a few theaters and are not accessible to a wide audience. The alternative distribution and exhibition network has also become weaker, and theatrical audiences have become selective in responding to independent films. In addition, young filmmaking communities have been swallowed by electronic media, and filmmakers are forced to work on prime-time soap operas or write scripts for advertisements. Senior independent filmmakers are struggling to keep their independence in the face of corporate television channels, such as Impress Telefilm and Channel 1, both owned by Impress Group. Also presenting difficulties is the fact that instead of patronizing independent filmmakers, the government of Bangladesh has hindered the growth and development of independent films by applying different censorship criteria to these films than they do to mainstream and commercial cinema.

REPRESENTING IDENTITY THROUGH NATIONALIST NARRATIVES

Most of the independent art films of Bangladesh are, in the words of Fredric Jameson, "necessarily . . . national allegories" by virtue of being Third World texts, which Jameson defines as having the experience of colonialism and imperialism (quoted in Ahmad 1994, 101). With few exceptions, these allegories mostly address the Liberation War or the political ideology derived through the experience of the birth of the nation. This is especially true for early independent films starting in the 1980s. Six of Tanvir Mokammel's nineteen films, six of Morshedul Islam's twelve films, and five of Tareque Masud's fourteen films focused on the Liberation War of Bangladesh. About this decision, director Tanvir Mokammel (n.d.) says, "It is curious to see that most of these short-film-makers began their career by venturing at least one film on the backdrop of 1971. The reason seems self-evident as during the 1971 war most of these young film-makers were in their boyhood, in their most sensitive and formative years. So the trauma they had experienced, resulted in 1971 war to appear again and again in their films, almost like a—*leitmotif*."

Though independent art cinema of Bangladesh does not have a wide audience, it has greatly contributed to the formation and sustainability of several specific identity discourses. Art cinema is accessed, appreciated, and analyzed by that academia-media-intelligentsia circle. While narrating the national history of the country on the screen, secular-modernist film directors have clearly taken a position on behalf of Bengaliness and against Muslimness and assume that the two identities are, and should remain, in conflict. According to Zakir Hossain Raju (2008, 134), culturalist-modernist art cinema filmmakers like Morshedul Islam and Tanvir Mokammel adamantly believe in a straightforward separation of the Muslim and Bengali identities of Bengali Muslims.

The basic notion of the birth of the nation in 1971 was an ultra-secular ideology regarding Bengaliness, which is seen repeatedly almost in every art form or piece. Independent filmmakers' ultrasecular point of view often portrays religious people as demons. In independent films related to the Liberation War, a kind of demon character called a *razakar*—a collaborator with the Pakistani army—is often present. Because *razakar*s collaborated with the Pakistani army during the Liberation War, the word is now synonymous with *traitor* in Bangladesh. In films, this type of character is heavily stereotyped, with Islamic mannerisms and features added to the character. He is often portrayed as a middle-aged man with a beard, clad in a white *pyjama-panjabi-tupi*, perceived as Islamic dress in the context of Bangladesh. It is true the *razakar*s were the members of some Islamic parties, but not all of them were middle-aged, and a lot of them were clean-shaven and wore Western clothing. Because of their westernized, secular worldview, the film directors do not differentiate scholastic Islam from political Islam. In their view, even popular Islam is synonymous with scholastic or political Islam. The diversity among Muslims is missing in these films, as religious identity is bundled into one stereotype.

The director Tanvir Mokammel shows clear support for Bengaliness, which comprises the idea of secularism and the saga of Bengali culture, frequently manifesting as anti-Islamic positions in his films.[5] In his films we see a kind of Muslimness that is primitive, antimodern, annihilating, and antinationalist. In *A River Named Madhumoti* there is one Islamist middle-aged character in a monstrous role. He collaborates with the occupying Pakistani army, kills freedom fighters, steals property, and abuses Hindu women. His nationalist guerrilla son finally kills his "demon" father at the end of the film.

A Tree without Roots, also directed by Tanvir Mokammel, portrays a different perspective on how Muslimness manifests itself in Bengali peasant society. It is the story of a hypocrite named mullah Majid, who appears in a village and cleans up an old dilapidated grave, declaring it a shrine to the famous *pir*, then promptly begins to worship it.[6] Over the years, the shrine provides Majid not only economic solvency but psychological domination over the community. He first marries Rahima, an obedient and hardworking peasant woman, but when Rahima fails to produce a child—and because of his polygamous sexual desires—he marries Jamila, a teenager, who eventually revolts against his repression. The film portrays Bangladesh as a totally fatalistic society, where in the name of Islam one can manufacture fear among Muslims, annihilate ordinary lives, and easily victimize women. Though this may be partially true (people like Majid can and do use Islam for their own worldly reasons), the film portrays a rigid and monolithic Islam. Majid, a shrewd, heartless, and rude person, is the caretaker of Islam there.

It must be noted that the Majid of the film is more monstrous than the Majid of the novel. The novelist Syed Waliullah portrayed Majid as a human being with limitations. His hypocrisy emerges from his situation in society rather than as a reflection of the individual. Also in the novel, he struggles with his hypocrisy. Hayat Mamud, the editor of the *Collected Novels* of Syed Waliullah, says, "Though we don't support the hypocrisy of Majid, our hatred doesn't rush to him; because his poverty and helplessness makes his fraudulence forgivable and makes him an ordinary and person of sorrow like us . . . gradually we are captured by a hidden sympathetic pain raised for Majid" (Mamud 1996, xi). But in the film *A Tree without Roots*, we do not see Majid with human limitations. He never feels sorry for his dishonesty. Instead, he is portrayed with shrewd eyes, as an aggressive ruler with the flag of Islam at his hand.

Like Tanvir Mokammel, Morshedul Islam also portrays Islam as a monolithic force and clearly sides with Bengaliness, considering these two identities to be essentially in conflict. Morshedul Islam has made several films related to the Liberation War of Bangladesh, including his first film, *Agami*, and his most recent film, *Anil Bagchir akdin* (A day in the life of Anil Bagchi, 2015). *Dollhouse* (2006) features a nationalist narrative, which includes the bravery of *mukti bahini* (freedom fighters), the brutality of Islamist collaborators (*razakars*), and the repression of the Pakistani army. Here, the jingoism of Bengaliness is clearly on display. The story line of *Dollhouse* does not focus on the bravery of *mukti bahini* and the brutality of Islamist collaborators; rather it is a story of the war victim Rehana, who passes a few days in an alienated and abandoned house with the naive and introverted Yakub, where they act as if they are playing in a dollhouse. In adapting the film from the novel of the same title by Mahmudul Haque, Morshedul Islam makes one major change. At the end of the film, Yakub, one of the main protagonists of the text, changes from the naive observer that he is in the book to an active participant. The novelist portrays Yakub as an inactive person in the tumultuous period of the war, when everybody either participates as a guerrilla or supports them—or at least is concerned with news and gossip of the war. This aloofness is common to almost all novels by Mahmudul Haque, but in *Dollhouse* Yakub was transformed into a potential guerrilla at the end. The director's choice to make Yakub willing to join the *mukti bahini* constructs a nationalist narrative of resistance that deviates from the novel and fulfills the director's desire, as well as the prejudices of the secular-modern target audience.

If *Dollhouse* highlights Bengaliness, Morshedul Islam's *Brishti* (Rain, 2000), adapted from a story by Alauddin Al Azad, deals with Muslimness and presents an anti-Islamic message. It shows a scholastic Islam that is very unkind, primitive, and even stupid. In the film, a village headman has declared a prolonged drought to be a curse from Allah, and the headman, along with the imam of the village mosque, declares that a pregnant divorced woman is the reason behind the curse. This unkind and primitive act is punished when the film shows that the headman's wife had sex with his adopted son at the same time as he and the imam were declaring the verdict of the trial in the village court and punishing the woman by stoning her to death. A horrifying anti-Islamic environment has been created in the film by the dress and mannerisms of the characters, as well as repeated and prolonged verses from the Qur'an recited by the imam and the headman himself to punish the woman. This example and others show Tanvir Mokammel and Morshedul Islam's nationalist-culturalist-modernist approach of Bengaliness and against Muslimness.

These films contribute directly or indirectly to sustaining the conflict between Bengaliness and Muslimness and widening the gap between the followers of the two approaches. On the eve of Victory Day and other national holidays, these films are shown widely on television. Sometimes they are re-released in theaters on national days. Many parents buy the DVDs to show their children. This trend is encouraged by the Awami League government. The Awami League has made it their policy to support films made about 1971. This is reflected in the selection criteria for government grants to filmmakers. Presently the Bangladesh government allocates grants for five films every year, out of which at least one film project on 1971 gets the national award. Also, Prime Minister Sheikh Hasina and other government officials often explicitly urge filmmakers to make films on the Liberation War.[7]

Arjun Appadurai (2001, 257) has said that "one man's imagined community is another man's political prison." Though he said this in reference to the majority's nationalist treatment of the minority within a nation, here, the relentless antagonistic treatment of Muslimness contributes to a widening gap between the followers of Bengaliness and Muslimness. Filmmaker Tareque Masud agreed with this proposition: "Independent films of Bangladesh are widening the gap between the conflicting secular and Islamist identity. Filmmakers are contributing to this polarization. They are reaffirming the secular and middle-class discourse. They are catering to this class position, reestablishing nationalist narratives and the dominant middle-class ideology. They are not questioning but catering to the audience. They are just perpetuating the dominant ideology" (personal interview with Masud, February 11, 2007).

The "catered-to audience" of these art films is urban middle-class people who typically identify with Bengaliness and dominate the discourse of national identity formation. Due to the *othering* of Muslimness, these films appear as "foreign" narratives to the followers of scholastic Islam. It is easy to understand why these films do not sit well with the followers of political Islam since the monolithic portrayal of Islam in the films positions Muslims as the "text of the opponent," which in turn alienates a large part of the Bengali population. This continuous negative portrayal has increased the chasm between secular-modern directors and mainstream audiences on the one hand and pro-Muslimness people on the other. Zakir Hossain Raju (2008, 140) agrees when he says, "As the art cinema authors are busy in the act of orientalizing Bangladesh for the global audience and westernized Bengali-Muslims, in most cases, their representation of Islam and Islamic education deepens the Islam-Bengali dichotomy."

Interestingly, this archetype of religious community in cinema has started to change in films such as *Joyjatra* (2004) by Touqier Ahmed and *Shyamol Chhaya* (2004) by Humayun Ahmed. Set against the Liberation War of Bangladesh in 1971, in both films people are in a boat trying to escape attack by the Pakistani military. In earlier films, the *razakar* and mullah characters took on the same symbolic meaning, but in *Joyjatra* the first protest against the Pakistani army comes from the imam of the village mosque, and the first man to join the Liberation War in *Shyamol Chhaya* is the protagonist, a *moulavi* (Muslim religious scholar). In *Joyiatra*, the first *shahid* (martyr) is a *moulavi*. In *Shyamol Chhaya*, when the boat people from the Hindu community are worshipping, Muslims ask them to stop from fear that the Pakistani army will attack them if it is discovered that Hindus are on the boat. But the *moulavi* resists them, telling them not to intervene in another religious community's rituals. This was quite unusual in 1971, when minority Hindus were the primary targets of the Pakistani army.

How has this reversed portrayal of religious people happened? The change comes from a new audience that dictates what they want to see. In the post-9/11 and Afghan-Iraq wartime, unjust aggression by global superpowers against Muslim countries has contributed to a global rise of Muslim fraternity. This has impacted the filmmakers of Bangladesh. Religious people are now forerunners of the Liberation War in contemporary films of Bangladesh. In earlier films the Muslim characters were portrayed as singularly negative characters, but in recent films, the Muslim characters are portrayed as singularly positive characters. This recent portrayal of identity issues can be seen as inconsistent with reality, like the earlier representations. The reality is always somewhere in between.

THE CLAY BIRD: A SENSIBLE REPRESENTATION OF NATIONHOOD

The Clay Bird by Tareque Masud deals with Bangladeshi issues that comprise all three aspects of identity: Bengaliness, Muslimness, and popular religion. The film makes a deliberate attempt to explore the presence of syncretic identity that includes popular religious practices in traditional Bangladesh. This exploration is unique as it is the first attempt of its kind on the screen.

Set against the backdrop of the East Pakistan independence movement in the 1960s, the film tells the story of Anu, a shy boy who has been sent to the madrassa by his orthodox father, Kazi, to protect him from "Hindu rubbishes" and other bad elements of the society. However, he has already been introduced to these "bad elements" by his secular and nationalist uncle Milon. In the madrassa Anu comes to know about two streams of Islam. The head teacher is in favor of political Islam, and he invites people in the path of jihad to protect Islam in East Pakistan. But another teacher, Ibrahim Hujur, believes in Sufi, or popular Islam. When the Pakistani army attacks the village, Anu flees with his mother, while Uncle Milon stays to resist the invaders with other guerrillas and dies. Anu's father does not leave home because he believes "the Muslim brothers" have come to keep the peace and not to kill people. But he is wrong, and his house is burned down by the army. Afterward, Anu and his mother find Kazi in a corner of the burned house and insist that he flee, but Kazi is left confused at the end.

Some important characters in *The Clay Bird* represent either Bengaliness or Muslimness. Kazi believes in Muslim brotherhood and follows scholastic Islam. But Milon, Kazi's younger brother, believes in Bengaliness and fights against the Pakistani military for the rights of the East Pakistani people. These two characters represent two opposite currents of the broader Bengali-Muslim identity. Milon is modern, liberal, and Marxist, while Kazi is zealous in his Islamic beliefs.

The director of *The Clay Bird* does not merely construct these two identities. He is aware of the limitations of both Bengaliness and Muslimness, and he clearly has endorsed popular religion in the film. It is apparent that he opposes Islamic dogmatism, but not emphatically so, as other filmmakers usually do. The pro-Islam character Kazi is portrayed with much sensitivity in the film. This pro-Islamic bearded man believes in Muslim brotherhood, and he does not take the breakup of Pakistan easily. In other films, he would have been portrayed as essentially a collaborator with the

Pakistani military and would have helped them in capturing freedom fighters. But here, he is dogmatic in his beliefs only. When the military comes to the village, his beliefs become confused. And when the military burns his house and Islamic books, his belief system is challenged. Kazi represents a lot of pro-Islamic people who fought the Pakistan state in the 1940s but are not often portrayed with the same nuance on film.

In the film, Kazi, who believes in Muslim brotherhood, is criticized by Milon, while the Marxist Milon is criticized by the boatman Karim, who believes in syncretic popular religion. In one scene Milon and Karim talk:

> MILON: There is only one way left, to fight for freedom.
>
> KARIM: Politics is just another game; there is no benefit for you and me. If only people knew what true freedom is . . .
>
> MILON: Blindly religious people like you are to blame for the mess our country's in today.
>
> KARIM: What did you say? "Blindly religious!" . . . Actually no true religion, be it Islamic, Hindu, or Christian, will ever make people blind. True faiths open your eyes.

The comment "True faiths open your eyes" confounds Milon, leaving him speechless.

Kazi contrasts with the head teacher of the madrassa, who supports jihad in order to impose Islam over everything. His extreme Muslimness is criticized by Ibrahim Hujur, the principal, who also believes in popular and mystic Islam. The head teacher tries to inspire students to follow jihad, but Ibrahim Hujur tells Halim Mia, another instructor, that it is not the role of a teacher to lead students to political extremism. He reminds Halim Mia that Islam in Bengal did not originate with the sword, but rather with creative and poetic inspiration from Sufi saints and those who converted to Islam.

The Clay Bird includes a lot of singing and debating by *bayatis*. A *bayati* sings folk songs with mystic and spiritual messages that debate religious and philosophical thoughts. When Anu returns from madrassa for the last time, after Dhaka City has been attacked by the military and people have fled the capital, a blind *bayati* starts singing a song that describes a "fratricidal war" between the grandsons of the Prophet. In another song at the end of the film, two *bayatis* are engaged in debate in order to establish the true way of Islamic living—*Shariah* (scholastic) or *Marfat* (mystic), the former rigid and the latter liberal. The *Marfat* wins at the end of the song, and again the director expresses his preference for popular religion and culture.

The title of *The Clay Bird* is influenced by mystic philosophical thoughts. The term "clay bird" is found in a song performed by a female *bayati* in a village concert, but the bird referred to here is not physical but a concept. In the song, the clay bird symbolizes the main theme of the film: freedom through mystic metaphor. As Sufism teaches us, the human being is made of clay, and the soul is always associated with a free bird. The soul is caged in a clay body, and the body is limited, transitory, fragile, and weak, while the soul has an immense desire to be free. The *bayati* sings:

> The bird is trapped in the body's cage
> Its feet bound by the worldly chains
> It tries to fly but fails. . . .
>
> The clay bird laments:
> "Why did you infuse my heart with longing
> If you didn't give my wings the strength to fly?"

The question of freedom versus various forms of human limitations—social, political, and religious—emerges at this point in the film. Anu's mother, Ayesha, wants to be free as a woman and as a human being; Anu wants to be free to do whatever he wants to do; Milon seeks national, territorial freedom, his own narrow sense of freedom; the boatman Karim talks about a greater, mystical, spiritual freedom. The theme of freedom recurs even against the backdrop of the political movements depicted in the film. The whole nation is pursuing an identity that is supposedly based on freedom. According to the director, the overriding theme is limitations versus freedom and is a tribute to Sufism and the religion's emphasis on the relationship between soul and body (Shaikh 2004). Thus, sensibly representing Muslimness, understating Bengaliness, and endorsing popular religions have made *The Clay Bird* a film that speaks about the greater freedom of people.

CONCLUSION

If identity is a "contingent, artificial and ideological invention" as Ernest Gellner (1983, 55) argues or an "artificial construct" as Gayatri Spivak (1990) suggests, this construction influences and is influenced by various cultural systems of representation, such as art, film, and literature. Independent cinema as a system of representation and as a cultural institution enthusiastically constructs Bangladeshi identity. Independent films tend to present an understanding of national identity that is based upon the Bengaliness interpretation of Bangladesh. In most cases, independent films engage in othering differing approaches to identity, especially Muslimness. As an influential cultural institution, cinema has contributed to widening the gap between the two conflicting identities among the general public, increasing societal conflict. If films depicted narratives of popular religion, an approach to identity that is more syncretic in nature, independent films could reduce this conflict instead of increasing it.

In recent independent and art house films, directors have begun to expand their lens to encapsulate a wider range of perspectives. Here filmmakers are more subjective; they are not obsessed with Liberation War narratives. They look at globalized and post-9/11 Bangladesh with different eyes than earlier filmmakers. In the film *Television* (2013) Mostofa Sarwar Foorki depicts how Muslimness responds to modernity as well as new technologies in postglobalized Bangladesh. This portrayal is sensible to the main protagonist, who is the religious as well as administrative leader in a peripheral village of Bangladesh. Some recent films portray the identity of urban spheres. Dhaka, the capital of Bangladesh, is one of the oldest cities in South Asia, but it was almost absent from cinematic depiction until recently, when it appears in popular independent films like *Piprabidya* (Ant story, 2015) by Mostofa Sarwar Farooki, *Under Construction* (2015) by Rubaiyat Hossain, *Aynabaji* (2016) by Amitabh Reza, and *Live from Dhaka* (2016) by Abdullah Mohammad Saad. These are still national allegories but with a clear thematic shift. This is a new beginning for the independent art cinema of Bangladesh.

NOTES

1 In Bangladesh, the independent film movement started in the mid-1980s. However, in the Bangladesh context, independent filmmakers are considered art house filmmakers because the mainstream industry rarely produces any artistic endeavors.

2 In the early twentieth century, during the last phase of British rule, the complex political dynamics in British India resulted in the idea of having different state(s) for Muslims living in greater India.

3 The two-nation theory was the basis for the Partition of India in 1947. This theory underpinned the proposal that Muslims and non-Muslims should be two separate

nations. Based on this theory, British India was divided into India and Pakistan. The east wing of Pakistan was liberated from the west in 1971 through a war, and Bangladesh was born as the new state.

4 In 1952, the central Pakistan government declared that Urdu (largely spoken in West Pakistan) would be the only state language in Pakistan. Bengalis from East Pakistan urged through protests that Bengali (largely spoken in East Pakistan) should also be declared a state language. After police killed students at a protest rally, the movement gained momentum throughout East Pakistan, and Bengali attained the status of a state language. The language movement had an impact on identity formation regarding Bengaliness, and the movement ultimately inspired Bengalis of East Pakistan to aspire to be liberated from Pakistan.

5 In Tanvir Mokammel's *Rabeya* (The sister, 2008), there is also an aged *razakar* character who orders the villagers not to bury the dead body of a freedom fighter killed by the Pakistani army. The brutal character appears as a demon when we see that the freedom fighter is his nephew. The film progresses with the conflict between the *razakar* and freedom fighter's sister Rabeya, who wants to bury her brother.

6 *Mullah* is the name for a Muslim cleric. A *pir* is considered a holy and spiritual man among Bengal Muslims.

7 On May 10, 2014, while distributing the National Film Award 2012, Prime Minister Sheikh Hasina called upon Bangladeshi filmmakers to portray the great achievements of the 1971 Liberation War and the history of sacrifices of the people through movies (*Dhaka Tribune*, May 11, 2014).

REFERENCES

Ahmad, Aijaz. 1994. *In Theory: Classes, Nations, Literatures*. London: Verso.

Anderson, Benedict. 2001. "Imagined Communities: Reflection on the Origin and Spread of Nationalism." In *The New Social Theory Reader: Contemporary Debates*, edited by Steven Seidman and Jeffrey C. Alexander, 224–30. London: Routledge.

Appadurai, Arjun. 2001. "Disjuncture and Difference in the Global Cultural Economy." In *The New Social Theory Reader: Contemporary Debates*, edited by Steven Seidman and Jeffery C. Alexander, 253–65. London: Routledge.

Chaterjee, Sudhir. 2005. *Gavir nirjan pathey* (In the deep isolate path). Kolkata: Ananda.

Dasgupta, Shashibhushan. 1976. *Obscure Religious Cults*. Kolkata: Firma KLM.

Gellner, Ernest. 1983. *Nations and Nationalism*. Ithaca, NY: Cornell University Press.

Hall, Stuart. 1999. "Culture, Community, Nation." In *Representing the Nation: A Reader*, edited by David Boswell and Jessica Evans. London: Routledge.

Haq, Fahmidul, and Shanthi Balraj. 2013. "Independent Cinema in Bangladesh: Its Roots, Growth, Challenges and Opportunities." In *Bangladesh's Changing Mediascape: From State Control to Market Forces*, edited by Brian Shoesmith et al., 277–95. Bristol: Intellect.

Levy, Emanuel. 1999. *Cinema of Outsiders: The Rise of American Independent Films*. New York: New York University Press.

Mamud, Hayat, ed.. 1996. Introduction to *Syed Waliullah: Uponnashsamogro* (Syed Waliullah: Collected Novels), edited by Hayat Mamud, ix–xiii. Dhaka: Pratik Prokashona Sangstha.

Mokammel, Tanvir. N.d. "Problematics of Alternative Cinema in Bangladesh: An Introduction." In *From the Heart of Bangladesh*, edited by Nurul Alam Atique. Dhaka: Bangladesh Short Film Forum.

Raju, Zakir Hossain. 2008. "Madrasa and Muslim Identity on the Screen: Nation, Islam and Bangladeshi Art Cinema in Global Stage." In *Madrasas in South Asia: Teaching Terror?*, edited by Jamal Malik, 125–41. London: Routledge.

———. 2015. *Bangladesh Cinema and National Identity.* London: Routledge.

Shaikh, N. 2004. "*The Clay Bird*: Asia Source Interview with Tareque Masud." *Asia Source.* http://www.asiasource.org/news/special_reports/masud.cfm

Spivak, Gayatri. 1990. *The Post-colonial Critic.* London: Routledge.

Umar, Badruddin. 1974. *Politics and Society in East Pakistan and Bangladesh.* Dacca: Mowla Bros.

van Schendel, Willem. 2009. *A History of Bangladesh.* New Delhi: Cambridge University Press.

Waheed, Karim. 2005. "Celebrating 50 Years of Our Cinema: Remembering *Mukh O Mukhosh* and Abdul Jabbar Khan." *Daily Star,* August 12, 2005. http://archive.thedailystar.net/2005/08/12/d50812140197.htm.

2 FEMALE FRIENDSHIP AND FORBIDDEN DESIRE

Two Films from 1960s Pakistan

KAMRAN ASDAR ALI

SA'ADAT HASAN MANTO (1912–1955), THE FAMOUS URDU SHORT story writer, in an essay written as an introduction to a collection of his short stories in the early 1950s, looks back at the time he spent in Bombay (twelve years) just before he migrated to Pakistan. He writes about the city with warmth and a sense of extreme loss, yet he is reconciled to the inevitable fact that he is now in Pakistan. But, he says, coming to the new country was full of uncertainty and anxiety:

> No one had given it a thought that after such a revolution things would not remain the same. Whether small alleys would become large highways or their existence would be completely lost, we did not have an answer. Would there be a difference between the governance by foreigners or by those we call our own, about this people were not sure either. How would the new cultural and social atmosphere nurture our thoughts and feelings? What would be the relationship between the state, government, community, and the individual? These were issues that we needed to seriously concentrate on.[1]

Manto's voice helps us rethink the moment in Pakistan's history when contesting voices of uncertainty and confusion, against an emerging nationalist framework, discussed and debated what shape Pakistan's social, political, and cultural life would take in the ensuing years. This was not an easy task. The question faced by the various intellectuals, and perhaps the state as well, was how does one even think, write about, or seek to build a future immediately after witnessing (and in many cases living through) a catastrophe or carnage like the killings, arson, disappearances, and rapes of the Partition. Entire communities that until recently had lived together turned against one another, and the carnage that followed undermined long held practices of shared existence and tolerance.

Despite Manto's apprehensions, the creation of Pakistan allowed the state and some of its inhabitants access to an imaginary future in which perhaps Muslimness could be their primary identity. At Pakistan's independence in 1947, when issues related to infrastructure development, settlement of refugee populations, and national security concerned the new state, debates related to Urdu as the national language and Islam's role in political life continued to play a major part in the state's internal discussions. In the first two decades of Pakistan's existence, there were several attempts to create a cultural politics of unity based on Islamic values.

Alongside these efforts, Pakistan's emerging cinema too struggled with the idea of defining the cultural boundaries of a new country. For example, as Iftikhar Dadi's (2016) article on the 1958 film *Zehr-e-ishq* helps us understand, the early years of Pakistani filmmaking were not a complete rupture from the dominant Bombay cinema (after all, many practitioners in the evolving industry had trained in Bombay) but a continuation in the form of repetition, parasitism, and doubling. Dadi has a layered reading of the film: he dwells on its historical and sociological context to discuss the tension the film raises between the pressures of modernity and the negation of backwardness and primitivism in a modern nation-state. He places it in the broader continuous genre of the Hindi-Urdu "social film," but he is also mindful of how the film excises the intimate Indic influences and denigrates non-Urdu-speaking local and "primitive" life worlds in order to emphasize the high Urdu of its bourgeois subjects. This desire to emphasize the new identity retains the post-independence fissures and fault lines in Pakistan's social fabric in the early years of its formation.[2] Dadi clearly understands this exclusionary cultural politics of Urdu (more dominant in Pakistan's first two to three decades of existence) and shows how popular aesthetic forms (film in this case) were used to create cultural hegemony in Pakistan.

Taking my cue from Dadi's research, in this chapter I discuss two films from the 1960s. I consider this decade as a time in Pakistan's history when the country had gained some distance from Partition (1947), and the ethnic- and sectarian-based politics that are prevalent today had not yet overwhelmed the social life of the country (although, with Bangladesh's independence in 1971, the question of national rights could not be ignored). In this chapter I analyze the films *Saheli* (1961) and *Neela Parbat* (1969) to foreground difference rather than cultural unity in the prescribed social order.[3] They also help me open up questions related to gender, sexuality, and "perverse" desire. I read the films using a theoretical and scholarly apparatus that helps me disrupt some of the entrenched moral arguments that encompass nationalist narratives. The chapter hence raises questions about how to represent the everyday and the unpredictable in order to contest more established social renditions of society. Within this context, we could understand my reading in light of what we have come to expect perhaps from contemporary Queer theory, a theoretical framework that depathologizes sexuality within public life and also makes it possible to revalue and document nonnormative ways of living (Cvetkovich 2007).[4] Hence the chapter will enable me to foreground other voices and narratives that the national project may have silenced or suppressed. *Saheli* was a blockbuster, while *Neela Parbat* failed at the box office. However, both deal with issues related to desire.

FEMALE FRIENDSHIP

As in other postcolonial societies, the Pakistani state has periodically tackled demands for female emancipation connected to discourses on cultural authenticity. Women's changing status in Pakistan has been portrayed as largely linked with the role of Islam in the modern state. One political question in the country's early history was how civil and gender rights that are common in Western societies could be reconciled with Islamic family law within a Muslim polity. The passage of the Muslim Personal Law in 1948, which gave women the right to inheritance under sharia, and the passing of the Family Law Ordinance in 1961 were seen as major victories. The Muslim Family Laws Ordinance provided some legal curbs against polygyny, expanded the right of women to initiate divorce proceedings, and also improved inheritance rights for women. Its impact on the lives of a large majority of women in Pakistan, whose literacy levels are low and who live under restrictive social conventions, has generally been minuscule (Rouse 1998, 55).

In passing this law, however, General Ayub Khan's government (1958–69) for the first time brought the regulation of the private sphere under the state's supervision and control. This move by the military government may not have been reflected in its cultural politics. The same year the Family Laws Ordinance was passed, the film *Saheli* (1960) received five President of Pakistan medals for different categories. The film's central theme was the friendship between two women (played by Shamim Ara and Nayyar

Sultana); it depicts one of them letting her friend marry her own husband as a second wife.

The film, although immensely popular at the box office (it also won four Nigar awards, Pakistan's most prestigious film award), has been criticized by liberal circles as normalizing the practice of polygamy in post-independence Pakistan (Gazdar 1998). Similarly, it may be considered an irony that a regime which had passed a law restricting polygamous marriages would bestow awards on a film that ostensibly promoted the same system. To be clear, the Muslim Family Laws Ordinance did not ban polygamy; it just made such marriage dependent on permission from the local authorities, who needed to receive consent from the current wife (or wives). In the film, the wife herself persuaded her husband to marry her friend, so the story did not challenge the path set out by the ordinance.

Let me offer a brief description of the film and then share a reading that questions its more obvious interpretive reception. The film was directed by S. M. Yusuf, a veteran of the Bombay film industry who had migrated to Pakistan in the late 1950s. This was Yusuf's first film in Pakistan, and he brought together a team that consisted of the experienced scriptwriter Hasrat Lukhnawi, the musical director A. Hameed, and a group of talented young actors including Darpan, Shamim Ara, Nayyar Sultana, and Aslam Pervez. The film tells the story of two female friends, Jamila (Shamim Ara) and Razia (Nayyar Sultana), who grow up together in Rawalpindi with Jamila's mother and her elder brother, played by a dapper Aslam Pervez.

When Razia is called away to her relatives in Hyderabad, the two friends are separated. They miss each other and write letters to stay in touch, but these are intercepted by Jamila's brother, who has a soft spot for Razia yet also has a mistress he keeps promising to marry. The friends are thus unable to communicate due to the brother not passing on letters to Jamila and not posting the letters she gives him for Razia.

Pining for her friend, Jamila fakes an illness and asks the doctor who comes to treat her to tell her mother that she should be sent to Razia to recuperate (or Razia should be invited back). During his visits to the house, the doctor, played by Darpan, falls in love with Jamila. She reciprocates his feeling, and their marriage date is fixed. On the day of the wedding, the doctor dies in a car accident. As the groom does not arrive, the guests leave, and Jamila, now traumatized, is left in a shock-like condition. The family, hearing of a doctor in Karachi who is a specialist in healing psychological problems, takes her there. When Jamila opens her eyes in the Karachi hospital, she sees the person who was supposed to be her husband. This is Darpan again, now playing the elder brother of the deceased doctor (who looks identical to his brother). This is Razia's husband. Jamila, of course, does not know this, and she is eager to marry the doctor. Her mother explains the situation to Razia, who asks her husband to marry her friend, as that is the only way she can recover her health.

Razia's husband initially rejects the idea. However, he is subsequently convinced by his wife. Jamila gets married, and for the time being Razia lives in a different house. One day Razia comes to visit Jamila. This scene is played very well. No one is a stranger to anyone, yet Jamila introduces her new husband to Razia (who is also married to him). Razia, a poet, sings a song at this juncture that became very popular: "Hum bhool gaye har baat, magar tera pyar nahin bhooley" (I have forgotten everything but your love; Naseem Begum was the playback singer). The song, of course, shows her love and affection for both of the people who make up her immediate audience—her friend and her husband. This is the classic mise-en scene moment in the film, which brings together the three main protagonists. Razia plays a grand piano in the middle of an elaborate living room set (with servants walking around in the background) and sings, while Jamila sits at her right looking at her friend with affection, as their mutual husband comes from the shadows into the full light, creating a triangle as he leans on the piano, directly facing Razia. The director creates this triangle to recap the entire narrative arc of the film. The song is melodious and soothing, but the lyrics remain ambivalent and suggest the underlying tension and conflict in an otherwise harmonious setting. Apart from Jamila, everyone else, including the audience, understands that the inherent contradiction may need a resolution. This is the climactic scene in the film, in which the characters, the song, and the setting bring the plot to a point where the central conflict has reached its intensity and the film has to move toward a conclusion. The next phase begins shortly afterward, as that evening, Jamila finds Razia speaking alone with their husband and in a fit of rage throws her out of the house. Even at that point Razia asks her husband not to divulge the truth.

Jamila's brother in the meantime takes the intercepted letters to her husband and convinces him that Razia was actually in love with him and was his childhood sweetheart. He offers the letters as proof. The letters, though addressed to Jamila, used only the term of endearment *habib* (my love), and were signed by Razia. After reading the letters, the doctor is convinced of his first wife's unfaithfulness and is willing to give her up (or kill her—he is shown with a gun). In the meantime, the doctor's loyal servant tells Jamila everything: how the person she was supposed to marry was dead and the person she married was the elder brother of the deceased, and also how Razia sacrificed her marriage for Jamila's happiness. Jamila calls Razia to apologize and while she is on the phone she hears Razia's shriek. Jamila's brother, who liked (or lusted after) Razia, had forcefully entered her house and is threatening to rape her. Sensing trouble, Jamila arrives at the house with a gun, confronts her brother, and shoots him through a broken windowpane of a locked door. He falls dead, with the unconscious Razia lying next to him. Jamila then goes and surrenders to the police.

The movie is actually a flashback that Jamila narrates in front of the judge hearing the murder trial. At the end of the movie another witness comes forward and says that Jamila's brother was killed by her bullet. This is the character played by Bahar: Jamila's brother's long-suffering mistress who is pregnant with his child. She killed him, she says in her testimony, because she could not see him ruin another life. The last shot shows the two friends embracing (both faces to the camera) and then riding back to their mutual home in a large convertible, the husband nowhere to be seen.

A READING

In her book *Between Women: Friendship, Desire, and Marriage in Victorian England* (2007), Sharon Marcus uses Victorian fiction to discuss female relationships in England of that era. She shows the intensity of these relationships in terms of mother-daughter dynamics, in female friendships, in the mutual investment of women in images of femininity, and in the different ways women associated with each other.

These homosocial relationships were deeply colored by ideas of altruism, generosity, and mutual indebtedness. Marcus argues that this was in contrast to the way emerging market forces were creating competitiveness, such that these friendships provided a critique of individuated relationships with their focus on reciprocity, an equal power balance, and gift-giving rituals. There was always a playfulness in their behavior, where women-to-women bonds created spaces for women to be more assertive and yet spontaneous in their relationships in comparison to those with men. The book concedes that the power of men, patriarchy, and the institution of heterosexual marriage defined the lives of these women, but also asserts that we need to understand the strong affective and complex bonds that women had with other women, which these forces could not always undermine.

Although the film can be read as a melodrama, following Marcus, we can also acknowledge that the two women protagonists of this film were very much part of a male-dominated society where they could be seen to perpetuate the institution of heterosexual marriage and even polygamy. But the viewer also witnesses that the bond between the Jamila and Razia is far stronger than what either could have with her male companion. At the beginning of the film, when the two are shown together for the first time, they address each other as *habib* and *mahboob*, terms of endearment used for lovers in the Urdu language. In fact, in their letters they do not address each other by name, but rather with these terms, which are normally reserved for relationships between men and women (a clear erotic message is conveyed, which the censors or the general public did not object to).

Since the strongest bond of affection in the film is between these two women, the separation created by Razia's departure to Hyderabad results in a creative dilemma that the script needs to resolve. This is akin to the tropes of *firaq* (separation) and *vasl* (meeting), so common in Urdu literary writings. In this case, irrespective of the conventional tropes, the reunion of these women could only happen with the removal of a male love interest. Hence, Jamila's fiancé had to be killed for the friends to be together again without the obstacle of conforming to the demands of two husbands. We may condemn the institution of polygamy, but in this film we may want to see it as cultural metaphor (a bowing to convention or a cinematic sleight of hand) that allows the two who truly desired each other to come together within the patriarchal tradition of taking a second wife. As mentioned above, despite the twists and turns, the relationship between the two women is the one that triumphs, and the last scene focuses on them, while the husband is off camera.

The film develops a triangle of desire between the two females and their mutual husband, but the male character remains superfluous and is used as a prop so that the story can come to a final resolution.[5] In *Saheli*, the affection between the two women is paramount, and the narrative arc creates an ending that shows them being together. This in itself was a radical decision by the director. He drives the narrative by subtly focusing attention on how women care for, provide support to, and also desire other women. In analyzing *Saheli*, I have borrowed from Marcus and used the word *desire* in its larger connotation of homosocial bonding and not merely in a narrow sexualized meaning. In the following section I invoke desire again to introduce *Neela Parbat* to the reader, as it deals directly with a more complicated notion of sexual attraction.

FORBIDDEN DESIRE

Neela Parbat, released in 1969 but under production for the entire decade, was one of the few films of its time to receive an adults-only label from the Pakistani censors (the other was the horror film *Zinda laash*, 1967). Produced and directed by Ahmad Bashir, a journalist and writer from Lahore, this film is experimental not only in terms of the theme, but also in its choice of music, playback singers, and dance performances. The story was penned by the famous short story writer and novelist Mumtaz Mufti, a friend and confidant of Ahmad Bashir. Mufti's early fiction dealt with Freudian themes, and the film shows this influence.[6]

Since independence in 1947, when Ahmad Bashir returned from spending time in Bombay with Mumtaz Mufti, he worked as a journalist and then for the government's Department of Films and Publications. In the early 1960s, he went to California on a state-sponsored scholarship to study filmmaking. On his return he borrowed money from friends and family and started working on *Neela Parbat*. In his semifictional memoir, *Dil bhatkay ga* (2012), Ahmad Bashir writes extensively about his trials in making the film on a low budget and also about his disadvantage in being an outsider to the Pakistani film industry. He also wanted to make an art film with classical South Asian music and dance sequences and chose a story that suggested incestuous desire.

The film was partly shot in Karachi at the Eastern Studios, which by the early 1960s was seeing a revival of filmmaking. Bashir, who was living in Karachi at the time, took advantage of the vibrancy of the city's cultural life to make the film.[7] However, the film was made in a fantasy landscape where the actors could frolic on the beach, enjoy songs on a boat, and also live in the scenic pine hills in the north of the country. In addition, the film relied on songs composed in the South Asian classical tradition. Ahmad Bashir was apparently a connoisseur of this music, and he brought in a classically trained music director, Pyaray Rang, and had the eminent classical singer Roshan Ara Begum (1917–1982) sing for the film.[8] Further, there was a dance sequence (which the film places in the studio of a music teacher) by the classically trained dancer Madam Panaa, which was combined Kathak, Bharatnatyam, and Manipuri, three distinct South Asian dance traditions. In the emerging world of Pakistani cinema, which was in the 1960s heavily under the influence of Bombay-based cinematic traditions with stereotypical story lines, Western-inflected song-and-dance sequences and commercialized aesthetics, *Neela Parbat* was a radical departure from the filmmaking tradition of the era. By introducing dances like Bharatnatyam and Manipuri, originally from the south and northeast of the subcontinent—areas that were not part of Pakistan and were linked with a devotional Hindu tradition—Bashir suggested a critique of the state-sponsored history of Muslim nationalism, where traces of Indic art were being actively eliminated from cultural life. It could in this sense also be read as a negation of Partition itself, or perhaps simply as a continuation of the pre-Partition filmmaking tradition that Dadi (2016) describes in his discussion of *Zehr-e-ishq*.

However, the most radical aspect of the film is its story. The film starts with the police arriving at an old mansion (Neela Parbat) to find four corpses. On interrogation, one of the servants tells the story in a flashback sequence (much like *Saheli*). The main protagonist in the story is a traditional and powerful feudal lord, Painda Khan, played by the character actor Agha Talish. He is a widower and lives with his adult son (Bakht Khan), played by the then young Mohammad Ali.[9] There is also a young woman in the house (played by a relative newcomer, Husna), the daughter of a deceased family friend who has come to live with them as Painda Khan's ward. Laila, this adopted adult daughter, pines for the young and dashing Bakht Khan, whose own love interest is his cousin, played by another newcomer to the industry, Komal (Rashida).[10] The intimate scenes between Mohammad Ali and Komal are quite risqué, and there is a long sequence in which a shirtless Mohammad Ali is shaving while Komal does an erotic dance with music playing in the background (there is no song in this shot, an unconventional choice for the director).[11] These instances of intimacy and erotic gyrations may have partly resulted in the adults-only designation by the censors.

The widower, a much older man, is shown to have feelings for Laila, his friend's daughter whom he has taken under his protection. He notices that Laila is attracted to his son, which creates tension between father and son, manifested in the father challenging his son to a duel in front of Laila and winning the round. In defeating Bakht Khan, he seeks to reaffirm his virility in the face of his athletic and handsome young son. Although oblivious to these tensions, Laila periodically has a dream in which she is trapped in a cave with reptiles and other animals and a large bat-like figure seeking to hurt her. She awakens screaming from this recurrent dream, and we see Painda Khan and others rush to comfort her.

In addition, Painda Khan sleepwalks, repeatedly ending near Laila's room. After being awakened from one of these episodes, he starts having insight into his desire for the young woman and is torn between his desire to maintain his respectability (as a father figure) and his yearning to possess

Laila. We witness his state of mind as he tries to restrain himself by tying himself to his bed. In one of the most dramatic scenes in the film, he unties himself and starts to sleepwalk, then there is the off-camera sound of a crash, which may suggest that he fell down in the passageway. Painda Khan, now awake, reenters the room and speaks directly to the camera, with the lighting clearly on his face. He expresses his repressed desire for Laila and then admonishes himself for having such base and indecent thoughts. The camera then shows Painda Khan's face half in shadow (echoing the uncertain emotions he is going through), and the scene culminates with him raising the temperature of the stove heater and burning his feet so that he cannot walk during his sleep.

Laila has a brother, who returns after many years to seek his sister (he had left the family for studies and was estranged from his deceased father). The widower is threatened by him, as he assumes that the brother will take his love interest away. He tries to persuade Laila that her brother is a miscreant and she should not see him. The brother lives with a music teacher and is himself a college professor. The brother and sister meet there, thus providing an excuse for the classical singing and dance sequences. Painda Khan eventually allows Laila to meet her brother, as he momentarily convinces himself that his "unnatural" desire for Laila is not worthy of a respectable and tradition-bound person like himself.

Toward the end, the entire extended family (along with Laila's brother, played by the character actor Kamal Irani) goes to visit a family elder in the mountains. There, over a meal, Bakht Khan and Rashida's engagement is announced, and everyone is happy. Soon afterward, the family elder, the host, asks for Laila's hand in marriage for his grandson. Painda Khan refuses, saying that she is too young and he is not really her guardian. The elder insists and says that she is under his care and like his own daughter and he should accept the proposal. Painda Khan gets flustered and in anger replies that Laila could never be his daughter (the scene clearly hints at the incestuous desire that only the viewing audience is aware of). This refusal creates a confrontation, as Laila's brother comes forward and asks to be her legal guardian so that he can accept the proposal. At this stage Laila faints and the scene ends.

That night, Laila again has the same nightmare, but this time in the dream she recognizes the person who is behind the monstrous mask: Painda Khan. In the dream Bakht Khan also appears, and the sleeping Laila is shown professing her love for Bakht Khan. At this moment Painda Khan enters the room and, on hearing Laila speaking in affectionate terms about his son, wakes her up and confesses that he loves her the most. While he is professing his love, she again loses consciousness. Painda Khan carries her on his shoulder and is about to leave when others, who have heard him, enter the room. Bakht Khan admonishes his father for his immoral behavior. Painda Khan runs away with Laila and takes her back to his ancestral house, Neela Parbat. Bakht Khan and Rashida rush after him. When Painda Khan reaches the house, the son again confronts his father for his immoral behavior. The father admonishes him for being disrespectful, but also pleads for understanding. Eventually, he challenges him to a sword duel and injures his son. He asks Rashida to take his son away and tells her that he has given all his wealth to her so that she can take care of his son. Thus he saves his own progeny from harm.

The music teacher and the brother also arrive at the house. The last scene is in a basement where Painda Khan laments that the two men have witnessed his humiliation and cannot be allowed to survive to ridicule him. He shoots them both. Then he professes his love again to the unconscious Laila and shoots himself. It is then that the semiconscious Laila slowly gets up, caresses the face of the dying Painda Khan, and puts the blood from his body on the parting in her hair, much like the *sindoor* (vermillion) that brides in South Asia traditionally put on during their wedding (again something that is very much part of an Indic tradition and not one that was fully embraced by Pakistani Muslim culture). She then stabs herself with a sword lying nearby. A traditional wedding song plays in the background.

THE EXPERIMENT AND THE UNCANNY

Ahmad Bashir uses the song-and-dance interlude particular to South Asian cinema to introduce creative and thematic breaks in the narrative structure. Although interrupting the story with songs composed in the classical South Asian music tradition rendered by the great Roshan Ara Begum may partly follow regional cinematic convention, by not rendering it in a popular form the technique forcefully breaks the linear trajectory of the narrative flow. Similarly, introducing classical dance sequences may pay homage to the genre's requirements, but it departs from the established conventions of contemporary South Asian cinema (where the camera cuts to exotic locales during song-and-dance scenes) and forces the viewer to adjust to a different temporal pace and music tradition (see Gopalan 2002). Hence these interruptions are conscious experiments to break the "magic" (the numbing experience) of the screen and to keep the audience alert. In another major intervention, the director uses the tradition of the occult by introducing Rashida's father's ability to predict the future by reading cards. In one scene, he asks his daughter, his wife, and Bakht Khan to look into a vessel. The movie cuts to a dance tableau that shows how in the future Komal and Bakht Khan would become partners. This experimental technique breaks the line of storytelling, destabilizing the viewer and helping her understand part of the ending. These experiments with storytelling and conventions may have led to the film not being successful at the box office, as the cinephelic South Asian filmgoer is more accustomed to certain kinds of interruptions (song and dance, interval, "censorship"; see Gopalan 2002). This bold departure from established filmmaking conventions may not have helped Ahmad Bashir's film.

This said, the film has many parts that need much deeper elaboration than what I can provide here. In alluding to the forcible possession of women, the film clearly raises taboo issues of incest, eroticism, and desire in old age. The main focus remains on Painda Khan's desire for a person who is young enough to be his daughter and is under his protection. Although Painda Khan's fantasy is not realized, as the conventions of storytelling or filmmaking in South Asia perhaps compelled the director to eliminate the immoral person, yet Painda Khan's actions can also be read sympathetically as the aging widower explicitly condemns his own feelings, tortures himself by burning his own feet, and when he cannot control these desires, kills himself. But still this is not entirely a neat moral resolution by the director, as the object of Painda Khan's desire puts *sindoor* in her hair and symbolically accepts being his bride (albeit in death).

The dream and sleepwalking sequences and their manifest and latent content notwithstanding, the film also hints at the notion of the uncanny as developed in Sigmund Freud's work ([1899] 2003). For Freud, an uncanny experience occurs when infantile complexes are revived or something that has been surmounted or repressed resurfaces as a reminder of our psychic past. For example, in premodern (or primitive) societies thoughts (or wishes) were thought to lead to injury and perhaps the return of the dead. However, even though the modern person does not believe in it, the old ideas may still linger in us, and when something happens that is in the realm of surmounted modes of thought, we second-guess ourselves and have a feeling of the uncanny. The ideas that death (or the future) can be predicted, that dreams can be fulfilled, and some kind of infantile desire can be rekindled are part of the complex Freudian argument on the uncanny.

The concept of the uncanny also helps Freud think about aesthetics and literature (and about audience reception). The film, very much like Freud's engagement of the uncanny in fiction, seeks to create a realistic world and a straightforward narrative but breaks this illusion by bringing forward uncomfortable desires, the monstrous, and the otherworldly. The director wants the viewer to partially look at the events through the eyes of Painda Khan, who is the only character who speaks directly to the camera while lamenting his repressed desire. We are asked to follow his invocation of tradition and respectability, which is then placed against his "unnatural" desire for his female ward (his daughter in terms of fictive kinship). This ambiguity in his character may create a moral discomfort in us, the viewing audience; we are made to understand his perspective, yet we are also repulsed by his actions.

Further, viewers may be conscious of such stories as part fantasy and part reality, based on their own social experience and surroundings. Fantasies, as Fredric Jameson (1983) writes, reflect our deepest desires and most fundamental hopes, but for them to be meaningful they also need to have a connection to our lived experience. For example, the story follows Laila's anxieties about being pursued by a bat-like monster in her dreams. This may resonate with women's anxieties about the sexually threatening private sphere, in which female viewers could find themselves in their everyday life. It would also be clear to them that most such sexual assaults are done by family members who are known to them. Rape and sexual violence against women are silenced life experiences in most societies, not only Pakistan.

This interpretation may be valid, but the film also shows both of the male protagonists (Painda Khan and Bakht Khan) treating the women harshly. Painda Khan's obsession with Laila is already discussed above, but Bakht Khan too is shown dragging a reluctant Rashida through the sand during an otherwise romantic scene of frolicking on the beach. Soon after in the same scene, he slaps her to make her respond to his romantic demands. In the final scenes we see him dragging Rashida again through dirt as she tries to stop him from following Painda Khan. This violence inflicted on women and those who are hierarchically inferior (in one scene, the audience hears an off-camera servant being whipped by Painda Khan) perhaps represents the artistic license taken by the director to depict the lifestyle of the feudal elite, yet it does betray a problematic aesthetic choice in terms of portraying violence against women without finding a resolution in the narrative. The women in the film remain passive recipients of the male gaze, are subordinated by their power, and are victims of their casual or formal acts of violence.

Various kinds of emotions are experienced by the viewer (and the protagonist, Painda Khan). The story subverts the moral resolution of killing the "evil" and desiring protagonist through an exchange and negotiation of desires by the dying Laila, who mysteriously affirms her fidelity to the man who sought to forcibly possess her. Painda Khan's suicide may represent his sense of respectability and propriety overcoming his "primitive" or infantile desire; in psychoanalytical terms, the adult and the rational suppress and surmount what needs to remain repressed. Yet Laila's surrender to him in her death destabilizes the moral basis of this reading.[12] Ahmad Bashir, in this unexpected (and problematic) move, escapes the larger moral tropes of South Asian filmmaking or fiction writing and transgresses the structures they inhabit.

Finally, although *Neela Parbat* focuses on the issue of desire, the film is shaped like a polyphonic text that includes classical song-and-dance sequences, horror-filled dreams, along with erotic intimate moments. The multiplicity of voices and themes and at times the nonlinear form of storytelling may also have strains of the older oral tradition and other forms of popular performance. Further, the story seeks to force concerns regarding sexual violence in the domestic/private sphere into a more public domain of popular viewing. In doing so Ahmad Bashir may have not only challenged the representational norms of filmmaking but also critically inserted a different narrative on the discussion of sexual desire that remains disturbing yet unique in the annals of filmmaking in Pakistan.

CONCLUSION

My reading of *Saheli* should not be understood as a misunderstanding of the power of how patriarchy functions in society (or as being supportive of polygamy). I would argue rather that the depiction of women's friendship in the film does not insist on the exclusivity of women, and it does promote heterosexual alliances and notions of domesticated femininity. Similarly, *Neela Parbat* opens up subjects of incest, domestic violence, and desire in old age and seeks to question the moral space of respectable Pakistani society.

Both films were bold experiments (one was commercially far more successful) in representing relationships that cannot be always encompassed by the normative explanatory tools we have. My analysis seeks to open up an argument about women's representation in popular media in Pakistan in order to create a different archive of cultural and sexual politics and histories. My revisiting (and rereading) of these two films may be a small step in starting a discussion on forms of cultural aesthetics in Pakistan and their representation of what may remain unsaid and silenced in national histories: the history of desire, of sexuality, of domestic violence, and of gendered subordination.

NOTES

1 Sa'adat Hasan Manto, "Jaib-e-Kafan" (The shroud's pocket), in *Manto Nama* (Lahore: Sang e Meel Press, 1990), 221–29. Published as the introduction to the volume of collected short stories, *Yazid* (1951; rpt. Lahore: Maktabah e Sher o Adab, 1975).

2 After Pakistan's creation in 1947, culturally, the Mohajirs (lit., refugees, those who migrated from India) along with the majority Punjabi ethnic group have been the most closely linked with Muslim nationalism and with Urdu as the Pakistani national language. Whereas English has remained the language of government and commerce, Urdu has retained its pivotal place at the risk of alienating other national cultures and languages in Pakistan.

3 Filmmaking had picked up in the late 1950s, and there were some attempts to make less formulaic films. Accomplished and highly educated people like the musical director Khursheed Anwar made some memorable films during this time. The veteran producer and director W. Z. Ahmed made *Roohi* (1948), which was the first movie to be banned in Pakistan as it was accused of spreading class hatred. It depicted an affair between a married rich woman and a poor unmarried man. He later made *Waada* in 1957, which was a commercial and critical success. The critically acclaimed *Jago hua savera* (the neorealist film by Ajay Kardar) was released in the late 1950s, and the early 1960s saw a new group of filmmakers ascending on the scene. A group of young educated men from Karachi consisted of Waheed Murad (producer and actor), Sohail Rana (musician), Pervez Malik (director), and Masroor Anwar (lyricist). This group, under the banner of Film Arts Production, produced some of the most successful films of the decade. Later in the 1960s, films like *Badnaam* (1966, Iqbal Shahzad) and *Lakhon mein ek* (1967, Raza Mir) created space for more serious cinema on a range of social themes.

4 It is obvious (historically speaking) that the directors of these films were not working from within the theoretical framework of a queer studies paradigm. Yet, significantly, as Ann Cvetkovich (2007) suggests, their work does allow me to move queer studies across historical and geographical boundaries, away from its recent history in the Western metropolis.

5 *Saheli*, which was released in December 1960, may have been influenced by the Indian movie *Chaudhvin ka chand*, released the same year (the love triangle is of course a common literary trope). Interestingly enough, while S. M. Yusuf, *Saheli*'s director,

may have borrowed the story line of *Chaudhvin ka chand* by using friendship as the central argument in his film, his treatment also subverts it. Rather than concentrate on the issue of male homosociality among rivals, he concentrates on female friendship and sacrifice.

6 See Mufti's collection *Unkahi* ([1944] 1975). Mufti later became a diehard Pakistani nationalist and also turned to mysticism under the tutelage of the civil servant and person of letters Qudrutullah Shahab (1920–1986, famous for his biography, *Shahab Nama*).

7 Eastern Studios was owned by Saeed Haroon, the youngest son of the Muslim League leader Abdullah Haroon. The family owned the Dawn group of newspapers, apart from other business ventures. Saeed Haroon had also started the pioneering English-language film magazine, *Eastern Films*.

8 According to a biographical essay by Mahmooda Ahmad Bashir (Ahmad Bashir's wife), Pyaray Rang was a worker in the press connected to Ahmad Bashir's workplace. Ahmad Bashir discovered him one day singing classical tunes. He employed him as a musician and composer and also changed his name from Qadri. See Bashir and Bashir (2016).

9 Mohammad Ali's first film was *Chiragh jalta raha* (The lamp kept burning, 1962) in which he played a villain. This may have been his second film. Production of *Neela Parbat* started in 1962–63, but the film was not released due to financial constraints until 1969. Mohammad Ali was by then a mature actor and a superstar of the industry. He and his wife, Zeba, were the number one couple of the Pakistani film world in the 1960s and 1970s.

10 In his semifictional biographical novel, *Dil bhatkay ga* (The heart shall wander), Ahmad Bashir discusses the problems that these two new entrants to the field caused during the shooting. I deal with this aspect of the film's making in a different text.

11 The dance scene ends with the two in what could be construed as suggestive love-making.

12 Perhaps the passive and scared young woman does finally take charge of her own desires and by performing her own death suggests the impossibility of truly possessing a woman's body. I take this argument from the filmmaker Luis Buñuel (1984, 250). It is strange to note that Buñuel made the film *That Obscure Object of Desire* in 1977 around a similar theme of desire in old age, almost a decade after Ahmad Bashir's film. I am certain that Buñuel had never seen or heard of *Neela Parbat*.

REFERENCES

Bashir, Ahmad. 2012. *Dil bhatkay ga* (The heart shall wander). Lahore: Sang-e-Meel Publications.

Bashir, Mahmooda Ahmad, and Ahmad Bashir. 2016. *Do tehreerain* (Two writings). Lahore: Sang-e-Meel Publications.

Buñuel, Luis. 1984. *My Last Sigh*. New York: Alfred A. Knopf.

Cvetkovich, Ann. 2007. "Public Feeling." *South Atlantic Quarterly* 106: 459–68.

Dadi, Iftikhar. 2016. "Lineages of Pakistan's Urdu Cinema: Mode, Mood and Genre in *Zehr-e-Ishq* / Poison of Love (1958)." *Screen* 57, no. 4: 480–87.
Freud, Sigmund. (1899) 2003. *The Uncanny*. New York: Penguin Classics.
Gazdar, Mushtaq. 1998. *Pakistan Cinema, 1947–1997*. Karachi: Oxford University Press.
Gopalan, Lalitha. 2002. *Cinema of Interruptions*. London: Palgrave Macmillan.
Jameson, Fredric. 1983. "Pleasure: A Political Issue." In *Formations of Pleasure*, edited by Hazel Carby, Lidia Curti, Iain Chamber, and Noel King. London: Routledge and Kegan Paul.
Manto, Sa'adat Hasan. (1951) 1975. *Yazid*. Lahore: Maktaba-e-Sher-o-Adab.
Marcus, Sharon. 2007. *Between Women: Friendship, Desire, and Marriage in Victorian England*. Princeton, NJ: Princeton University Press.
Mufti, Mumtaz. (1944) 1975. *Unkahi* (The unsaid). Lahore: Maktaba Urdu.
Rouse, Shahnaz. 1998. "The Outsider(s) Within: Sovereignty and Citizenship in Pakistan." In *Appropriating Gender*, edited by Patricia Jeffery and Amrita Basu, 53–70. New York: Routledge.

3 BRINGING BACK SIKHS AFTER THE 1984 POGROM

The Politics of Picturization in Hindi Cinema

AMIT RANJAN

THE HINDI FILM INDUSTRY HAS BEEN PIVOTAL IN REINFORCING INDIAN nationalism as articulated by the country's Hindu majority. The construction of a single national identity at the cost of plurality/diversity typically is supported by an assortment of myths and "shared values" about the "united selves,"[1] as well as a clear enumeration of differences between the religious majority and the "alien" other(s) (Anderson 1983; Hobsbawm 1992). Such myths habitually create and codify a common enemy in order to rally support and create an us-versus-them binary. The other does not have to be an exogenous enemy but can be an endogenous other that has been imagined, conceived, groomed, and sustained. Seen in this light, the grooming and sustenance of the Sikh identity by Hindi film narratives has been particularly complex insofar as it has involved contradictory processes of invisibility, alienation, and assimilation and reassimilation.

Admittedly, some concession must be granted here to the popular cultural productions of India as a postcolonial state. Not unlike most postcolonial states, India continues to face insurgency-related violence. The loyalties of ethnic and religious minorities toward the nation are repeatedly called into question, with the situation compounded by intercommunity conflicts. One characteristic way in which the Hindi film industry deploys accounts of such communal rifts to articulate a national identity is through depicting narrative resolutions of conflict that reproduce the other and reinforce dichotomy. Such nationalist formations of the ideal and the alien appeared on the Hindi screen way back in the 1930s, when Hindu and Muslim filmmakers began to differentiate their respective religious identities. Even though appeals to harmony between religious communities did counteract these communal trends through the early 1940s in films such as *Padosi* (1941) and *Bhalai* (1943), such appeals gave way to communalist narratives in the face of the Pakistan movement. After the independence of India in 1947, the Hindi film industry came to be deeply engaged in constructing abstractions wherein "other national/ethnic/socio-religious identities [were positioned] in stereotypical ways under an overarching North Indian, majoritarian Hindu identity" (Vasudevan 2000, 132). The complexity of narrating a Sikh identity lies precisely in this majoritarian drive of the Hindi cinema. Historically, the Sikhs as a socioreligious group of North India have been subsumed by the majority, since both socially and constitutionally they have been accepted as Hindu (even though the Sikhs themselves do not accept this identification). This relationship between Hindus and Sikhs was constitutively altered after the 1984 anti-Sikh pogrom. Whereas questions regarding the uniqueness of the Sikh identity had not been germane in previous eras of Indian cinema, post-pogrom Hindi film began to feature Sikh characters in leading roles. By the 1990s, these filmic narratives were striving to suppress memories of conflict and difference by reassimilating the community back into the Hindu religious fold. This chapter demonstrates how two well-known films, J. P. Dutta's *Border* (1997) and Anil Sharma's *Gadar: Ek prem katha* (Tumult: A love story, 2001), enact this assimilation by dramatizing the idea that Sikhs are part of the Hindu community.

These two commercially successful films presenting Sikhs as brave warriors willing and able to fight for India form the gateway to a series of films casting Sikhs in leading roles. The series includes such well-known films as *Ab tumhare hawale watan saathio* (We entrust this nation to you friends, 2004), *Singh Is King* (2008), *Rocket Singh: Salesman of the Year* (2009), *Son of Sardar* (2012), and *Bhag Milkha bhag* (Run Milkha run, 2013). This wave of Sikh-hero narratives marked a change from the stereotyped characters of clown, comedian, or brave man (Roy 2012) appearing on the Hindi screen prior to the 1990s. For example, Rajendra Nath, a leading comedian of the 1960s and 1970s, played many a Sikh role, including Makhan Singh in *An Evening in Paris* (1967). Even where they appeared as brave men, Sikh figures typically remained on the periphery, with a Hindu character in the lead. A case in point is the war film *Upkar* (1967), which depicted Sikh soldiers in the background. The characteristic subordination of Sikh heroism in prepogrom Hindi cinema is only reinforced by a production such as *Jevan mrityu* (Life death, 1970), which shows the protagonist (Dharmendra) turning into a Sikh character to conceal his identity while seeking vengeance. The rise of the Sikh hero in selected films of the 1990s marks a departure not only from this earlier history of subordinate characterization but also from prevalent treatments of territorialism in films of the period.

One way that Hindi films in the 1990s tried to extend the territory of the nation was by including the diaspora and Non-Resident Indians (NRI) in its scope to support the New Economic Policy adopted by the Indian state in 1991. Marking the advent of what Sangita Gopal (2011) calls the New Bollywood genre, these NRI-based films pivot on family values, traditions, culture, and belongingness. One of the early films of this New Bollywood genre, *Dilwale dulhania le jayenge* (The big-hearted will take away the bride, 1995) remains popular to this day. Another theme through which territorialism found space in the Hindi cinema of the era, and which persists to this day, is looking at Muslims as others or outsiders. This genre responded to a rise in Islamist militancy hand in hand with the tilt of the Indian middle classes toward Hindu right-wing politics. Mani Ratnam's *Roja* (Rose, 1992) was an early effort in that direction. It shows that the god in a temple in Kashmir is no different from gods in temples in Tamil Nadu, thus offering Hinduism as a framework not only to transcend regional differences but also to extend the national territory (Vasudevan 2010, 217). By contrast to the Muslims, the Sikhs began to be territorialized on the 1990s Hindi screen not as others but as turban-wearing heroes voicing Hindu constructs of society and nation. Let me note in passing that alternative and critical films on the 1984 pogrom, by contrast, were either banned (for example, *Dilli 1984* [2014]) or released only after significant cuts were made by the Central Board of Film Certification (CBFC) (for example, *Amu* [2005]).[2]

This chapter focuses on the narrative politics of reassimilating Sikh masculinity into dominant Hinduness, while further illuminating the representative role taken by a female character in these politics. The glorified role consolidates the position of the Sikh as a national Indian hero by depicting how a devoted woman yields her body and her faith to preserve the honor of his family-qua-nation. Predictably, this affirmation of the Sikh man's Hinduized Indian identity plays out on the body of a Pakistani Muslim woman in the film *Gadar: Ek prem katha*. To account for the shifting relations of Sikh-Hindu identities on the Hindi screen, this chapter takes a brief detour into the historical background of Sikhs in India and the 1984 pogrom.

THE INDIAN STATE AND SIKHS

The Hindu majority has alienated nearly every other group in India with the notable exception of the Sikhs. Upper-caste (non-Mazhabi) Sikhs are accepted as pure by the Hindu upper caste, and thus there has typically been little religious- or caste-based discrimination practiced by the Hindus against the Sikhs.[3] Strong communal bonding between the Hindus and the Sikhs stems from religious linkages as well as historical common enemies: Muslims. However, most Sikhs do not accept this Hinduized interpretation of their identity. Based on principles of egalitarianism, Sikhism was launched as an antithesis to the hierarchical practices and structures of Hinduism, which posits that inequality is inherent to the human condition (Oberoi 2001).

During the Partition of India, Sikh leadership under Master Tara Singh demanded a separate territory, which was not accepted. A substantial section of the Sikhs joined the Hindus after they were attacked by the Muslim *razakars* during the Partition-related violence. After Partition, the majority of Sikhs adopted India as their country while a few remained in Pakistan. In India, despite their claims of belonging to a different religious group, Sikhs were subsumed as a community within the Hindu religion (Grewal and Banga 2000).

The 1984 anti-Sikh pogrom started in Delhi, a day after the then prime minister of India, Indira Gandhi, was assassinated by her Sikh bodyguards on October 31, and spread to other parts of the country. The assassins were enraged over Operation Blue Star, carried out by the Indian Army in June 1984 to flush out Sikh militants from the Golden Temple. In that operation, Jarnail Singh Bhinderwale, leader of Damdami Taksal, earlier chosen as a political protégé by the Congress leadership, was killed along with his supporters (Suri 2015). During that operation, as narrated by a former Union minister of India, Balwant Singh Ramoowalia, the Indian Army lined up around thirty Sikh youths, mowing them down with a machine gun (Dogra 2016).

From its early days, Sikh militancy found support in the Pakistani establishment. This is clear from the fact that hours before the Indian Army cleared militants from the Golden Temple, five Sikh youth with automatic rifles and a metallic box that was possibly a transmitter came to Akali Dal president Harchand Singh Longowal and then Shiromani Gurudwara Prabandhak Committee head Gurcharan Singh Tohra and told them that the box was connected with General Zia-ul-Haq in Pakistan and asked them to declare the formation of Khalistan, so that the Pakistan Army could launch an attack on India. Tohra told them it was a battle between Indira Gandhi and Bhinderwale (Dogra 2016). Even today, there is ample proof of the Pakistani establishment's support for Sikh separatist groups such as Khalistan Zindabad Force (Long Live Khalistan Force; Jacob 2017).

Prior to the pogrom, the ten million Sikhs of India had been well represented in all the major fields and institutions, but after 1984 the community realized for the first time that, despite their large numbers, they constituted merely 2 percent of the total population of India (Chakravarti and Haksar 1987, 23). One of the demands of the Sikh militants was to recognize Sikhism as a different religion. Raising this issue in February 1984, some militant Sikh leaders publicly defaced copies of the Indian Constitution in many cities across Punjab (Oberoi 2001). Later, the 1986 Declaration of Khalistan[4] stipulated that "the Sikh religion will be the official creed of Khalistan" (Tully and Jacob 1985).

To deal with the troublesome situation, the Indian state used both coercive and democratic means. One bold political step to reconcile with the Sikhs came in 2005, when Dr. Man Mohan Singh, the first Sikh prime minister of India, issued a public apology for the anti-Sikh pogrom of 1984. Standing before the Indian Parliament, he stated, "I have no hesitation in apologizing to the Sikh community. I apologize not only to the Sikh community but to the whole Indian nation because what took place in 1984 is the negation of the concept of nationhood enshrined in our Constitution" (Suroor 2011).

The Hindi film industry has played a significant role in this reconciliation process by giving space to turban-wearing Sikh characters in leading roles. A striking exception to the subordination of Sikh characters in pre-1984 films was *Vijeta* (The victor, 1982) a parallel film directed by Govind Nihalani. Unlike *Vijeta*, post-1984 films were commercial in nature. Before the arrival of the turbaned Sikh as a hero in Hindi films, "both *mona* (shaved) and turbaned Sikhs' bodies had been inscribed as signs of pleasure in Bhangra music videos and Bollywood song and dance sequences" (Roy 2012). Gurdas Maan was a popular singer on Indian television in the late 1970s and 1980s. The next section discusses how the films *Border* and *Gadar: Ek prem katha* change this trend by reconciling Sikh identity with the dominant Hinduized version in consonance with the Indian state policy upheld by the Constitution. In this light, the Sikh emerges as a savior of the nation, exemplary in patriotism.

RECONCILING WITH SIKHS, ASSIMILATING THE OTHER IN *BORDER* (1997) AND *GADAR* (2002)

Border and *Gadar* work at multiple levels to subsume Sikh identity under a Hinduized Indianness—not only by showcasing them as brave warriors who protect the country while assimilating into the Hindu religious fold, but also by depicting them as fighters who band with Hindus against the Muslim Pakistan enemy. What changes in these films is the religious identity of the patriotic warrior who is pitted against a national enemy. Earlier war films made by the Hindi film industry invariably placed Hindu characters in the lead roles. Take, for instance, the leads in films such as *Haqeeqat* (Reality, 1964), featuring a heroic Indian war against the Chinese, or *Hindustan ki kasam* (Swear to India!, 1973), which came in the wake of the Bangladesh Liberation War and openly named Pakistan as the enemy (altering a long-standing tradition of anonymous depiction) (see Kumar 2012). The persistent glorification of Hindu heroism in this line of Bollywood war cinema was transformed in *Border.*

Border is a story about the war between India and Pakistan over the liberation of Bangladesh (formerly East Pakistan) in 1971. In *Border,* as in his other films, J. P. Dutta uses masculinity, male bonding, a multi-star cast, and violence (Gopalan 2002) to underpin a cinematic adaptation of the battle fought at Longewala sector, Rajasthan, where soldiers from the 23rd Punjab Regiment, under the command of Kuldip Singh Chandipuri (Sunny Deol), held back a well-armed Pakistan Army brigade for an entire night until Indian Air Force fighter planes, led by its commander (Jackie Shroff), came to their assistance in the wee hours. It is one of the rare films in the world in which a real flag of an enemy state is included in its last visual sequence (Singh 2008).

In *Border,* while fighting against Pakistan, the Sikh soldiers raise the battle cry used by their last guru, Gobind Singh: *Sava lakh se ek ladaun tabhi gobind singh naam kahaun* (One Sikh is equal in strength to 1,250,000 of his enemies). Many Hindus have politicized the fact that Sikhs and Hindus historically shared a common enemy, and on this basis, they want to consider Sikhs as belonging to the Hindu faith. The holy war cry of the Sikhs invoked in *Border* is meant to highlight precisely the sentiment that, on the imperiled ground of Longewala, Sikhs join Hindus in a holy battle launched by a community of the faithful against the common enemy and in defense of national (or communal) territory. Similarly, *Gadar*'s dialogue includes popular political statements that clearly reflect and reinforce the views of Hindu nationalists. Significantly, in both films the Sikh protagonists repeatedly express love for their "own land"—India. This negates the possibility of a separate homeland for the Sikhs, which militants demanded during the militancy in the Punjab.

In *Border,* the leading characters are Punjabi Hindus and Sikhs, while Bhairav Singh (Sunil Shetty) is a Rajput from the Indian state of Rajasthan.

In this high-octane, jingoistic film, Sunny Deol's character as a commanding officer in the Indian Army is a Jat Sikh who bravely carries out his duty to protect the Indian border against invasion by a foreign enemy. Here, when Kuldip Singh mentions *desh ka dushman* (enemy of the country), he is referring to Pakistan. To substantiate the communal bond between the two communities, in the film the Sikh protagonist uses the word *we*, suggesting that Sikhs and Hindus are a united group. By contrast to the Sikhs, Muslims are not trusted and are treated largely as outsiders (Naqvi 2016). This is reflected in many other Hindi films, such as *Sarfarosh* (1999). Likewise, in *Border* Bhairav Singh accuses the villagers on the borderland of harboring informants and enabling transgressive crossings. The people who inhabit the borderlands are shown to be reluctant members of the Indian nation, who, if not adequately policed, would prefer to maintain their affiliations with villagers on the Pakistani side rather than demonstrate the patriotism for India that the heroes of the film so vocally espouse (Athique 2008). The scene is akin to the current situation in the Indian side of Jammu and Kashmir, the only Muslim-majority state, where India faces militant movements attributed to backing by Pakistan since 1989.

Border repeatedly sends the message that, for Sikhs, country supersedes family and community. In an early scene, Major Kuldip Singh's wife, played by Tabu, pleads with her father to get her husband transferred off the battlefield. Overhearing the conversation, Kuldip Singh asserts that his love for his country is not second to his family. By contrast, Naib Subedar Mathura Das (Sudesh Berry), a Hindu, had requested leave to see his bedridden wife after war was declared. While he is at the front, he gets the news that his leave has been sanctioned and leaves his comrades in the midst of war to go to his wife (although he does return to the battlefield and subsequently lays down his life). Unlike him, none of the Sikh soldiers or commanders, despite problems back home, request leave while the war rages. The longings of parents and of a new bride unfold on-screen as a sentimental song plays on in the background about messages that come (*sendeshe aate hain*) and promises of return (*main ghar aaunga* [I will come home]). Overall, the emotions created on-screen are for a nation where sacrifice for the country is the most applauded value. The soldiers who are shown fighting at Longewala represent this value. Many dying in the war hold onto the promise that in their next life they will fulfill their responsibilities toward parents or wives.

In many ways, *Border* is an effort to reestablish a relationship between the Indian Army and the Sikhs. Sikh soldiers have been a very important component of the Indian Army since the colonial period, but after the rise of militancy in Punjab, particularly after Operation Blue Star in 1984, many Sikh soldiers deserted their military positions to fight for the Sikh cause. A good number joined the Bhinderwale group against the Indian state. Prominent among them was Major General Shabeg Singh Bhangu, a decorated army officer who fought in the Bangladesh Liberation War of 1971. He trained many militants to fight against the Indian state and was killed with Bhinderwale during Operation Blue Star. After Blue Star, some Sikh soldiers rebelled against Hindu commanding officers and attacked Hindu comrades. One such incident occurred at the Sikh Regimental Center in Ramgarh District, Jharkand, where commanding officer Brigadier R. S. Puri was killed. Likewise, General Arun Vaidya, the chief of Indian Army staff who oversaw Operation Blue Star, was assassinated in 1986 by Sikh militants in Pune. *Border*, by depicting Sikh soldiers led by a Sikh commanding officer, shows Sikhs as saviors of the country integrated into the Indian Army. The film is poised to erase bitter memories of the 1984 pogrom.

The narrative of *Gadar*, opening on a scene set in the last days of pre-Partition India, deals with the complex history of the Partition in relation to the formative days of sovereign India and Pakistan. In this plot, Partition-related brutality leads to the loss of Tara Singh's (Sunny Deol) family members and drives him to enter a Sikh gang engaged in killing Muslims. Meanwhile Sakeena (Ameesha Patel), who has known Tara Singh from her school days and is the daughter of a prominent Muslim politician of the Punjab, is left stranded on a platform. She has been separated from her family after failing to board an overcrowded train headed to Pakistan. Seeing her all alone and recognizing that she is a Muslim, Tara's gang pursues her, wanting to attack and rape her, thus violating her honor and that of her Muslim community. As Sakeena flees in a desperate bid to save her honor and escape physical violence, Tara Singh suddenly recognizes her as his schoolmate and leaps to the rescue. He warns the chasers not to touch her, and he fights his own gang in order to protect her. In a final flourish of protectiveness, Tara Singh anoints Sakeena's forehead with his own blood. He then yells out to the attackers that she has now become a Sikh. This symbolic act of marking the woman's forehead with vermillion signifies the Hindu marriage ritual of transforming a (virginal) female body into that of a bride protected and owned by the husband (and as such, inaccessible to other men).

Subsequently, Tara Singh and Sakeena fall in love, get married, and have a son. About halfway through the narrative, Sakeena reads about her lost family in a newspaper report and expresses a desire to meet them, to which Tara Singh agrees. Arriving in India, her father takes Sakeena back to Lahore and subsequently demands that she leave her Sikh husband and marry a Muslim man of his choice. Sakeena is steadfast in her refusal. Meanwhile Tara Singh, receiving no information about his wife, decides he must go to Pakistan to look for her, illegally crossing the border with his son and a trusted friend. Eventually, Tara Singh has to publicly agree to accept Islam so that he can reunite with his wife. In the same cause, he is even willing to chant nationalist slogans such as "Pakistan zindabad!" (Long live Pakistan!). However, he draws the line when he is asked to say, "Hindustan murdabaad" (Destruction to India). He is intransigent in this matter.

Here, as in *Border*, national identity is paramount for the Sikh protagonist. Tara Singh's readiness to accept Islam is different than pronouncing an anti-India ideology. Whereas in accepting Islam, he has presented himself as a representative of secular India who has an equal respect for all religions, in unflinchingly standing by his country, he effectively reclaims for himself an Indian identity at odds with Pakistan and Muslimness. Furthermore, the narrative elsewhere decisively establishes Tara Singh's supremacy over Pakistan through dialogues in *Gadar* such as "Pakistan tera baap hain Hindustan" (India is the father of Pakistan). This type of dialogue gives Indian men the upper hand over Pakistani Muslim men, as is dramatically shown in the denouement, when a Jat Sikh hero single-handedly defeats the entire Pakistani army, armed with Apache helicopters, which were a point of pride for the Pakistan defense forces in 2001.

Gadar is explicit in embodying extreme forms of Hindu nationalist sentiment through the masculinity of its Sikh protagonist. For instance, Tara Singh asserts at one point that Pakistan was able to stand on its feet only because India had provided "fifty-five crores of rupees" to help the country soon after Partition in 1947. Note that this was the precise reason cited by the Hindu extremist Nathu Ram Godse in assassinating the foremost leader of the Indian national movement, M. K. Gandhi, on January 30, 1948. In this light, it could hardly be a coincidence that *Gadar* was released in 2001 under the Hindu right-wing National Democratic Alliance (NDA), led by the Bhartiya Janta Party (BJP). Even as this filmic narrative ostensibly extends a generous secular hand to Islam, it subjugates the common other by glorifying the symbolic sexual prowess of the Sikh man over feminized and dehumanized Pakistani Muslim manhood. And precisely through this narrative and symbolic invasion of the inimical body by the martial Sikh in the name of patriarchal Hindustan, the Sikh is embraced back into the Hindu communal fold.

RECLAIMING THE SIKH INTO THE HINDU FOLD: RELIGIOUS NATIONALISM AND THE WOMAN IN *GADAR: EK PREM KATHA*

Both *Border* and *Gadar: Ek prem katha* try to reconstruct Indian Sikh identity in the Indian/Hindu patriarchal mold. Drawing upon Frantz Fanon's work, Homi Bhabha (1990) maintains that a homogenous identity is a relational formation, which takes shape through clarifying the interests and commitments of one group in correspondence with or in contrast to another. Working along these lines, both *Gadar* and *Border* align the Sikh with Hindu Indian identity by narrating the former's commitment to the moral ideals of Hindu behavior toward Muslims. One striking scene of *Border*, for example, shows the Sikh protagonist Bhairav Singh rushing into flames and emerging with the Holy Quran in his hand. His valiant act is meant to allay the distress of an Indian Muslim man whose village bordering Pakistan is under attack by enemy tanks. Subsequently the heroic Singh is shown responding to the Muslim villager's gratitude with the observation that *Hindus* (not Sikhs) believe in protecting others; the villager answers with utter gratitude: "And some say you are our enemy." This role of towering moral guardian, standing for Hindu Indian identity, is shared in *Gadar: Ek prem katha* by the more ambivalent figure of a woman subjected to multiple patriarchal religious claims.

In defining the homogenous identity of any group, community, or nation, the ideal woman historically has functioned as the key symbol. As such, respectable women are burdened with the responsibility to protect their honor in the name of the patriarchal community to which they belong. The ideal woman must remain pure since violation of a woman's sexual purity means that the male members of her community lose their status as patriarchs able to control and protect their women and preserve their bloodline against violators. As such, voluntary self-annihilation by honorable women—when threatened with violation in the absence or following the death of their male protectors—has come to constitute one of the more esteemed values enshrined in the legends of patriarchal societies, a value reinvented in modern nationalist representations. One such Indian legend of women's mass suicide, glorified as self-sacrificial martyrdom, was recently revived in a controversial Bollywood production in 2018. Deriving from a tradition of chivalry in western India, the myth in question deifies Queen Rani Padmavati. Padmavati is said to have led the women of her palace into the ritual act of *jauhar* (mass suicide by immolation) to secure the honor of the men of her Hindu Rajput clan in the face of an attack by the Muslim ruler Alauddin Khilji. This value of sexual honor, glorifying communal solidarity in the face of masculine strife, also riddled the history of gender violence during Partition. On the one hand, sexual assault was wielded as an invasive cudgel on a mass scale. Around 75,000 women were raped or abducted (Butalia 1998, 5). Governments on both sides of the border strove hard to recover the women and children (Bhattacharya 2011) and passed almost identical laws (the Abducted Persons Recovery and Restoration Act, 1949). On the other hand, women's mass suicides in defense of patriarchal honor were widespread. For example, ninety Sikh women and children committed mass suicide in the village of Toha Khalsa, in the district of Rawalpindi, now in Pakistan (Butalia 1998). Many were poisoned or killed by their own parents.

As illustrated by these narratives and entwining historical records with cultural myths and assumptions, women's bodies become sites of contestation and confrontation during times of intercommunal conflict. The representation of ideal womanhood in *Gadar: Ek prem katha* reinforces the instrumental role of female identity in this space of contestation. As described in the previous section, the Indian Sikh hero wins the argument against militant men from his own community by transforming the body of a Muslim woman into that of a Sikh. When Tara Singh's Sikh gang members attempt to acquire and control Sakeena's body because she is a "Musulman," a hated other (Bhattacharya 2011), Tara Singh protectively marks her forehead with his blood. In effect, he has appropriately placed on her forehead the vermilion mark signifying sacred wedlock in *Hindu* religious symbolism. In other words, Tara Singh has symbolically converted a Muslim into his respectable wife, a Sikhni, in the only way acceptable to the majority Hindu community of India. While in this manner Sakeena becomes pure and honorable in the eyes of the Indian men who had wanted to control her through sexual violation, at the same time the Muslim female body comes to be instrumentalized as a communally porous object open to competing masculine claims and conquests.

Along these lines, the narrative makes Sakeena wear multiple identities other than her own. At the outset, as a Pakistani Muslim woman, she tries to defend her family's and community's honor; after marriage, she is shown struggling to preserve her Indian Sikh/Hindu identity against intrusion by her parents and her society (Perckel 2008). Although *Gadar* ostensibly is a love story between a Jat Sikh and a Muslim woman, it rests on a larger

India-Pakistan drama with roots in the Partition. Sikh identity was subsumed after Partition, assimilated into Hinduism and positioned as such by Article 25(2b) of the Indian Constitution. *Gadar: Ek prem katha* reasserts and reenacts this assimilation in the postpogrom era, for what the narrative implicitly erases is the memory of the Sikh militant and radical voices who had refused identification with the Hindu majority and fought instead for a distinct legal and social status. Fulfilling the erasure and amnesia, Tara Singh tells people in Pakistan—where he has gone to reclaim his wife from the inimical in-laws—"We Hindus, we don't buckle down to you Muslim people" (Banaji 2008). Following her husband's trail of communal/national loyalty, Sakeena hastens to take up the responsibility of guarding the honor of her (circumstantially turned) religious family and nation.

Sakeena, born a Pakistani Muslim to whom Hindus had been described as the other earlier in the plot line, takes it upon herself to perform the role of a married Hindu (not Sikh) woman at all costs. She refuses to pull out her *mangalsutra* or to stop wearing the vermillion mark on her forehead, thus clinging to the sacred Hindu signifiers both of active marital status (as against Hindu widowhood) and of loyalty to her husband and patriline. All in all, the narrative positions Sakeena as oscillating between two patriarchal loyalties: toward her husband and toward her father. The porosity of the woman's identity, symbolized through the control imposed on her body by the men in her family, is vindicated by the readiness with which Sakeena transfers her allegiance. Claimed both by the father and the husband, after her marriage, she fights her parents to maintain the honor of her husband.

If the body of Pakistani Muslim Sakeena earlier in the narrative represents a "fractious locus for [her] identification [as] citizen," at the close it is explicitly transported and transmuted (Bhattacharya 2011, 142). Tara Singh is shown crossing the border with his Pakistani wife and visibly altering her (patri-)location together with her national identity. Moreover, this transformation of the woman and her national/familial position has been sealed by one more implicit Hindu patriarchal marriage rite. The denouement depicts Tara Singh being reunited with Sakeena only after winning the heart of her once-alienated Pakistani father by single-handedly defeating the Pakistan Army. Her father, Ashraf Ali (Amrish Puri), ends up giving his unequivocal consent. In effect, this closing episode dramatizes the custom of *kanayadan*—the father or a male family elder "donating" the bride to the groom—which is crucial to solemnizing the Hindu ritual of marriage.

Gadar: Ek prem katha consistently celebrates the bravery of the Sikh hero (through scenes of Tara Singh blowing up bridges, trucks, and people), as if to suggest that his act against the (common) Muslim enemy justifies his assimilation into the patriarchal fold of the Hindu/Indian nation.

PATRIOTIC HINDI CINEMA AND MARGINAL MEMORIES: VIEWS FROM THE FIELD

This chapter has argued that these two films were part of the process in reintegrating the Sikhs into mainstream Indian society and politics. The films portray Sikh men both as saviors of India and as a part of the Hinduness of the nation. These high-octane films were cinematic attempts to anchor the faith and identity of the Sikhs, especially the Jat Sikhs, into the official narrative of India's history. Both *Border* and *Gadar* did very well at the box office. *Border* was a major hit of the year and earned around $22 million, whereas *Gadar* grossed $23 million in 2001. Moreover, the rating of *Border* further increased after a limited war between India and Pakistan in the Kargil sector in 1999. The complexity of this film's appeal lies also in the fact that the director, J. P. Dutta, promoted the film as an antiwar narrative, pointing especially to a song (addressing *mere dushman* [my enemy]) that calls for giving up war and destruction through befriending the enemy. The narrative of *Border* revolves around a jingoistic India-Pakistan drama. To this day, these two films lead the patriotic canon of Hindi cinema, regularly returning to the air on such appropriate occasions as India's Independence Day or Republic Day. By contrast, critical films faced censorship when they tried to present a different narrative of the 1984 pogrom.

Sikhs still have not overcome stereotypical images. Popular Hindi comedian Johnny Lever played a shaved Sikh clown in *Raja Hindustani* (1996) and then a bearded one in *Paying Guest* (2009). Not only on the big screen but in many television serials, which occupy significant space in post-liberal Indian households, Sikhs have been shown in stereotyped roles. For example, in one of the most popular television serials, *Tarak Mehta ka oolta chashma* (Tarak Mehta's inverted spectacles), running since 2008 on SAB TV, a Sikh character named Roshan Singh Sodhi, played by a Sikh actor, Gurcharan Singh, is shown as a clown, driver, garage owner, and brave man. The other characters in this serial too have been stereotyped according to the community they represent on the screen

It is important to note that the success of the majoritarian portrayal of Sikh heroism must also be attributed, at least in part, to hierarchies internal to the Sikh community. The Jat Sikhs were relatively open to the assimilationist strategies we find in *Border* and *Gadar: Ek prem katha*; the group as a whole was inclined to reconcile with the Indian establishment and forge anew its historical bond with national structures. By contrast, other Sikhs—who were the real victims of the pogrom—have never appeared in dominant nationalist narratives nor on the Hindi screen because of their lower socioeconomic status. Thus, even if we consider nationalist measures, including the production of popular cinema, to be somewhat effective in reconciling the Sikh community with mainstream India, we must note that not all community members have been included in this process.

Many Sikhs still live with grief and deep-seated animosity toward the Indian state. I observed these feelings while researching this paper in Delhi in October 2014. My respondents were mainly individuals belonging to the socioeconomic class that suffered the most in 1984. While passing through Tilak Vihar, a locality in west Delhi, in October 2014, I asked my hired driver to show me the place where the victims of 1984 anti-Sikh riots lived. He replied that his own family had also been victimized during the pogrom. Like other Sikh children, he had long hair, but his father cut it in 1984 to conceal his Sikh identity. Ever since, he has never grown his hair or beard long again. When I tentatively asked about his views on the pogrom and whether anything had changed since then, he categorically said, "Na bhule hain na maaf kiya hain unko" (We have not forgotten nor forgiven them).

My field notes also confirm that a chasm has appeared between the two communities. One of my respondents informed me that, like Muslims, Sikhs preferred self-ghettoization following the pogrom, so that they might fight back collectively if attacked. One of my respondents informed me that when Rajiv Gandhi, then prime minister of India, was assassinated on May 21, 1991, by a suicide bomber from the Liberation of Tamil Tigers Elam, many Sikhs in Delhi feared reprisal from the Hindu majority because of persistent ethnic prejudice against the community; for this reason, Sikhs from East Delhi sought shelter in what were thought to be the relatively safe zones in the city or fled to the Punjab.

Even today, despite many attempts to erase the memory of violence faced by the Sikh community in 1984, Jarnail Singh Bhinderwale remains a salient symbol of Sikh resistance. Hartosh Bal notes, "In many cities of Punjab slogans eulogizing Bhinderwale can be seen written on the walls or one can pass by youths wearing T-shirts . . . [displaying] his picture. This is not limited to Punjab only; it is also spreading into the nearby state(s) where the Sikhs are substantial in number" (Bal 2014). On June 8, 2015, a handful of Sikhs, wearing T-shirts with Bhinderwale's face, waved the Pakistani flag and chanted pro-Khalistan slogans in Jammu (Mustafa 2015). In addition, Sikhs who fled to foreign countries during the days of militancy in the Punjab or were affected by the anti-Sikh pogrom of 1984 occasionally raise the issue of injustice done to the community by distributing pamphlets and leading protests when prominent Indian leaders visit their adopted country.

NOTES

Please note that the views of this chapter are solely those of the author and do not reflect the position of his affiliated institution.

1 This united self has been created by constructing a narration that those who are not Muslims or Christians or part of any other religion are Hindus. This includes the Dalits, who even today face social and caste-based discrimination from upper-caste Hindus, and tribals who do not belong to any religious fold, though many have been converted into Christianity by the missionaries.

2 *Dilli 1984* is based on the life of Bibi Jagdish Kaur, whose entire family was murdered during the 1984 anti-Sikh pogrom in Delhi. The CBFC banned the film, unanimously stating that the movie was "not fit for public viewing." The reason given was that its public screening could disturb the peace across India (*Sikh24* 2014). *Amu* is a story about an American woman's visit to Delhi, where she accidentally meets the son of a man who was responsible for killing her father during the 1984 anti-Sikh pogrom in Delhi. The film was released with an A certificate, so that only adults could view it.

3 Hinduism is hierarchical. It categorizes groups according to their defined traditional occupation and the level of purity of such occupations. On this basis the upper castes—Brahmin, Kshatriya, and Vaisya—are considered to be pure, while others are treated as impure, and some are even regarded as untouchables. There is also discrimination and hierarchy *within* castes based on region, diet, and language (see Gupta 1991).

4 Land of Khalsa. Khalsa means an army of all initiated Sikhs led by a leader.

REFERENCES

Anderson, Benedict. 1983. *Imagined Communities: Reflections on the Origins and Spread of Nationalism*. London: Verso.

Athique, Adrian. 2008. "Aggression and Transgression on the India-Pakistan Border." In *Filming the Line of Control: The Indo Pak Relationship through the Cinematic Lens*, edited by Meenakshi Bharat and Nirmal Kumar, 21–39. New Delhi: Routledge.

Bal, Hartosh Singh. 2014. "The Shattered Dome: The Story of the Gandhi's Biggest Mistake, and How It Still Haunts Punjab." *Caravan* 1 (May): 44–59.

Banaji, Shakuntala. 2008. "Fascist Imaginaries and Clandestine Critiques: Young Hindi Film Viewers Respond to Violence, Xenophobia and Love in Cross Border Romances." In *Filming the Line of Control: The Indo Pak Relationship through the Cinematic Lens*, edited by Meenakshi Bharat and Nirmal Kumar, 157–77. New Delhi: Routledge.

Bhabha, Homi K. 1990. *Nation and Narration*. New York: Routledge.

Bhattacharya, Nandini. 2011. "Imagined Subjects: Laws, Gender and Citizenship in Indian Cinema." In *Bollywood and Globalization: Indian Popular Cinema, Nation, and Diaspora*, edited by Rini Bhattacharya Mehta and Rajeswari V. Pandharipande, 129–44. London: Anthem Press.

Butalia, Urvashi. 1998. *The Other Side of Silence: Voices from the Partition of India*. New Delhi: Penguin.

Chakravarti, Uma, and Nandita Haksar. 1987. *The Delhi Riots: Three Days in the Life of a Nation*. New Delhi: Lancer International.

Dhulipala, Venkat. 2015. *Creating a New Medina: State Power, Islam, and the Quest for Pakistan in Late Colonial North India*. New Delhi: Cambridge University Press.

Dogra, Chander Sutta. 2016. "Operation Blue Star: The Untold Story." *The Hindu*, June 6, 2016. http://www.thehindu.com/news/national/operation-blue-star-the-untold-story/article4798102.ece.

Gopal, Sangita. 2011. *Conjugations: Marriage and Form in New Bollywood Cinema*. Chicago: University of Chicago Press.

Gopalan, Lalitha. 2002. *Cinema of Interruptions: Action Genres in Contemporary Indian Cinema*. London: British Film Institute.

Grewal, J. S., and Indu Banga. 2000. "Pakistan, Khalistan and Partition." In *The Partition in Retrospect*, edited by Amrik Singh, 159–77. New Delhi: Anamika Publishers.

Gupta, Dipankar. 1991. "Hierarchy and Difference: An Introduction." In *Social Stratification*, edited by Dipankar Gupta, 1–22. New Delhi: Oxford University Press.

Hobsbawm, Eric J. 1992. "Inventing Tradition." In *The Invention of Tradition*, edited by Eric Hobsbawm and Terence Ranger, 1–14. Cambridge: Cambridge University Press.

Jacob, Jayant. 2017. "Pakistan Supporting Sikh Militants, Say Fresh Intelligence Inputs." *Hindustan Times*, September 5, 2017. https://www.hindustantimes.com/india-news/pakistan-supporting-sikh-militants-say-fresh-intelligence-inputs/story-KJTEQPdHMj9FBawDC2gOrN.html.

Kumar, Raksha. 2012. "How Bollywood Views on Pakistan Evolved." *New York Times* blog, August 12. https://india.blogs.nytimes.com/2012/08/16/how-bollywoods-views-on-pakistan-evolved/.

Mustafa, Seema. 2015. "Governments Cower as Bhinderwale Re-emerges." *The Citizen*, June 8, 2015. www.thecitizen.in/index.php/NewsDetail/index/1/3914/GOVERNMENTS-COWER-AS-BHINDRANWALE-RE-EMERGES.

Nanda, Reena. 2018. *From Quetta to Delhi: A Partition Story*. Delhi: Bloomsbury.

Naqvi, Saeed. 2016. *Being the Other: The Muslim in India*. New Delhi: Aleph.

Oberoi, Harjot. 2001. "Sikh Fundamentalism." In *Politics in India*, edited by Sudipta Kaviraj, 318–28. New Delhi: Oxford University Press.

Perckel, Claudia. 2008. "Millions of Daughters of Punjab Weep Today: The Female Perspective in Partition Films." In *Filming the Line of Control: The Indo Pak Relationship through the Cinematic Lens*, edited by Meenakshi Bharat and Nirmal Kumar, 71–86. New Delhi: Routledge.

Roy, Anjali Gera. 2012. "Representation of Sikhs in Bollywood Cinema." Paper presented at the conference Sikhi(sm), Literature and Film, Hofstra University, October 19–21, 2012. The draft has been cited with the author's permission.

Sikh24. 2014. "Dilli 1984: Film Based on the Life Story of Bibi Jagdish Kaur Banned in India." August 16, 2014. https://www.sikh24.com/2014/08/16/dilli-1984-film-based-on-the-life-story-of-bibi-jagdish-kaur-banned-in-india/#.WrQ8qmpuaUk.

Singh, Sunny. 2008. "Defining a Non-Pakistan-centric Post-globalisation Self in Hindi Cinema, 1996–2006." In *Filming the Line of Control: The Indo Pak Relationship through the Cinematic Lens*, edited by Meenakshi Bharat and Nirmal Kumar, 111–27. New Delhi: Routledge.

Suri, Sanjay. 2015. *1984: The Anti-Sikh Violence and After*. Noida, India: Harper Collins.

Suroor, Hasan. 2011. "Manmohan Singh's Apology for Anti-Sikh Riots a 'Gandhian Moment of Moral Clarity,' Says 2005 Cable." *The Hindu*, April 22, 2011. http://www.thehindu.com/news/the-india-cables/manmohan-singhs-apology-for-antisikh-riots-a-gandhian-moment-of-moral-clarity-says-2005-cable/article1715620.ece.

Tully, Mark, and Satish Jacob. 1985. *Amritsar: Mrs Gandhi's Last Battle*. New Delhi: Rupa Publications.

Vasudevan Ravi S. 2000. "The Politics of Cultural Address in a 'Transnational' Cinema: A Case Study of Indian Popular Cinema." In *Reinventing Film Studies*, edited by Christine Gledhill and Linda Williams, 130–64. London: Bloomsbury Academics.

———. 2010. *The Melodramatic Public: Film Form and Spectatorship in Indian Cinema*. Ranikhet: Permanent Black.

4 SILENCING FILMS FROM THE CHITTAGONG HILL TRACTS

Indigenous Cinema's Challenge to the Imagined Cultural Homogeneity of Bangladesh

GLEN HILL AND KABITA CHAKMA

IN HIS FORMATIVE TEXT, *BANGLADESH CINEMA AND NATIONAL Identity: In Search of the Modern*, cinema scholar Zakir Hossain Raju (2015) characterizes the recent cinema of Bangladesh as Bengali-Muslim cinema. Recounting the transformation of Bangladesh cinema in the second half of the twentieth century, Raju observes that Dhaka-based Bengali cinema developed as a secular cultural cinema during 1950s and 1960s. Raju suggests that it was only after the 1971 war for independence from Pakistan, when Bangladesh experienced industrialization and homogenization to meet postcolonial Bangladesh's nationalist state aspirations, that cinema began to conform to Bengali and Muslim representations of hegemonic Bangladesh identity. In alignment with nationalist state aspirations, the film industry in Bangladesh now presents itself as monolingually and monoculturally Bengali, and monoreligiously Islamic.

While Bengali is the dominant ethnicity, culture, and language of Bangladesh, and Islam the dominant religion, the country nevertheless has a diversity of ethnically distinct minorities. Raju (2006, 132) argues that "the attempts of the state and middle-class Bengali Muslims to turn Bangladesh into a Bengali-Muslim nation-state, as demonstrated in the hegemonic representational politics of contemporary popular cinema, clearly undermine the cultural identity of minority groups like non-Muslims and non-Bengalis such as hill-tribes [i.e., the indigenous communities of the Chittagong Hill Tracts] living in Bangladesh."

Raju's brief but insightful comment about the potential colonizing effect of the consumption of mainstream film by indigenous minorities has been raised in connection with other indigenous communities. Discussing Australian indigenous cinema, Therese Davis (2009) endorses Faye D.

Ginsburg's claim that "studies of Indigenous film production and culture have been 'haunted' by the question of 'whether minority or dominated subjects can assimilate media to their own cultural and political concerns or are inevitably compromised by its presence.'"

Through documentation of the history of the consumption and production of cinema in the Chittagong Hill Tracts (CHT), this chapter questions the cultural hegemony of Bengali nationalism represented in Bangladesh cinema and suggests that film has not only been used to impose multiple subjectivities on Bangladesh's indigenous peoples, but has also been used by the indigenous communities themselves to attempt to resist the imposition of identities and to actively construct their own diverse subjectivities. The chapter contends that the state's control over the construction of subjectivity in Bangladesh cinema is no longer appropriate or viable in the contemporary landscape of transnational flows of production and consumption of cinema. By portraying the ethnic and cultural diversity of Bangladesh, Indigenous Cinema, although repressed by censorship and prejudice, has the potential to act as an agent of change toward a more heterogeneous self-identity for Bangladesh.

THE CHITTAGONG HILL TRACTS

The CHT is located in the southeastern hilly region of present-day Bangladesh, on the fault line between South Asia and Southeast Asia. It is the traditional homeland of at least eleven indigenous peoples, who collectively call themselves the Jumma, after their shared "jum," or swidden, agricultural practices (van Schendel 1992). Jummas are linguistically and religiously diverse. Each indigenous Jumma community has its own language, distinct from Bengali, and the communities follow religions that include Buddhism, Hinduism, Krama, Animism, and Christianity, rather than Islam, the major religion in Bangladesh.

The CHT has a different precolonial, colonial, and postcolonial history from the rest of Bangladesh. Resistance to the British colonial incursions by the indigenous peoples of the CHT meant that the CHT was not annexed by the British until 1860, one hundred years later than adjacent Bengal (the eastern part of which is now Bangladesh). Even after annexation, the CHT remained relatively autonomous, retaining its traditional monarchical governance system alongside the British administration. At the departure of the British from India in 1947, the CHT was left under the control of a new "colonial" power, East Pakistan. Control of the CHT moved to Bangladesh when it gained independence from Pakistan in 1971.

The 1972 Bangladesh constitution did not provide a constitutional safeguard for the autonomous status the CHT had enjoyed during the British- and to a lesser extent the Pakistani-administered periods. Soon after rejecting the demand by CHT leaders to maintain CHT's autonomy in the new constitution, the government began to suppress the early stages of a struggle for autonomy that eventually saw the emergence of an armed guerrilla group, the Shanti Bahini (Peace Force). The CHT became militarized in August 1975, when Bangladesh was brought under military rule. Since 1975 Bangladesh has had both military and democratic governments, but the CHT has remained under military occupation. In 1991 the CHT Commission, an international human rights panel, noted the extraordinary numbers of military personnel in the CHT, estimating that there was one member of the security force for every ten hill people in the CHT (Chittagong Hill Tracts Commission 1991, 42).

The high military presence did not change even after the signing of the CHT Accord in December 1997, which ended more than two decades of armed struggle for autonomy. While the indigenous militia demobilized as part of the Accord, the Bangladesh government, in contravention of the Accord, maintained its heavy military presence in the CHT. A 2011 UN study (UN Economic and Social Council 2011, 16) noted that one-third of the Bangladesh military was stationed in the CHT, which constitutes only a tenth of the land area of the country, with an indigenous population of less than one percent of Bangladesh's population. The report recorded the occurrence of "arbitrary arrests, torture, extrajudicial killings, harassment of rights activists and sexual harassment."

The occupation of the CHT by the Bangladesh military was accompanied by systematic colonization of the CHT by Bengali settlers. This was carried out by two means: a government policy of transmigration involving mass settlement of four hundred thousand Bengalis from the plains to the CHT, and a policy of state acquisition of the lands of indigenous people (Adnan 2004, 57). However, lack of usable land in the CHT, which had already been exacerbated in the early 1960s, when the valleys of the CHT were flooded to create the vast Kaptai Lake and hydroelectric facility, meant that it was impossible to allocate the promised amount of land to the large number of Bengali settlers, leading to conflict between the indigenous inhabitants and the newly arriving Bengali transmigrants. After over thirty years of sustained transmigration, Bengali settlers now represent half of the population of the CHT. Dispossession of land and violence perpetrated by the Bangladesh military and Bengali civilian militia have transformed the indigenous peoples' homeland into an often dangerous and frightening landscape.

CONSUMPTION OF CINEMA IN THE CHT

Because of its remote location, the CHT remained longer on the margins of European technologies than the rest of Bangladesh. The technology of still photography had been used to document the CHT and its people from at least the 1860s, but few critical studies have been undertaken to ascertain when indigenous peoples began autonomous portrayal of themselves as subjects (van Schendel, Mey, and Dewan 2000; van Schendel 2002). Likewise, the infiltration of the technology of film into the CHT is not well documented. An early silent clip (*Chittagong Hill Tracts Nov 1935*), recording the governor of Bengal Sir John Anderson's 1935 visit to the CHT, is perhaps the first film shot in the hill tracts.

In the large population centers of what is now Bangladesh, films had been shown from around 1900, when the British raj administered India. Public exhibition of films was introduced into the CHT after the Partition of India, when the CHT, along with the rest of current-day Bangladesh, fell under the political administration of Pakistan. During the Pakistan era, the Department of Publicity showed films throughout East Pakistan (now Bangladesh), including the CHT, in public places such as community halls, markets, and open fields. These public relations exercises conveyed political messages, public policy, and information about social welfare schemes.

The first permanent cinema hall in Bangladesh, known as the Picture House, began operating in Dhaka (now the capital of Bangladesh) around 1913–14. But it was not until 1955 that the first cinema hall, the Indrapuri, was built in Rangamati, the largest town in the CHT. Some Jummas, particularly the elites, were already familiar with cinema from at least the end of the second or early third decade of the twentieth century. They watched films at cinemas in metropolitan Calcutta (now Kolkata), where CHT elites went for official visits and luxury trips and sent their children for education. In the 1940s and 1950s, before the Indrapuri cinema house was built, most CHT elites and some ordinary people attended the cinema in the adjacent city of Chittagong (Roy 2003, 115). Other cinema halls were established later in the CHT: the Olympia was established in Kaptai in 1962, the Kakoli cinema at Garjantali in Rangamati in 1977, the Mitali at Khagrachari Bazar in 1980, the Banashree at Madhyam Para in Bandarban in 1983, and the Moonmoon at Panchari in 1984. From the late 1980s to the 1990s, cinema audiences declined all over Bangladesh as new technologies for showing films became available, alternative viewing sites (particularly home viewing) became possible, and access to a larger, often international, range of films became available. As a result, all of the cinemas in the CHT except the Kakoli closed or functioned irregularly.

THE PRODUCTION OF CINEMA IN THE CHT

As early as the period of Pakistan administration (1947–71) the CHT had become the site of cinema production. There were two principal drivers for filmmaking in the CHT. First, with its unique landscape of hills and forest, which is so different from the vast deltaic plains of much of the rest of the country, the CHT became an exotic location for commercial narrative filmmaking.[1] For a quite different reason the CHT was also the site of documentary film production. Kaptai Lake was a major technological feat. For the government it was a source of great pride, demonstrating the technological achievement of neocolonial post-1947 Pakistan. After independence in 1971, the Kaptai hydroelectric facility became a signifier of Bangladesh's entry into modernity. Many state guests' visits to the new nation-state included a visit to the CHT accompanied by extensive visual documentation. The significant post-independence film *Bangladesh I Love You* (dir. Reginald Massey), which documented the 1978 state visit of the heavyweight champion Mohammad Ali, was partly shot in the CHT.

Ironically, the technological feat of constructing a vast lake that transformed ancient hills into green islands created yet another layer of aesthetic contrast that added to the CHT's appeal as a location for narrative filmmaking. For the indigenous people of the CHT, however, the creation of Kaptai Lake did not have a positive outcome. The lake inundated Rangamati town, the major administrative headquarters of the CHT, including the residence of the Chakma royal family. It submerged many villages and destroyed the best arable land in the region. Ultimately it rendered one-third of the entire CHT population homeless. As an aside, the lake also inundated the CHT's first cinema, the Indrapuri.

In the brief history of filmmaking in the CHT, the filmic portrayal of the CHT and its indigenous peoples has varied dramatically, resulting in significantly different constructions of indigenous subjectivity. At least three different types of filmic portrayal are identifiable, each of which constructs quite distinct indigenous subjectivities. One category, here called scenographic films, takes the CHT and its indigenous people as an exotic backdrop, providing little or no insight into issues of consequence to the CHT and its peoples. A second category, exogenous, takes the CHT or its people as a significant theme, but from a perspective that may be other than that of the indigenous peoples. A third category, endogenous, takes the CHT or its people as a significant theme and does so from the perspective of the indigenous peoples themselves.

SCENOGRAPHIC CHT FILMS

The Dhaka-based Bangladesh Film Development Corporation (BFDC), Bangladesh's national filmmaking institution, has produced most of the commercial films made in Bangladesh. Of the thousands of films it has produced to date, all have been Bengali-language films, even though over forty-five non-Bengali languages are spoken in Bangladesh. This monolingual focus contrasts with other South Asian cinemas, such as India, Sri Lanka, and Pakistan, where state-supported commercial films are often multilingual. Thus, of the many films funded by the BFDC that are set in the CHT, none are in a local CHT language.

The treatment of the CHT and its indigenous people in Bengali narrative films, particularly in the early period of filmmaking, constructed the people and place as an exotic other. The representation of the indigenous people generally bore no resemblance to reality. While each of the eleven indigenous groups in the CHT has its own individual language, cultural practices, and unique and identifiable mode of dress, Bengali films set in the CHT made little attempt to give specificity to any of the unique CHT cultures, nor was there any connection between the location where the scenes were set and the indigenous people portrayed as living there. As if to avoid portraying genuine otherness, when indigenous characters (known as *paharis*) were required, they were generally played by Bengali actors. In 1970s films such as *Anek din ager katha* (Tales of long ago) and the box office hit *Jokhon bristi elo* (The rain), indigenous men are played by Bengali actors, some wearing extravagant moustaches (never normally grown by *pahari* men), while indigenous women are attired in exotic dress that has no connection to any cultural group in the CHT.

EXOGENOUS CHT FILMS

Perhaps the earliest significant commercial-release narrative film that attempts to take seriously the portrayal of the CHT and its indigenous inhabitants is the acclaimed 1976 Bengali film *Megher onek rong*, literally meaning "Many Colors of Clouds" or "Many Colors of the Sky" (a title that resonates with the rainbow that arches over the opening scene of the film). The film, directed by the nonindigenous filmmaker Harunur Rashid, depicts a young Bengali doctor, Dr. Omor (Omor Elahi), who, along with his wife, Ruma (Dr. Rowshan Ara) and young child, Adnan (Master Adnan), is caught up in the violence of the war of independence from Pakistan. In the tumult, the husband becomes separated from his wife and child. His wife is gang-raped by Pakistani soldiers and she and her child left for dead. The doctor believes his family has been killed and begins a new married life with an indigenous woman from the CHT, Mathin (Rina Sarki).[2] After the war is won, he moves with his new wife to the CHT to practice medicine. Ruma, the doctor's first wife who has survived but is psychologically scared, unwittingly moves with her son to the CHT for rehabilitation. Ruma recognizes her husband when he visits the rehabilitation center, but because of her shame she cannot face him. She chooses instead to anonymously leave her son with the doctor and his new wife and commit suicide, a depiction now critiqued by feminists (Gayen 2015).

Megher onek rong is a powerful epic that won five national film awards (Best Film, Best Director, Best Child Artist, Best Cinematography, and Best Music Director). While the primary theme revolves around the war of independence and its devastating impact on the protagonists, the issue of who has the right to belong in the new state of Bangladesh is also prominent.

Unlike earlier narrative films set in the CHT, the CHT and its indigenous inhabitants are no longer merely exotic backdrops to the film's action. The film attempts to be authentic to its location, inserting specific scenes of the landscape and traditional life of the CHT, including *jum* (swidden) agriculture, and the Marma chief Bohmong's ceremonial procession to a Buddhist temple. The use of actors from the CHT, particularly Mathin in the leading role, is a shift away from using Bengali actors to play *paharis*. The characters of the *paharis* are not subordinate or simple, but are treated respectfully. Dr. Omor's colleague in the Chandraghona Christian Missionary Hospital, a real location in the CHT, is an indigenous doctor played by Dr. Swehla Mong Chowdury, an actual Marma doctor. He is presented attired in a smart modern Western suit, the equal of his fellow Bengali doctor. Dr. Omor's second wife, Mathin, who is played by a CHT woman of Tripura and Nepali origin, is presented as modern and sophisticated. She dresses in fashionable Western and Bengali clothing. She speaks with the intonations of an educated Bengali. She reads *Time* magazine. The repartee between her and her husband is vibrant, and neither is portrayed as subordinate.

Although Mathin speaks Bengali throughout most of the film, there are intimate moments when she speaks in either Marma or Chakma. On the long drive into the remote forested hills of the CHT, Mathin sings a popular Chakma song. In a parting scene, Mathin and Dr. Omor exchange farewells in Marma. Perhaps the most poignant use of the local language is the scene in which Omor's son, Adnan, addresses Mathin using the Bengali word for mother, *ma*, and Mathin corrects him, insisting that he address her with the Marma word for mother, *omoi*. In this way Mathin not only differentiates herself from Adnan's Bengali birth mother but also emphasizes her Marma identity.

In the film's depiction of the new nation of Bangladesh emerging out of the violence of war, the question of who should belong is foregrounded. An intense scene that broaches the issue of the place of non-Bengali minorities in the new state of Bangladesh occurs when Mathin, a nurse who has been caring for wounded freedom fighters and is clearly committed to the new nation, has her allegiance questioned by Dr. Omor. Mathin, articulating why one would fight for one's country, argues, "Life without mission is death; that is why there is this fight for freedom." But Dr. Omor dismisses this with the question "Is this fight for freedom yours too?" As if to emphasize the point, he states, "[You use] borrowed ideas," indicating that non-Bengalis do not have genuine reasons to fight for the new nation.

From the perspective of the indigenous people of the CHT, one of the most controversial lines of the film is Mathin's rejoinder to Dr. Omor's questioning of her allegiance: "You do not want to accept us as Bengali, but I belong to this land!" Her use of the word *Bengali* brings uncertainty to the film's message. With these words, does the indigenous character Mathin locate herself as an outsider who is thwarted in her aspiration to become a Bengali? Should we understand her as an indigenous woman who has acquired almost everything—education, affluence, Western affectations—and the final step in her rise above her *pahari* status is to be accepted as a Bengali? This reading is reinforced by a speech given in the CHT by the prime minister of Bangladesh, Sheikh Mujibur Rahman, shortly before the film was made, in which he said, "The hill people would be known as Bengali and they would have no other identity" (Chakma 2010, 287), an unequivocal call for the communities of the CHT to abandon their own culture and be integrated into Bengali culture.

But would the implication have been different if Mathin had used the only available alternative expression and exclaimed, "You do not want to accept us as *Bangladeshi*"? While *Bangladeshi* was at the time a neutral descriptor yet to be colonized by Bengali Muslim nationalism (and as such advocated for use by indigenous people themselves), Amena Mohsin (2013) notes that it had little currency in Bangladesh in this period. Its unfamiliarity would therefore have made it difficult to use in the film's script. The telling point here is that there was, and still is, no accepted word for an inhabitant of Bangladesh that does not also imply the exclusion of its non-Bengali, non-Muslim minorities.

This lacuna in language may in fact allow a more generous interpretation of the film. It may be that the *pahari* voice of Mathin is pleading that, at the very outset of this new nation, the category *Bengali* (at the time the most accepted word for a citizen of Bangladesh) should be *expanded* to include all of the culturally diverse peoples of Bangladesh. The film title's reference to a rainbow perhaps reinforces this interpretation: just as each color of a rainbow retains its identity within a rainbow, the non-Bengali minorities might retain their identities within the overarching "multicolored" state of Bangladesh.

Karnaphulir kanna (The teardrops of Karnaphuli, 2005), an hour-long documentary film made by the eminent Bengali film director and writer Tanvir Mokammel, also takes seriously the portrayal of the CHT and its indigenous inhabitants. Although the filmmaker is not from the CHT, the film empathizes with the indigenous people's perception of oppression and violation by both the Bangladesh military and Bengali transmigrants.

Using the familiar ethnographic documentary filmmaking trope of the interview, *Karnaphulir kanna* juxtaposes the views of local indigenous inhabitants with alternative views from Bengali transmigrants. In this way, the film effectively highlights the loss of the indigenous people's traditional way of life, land, and livelihood as a result of both the building of the Kaptai dam and the influx of Bengali settlers. It also reveals the almost total lack of communication, understanding, and trust that exists between the indigenous inhabitants and their transmigrant Bengali neighbors.

Because of its uncompromising portrayal of conditions in the CHT, *Karnaphulir kanna* was subject to one of the most highly publicized attacks by the Bangladesh state on a cultural work relating to the CHT, when upon release it was banned from public exhibition. The ban appeared to support the claim that the state was attempting to conceal Pakistan and Bangladesh government oppression in the CHT. Defending the censorship, the government explained that "the film has been banned as per Criminal Procedure Code Act 99(A) for depicting objectionable messages against the interests of the country as well as its people (*bdnews24.com* 2005)." However, a High Court challenge in 2006, which overturned the ban on *Karnaphulir kanna*, demonstrated the weakness of the government's legal case, exposing the ban as politically motivated.

Banning or impeding the presentation of CHT cultural works through government intimidation of cultural workers is not new. From the mid-1970s, the CHT has experienced cultural oppression, including the arbitrary banning of cultural, political, economic, and human rights activities (Chakma and Hill 2013, 148–49; CHT Commission 1994, 23–24). Unlike the case of *Karnaphulir kanna*, however, these incidents have had limited or no coverage in the national media and remain largely unnoticed by the people of Bangladesh.

As a result of the ban, *Karnaphulir kanna* has had limited public exposure. It has been screened in noncommercial theaters, universities, and film festivals in Bangladesh and India. It has also been shown in a number of prestigious international venues, including the Kathmandu documentary film festival and at the Musée Guimet in France. *Karnaphulir kanna* earned prestige in the South Asian filmscape by being selected by Film South Asia in 2005 as one of the best fifteen films of the year and now travels as part of Film South Asia's catalog.

ENDOGENOUS CHT FILMS

Films produced in the CHT and made from the perspective of the indigenous peoples themselves fit within the scope of Barry Barclay's (2003) definition of Fourth Cinema. In 1990, Barclay, a Maori filmmaker and cinema critic from Aotearoa, New Zealand, introduced the term *Fourth Cinema* to describe Indigenous Cinema. Barclay suggested Fourth Cinema as an addition to Fernando Solanas and Octavio Getino's (1983) framework of First, Second, and Third Cinema, which they proposed in their 1969 essay *Towards a Third Cinema*. In this framework, First Cinema refers to Hollywood movies, Second Cinema to the form of European art cinema that rejects Hollywood conventions and instead focuses on an auteur director, and Third

Cinema to film from the postcolonial world, such as the authors' home region of Latin America, which accommodates the particular cultural thinking pattern of the colonized projected though the eyes of the repressed (Barclay 2003). Barclay's Fourth Cinema also relates to the older term *Fourth World*, coined in the late twentieth century (Wilson and Stuart 2008, 9) as part of the emergence of collective international indigenous activism. Recognizing that indigenous peoples' cultures are unmatched to the cultural paradigms of modern nation-states, Fourth Cinema is an ideology that does not necessarily conform to the modern nation-state's cultural goals and aspirations. Barclay argues that Fourth Cinema introduces views outside the convictions of the cinema of modern nation-states, calling on it to "seek to rework the ancient core values to shape a growing Indigenous cinema outside the national orthodoxy." The discourse of Fourth/Indigenous Cinema has since been extended in the work of cinema scholars and activists like Faye D. Ginsburg (1996, 2002), Stuart Murray (2008), Jennifer Gauthier (2008), Michelle Raheja (2011), Joanna Hearne (2012), Joanna Hearne and Corinn Columpar (2012), Hester Joyce (2013), and others.

The number of Fourth Cinema productions by indigenous CHT filmmakers is small relative to the volume of films produced throughout Bangladesh. For example, in 2005, a year when over a hundred popular Bengali feature films were also released (produced by the Dhaka-based Bangladesh Film Development Corporation), only two feature-length films about the CHT were made (*Karnaphulir kanna* and *Dulu kumuri*, a 2005 film released in 2006). The number of films produced in the CHT has been limited by demography, technology, and politics. The indigenous population of the CHT is approximately 750,000, compared to an overall Bangladesh population of over 150 million. This not only implies reduced potential for production but also means that the market for consuming minority-language or -themed films is limited. Technologically, filmmaking in the CHT emerged using low-cost film formats. However, commercial theaters have until recently been equipped to show only 35 mm films, and without state support 35 mm film production is financially prohibitive. Only in the last few years has the screening of digital film in commercial cinemas become possible. Politically, films made in the CHT have been, and continue to be, the subject of state censorship. This is particularly pertinent for commercial-release films, as public cinema screening is regulated by the Bangladesh Censor Board.

Like all cinema, CHT's Indigenous Cinema involves a complex nexus of transactions of production, exhibition, distribution, and reception. The last decades of the twentieth century saw a revolution in the possibilities for film production and consumption. In 1979 VCR technology was introduced into Bangladesh. As a result, cinema audiences across the country dwindled, as people were able to access South Asian, particularly Indian Bangla and Hindi, films. Subsequent digital media and satellite television technologies had a further impact as audiences chose to watch higher-quality non-Bangladeshi films at home instead of going to theaters, which continued to show predominantly 35 mm Dhaka-based Film Development Corporation Bangla-language films. With the arrival of new technology and the fading of celluloid cinema screening, CHT's Indigenous Cinema found a local niche, and the first narrative film from the CHT, *Aandalat phor* (Penumbra), was released in 1996.[3] Encouraged by the availability of more affordable technology for making and showing films, the early 2000s saw the emergence of a small but significant group of young indigenous CHT filmmakers, including Jnana Kirti Chakma, Tarun Chakma (Monibo), and Shuvashis Chakma (Ittukgula).

CHT's indigenous filmmakers produced both documentary and narrative films in a number of languages. Documentary films have either had ethnographic themes[4] or human rights themes.[5] Narrative films have dealt with CHT folklore (*Dulu kumuri*) or themes relating to the everyday life of indigenous CHT people.[6] Indigenous CHT films are mostly made in indigenous languages (the commonest being Chakma, the largest language group), though some have been made in Bangla,[7] and more recently in English.[8] English-language indigenous CHT films are particularly favored by filmmakers from the international indigenous CHT diaspora based in countries that include the United Kingdom,[9] Canada,[10] and Australia.[11] While documentary and narrative films have been mostly low budget and variable in quality, exceptions include *Khumi i awmnai reta* (Khumi lives, 2007), *Life Is Still Not Ours: A Story of the Chittagong Hill Tracts* (2014), *Rajanagar* (2016), *Ranjit Dewan: A Living Legend of Chakma Music* (2013), *Swaban nahi pattam* (Dream or reality, 2015, which received the Tarek Masud Film Award 2015), and the international award-winning *Maw theng gaari* (My bicycle, 2014), which has yet to be allowed commercial screening in Bangladesh.

The exhibition and distribution of CHT Indigenous Cinema has to date been relatively limited. Because of both format restrictions and censorship, such films have not been shown in mainstream commercial theaters. However, many have been screened in alternative theaters, and many more have been viewed in domestic settings. CHT cinema's public exhibition is often at local fairs and festivals. The first public screening of Tarun Chakma's 2005 debut film, *Dulu kumuri*—a feature-length Chakma-language film produced by the Jum Aesthetic Council (JAC) of Rangamati and the first to be directed by and feature indigenous peoples from the CHT—occurred during the 13th Adibasi Sanskriti Mela (Indigenous Peoples Cultural Festival) in April 2006 in Rangamati. The primary distribution sites for CHT Indigenous Cinema have been largely limited to the CHT and indigenous CHT communities across the border in India. While the audience is not large, it is not insignificant. Within a year of its release, *Dulu kumuri* is estimated to have been viewed by over 200,000 people in Bangladesh and India. There has also been formal, informal, national, and transnational distribution of films involving audiences that are local, national, and international, facilitated by new international media platforms such as YouTube.

INDIGENOUS CHT CINEMA'S CONSTRUCTION OF SUBJECTIVITY

In the majority of indigenous CHT films to date, indigenous subjectivity is constructed in the shadow of militarization and the loss of traditional ways of life. This is perhaps most powerfully illustrated in the recently completed *Maw theng gaari* (My bicycle), which sets the mundane details of the struggles of everyday life in the CHT against a changing cultural and technological landscape and the unsettling backdrop of military occupation.

Maw theng gaari is a sixty-one-minute, digitally produced, Chakma-language film written and directed by Aung Rakhine, an indigenous Rakhine from Cox's Bazar, a district adjacent to the CHT. After living for some time in the CHT, he decided to focus his drama on the Chakma community, because, as he states, "they struggled more than any other indigenous group of the country" (Chakmapedia n.d.).

The plot of *Maw theng gaari* centers on an unemployed indigenous CHT Chakma youth, Kamal (Kamal Mani Chakma), whose life revolves around his much-loved bicycle. After losing his job in the city, Kamal returns home with his bicycle, which is a novelty in his remote village. He hits upon the idea of earning an income by ferrying people and goods with his bicycle. But his entrepreneurial endeavors are disrupted by run-ins with both the powerful locals and hoodlums in the village. Eventually Kamal's bicycle is stolen, and he finds it discarded and damaged, the wrecked bicycle a metaphor for his shattered dreams. In the final scene Kamal is shown leaving the CHT just as he arrived—a passenger sitting with his (now broken) bicycle in a small one-oared boat on the river Karnaphuli. The one-oared boats that pass by him slowly from the opposite direction carry even more contemporary technologies than his beloved bicycle: one carries a motorcycle; another, a television set.

In its reflection of the experience of living in the CHT, *Maw theng gaari* subtly evokes an ambient threat of violence. However, here the primary threat is from the criminal activity of fellow indigenous villagers rather than the security forces. While the presence of the military is menacingly alluded to, only rarely are soldiers actually encountered. In one brief scene soldiers are shown marching over a child's toys as the child withdraws to his mother in trepidation. To cloud the interpretation further, the military uniform evident in this scene (camouflage and sneakers) is not precisely that of the Bangladesh military, leaving open other interpretations.

Maw theng gaari premiered at the 13th International Short and Independent Film Festival in Dhaka in December 2014, and was subsequently shown at numerous film festivals all over the world including Italy, the United Kingdom, Estonia, Kolkata, Finland, Sweden, Tanzania, and Canada. It won international awards, including Best Script at Russia's Silver Akbuzat International Festival of National and Ethnic Cinema in 2015.

In its construction of indigenous subjectivity, the endogenous narrative film *Maw theng gaari* differs significantly from earlier films. There are, for example, significant differences between *Maw theng gaari* and the notable exogenous documentary film *Karnaphulir kanna*. Like much orthodox ethnographic filmmaking, *Karnaphulir kanna* constructs the indigenous inhabitants of the CHT as authentic autochthonous inhabitants, fixed in a traditional way of life. When indigenous people appear in shot, the montage of images with which they are portrayed shows them engaged in traditional *jum* agriculture, undertaking traditional cultural activities (such as *ben* weaving and bamboo dancing), wearing traditional dress, and so on. The film, deliberately or otherwise, creates a sense of nostalgia for a lost utopic way of life before the building of the dam and the arrival of Bengali transmigrant settlers. As the opening text scrolls down, the viewer is told that the dam was "the first crisis in the *peaceful life* of the Chittagong Hill Tracts" (emphasis added). This "peaceful life" is to some extent mythic, as it involves a selective forgetting of events such as internecine violence and environmental hardships. Not unlike the early naive scenographic cinematic portrayals of indigenous peoples from the CHT, *Karnaphulir kanna*'s portrayal, while empathetic, still reduces the diversity of CHT communities to a somewhat homogeneous ethnographic stereotype: traditional people belonging to the past and longing for the past. This reductive tendency in ethnographic cinema is described by William Lempert (2012), who, drawing upon the postmodern scholar of Native American identity politics Sandy Grande, argues that in these cinematic contexts indigenous peoples are not free to reinvent themselves or transgress the borders of difference imposed upon them.

By contrast, the indigenous subjects of the endogenous film *Maw theng gaari* actively reinvent themselves and transgress ethnographic stereotypes. The principal indigenous protagonist is portrayed improvising ways to survive in the face of contemporary conditions of life—not simply in response to the difficult context of military or transmigrant occupation but also (and perhaps even more significantly) in response to an ever-changing technological and cultural milieu. The bicycle with which he reconstructs his life is the central technological motif in the film. But other technologies that have been imposed on the CHT, such as the dam that signifies industrial progress or the guns of the military, have also required the indigenous inhabitants to creatively reinvent their lives. In *Maw theng gaari* indigenous subjectivity is therefore not fixed in time, but rather is in a state of ongoing transformation (hence the power of the final scene, where the audience is left to imagine the existential implications of the two new technologies, the motorbike and television, which arrive, ironically, on traditional one-oared boats). As well as not being fixed in time, indigenous subjectivity in *Maw theng gaari* is not treated as homogenous. Unlike *Karnaphulir kanna* and Bangladesh's earlier mainstream commercial films, *Maw theng gaari*'s protagonists are constructed with a diversity of qualities (and moralities) without losing the specificity of their indigenous Chakma identity.

Despite the cinematic quality of *Maw theng gaari* and the acclaim it has received at festival screenings, the film's quiet but powerful mode of representing the indigenous experience of life in the CHT has led to the politicizing of the film and the blocking of its commercial release. Although the Bangladesh Censor Board initially issued a viewing date of July 22, 2015, for the film's review, it deferred this viewing based on a written complaint from Lt. Colonel Mohammad Jahangir Alam that claimed Rakhine's film had been screened without censor approval, even though no approval is required for film festival screenings.[12] The same letter asserted that the film contained scenes and dialogue detrimental to the Bangladesh government and security force.

Rakhine, the filmmaker, stresses, however, that the scene showing uniformed military personnel passing by is symbolic, and that the film does not specify them as being from the Bangladesh Security Force (Deutsche Welle 2015). To understand his point, it must be understood that in the post-Accord CHT, military uniforms and arms commonly fall into the hands of those involved in criminal activities like extortion and kidnapping (perhaps, some suggest, to legitimize the military's presence in the post-Accord CHT).

Even though the scenes that offended the Bangladesh Censor Board appear relatively innocuous, and there is well-publicized support for the film in the Bangladesh media and the film's funders are majority Bengali, *Maw theng gaari* remains banned in Bangladesh.

CONCLUSION

Indigenous CHT cinema exists as a small but diverse transnational enterprise of film production and consumption. Through cinema, the CHT connects to an indigenous diaspora in India, the United Kingdom, the United States, Australia, Canada, and beyond, and presents itself to a worldwide audience via international film festivals and globally networked online digital media platforms.

Yet within Bangladesh, indigenous CHT cinema has still to breach the barrier of nationalist prejudice and censorship. The Bangladesh state continues to maintain what appears to be an increasingly anachronistic attempt to control the construction of Bangladeshi subjectivity. At present the only lives reflected back in the mirror of Bangladeshi cinema are Bengali-Muslim lives, perpetuating the myth of the homogeneity of the Bangladesh nation. This attempt to control the construction of subjectivity is set against the reality that the flows of diverse international media (from Bollywood to Hollywood) are already reshaping the subjectivity of the inhabitants of Bangladesh outside government control. It is also set against the reality that Bangladesh is home to a diversity of ethnically, culturally, and religiously distinct minorities. If Indigenous Cinema were to be allowed a place within the frame of the mirror of the Bangladesh filmscape, the potential exists for it to positively transform the self-representation of the Bangladeshi film industry and to act as an agent of change toward a more heterogeneous identity for Bangladesh.

NOTES

1 For instance, Zahir Raihan's box office hit *Sangam* (Confluence, 1964, Urdu) was partly shot in the CHT; and Azizur Rahman's box office hit *Chutir ghanta* (The bell of departure, 1980) was mostly shot in the CHT.

2 The marriage of a *pahari* to a Bengali would also have been frowned upon by the vast majority of the indigenous inhabitants of the CHT. This is especially true as its portrayal comes at a time when the army had just occupied the CHT to put down the beginnings of a popular insurgency, and before a secret memorandum (1983) was circulated to all army officers in the CHT encouraging them to marry tribal women (CHT Commission 1991,109).

3 *Aandalat phor* (Penumbra, 1996), a coproduction of Jum Aesthetics Council, Rangamati, and Aranyak Natyadal, a leading Dhaka theater group, is the first Chakma-language film filmed in the CHT. Originally written and directed as a stage drama by Jhimit Jhimt Chakma, his script was later made into a film under the direction of Faiz Zahir and Aranyak Natyadal.

4 Shuvashis Chakma's *Khumi i awmnai reta* (Khumi lives, 2007), and *Life on the Margins* (2009). Zhantu Chakma's *Shikarer kanthaswar* (Voices from the roots, 2010), *Pratishruti o sangramer galpa* (A tale of promise and struggle, 2011), and *Balancing Harmony* (2013). Jimi Chakma and Salit Chakma's *Ranjit Dewan: A Living Legend of Chakma Music* (2013), and *Ratikanta Tanchangya—Pioneer in Trending Art in CHT* (2013); Jimi Chakma and Anmoy Kiron Chakma's *Ramani mohan gengkhuli* (2015); Arnab Dewan's *Rajanagar* (2016, not yet released); Monoj Bahadur's *Parbatya chattagramer Marma janagoshthi* (Marma people of the CHT).

5 Shuvashis Chakma's *Terrified Voices* (2003), *Rendering Homeless: Sajek, CHT* (2005), *Hills in Flames* (2005), *Ballad of Land Alienation* (2006), and *How Can I Become Bangali* (2013); CHTnews online service's *Bogachari: Sena-Setller Tandab 16 December 2014* (Army-settlers' attack in Bogachari on December 16, 2014); Jummo Chokh Media's 2015 productions *Interviews of Panchari Massacre Panchari* (1986), and *Taindong Attack*, part 1–4 (2013); Arnab Dewan's *Life Is Still Not Ours: A Story of the Chittagong Hill Tracts* (2014).

6 Feature-length films include Tarun Chakma (Monibo)'s *Debangshir aandhaar haalaa saabaa* (Black shadow of the divine, 2009); Shantomoni Chakma's *Chittopunor degree paaj* (Graduation of Chittopuno, 2010–11). Short films include *Aandalat phor* (1996); Kolin Chakma's *Killer* (2014); Sarbajo Bouddha Parishad's *Pohr phudok* (Let there be light); Adit Dewan's *Claims of 2 Rooms* (2015), *Swaban nahi pattam* (Dream or reality, 2015), and *Ramani mohan gengkhuli* (2015); Aungkon Chakma's *Uvoloc* (Demand, 2016); Nirupam Chkma's *Faghara* (Fraud, 2015); Komico Chakma's *Light* (2016), and *Budung Badang* (Aimless, 2016).

7 Rajbana Bihar Meditation Centre Katachari's *Alokita jibaner sandhane* (In search of enlightened life).

8 For instance, Arnab Dewan's two films, *Life Is Still Not Ours: A Story of the Chittagong Hill Tracts* (2014), and *Rajanagar* (2016, not yet released).

9 Joyoti Grech, *Chittagong Hill Tracts* (1997).

10 Fuad Chowdury, *War and Peace in the Hill Tracts* (2016). Based on the life of Dr. Chiranjib Talukdar, a Canadian Chakma pediatrician. Screened at the 2016 IFFSA Toronto, the largest South Asian film festival in North America, it won one of the fifteen Best Film awards.

11 Dibos Dewan, *CHT Jummas Global Rally* (2010); Saikat Khisa (Suja), *Chittagong Hill Tracts and Moanoghar—Towards a Better Future* (June 2015).

12 Memo No: Bachsebo-11 (bibidh-2)/2014/1063, July 12, 2014; letter from the Censor Board to the filmmaker, Rakhine. Letter no. 10(9)/2014/1011, June 29, 2015 (both documents in the possession of the filmmaker).

REFERENCES

Adnan, Shapan. 2004. *Migration Land Alienation and Ethnic Conflict: Causes of Poverty in the Chittagong Hill Tracts of Bangladesh*. Dhaka: Research and Advisory Services.

Barclay, Barry. 1990. *Our Own Image*. Auckland: Longman Paul.

———. 2003. "Celebrating Fourth Cinema." *Illusions* 35: 7–11.

bdnews24.com. 2005. "Mokammel Reacts Sharply at Ban of His Documentary *Karnaphulir Kanna*." August 21, 2005. https://bdnews24.com/politics/2005/08/20/mokammel-reacts-sharply-at-ban-of-his-documentary-karnaphulir-kanna.

Chakma, Bhumitra. 2010. "The Post-colonial State and Minorities: Ethnocide in the Chittagong Hill Tracts, Bangladesh." *Commonweath and Comparative Politics* 48, no. 3 (July): 287.

Chakma, Kabita, and Glen Hill. 2013. "Indigenous Women and Culture in the Colonized Chittagong Hill Tracts of Bangladesh." In *Everyday Occupations: Experiencing Militarism in South Asia and the Middle East*, edited by Kamala Visweswaran, 132–57. Philadelphia: University of Pennsylvania Press.

Chakmapedia. N.d. *Mor Thengari—First Chakma Feature Film in Bangladesh*. Accessed February 4, 2019. http://chakmapedia.blogspot.com.au/2015/09/mor-thengari-first-chakma-feature-film-in-bangladesh.html.

Chittagong Hill Tracts (CHT) Commission. 1991. *Life Is Not Ours: Land and Human Rights in the Chittagong Hill Tracts Bangladesh*. Copenhagen: International Work Group Indigenous Affairs.

———. 1994. *Life Is Not Ours: Land and Human Rights in the Chittagong Hill Tracts Bangladesh*. Update 2. Copenhagen: International Work Group Indigenous Affairs.

Chittagong Hill Tracts Nov 1935. Archived at the Centre for South Asian Studies, University of Cambridge.

Davis, Therese. 2009. "Indigenising Australian History: Contestation and Collaboration in *First Australians*." *Screening the Past* 26: 1–9. www.screeningthepast.com/2015/01/indigenising-australian-history-contestation-and-collaboration-in%C2%A0first-australians/.

Deutsche Welle, Bangladesh. 2015. "Chakma Bhashai Chalacittra: Apatti Senabahinir" (Film in Chakma language: Objection by army). Radio broadcast, December 15, 2015.

Film South Asia. 2007. *Festival of Southasian Documentaries, Kathmandu, Nepal: Karhaphulir Kanna (Teardrops of Karnaphuli)*. www.filmsouthasia.org/archives/fsa-2007/.

Gauthier, Jennifer. 2008. "'Lest Others Speak for Us': The Neglected Roots and Uncertain Future of Maori Cinema in New Zealand." In *Global Indigenous Media: Cultures, Poetics and Politics*, edited by Pamela Wilson and Michelle Stewart, 59–72. Durham: Duke University Press.

Gayen, Kaberi. 2015. "Women, War and Cinema: Construction of Women in the Liberation War Films of Bangladesh." *French Journal for Media Research* 3. http://frenchjournalformediaresearch.com/index.php?id=478.

Ginsburg, Faye D. 1996. "Mediating Culture: Aboriginal Media and Social Transformation of Identity." Paper presented at the Conference of Communication and Empowerment: Uses of Media and Information Technologies in Developing Countries, Program in Development Communication, Annenberg Centre for Communication, University of Southern California, April 11–13, 1996.

———. 2002. "Screen Memories: Resignifying the Traditional in Indigenous Media." In *Media Worlds: Anthropology on New Terrain*, edited by Faye D. Ginsburg, Lila Abu-Lughod, and Brian Larkin, 37–57. Berkeley: University of California Press.

Guhathakurta, Meghna. 2010. "Representing the Khumi of the Chittagong Hill Tracts: The Making of a Film." Paper presented at Asian Borderlands: Enclosure, Interaction and Transformation, Chiangmai, Thailand. https://www.academia.edu/6303248.

Hearne, Joanna. 2012. *Native Recognition: Indigenous Cinema and the Western*. Albany: State University of New York Press.

Hearne, Joanna, and Corinn Columpar. 2012. *Unsettling Sights: The Fourth World on Film*. Carbondale: Southern Illinois University Press.

Joyce, Hester. 2013. "Maori Cinema as 'Fourth Cinema,' Taonga (Cultural Treasures): Reflections on Maori Storytelling in the Cinema of Aoeteroa/ New Zealand." In *Storytelling in World Cinemas: Contexts*, vol. 2, edited by Lina Khatib, 21–34. New York: Columbia State University Press.

Lempert, William. 2012. "Telling Their Own Stories: Indigenous Film as Critical Identity Discourse." *Applied Anthropologist* 32, no. 1: 23–32.

Mohsin, Amena. 2013. "The Two Meanings of 'Bangladeshi.'" In *The Bangladesh Reader: History, Culture and Politics*, edited by Meghna Guhathakurta and Willem van Schendel, 332–33. Durham: Duke University Press.

Mokammel, Tanvir, dir. 2005. *Karnaphulir kanna*. Bangladesh.

Mro, Sing Yong. 2005. "Mro bhasha o barnamala" (Mro language and scripts). In *JAC'er 25 barsha purti sankalan* 2005 (JAC's 25th anniversary monograph 2005), edited by Shishir Chakma, 77. Rangamati: Jum Aesthetic Council.

Murray, Stuart. 2008. *Images of Dignity: Barry Barclay and Fourth Cinema*. Wellington, NZ: Huia.

Raheja, Michelle. 2011. *Reservation Reelism: Redfacing, Visual Sovereignty, and Representation of Native Americans in Film*. Lincoln: University of Nebraska Press.

Raju, Zakir Hossain. 2006. "Bangladesh: Native Resistance and Nationalist Discourse." In *Contemporary Asian Cinema: Popular Culture in a Global Frame*, edited by Anne Tereska Ciecko, 120–32. Oxford: Berg.

———. 2015. *Bangladesh Cinema and National Identity: In Search of the Modern*. London: Routledge.

Rakhine, Aung, dir. 2014. *Maw theng gaari*. Bangladesh: Era Motion Pictures/ Khona Talkies.

Rashid, Harunur, dir. 1976. *Megher onek rong*. Bangladesh: Ratna Kothachitra.

Roy, Raja Tridiv. 2003. *The Departed Melody (Memoirs)*. Islamabad: PPA Publications.

Solanas, Fernando, and Octavio Getino. 1983. "Towards a Third Cinema: Notes and Experiences for the Development of a Cinema of Liberation in the Third World." *In Twenty-Five Years of the New Latin American Cinema*, edited by Michael Chanan, 33–58. London: BFI/Channel 4 Television.

UN Economic and Social Council. 2011. *Study on the Status of Implementation of the Chittagong Hill Tracts Accord of 1997*. February 18, 2011. E/C.19/2011/6.

van Schendel, Willem. 1992. "The Invention of the 'Jummas': State Formation and Ethnicity in Southeastern Bangladesh." *Modern Asian Studies* 26, no. 1: 95–128.

———. 2002. "A Politics of Nudity: Photographs of the 'Naked Mru' of Bangladesh." *Modern Asian Studies* 36, no. 2: 341–74.

van Schendel, Willem, Wolfgang Mey, and Aditya Dewan. 2000. *The Chittagong Hill Tracts: Living in a Borderland*. Bangkok: White Lotus Press.

Wilson, Pamela, and Michelle Stuart, eds. 2008. *Global Indigenous Media: Cultures, Poetics and Politics*. Durham: Duke University Press.

5 PAKISTAN, HISTORY, AND SLEEP

Hassan Tariq, a Progressive Patriarch, and Neend

NASREEN REHMAN

THIS CHAPTER IS A FRAGMENT OF MY LARGER RESEARCH PROJECT to study how the cinema is imbricated in the political economy of subjectivity, emotions, and aesthetics across time. Here I focus on a feature film called *Neend* (Sleep, 1959), released at the advent of Ayub Khan's era of military dictatorship (1958–69), the first of forty-four films directed by Hassan Tariq (1933–1988), a leading Pakistani auteur with politically progressive leanings. Any film is open to several readings. I interrogate *Neend* to understand how Tariq's aesthetic vision and deployment of the trope of sleep intersect with the official discourse of the Pakistani state on what it means to be a gendered Pakistani national and moral subject.

I explore *Neend* as a multisensory archive that shapes and is shaped by political, economic, social, and cultural constellations and argue that art and aesthetic articulations are not mere reflections of history and political subjectivity; rather, they are the political. Hence, "art as such is more than a collective noun. It is a configuration of a will to power" (Heidegger 1991, 69–77). I buttress this insight with Jacques Rancière's (2000) disquisition that the logic of fiction and the logic of history are shaped in the same crucible. As the philosopher Slavoj Žižek (2000, 77) asserts, art and poetry are "not just secondary illustrations of an underlying ideological struggle, but the very terrain of this struggle."

I examine moving images, dialogue, songs, the dramatis personae, as well as economic and social relations to probe the many moods of the sleeping, awake, angry, quiescent, rebellious, compliant, willing or unwilling, aware or unaware, nationalist, patriotic and dissident gendered Pakistani subject. I use the word *mood* as a *rasa* (a mood aesthetic), as described in the Nāṭyaśāstra (Rangacharya 1996), to create an *asthāī bhāva* or a sustained state of emotion/temper/rapture. A sustained *rasa* can compel the subject to action or inaction. It is the coalescence of *rasa* and subjectivity that makes art possible in an exchange whereby the subject is both creator and interlocutor (*rasīkā*), an engaged member of an audience.

Neend provides insights into the gendered Pakistani subject's relationships within family, community, and state, as well as with conceptions of religion, economic development, and honor (*izzat*) (Ahmad 2016; Ali 2016). I contend that the subject can hold, individually and collectively, multiple subject positions that do not necessarily cohere (Moore 2007) and conclude that although *Neend* is a searing anticapitalist critique of Pakistani masculinity and an uncaring state, it is simultaneously in harmony and in counterpoint with official and dominant discourses. The film dislocates pervasive ideas of class, gender, religion, and nationalism, yet it reasserts formidable patriarchal masculinities (Lindisfarne 1994). The value and function (real or spectral) of the woman is consigned to the sexual and reproductive—as an object of male desire in the present and as a mother of sons, the Pakistani male subject of the future.

Neend stands halfway between the creation of Pakistan and its breakup in 1971, after a genocidal civil war and the secession of East Pakistan as the independent state of Bangladesh. It tells the story of Sanvari, a Hindu coal picker, essayed by Noor Jehan (1926–2000), the iconic singing star of South Asia. Sanvari lives with other Hindu families in a shantytown abutting a textile mill. To escape the depredations of real life, she retreats into sleep from time to time through the day. Jimmy, a rapacious Muslim mill owner, lures, grooms, impregnates, and abandons Sanvari with an illegitimate baby son. In their final encounter, Sanvari kills Jimmy before she shoots herself and retreats into what Teju, the Hindu antihero, calls eternal sleep (*hameshā kī neend*).

In my analysis of the film I rely on three ideas as heuristic devices. First, I juxtapose, as two contradictory conceptions of citizenship, Jinnah's vision of a Pakistan where the religion of a citizen should be of no consequence for the business of the state (Jinnah 2009) with the Objective Resolution (1949), whereby Islam became the guiding principle to underwrite sovereignty and citizenship. Second is a view of the Ayub decade of military dictatorship as one of unprecedented industrial expansion and economic growth. And third, a nostalgic vision of the Ayub years as a golden age of Pakistani liberalism. Before I analyze the film, I explore briefly Tariq's early life and his entry into the film world in order to contextualize his worldview.

EARLY LIFE AND CAREER OF HASSAN TARIQ (1933–1988)

In an interview in Lahore, Asma Riaz, a sister of Hassan Tariq, confirmed that he was born in 1934 into a moderately prosperous bourgeois Muslim family in Amritsar (personal interview, September 9, 2017). Two brothers and three sisters preceded Tariq, the youngest offspring. Their father, Khwajah Muhammad Hassan, worked for the Amritsar Municipal Corporation and dabbled in "business" (*kārobār*) as well as "a bit of politics" (*aur thoṛī bahaut siyāsat*). Nevertheless, Khwajah Sahib looked down upon businessmen and wanted his sons to be educated bourgeois professionals. He turned away from politics, equally disenchanted by the "shenanigans of the Congress and the Muslim League" (*Congress aur Muslim League kī kārastānīyāṅ*). Tariq's mother, Chand Begum, also from Amritsar, had passed her school matriculation certificate "sometime in the mid-1920s." Asma recalled the reading room in their house had over five hundred books, and described how their parents favored a gendered education for their offspring. Tariq's sisters were sent to English-medium schools and later to colleges to be groomed as good wives.

In 1947, Tariq's family fled to Pakistan to escape the massacre of Muslims by Hindus and Sikhs in what became Indian Punjab. In Lahore, the young Tariq enrolled in the Central Model School and later Government College (GC).

HASSAN TARIQ THE FILMMAKER

Tariq's filmmaking career began in a rupture that brought an era of filmmaking to an end engulfed in an orgy of communal killings. Before the two independent states of India and Pakistan came into being, colonial Lahore was part of regional and international film distribution circuits. Importantly, its small but vibrant film industry produced regular all-India box-office triumphs with an exchange of talent and capital with Calcutta and Bombay (Rehman 2015). In Muslim-majority Pakistan, Lahore was cleansed of most Hindus and Sikhs, who either had been slaughtered or had flown their city. Those who fled included men and women such as Shorey, Pancholi, Nanda (leading film producers); Pran and Ramola (stars); P. N. Malhotra (cameraman); Ishan Ghosh (sound recordist); Dinanath Madhok (lyricist)—and countless others, including musicians, technicians, exhibitors, distributors, film journalists like B. R. Chopra, and box office and front of house staff.

In 1948 Lahore saw the return from Bombay (now in Hindu-majority India) of several artists, including the composer Master Ghulam Haider, Noor Jehan and her husband, the director Shaukat Husain Rizvi. All had risen to fame from the old Lahori industry after the box-office triumphs of *Khazanchi* (dir. Moti B. Gidwani, 1941) and *Khandaan* (dir. Shaukat Husain Rizvi, 1942), produced in Pancholi's atelier. Invitations from a much larger industry lured them to Bombay in 1942. Their return to Lahore was precipitated by the burning, during communal riots, of the studio of the Muslim producer Shiraz Ali Hakim (P. K. Nair, personal communication, May 30, 2000). They arrived as refugees from India to claim the remains of the abandoned old Lahori studios and built a new Pakistani film industry.

Undoubtedly, Lahori film production shrank temporarily after 1947. The post-independence industry, which Tariq joined in the late 1950s, carried several continuities from its colonial incarnation, but with different national, economic, political, religious, and cultural contingencies (Rehman 2015). The terms of engagement for the articulation of subjectivity in artistic practices changed. India had transformed from a colonial project for economic extraction into two new independent and antagonistic nation-states. Where old distribution and exhibition circuits had covered the whole of colonial India, Burma, and beyond, now nationalist cultural movements and trade wars constrained the circulation of films between India and Pakistan, as well as the exchange of talent between production houses in Lahore, Calcutta, and Bombay, a hallmark of the pre-1947 Indian film industries. Lahori and later Pakistani cinemas remained part of a fraught cinematic discourse across South Asia, beyond the scope of this chapter.

Tariq describes his entry into filmmaking in a gendered monthly feature, *Men and Ideas*, in the July 1968 issue of the Pakistani film magazine *Eastern Film*. His words echo bourgeois discomfort with the allure of the cinema, particularly as a profession. He explains how as a student at GC uninterested in the cinema or even going to the movies, he preferred to hang out at coffee houses with "writers and intellectuals." At the time, his friend Anwar Jalal, a screenplay writer, was working on *Muskaraahat* (dir. N. E. Akhtar, 1959). Unable to meet his deadline, Jalal, who knew that Tariq had written a few short stories, asked the latter to write the dialogue for his screenplay. Tariq took up the offer and was "struck by the potentialities of the cinema at human self-expression."

Asma remembered that their father wanted Tariq to train as an engineer. She switched from a medley of English and Urdu to Punjabi, and laughed as she quoted her father: "Will you go on pointlessly making films! After all, you have to settle down" (*Aivaiṅ, filmāṅ banāndā rai gā! Ākhīr* settle *vī te honā ai*). Nevertheless, Tariq Hassan switched his name to Hassan Tariq and made his entry into the film world as an assistant director in *Saat Lakh* (dir. Jaffar Malik, 1957).

On the set, he began a love affair with Nighat Sultana, an actress with a supporting role in the film. Tariq's relationship with Nighat smacks of the casting couch and the pervasive practice of directors' exploitative relationships (often including marriage) with their heroines, a matter commented upon by Manto and the actor/songstress Mukhtar Begum (Manto 1991, 320–29; Ramnagri 1935). Closer at hand was the example of Noor Jehan and her ex-husband, director Shaukat Hussain Rizvi. Film legend has it that Nighat's Bengali father had migrated during the First World War to Iraq, where he married her Baghdadi mother. Nighat was born in Baghdad. In 1948 the family came to Karachi, where she trained as a nurse and worked in a military hospital.

Nighat introduced Tariq to the producers S. M. Malik and Zakaullah Kitchlew. Asma recalled how all the discussions for *Neend* happened at Nighat's house, and Tariq married her during the shoot. He selected the Marxist Riaz Shahid as his scenarist and, in a casting coup, he signed Noor Jehan as his heroine. She dominated the firmament of South Asian cinemas, unrivaled as a singing star. As Baby Noor Jehan, she became a child star after her debut in the Punjabi film *Sheila urf Pind di kurri* (dir. K. D. Mehra, 1935), produced by Calcutta's Madan Theatres. Noor Jehan rose to fame in 1942, as Zeenat, the heroine in *Khandaan*, the first "Muslim social" film, released on Indian film circuits. In *Neend*, too, she sang for herself and gave an accomplished performance.

Tariq cast Aslam Pervez, a successful hero, as the evil Jimmy, and set him on a new career trajectory as one of the most popular villains of Pakistani cinema. Allaudin as Teju reinforced *Neend*'s box-office appeal—the same year he starred in *Kartar Singh* (dir. Saif-ud Din Saif, 1959), which swept the annual film awards and has acquired cult status among films on the Partition of India. Tariq cast Nighat Sultana as Rachna, the vamp.

THE PLOT OF *NEEND*

As white credits roll on a black screen, Noor Jehan's voice is heard singing a warning to the audience that a tragic love story is about to unfold.

> Darling, if I knew love really hurts [*prīt kare dukh hoe*]
> I'd have warned the world
> Don't fall in love [*prīt nā karīo koī*].

A man (Teju) and a woman (Rachna) in simple rustic attire bring a five-year-old boy for admission to a top boys' prep school. Rachna's head is covered demurely with a phulkari. The boy's shorts and tucked-in shirt indicate he probably belongs to an urban middle-class family. The headmistress asks the boy's and his father's names, and promises to put him on the waiting list. Teju tells her the child is his late sister's son and begins to recount Sanvari's story. Ninety-seven percent of *Neend* is in flashback.

The audience enters the world of Teju's story in a scene with Sanvari and her friends picking coals and singing a song that describes their times.

> Don't go out alone, times [*jamānā*] are tricky [*nājuk*]
> You'll to regret it; times are tricky. (Lyrics by Tanvir Naqvi)

The lyricist transformed the *z* of *zamānā* and *nāzuk* to a *j*—thus *jamānā* and *nājuk*, to imbue rustic charm and innocence. References to *zamānā* are pervasive in Urdu literature, film dialogue, and songs: the word encapsulates and transcends time and space, diachronically and synchronically, and refers to both ideas and practices. In the universe of early Indian talkies, *zamānā* was usually against the protagonist. The song underpins the story of *Neend*: a woman alone should be vigilant because times are "tricky," but in this tale Sanvari, the heroine, keeps falling asleep.

The action unfolds and moves between a mill compound near a railway line and a local bazaar, supported by the shantytown where Sanvari, her sister Bindiya (Neelo), niece Baela, and Baba, her blind father, live alongside other coal pickers.

Like the song, the next scene makes it clear that "tricky times" signify men preying on women for sexual gratification. A man informs Sanvari that there's a buyer for her coal. She goes to meet the person, and someone grabs her from behind a gate. The camera catches Sanvari's bare legs and sounds of a struggle. She fights off her attacker and heads back to her friends. Sanvari's escape presages the later covert assault that she cannot escape. As the group of friends (*sahelīyāṅ*) gossip about Rachna, who is retained by Munshi for sexual favors, Sanvari falls asleep.

In a powerful shot, the narrative turns to Jimmy, a mill owner and Munshi's boss, who sits with his back to the camera, facing the tall chimney of

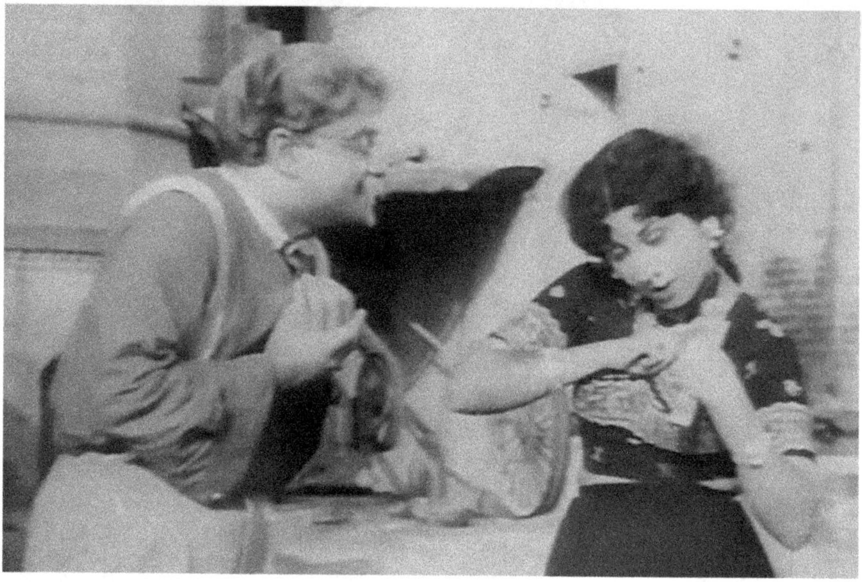

FIGURE 5.1. Rachna flirting with Munshi. (Source: *Neend*, dir. Hassan Tariq, 1959)

the mill, framed in the open window. The mill had become a powerful sign of capitalist exploitation in the cinema after *Mill* (dir. Mohan Bhavnani, 1934), written by Munshi Premchand (1880–1936). Jimmy is with his Anglo-Indian secretary Vicky (played by Rakshi), with whom he has an amorous relationship.

The concise dialogue and accomplished editing draw attention to Tariq's comments on filmmaking in his *Eastern Film* interview: "The Director should economise on the use of dialogue, the film should convey more through other methods, like an actor's expression, for example. Silent shots should also replace dialogue, wherever possible."

The following scene in the local bazaar establishes the female subject as a commodity desired by male vendors of various Pakistani ethnicities, Pathan, Punjabi, Sindhi, and Mohajir (Urdu-speaking refugees and migrants from the United Provinces of India). Rachna flirts with Munshi, and extracts money from whomever she can. She spots an honorable and weak young man (Jaffery), named Babu at birth. He works in Jimmy's office as a clerk and is saving money to ask Sanvari's father for her hand in marriage. Rachna tells him Sanvari's father is unwell and needs money for his medicines.

The camera cuts to Sanvari asking Khan the Pathan tea seller to settle his account. She describes problems faced by coal pickers because of the

FIGURE 5.2. Jimmy in his office with Vicky and the mill as the backdrop. (Source: *Neend*, dir. Hassan Tariq, 1959)

government's disregard for the poor. "Where can we find coal these days? We got it from trains, but now the government runs them on oil. I hear, from next year the cloth *phactory* will also run without coal."

Back in the office, Vicky is late. A furious Jimmy turns away from her to look out of the window. He spots the sleeping Sanvari. The camera catches his licentious intentions. Jimmy summons Munshi and asks him, "I want to buy some goods. What's the going rate?" (*Maiṅ māl kharīdnā chāhtā hūṅ, Munshī bhāo batāo*), and points to Sanvari. To leave the audience in no doubt that Sanvari's body is the commodity, Munshi responds, "I'll have to check the rate" (*Bhāo patā karnā paṛe gā*).

In the following scene, Rachna establishes herself as the most successful trader in the bazaar. Unabashedly selling her body, she arrives playing her harmonica and singing.

> Just one heart [*dil*] and so many punters [*gāhak*]
> Whom do I choose among the hunters?
> (Lyrics by Qatil Shifai)

Babu has sold his bicycle and gives the money to Rachna for Sanvari's father, but she shares it with Chachi, the procuress with whom she lives.

Munshi approaches Sanvari with an offer to sell her body. She slaps him across the face; he reports this to Jimmy, who commands him to "be fox-like to get your way" (*lomṛī ban kar kām nikālo*). Rachna advises Munshi that Sanvari will never give herself to a man she does not love.

Unlike Sanvari, Rachna is a light sleeper. One night, she wakes up and sees Teju peering through her window. He has returned after serving a prison term for attacking a man who exploited Rachna sexually and possibly fathered her son. Munshi thinks the child is his. Rachna screams and alerts the entire shantytown. Teju is protective toward all the girls in the community and considers them his sisters, except for Rachna, whom he loves despite her transgressions and indifference.

Jimmy and Munshi concoct a plan in which Jimmy "accidentally" encounters Sanvari. He asks her to deliver coal to his house. Sanvari takes her consignment and falls asleep on a bench in Jimmy's garden. She wakes to find the cool air of a table fan trained on her. Jimmy arrives and speaks to Sanvari of how the false lifestyles of the rich "empty their hearts and heads of human sympathy" (*diloṅ ko insānī hamdardī se khālī kar detā hai*). Sanvari addresses Jimmy as Babu, meaning "Sir" or "Mr."

The next time Sanvari delivers coal, she overhears Jimmy and Munshi having a staged conversation. Jimmy tells Munshi he will only marry a girl

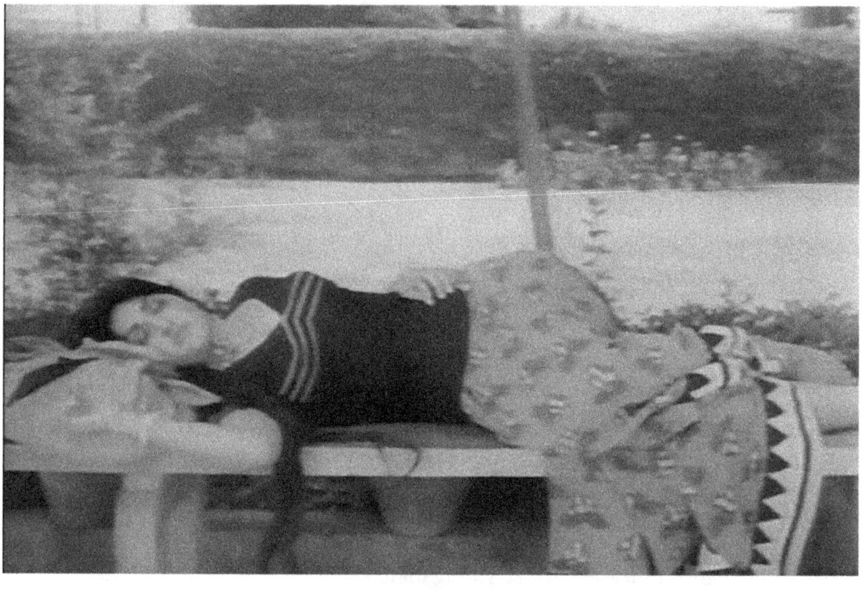

FIGURE 5.3. Sanvari sleeping on a bench in Jimmy's garden. (Source: *Neend*, dir. Hassan Tariq, 1959)

who loves him and not his wealth (*daulat*). Sanvari falls for the ruse. Jimmy asks her to meet him at the ancient ruins. The ruins where Sanvari meets her beloved (like countless South Asian film heroines) are symbolic of her fate. She goes to the assignation and falls asleep. Jimmy arrives and wakes her up. She sings and dances for him to a song that became a box-office hit.

> Chhun, chhun, chhun chhun, my anklets tinkle,
> *Sāṅvarīyā*!
> (Lyrics by Tanvir Naqvi)

After their union results in Sanvari conceiving their child, Jimmy turns away from her. When Baba hears of Sanvari's pregnancy and shame, he wants to kill her but relents when Sanvari pleads with him and foretells her tragedy: "Don't color your hands with my blood [*Merā khūn apne hāthoṅ par mat le*]. I promise you I will kill myself. But if you wish, show your power against your blameless daughter [*nirdosh biṭyā*]."

When Babu the clerk hears Sanvari's news, he writes a resignation letter to Jimmy and leaves the colony forever. Sanvari gives birth to a son. She goes to Jimmy and implores him to look after his son and leaves the infant on his bed. Jimmy denies paternity and refers to the infant as a bundle of Sanvari's sins; he pulls out a pistol and threatens to shoot the baby. With maternal strength, Sanvari wrests the pistol from Jimmy's hand. Convinced Sanvari will never harm him, Jimmy grabs the baby and threatens to fling him from the balcony. Sanvari pleads with Jimmy. When she sees that Jimmy will kill her baby, Sanvari shoots and kills Jimmy. The final scene returns to the headmistress's office.

> TEJU: And matters took a turn. The bullet meant to protect Babu ripped his chest apart.
>
> HEADMISTRESS: And then what happened?
>
> TEJU: Before the hand of justice could reach her, Sanvari turned away from the world. She embraced eternal sleep, saying, "He is the son of a *distinguished* father [emphasis mine]. I leave my justice to Him." This child is a testament to the mother who lost her life in the battle between the maternal and conjugal imperative. He is the son of a father who couldn't distinguish between hatred and love. . . . I hope he will grow into an educated young man, with his father's physical strength and his mother's heart. Help me make something of his life

so he can confront the world to remove all obstacles between the high and low.

HEADMISTRESS: Indeed, I will help you. I'll offer him a place.

TEJU: I am very grateful to you.

HEADMISTRESS: Nanhe . . . oh . . . he's fallen asleep.

TEJU: Let him sleep, Memsahib. He is the son of a mother who embraced sleep. I never wake him up from his sleep. I'll return with him tomorrow.

HEADMISTRESS: All right then.

TEJU: Ah well, Salam.

Teju lifts the sleeping child and goes to the garden, where Rachna is waiting for him. They walk across a playing field full of schoolboys (Pakistan's future) running around. Sanvari's son continues to sleep peacefully in Teju's arms, as happy music underscores the scene for the audience.

PAKISTAN, THE HEROINE, AND THE *ASTHĀĪ BHĀVA* OF SLEEP

Ten years after the Objective Resolution, Sanvari, the Pakistani heroine, is a Hindu who embodies Jinnah's Pakistan and, as the mother of a son, its futurity. Sanvari is an archetypal sacrificing heroine (as a daughter, lover, and mother), ruled by her heart and not her head. Sanvari tells Jimmy, "My head says that everything you say is a lie, but my heart says that all your talk of love is true." Importantly, she uses the language of a devotee, or *bhakt*, of the god Krishna. She addresses Jimmy as *Sāṅvarīyā*, or the dark one, a reference to Krishna's complexion, and longs for what Christopher Pinney calls corpothetic *darśan* of her beloved, in an act of encountering, seeing, and becoming one with the beloved (Rehman 2015, 102–5; Pinney 1998, 19).

Thirsty for *darśan*
I am a slave at your feet [*charan kī dāsī*].
(Lyrics by Tanvir Naqvi)

Tariq and Shahid's message to the female subject is clear: death is the price you pay if you are unmindful of male predators. It is the *asthāī bhāva* of sleep that transforms Sanvari from a stereotypical heroine who loves blindly into a moral agent and harbinger of an anxiety-ridden gendered patriarchal history. Sleep is symbolic of Sanvari's lack of awareness of danger (unlike her blind father). Furthermore, because of repetition, sleep is no longer merely symbolic of Sanvari; rather, it constitutes her, the female subject. Sanvari's regular retreats into sleep are not those of the proverbial Sleeping Beauty, whose prince will kiss and awaken her to a world of happiness. Sleep is not a sanctuary for Sanvari, but a withdrawal from historical time and space—a loss of agency. In her last moments she recovers her agency, but it is contingent on male violence and motherhood, and on death, where she transforms into the spectral.

Importantly, Sanvari's transformation into a tragic spectral form tempers the abuse she confronts when (like countless other women), she finds herself pregnant as a result not of love but of grooming and rape. With no recourse to public health and birth control clinics in Pakistan at the time (Khan 1996), Sanvari has no choice. She faces the shame of motherhood out of wedlock and embraces eternal sleep—death. It is the alert Rachna who survives.

THE TEMPTRESS, THE VILLAIN, THE ANGLO-INDIAN VAMP, AND THE ANTIHERO

Rachna, the Hindu temptress, stands in stark contrast to the sleeping and gullible Sanvari. She is a light sleeper, and when she senses danger, she screams—and arouses the entire community. She can wind around her little finger any man in her vicinity and has no delusions about love. She uses her body without shame to earn as much as she can to live a comfortable life. Rachna struts through the colony and the bazaar, dancing, singing, and playing her harmonica to entice men. In the opening song, when Sanvari and her friends sing about hiding their beauty in *nājuk* times, Rachna responds,

> Why not fire arrows [*tīr*] of love with our eyes
> Ram gave us beauty [*rūp*], why should we hide?
> (Lyrics by Tanvir Naqvi)

Rachna hoodwinks Munshi, who desires and delusionally values her as the mother of his son. Nevertheless, at the end of the narrative, Rachna's rebellious agency is diminished. She is redeemed by Teju's love: an independent woman, once in control of her life, walks into the future in the shadow of her male savior with her head demurely covered and body swathed in a chador. In an alternative and less likely reading, Rachna may have dressed to impress the school authorities. This fashioning of a subdued Rachna alerts us to the importance of interpreting sartorial choices in light of the historian C. A. Bayly's (1986, 286) insight into "cloth as a thing that can transmit spirit and substance."

Significantly, in Riaz Shahid's narrative, the archvillain is Jimmy, a wealthy and powerful Muslim capitalist mill owner and Sanvari's love interest. In South Asian cinemas, the Jimmy typology has roots in anticolonial times, when filmmakers often fashioned the villain or buffoon as an anglicized, deracinated *desi*. In *Neend*, the wealthy Muslim Jimmy conducts a love affair with Vicky, his vamp-like secretary, and grooms and rapes Sanvari—both girls from less well-to-do religious minority communities.

Vicky is an anticolonial fashioning of a wicked Western woman but, alas, also a profoundly racist and religiously motivated vision of the Anglo-Indian Christian woman as the stereotypical vamp. Again, when Jimmy wishes to marry (in a mock *nikāh*) the poor Hindu Sanvari, no questions are asked. Does this augur the abduction in Sindh by powerful Muslim men of Hindu girls whom they coerce into marriage?

In a film that foregrounds rape by predatory men as an omnipresent risk to women and features no conventional hero, it is not Sanvari's Muslim sweetheart but Teju, a poor, uneducated Hindu laborer and jailbird, who embodies the heroic. He stands tall in contrast with every other Muslim male in the film. Teju is a protector of women. Moreover, he is a reformer of women who falter. Critically, in contrast with the rapacious Jimmy, he assumes the guardianship of Rachna and Sanvari's illegitimate sons. Yet, in a patriarchal narrative, Teju's triumph renders both Sanvari (the heroine) and Rachna (the vamp) into mere ciphers.

OTHER DRAMATIS PERSONAE AND PAKISTAN

It is possible to construe the fashioning of the Pakistani, Hindu and Muslim, subject and the vision of the *jhuggi* (shanty), factory, and bazaar as microcosms of Jinnah's Pakistan, albeit flawed. The male vendors in the marketplace embody stereotypical imaginings of Pakistani provincial men and include Khan the Pathan, a Punjabi, an Urdu-speaking refugee, and a Sindhi—all identifiable by their dress and accents. Since the story unfolds in West Pakistan, it is possible to overlook the exclusion of East Pakistan, but Baluchistan is a glaring void. Does *Neend* hold a mirror to the future when it articulates a

Pakistan with East Pakistan and Baluchistan occluded from view? Yet Pakistani subjectivity as fashioned in *Neend* is more inclusive in accepting ethnic and religious difference compared with how the country developed (Rahman 2016)—and less punishing of women who are seen to err.

Along with religious and provincial markers, the dramatis personae conform to mythical typologies across South Asian cinemas. Sanvari's blind father, Baba, is the indigent, helpless head of a family, and Rachna's Chachi, an exploitative procuress—the approximation of the madam of a brothel.

Perhaps the most complex exploration of subjectivity in *Neend* is that of Babudom, in the persons of Jimmy (addressed as Babu by Sanvari and Teju), Munshi, and Babu the young clerk. When Sanvari addresses Jimmy as Babu, she gestures to a class of qualified bureaucrats and entrepreneurs. In a trenchant critique of capitalism, *Neend* captures the dilemmas of those trying to survive on the fringes of the bourgeoisie. Munshi, who does Jimmy's dirty work, is, of course, the horrid middleman, reviled as the scourge of society in cinemas across South Asia. In Pakistani cinema, Iftikhar Dadi (2016) has written about the munshi in *Armaan* (dir. Pervez Malik, 1966) and relied on the following insight: "Aficionados of Hindi films since the 1960s will recognise the character of the *munshī* as the accountant and henchman of the cruel and grasping zamīndār, greasily rubbing his hands and usually unable to protest the immoral demands of his master" (Alam and Subramnyam 2004).

Undoubtedly, the most nuanced cinematic rendition of the Munshi/Babu typology is *Jana aranya* (The middleman, dir. Satyajit Ray, 1976). In Babudom, as articulated in *Neend*, Munshi stands in the middle, between the worlds of the capitalist mill owner Jimmy Babu and the young petit-bourgeois clerk named Babu at birth. His words to Sanvari's father capture the financial and emotional tightrope the less successful members of Babudom must walk—across a chasm between aspirations and reality: "Office clerks dwell in a world apart. We spend our lives dreaming about increments in our pay . . . and this year instead of a rise, I had a ten-rupee cut." Unlike Teju, Babu is not cast in a heroic mold; although he loves Sanvari, when he hears of her plight, he resigns from his job and leaves town. In fashioning Babu, Tariq is somewhat closer to his fantasy of creating films in the social realist mode, as reported in his interview in *Eastern Film*: "He thinks even fantasies have a reality of their own. He believes that the life of a clerk should be depicted as it is in reality; his clothes or his manner should not belie his profession."

LANGUAGE, DEVELOPMENT, LIBERALISM, AND ILLEGITIMACY

LANGUAGE

The dialogue of *Neend* evinces a Pakistan where everyone speaks or attempts to converse in Urdu and draws attention the ongoing debate over the national language of Pakistan. While the characters who live in the shantytown speak a bizarre filmi patois that is neither Urdu nor Hindi or Avadhi, the vendors in the bazaar use pidgin Urdu with Pashtu, Punjabi, and Sindhi inflections. The rich Jimmy, bourgeois Munshi, and petit-bourgeois Babu speak Urdu. In an essay dated October 1948, Hassan Askari, a leading Urdu scholar and literary critic, had this to say: "Urdu may not be the language of any area of Pakistan, yet Muslims have decided that Urdu will be the tool of their national unity" (Askari 2015, 1132).

Of course, this was not the case. The struggle for an independent Bangladesh was rooted, among other factors, in East Pakistan's resentment at the imposition of Urdu as the national language, as early as 1948. The dialogue in *Neend* suggests echoes of a polyphonic Pakistan but without any acceptance of linguistic diversity (Rahman 2016).

DEVELOPMENT

In a film where the heroine is a coal picker, it is worth setting the economic expansion of the Ayub era against the backdrop of an industrial wilderness in the early 1950s with a shortage of coal (Jaffrelot 2015, 91). Kamran Asdar Ali (2016) describes *Behan bhai* (dir. Hassan Tariq, 1968), a film released a decade after *Neend*, as "a fantasy of progress of the Ayub era." He concludes rightly that economic development in Pakistan did not fulfill the promise of the film. Indeed, coeval with the release of *Behen bhai*, in a speech in Karachi, Mahbub ul Haq, chief economist of Ayub Khan's Planning Commission, had embarrassed the government when he asserted that the fruits of economic growth had benefited merely twenty-two families and not touched the lives of the majority of Pakistanis, who remained poor (Haq and Ponzio 2008).

Neend was released before the Ayub government launched its expansive family planning program in 1959, with Asghari Manzur Qadir as its president—too late for Sanvari to benefit from it (Wellcome Library, C4/5 and C4/7). Nevertheless, Zulfiqar Ali Bhutto (1971–78) stepped back from family planning initiatives (Khan 1996) under perceived pressure from religious zealots. In 1974, Tariq revisited Sanvari's story as *Begum Jan*, starring Rani, his wife at the time. The Hindu heroine transformed into a Muslim Pathan cloth seller, who kills the rich Shahid Khan, after he grooms and impregnates her, then denies paternity. She goes to prison for murder. At the end of the film she leaves prison and walks to freedom with her illegitimate son.

In 1979, Zia-ul-Haq introduced the Hudood Ordinances, according to which a man and a woman commit the crime of *zina* if they "willfully have sexual intercourse without being married to each other." The penalty was a hundred lashes or death by stoning. For the Sanvaris, Rachnas, and Begum Jans in Pakistan, pregnancy was proof of consensual sex with a man outside marriage. The men who groomed them could easily deny paternity in an age before DNA testing. The Protection of Women (Criminal Laws Amendment) Act 2006, has reduced the penalty of a hundred lashes or death by stoning to a prison term of between five to ten years.

LIBERALISM

Just as the fruits of economic growth and development failed to reach the vast majority of Pakistanis, the golden age of liberalism under Ayub Khan was a hell for many progressives. Pakistan leaned toward a pro-America foreign policy, and liberalism in Ayub's Pakistan mirrored American McCarthyism: the state crushed movements for social, economic, and political justice, and many political activists, journalists, and literary figures were in and out of prison. Asdar Ali (2016) gives a chilling account of how the government picked up the activist Hassan Nasir from a shantytown in Karachi in 1960 and moved him to the dreaded Lahore fort, where he was tortured and killed. When exhumed for identification and burial, Nasir's mother refused to accept the body, since she did not recognize it as that of her son—a punishing message in any society but particularly in one with a high premium on sons.

Yet in his discussion of the cinema in Pakistan, Mushtaq Gazdar (1997, 72) sees the certification of censorship for *Jago hua savera* (dir. A. J. Kardar, 1959), and *Neend*, as a sign of the military government's inflection toward a liberal worldview. Members of the Pakistan Board of Film Censors (PBFC) were selected, like their colonial forebears and as they are today, by the bureaucracy (Rehman 2015), and were advised to curtail "anything that might cast aspersions on the government, civil service, judiciary and the law enforcing agencies" (Gazdar 1997, 72). Of course, Gazdar was writing from a vantage point after Zulfiqar Ali Bhutto and Zia had inserted obscurantist interpretations of Islamic shariah into the law and governance. Religion has been used to terrorize minorities and Muslims, to diminish their rights as citizens and for moral policing. There are no Hindus in *Begum Jan*, and in 1974, the same year that the film was released, the Parliament under Bhutto demonstrated its right to decide who is a Muslim and unanimously declared Ahmadiyas as non-Muslim. Under Zia and Nawaz Sharif (1990–93, 1997–98, 2013–17), the colonial blasphemy law was strengthened for the same purpose.

ILLEGITIMACY

A film that ends with the future of Pakistan embodied in the illegitimate son of a Muslim father and a Hindu mother provides a compelling frame to examine what the trope of illegitimacy signifies for Pakistani masculinity and subjectivity. Faisal Devji has alerted us to the "lineaments of a bastard history" as he problematizes the urge to trace the genealogy of Gandhi's politics of nonviolence and a new moral relationship between Hindus and Muslims to the conflict of 1857 (Devji 2012). *Neend* disrupts Muslim or Hindu patriarchal and religious claims to nationhood, as it foregrounds and disrupts the possibility of such a history. The harbingers of history are two Pakistani Hindu women, and the country's future is linked by birth to a religious minority community. The illegitimate future male subject heralds patriarchal masculine anxiety in the present and renders unstable the Muslim male subject's claim to futurity. This reading applies equally to claims by Hindu nationalists to an India cleansed of Muslims.

CONCLUSION

This essay summarized the early life and career of the film director Hassan Tariq and located him simultaneously in old colonial and new national fields of practice. It explored his first film, *Neend*, and interrogated Tariq's articulation of the *asthāī bhāva* of sleep and gendered Pakistani subjectivity. I interpret *Neend* as a patriarchal anxiety-ridden attack on Pakistani male subjectivity. The film disrupts the claim to paternity and the legitimacy of the male subject. Nevertheless, the woman subject remains a sexual commodity; alive or relegated to sleep, death, and the spectral, the focus is on her reproductive function as the mother of a son. In a narrative of hope, the alert and transgressive Rachna is redeemed by male love and walks into the future as Teju's chastened appendage.

Neend continues to pose several questions for Pakistani storytellers, the religious establishment, and lawmakers. Can Pakistani masculinity fulfill its promise only by deploying the power of storytelling to claim the woman's sexual and reproductive function—spectral or real? Is motherhood a Pakistani woman's only destiny—even in a politically progressive narrative? Why does the sleeping female subject morph into a sleeping male child?

In post-*Neend* Pakistan, patriarchal masculinities have deployed the might of religious and secular law to thwart the sexual, cultural, economic, and political rights of minorities and the woman subject. Although Begum Jan is a Muslim woman who walks with confidence into the future with an illegitimate son, there are no Hindus in the narrative. Pakistani women—Muslims and members of religious minorities, human rights activists, storytellers, and filmmakers—know a different truth. Viewed today, alongside the quotidian exigencies of Imran Khan's Pakistan in the wake of Bhutto, Zia, and Sharif, the world of *Neend* is a dystopian utopia for women and minorities.

REFERENCES

Ahmad, Sadaf. 2016. "Punctuating Gendered Values: Exploring the Phenomena of Slaps in Commercial Pakistani Films." In *Cinema and Society: Film and Social Change in Pakistan*, edited by Ali Khan and Ali Nobil, 263–85. Karachi: Oxford University Press.

Alam, Muzaffar, and Sanjay Subramnyam. 2004. "The Making of a Munshi." *Comparative Studies of South Asia, Africa and the Middle East* 24, no. 2: 61–77.

Ali, Kamran Asdar. 2015. *Communism in Pakistan: Politics and Class Activism, 1947–1972*. London: I. B. Taurus.

———. 2016. "Cinema and the City: The Ayub Years." In *Cinema and Society: Film and Social Change in Pakistan*, edited by Ali Khan and Ali Nobil, 101–14. Karachi: Oxford University Press.

Askari, Mohammad Hassan. 2015. "Taqsīm-i Hind ke b'ād." In *Majmū'āh*. Lahore: Sang-i Meel Publications. (Urdu)

Aziz, K. K. 2008. *The Coffee Houses of Lahore, A Memoir, 1942–1957*. Lahore: Sang-e-Meel Publications.

Bayly, C. A. 1986. "The Origins of Swadeshi (Home Industry): Cloth and Indian Society, 1700–1930." In *The Social Life of Things: Commodities in a Social Perspective*, edited by Arjun Appadurai, 285–322. Cambridge: Cambridge University Press.

Bhavnani, Mohan, dir. 1934. *Mill aka Mazdoor*. India: Ajanta Cinetone. (Hindustani)

Dadi, Iftikhar. 2016. "Modernity and Its Vernacular Remainders in Pakistani Cinema." In *Cinema and Society: Film and Social Change in Pakistan*, edited by Ali Khan and Ali Nobil, 77–100. Karachi: Oxford University Press.

Devji, Faisal. 2012. *The Impossible Indian: Gandhi and the Temptation of Violence*. London: Hurst.

Gazdar, Mushtaq. 1997. *Pakistani Cinema, 1947–1997.* Karachi: Oxford University Press.

Haq, Khadija, and Richard Ponzio. 2008. *Pioneering the Human Development Revolution: An Intellectual Biography of Mahbub ul Haq.* Karachi: Oxford University Press.

Heidegger, Martin. 1991. *Nietzsche*, vol. 1, *The Will to Power as Art*, and vol. 2, *The Eternal Reurrence of the Same.* Translated by David Farrell Krell. New York: Harper Collins.

Jaffrelot, Christophe. 2015. *The Pakistan Paradox: Instability and Resilience.* London: Hurst.

Jinnah, Muhammad Ali. 2009. "Farewell Message to East Pakistan." In *Jinnah: Speeches and Statements, 1947–48*, 173–74. Karachi: Oxford University Press.

Kardar, A. J., dir. 1959. *Jago hua savera.* Dhaka: East Pakistan Film Development Corporation. (Urdu/Bengali)

Khan, Ayesha. 1996. "Policy Making in Pakistan's Population Programme." *Health Policy and Planning* 11, no. 1: 30–51.

Lindisfarne, Nancy. 1994. "Variant Masculinities, Variant Virginities: Rethinking Honour and Shame." In *Dislocating Masculinity: Comparative Ethnographies*, edited by Andrea Cornwall and Nancy Lindisfarne, 82–97. London: Routledge.

Manto, Saadat Hasan. 1991. *Manto Nāmāh.* Lahore: Sang-i Meel Publications. (Urdu)

Mehra, K. D., dir. 1935. *Sheila urf Pind di Kurri.* India: Indira Movie Tone. (Punjabi)

Mookherjee, Nayanika. 2015. *The Spectral Wound, Sexual Violence, Public Memory and the Bangladesh War of 1971.* Durham: Duke University Press.

Moore, Henrietta L. 2007. *The Subject of Anthropology: Gender, Symbolism and Psychoanalysis.* London: Polity.

Pinney, Christopher. 1998. *Camera Indica: The Social Life of Indian Photographs.* Chicago: University of Chicago Press.

———. 2003. *Photos of the Gods: The Printed Image and Political Struggle in India.* London: Reaktion Books.

Rahman, Tariq. 2016. "Language and Ideology in Pakistani Cinema." In *Cinema and Society: Film and Social Change in Pakistan*, edited by Ali Khan and Ali Nobil, 285–97. Karachi: Oxford University Press.

Ramnagri, Gauhar. 1935. *Filmī Parīyāṅ.* Lahore: Prem Shastra Book Depot. (Urdu)

Rancière, Jacques. 2000. *The Politics of Aesthetics.* Translated by Gabriel Rockhill. London: Continuum.

Rangacharya, Adya. 1996. *The Nāṭyaśāstra.* Translated by Munshiram Manoharlal. New Delhi: New Delhi Publishers.

Ray, Satyajit, dir. 1976. *Jana Aranya.* (Bengali)

Rehman, Nasreen. 2015. "A History of the Cinema in Lahore, c. 1919–1947." PhD diss., University of Cambridge.

Rizvi, Shaukat Hussain, dir. 1942. *Khandaan.* Lahore: Pancholi Pictures. (Urdu)

Tariq, Hassan, dir. 1959. *Neend.* Pakistan: Movietone. (Urdu)

———, dir. 1977. *Begum Jan.* Lahore: Mughal Films. (Urdu)

Žižek, Slavoj. 2000. "Afterword." In *The Politics of Aesthetics*, by Jacques Rancière. Translated by Gabriel Rockhill. London: Continuum.

PART II

TRANSREGIONAL CROSSINGS

6 THE PUBLIC IN THE CITIES

Detouring through Cinemas of Bombay, Calcutta, and Lahore (1920s–1930s)

MADHUJA MUKHERJEE

BY EXPLORING THE DECISIVE *INDIAN CINEMATOGRAPH COMMITTEE Report, 1927–28* and considering Kaushik Bhaumik's (2001) proposition that early industrial conditions were like a bazaar, I reconsider the public viewing cultures of Bombay, Calcutta, and Lahore during the late 1920s. I argue that such cities could be remapped through their locations of consumption, leisure, and cultural transactions. I demonstrate that through active film cultures, these places became sights/sites of vibrant cosmopolitanism. I contend that a close reading of cinema practices with regard to *places and spaces* brings forth a complicated history of the era that is marked by multiple—and often conflicting—trajectories. Through such analyses, I draw attention to the industrial and cultural linkages among the major cities of Bombay, Calcutta, and Lahore, and in examining the accounts of the cinemas and theaters, I study the manner in which cinema halls became locations of both *transregional* and *transnational* dialogues. I delve into the many itineraries of cinema, its movement across cities and territories, and the effect that film culture had on public life. Through this exploration, I question existing models of national cinema(s) and argue for a new historiography.

As proposed in the forthcoming volume *Industrial Networks and Cinemas of India* by Monika Mehta and myself, ideas of nation and nationalism have been predominantly used as categories to study cinema histories and public cultures, particularly during the first phase of cinema studies in India during the 1990s.[1] Such studies have drawn from the theorization of geopolitics and socioeconomic transformations, and the attempts have by and large read the complicated accounts of film cultures in relation to the nation. Broadly speaking, national cinema frameworks—such as all-encompassing readings of African cinema, Chinese cinema, or Latin American cinema—aspire to produce a cinema of and for the nation or larger geopolitical area.

These tend to adhere to the borders of the state or continent, and rarely explore the densities and complexities of intra- and international transactions.[2]

Over the last decade, studies of Bollywood and Indian diaspora films have explored transnational travels of mainstream Hindi films, though more recent studies have reflected on industries located in disparate regions or territories of South Asia. This analytical shift has reassessed regional cinema as a category, which has replicated political and linguistic divisions vis-à-vis the states (or provinces) and has produced classifications such as Bengali cinema, Tamil cinema, Telugu cinema, Marathi cinema, Gujarati cinema, and so on. At the local level, the same limitations, which hinder national cinema studies, have been reproduced. Certain recent studies, however, question the dominant approach of national and regional cinema categories. Through close readings of production, exhibition, stars, fan cultures, genres, and practices, they demonstrate the presence of multiple language cinemas within the regions as well as transference of stories, styles, and techniques, along with travels of stars, artists, and technicians across regions, and in this manner, highlight the problems of national and regional cinema models (see, e.g., Hughes 2010; Radhakrishnan 2015; M. Mukherjee 2016).

By the early 1930s, film production, circulation, consumption, and varied conventions of making and viewing were more or less established across the globe (Nowell-Smith 1997). While film historians have long studied the modes of Hollywood film production, its technological transformations, and its wide range of styles and genres, there has been significantly less scholarly research pertaining to the film industries of the Indian subcontinent, especially during the formative decades of the 1920s and 1930s.[3] My own research (2008) on film studios based in Calcutta, the city's public cultures, technological advancements, evolving film styles, and early aural stardom, as well as more recent research by other scholars focusing on Bombay cinema have focused on the dynamic relationship between debates on modernity, emergent urban cultures, and cinema of the period (see also Dass 2015). Debashree Mukherjee (2015) situates Bombay cinema at the intersection of historical debates on colonial surveillance, financial modernity, Indian femininity, workers' struggles, and public and urban spaces. She argues that the early talkie industry played a crucial part in defining the textures and temporalities of the city's unique brand of modernity, which she describes as Bombay Modern.[4]

In his 2001 dissertation, "The Emergence of the Bombay Film Industry, 1913–1936," Kaushik Bhaumik draws a wide map of the industrial networks and considers the consolidation of Bombay cinema in relation to its transregional circuits. He analyzes the acceptance of the "Socials" or social reform films (and realist trends) vis-à-vis what he calls Cosmopolitan Bazaar Cinema (see also Vasudevan 1995; Bhaumik 2011). In his study, the function of film journalism is perceived as pivotal (see also M. Mukherjee 2012; D. Mukherjee 2013a). Critically, Bhaumik (2001, 140) articulates that "this cinema was itself located in the *bazaar*," a bazaar that was jam-packed with cosmopolitan culture.

The *Indian Cinematograph Committee Report* (*ICCR*) holds a mirror to the colonial history and politics of India, and it is through cinema and its many courses in public life that the complications of colonial rule, the economy, cultural-political negotiations, tussles over modernity, and international connections may be revisited and retold. While the *ICCR* frames the viewers in India and their tastes as more or less homogeneous, close reading of the various interviews highlights the ways in which places and people were heterogeneous. Through the oral and written accounts of S. D. Puri, the proprietor of Gaiety Theatre Lahore; Ram Prased Marwa, manager of the Star Cinema in Lahore; Rustomji Dorabji, proprietor of the Wellington, West End, and Venus Cinemas, Bombay; S. A. Alley, manager of Purna Theatre, Calcutta; N. C. Laharry, the secretary of Globe cinema, Calcutta, among others, this chapter underscores the close linkages between Lahore, Bombay, and Calcutta.

While is it evident from such testimonies that films like D. G. Phalke's landmark mythological films and *The Light of Asia* (dir. Franz Osten and Himanshu Rai, 1925), based on the life of Buddha, were popular, Hollywood stunt films like *The Thief of Baghdad* (dir. Raoul Walsh, 1924) became cult favorites. Such information effectively presents the varied nature and densities of public preferences and political contestations over cinema. A study of theaters also draws attention to the material history of cinema, which involves the history of celluloid and machines, along with the history of workers, laboratories, and localities in which theaters were built. Cinema halls entail a sensorial experience produced by grease, sweat, dust, heat, light, aroma, and movement. It also comprises viewers' active involvement, which is played out in and via the physical places of cinemas and various publicity materials. Close reading of archival materials, such as the *ICCR*, helps to forge alternative methods of interpreting cinematic history. By exploring the archaeology of cinema and the material history of film, we can piece together a more nuanced understanding of early Indian film and the spaces it occupied (see also Huhtamo and Parikka 2011).

CHRONICLES OF CINEMA: *INDIAN CINEMATOGRAPH COMMITTEE REPORT, 1927–28*

The Indian Cinematograph Committee (ICC), conceived by the empire, was created to investigate the Indian film bazaar. The committee aspired to verify mechanisms of production-distribution-exhibition, as well as the growing popularity of American films across British India, and thereafter implement direct control over the evolving film market in India and so-called gullible audiences (or "subjects"). The ICC, which was made up of three Indian men and three Englishmen, examined the validity of the embryonic indigenous film industry. They inquired about the milieu of the theaters, working conditions in the studios, the economic and physical risks involved in making and screening Indian films, and the source and amount of capital investment. Questions were also asked about the types of films being shown in the cinemas and the composition of the public in the theaters, specifically about their religious identities. They looked into the circumstances under which Indians were watching Indian and American films and the effects American films had on them.

The scope of this investigation was quite wide since it comprised personalities from territories like United and Central Provinces, North-West Frontier Province, Bengal, and Burma, as well as cities such as Karachi, Lahore, Peshwar, Bombay, Lucknow, Nagpur, Calcutta, Madras, Rangoon, Mandlay, and other places of British India. The ICC particularly interviewed respectable people and officials such as members of the legislative committee, police officers, judges, professors, teachers, doctors, political leaders, eminent actors, producers, filmmakers, theater/hall owners, and members of the Censor Boards. The questionnaire, sometimes accompanied by an oral interview, contained twenty-seven multipart questions. On the surface, the questionnaire inquired about the notion of good cinema, the quality of the films, technical standards, themes, and styles of Indian and American films; however, the subtext of the questions, especially in the oral interviews, involved the immoral effects of cinema, as well as details on gullible and unruly Indian crowds.

While M. Madhava Prasad (2003) and Manisita Dass (2009) consider the ideology of *ICCR*, I take a different approach and explore the margins of the report and read between the lines in order to glean information regarding production, labor, involvement of women as workers, day-to-day activities, the physical conditions of the theaters, and participation of the public.[5] Indeed, the volumes provide a plethora of information regarding the industrial conditions, exhibition networks, and public culture in cities such as Bombay, Calcutta, and Lahore. As Priya Jaikumar (2003, 103) notes, "These ICC interviews reveal various aspects of the changing relationship between the British Indian state and the Indian film industry" (see also Jaikumar 2017). One may suggest that the *ICCR* reveals many contours of colonial history and politics, and by and large, it is through cinema and its many trajectories in the public domain that the complex histories of colonial rule, the economy, cultural-political strife, tussles over modernity, and connections with international histories may be addressed.

CIRCUITS OF CINEMA: FROM CALCUTTA TO LAHORE VIA BOMBAY

In my recent work on Calcutta cinemas, "Inside a Dark Hall" (2017a), I underscore the significance of place and locality, and illustrate how theaters developed in three areas of Calcutta—Beadon Street (now Bidhan Sarani, North Calcutta), the Sealdah Station area, the Dharmatala-Chowringhee–New Market area (Central Calcutta), and Bhawanipore (south of Calcutta)—locations that were marked by the peculiarities of the bazaar and middle-class habitats, and were reframed through such community-oriented houses of leisure (see also M. Mukherjee 2013). The neighborhoods, I contend, were reoriented via new locations of consumption and leisure; thus, through film cultures specifically, they became sites of vibrant cosmopolitanism.

This was also true in Bombay. Kaushik Bhaumik (2001), embarking on a rereading of the structures and architecture of the cityscape, remaps Bombay via cinema halls. Most cinemas were located in two zones—the Fort area and the ever-growing Native Town. Bhaumik discusses how Sandhurst Road in Bombay became a hub of activity and cinema halls developed all along the road. These included the Coronation, the American-India, the Olympia, and the New Alhambra. The area was also packed with shops, hotels, office buildings, and residential homes. The road led to a bazaar of sorts and drew crowds "from Charni Road, Null Bazar, Lohar Chawl, Kalbadevi Road and Girgaum Road" (Bhaumik 2001, 24). From 1917 onward, the attention to cinema hall construction shifted to the Grant Road–Lamington Road axis. The Imperial and El Dorado opened in the same year, while the Majestic and the Precious opened in 1918.

Testimony by Rustomji Dorabji (proprietor of the Wellington, West End, and Venus Cinemas, Bombay) and the manner in which he describes patterns of viewership in Bombay are telling. The following is Dorabji's response to a series of questions from the committee:

> CHAIRMAN. Mr. Dorabji, you have been 12 years in this line, is it not?
>
> A. Yes, Sir.
>
> Q. Do you do this business alone or have you any other business?
>
> A. I am doing other business also. I am the proprietor of Wellington Motor and Cycle works. I am also the proprietor of three theatres in Bombay which are all situated in different localities, one at Dhobi Talao, one in Charni Road, and one in Parel. The theatre at Dhobi Talao is generally patronised by educated Indians, the one in Charni Road is patronised by Anglo-Indians and educated Indians and the one at Parel is patronised by mill hands [laborers].
>
> Q. Which is that one, is it the Venus?
>
> . . .
>
> A. Do you exhibit any Western films in the last?
>
> Q. I did try some Western films in the Venus, but it was not successful, so that I show only Indian films there. (*ICCR*, vol. 1, 350)

In the latter part of the interview, Dorabji narrates his experiences of screening different language films (or films with intertitles in different languages) in the three theaters located in three distinct areas. He mentions how when *Krishna janma* (Life of Krishna, dir. D. G. Phalke, 1918) was screened in one of his theaters, the entire one-hundred-foot road in front of the theater was jammed with traffic. Furthermore, his profits were so huge that he could not physically carry the money and had to transport it by rickshaw. Nevertheless, Dorabji was against screening Indian productions—including *The Light of Asia* (dir. Franz Osten and Himanshu Rai, 1925)—in the Wellington cinema, and he discusses how, following the screening of *Lanka dahan* (dir. D. G. Phalke, 1917) at Wellington he had to stall screenings, disinfect the theater, and therefore incurred losses (figure 6.1).

Virchand Dharamsey, in his meticulously researched article, "The Early World of Cinema: Bombay/Mumbai Theatres," divides the Bombay cinemascape into seven areas. Dharamsey argues:

> A myth that we see created in the Indian Cinematograph Committee Report of 1928 through a particular trajectory of questioning is that it was a mainly illiterate class of audience that frequented the cinema theatres

FIGURE 6.1. Capitol Cinema, Bombay, now defunct. (Photograph by the author)

> showing Indian films. To consider the residents of Kalbadevi, Girgaum or Mandvi as being uneducated is a colonial prejudice that we see lurking in the report. The main theatres screening Indian films—Majestic, Imperial and Krishna—were being visited by a wide range of audience including the Indian intellectual and cultured classes.

It is clear from the two disparate opinions that a "wide range of audience" and mixed groups were visiting the theaters, and that varied types of films were screened at theaters located in different areas in each city. The question of public taste may be further problematized if we consider the testimony of S. A. Alley, manager of Purna Theatre, Calcutta, apparently the only independently owned first-class cinema of the city. In his written evidence, Alley stated that "to the cultured and educated Indian, I should think the superior class of Western [American] features and social subjects, or adaptation of well-known literary and classical works of fiction" was acceptable, while, with "the masses, serials, adventurous subjects, comedies, and Indian production based on Mythological themes" were popular (*ICCR*, vol. 2, 812–17). Alley designates diverse genres (like comedies, action films, and mythological films) for the Indian masses. Furthermore, in his oral testimony before the committee, besides narrating his experiences in Rangoon, Burma, and describing the popularity of Bengal productions in the area, Alley responds:

Q. What class of people go your theatre?

A. That depends on the class of pictures. When I show serials, I get illiterate classes as a rule.

. . .

Q. They do not come for these social dramas?

A. No.

Q. They are not affected by social dramas?

A. No.

Q. Who patronises Western social dramas?

A. Mostly educated class who understand and follow captions.

Q. Bhowanipore is the place where the *vakils* [lawyers] live and other educated people?

A. Not only *vakils*, but the clerical class, the middle-class population, students etc.

. . .

Q. What percentage of sex films do you show?

. . .

A. I do not think I have shown more than two or three of that during all this period. [Purna had been operational since 1923.]

Q. Kissing going on all over the body, kissing on the neck, shoulder and so on.

A. I have not seen any. (*ICCR*, vol. 2, 817–26)

Alley's account complicates the history and apparently refined public culture of the Bhadralok localities in Calcutta. For instance, who was watching the so-called sex films? Were they the *vakils* and the middle-class population, or students or illiterate people or all? Alley also elaborates on the financial difficulties in acquiring and screening Bombay productions and the challenge due to the demographic divide between North and South Calcutta, considering that the former neighborhood was inhabited by a non-Bengali populace despite Calcutta being imagined as Bengal's capital, and North Calcutta being described as the hub of Black Town (Chaudhuri 1995). Moreover, the popularity of social dramas among the Calcutta elite, and the lack of such in Punjab shows how popular sensibilities fluctuated from territory to territory, city to city, and even from neighborhood to neighborhood (figure 6.2).

Like Calcutta and Bombay, "Lahore's film culture was a *bazaar*-oriented one" (Bhaumik 2001, 140). Theaters were located broadly in two areas, the posh McLeod Road and Bhatti Gate areas. Indeed, "Lahore's film culture

FIGURE 6.2. Purna façade. (Courtesy of Bitan Basu)

incorporated the din and culture of the *bazaar* into the film-watching experience" (140). Films were advertised in a performative style, and in the theaters, vendors sold cigarettes, boiled eggs, peanuts, *chilgozas* (pine nuts), and sugar candy. Relating to Punjab (on the Pakistan side), the *ICCR* offers a wide range of testimony, facilitating the production of new histories of the subcontinent and the networks between cities. For example, interviewees from the Punjab territories and North-Western Province include members of the Lahore Censor Board (vol. 2); Lala Lajpath Rai, member of the Legislative Assembly and later prime minister of India (vol. 2); C. J. Mehta, manager of the Palace Theatre, Karachi (vol. 4); R. Pancholi, Capital Theatre, Karachi (vol. 1); L. K. Chand, Imperial Bioscope, Peshwar (vol. 2); Ram & Sons, Frontier Cinema, Bannu (vol. 4); S. D. Puri, Gaiety Theatre, Lahore; and R. P. Marwa, manager of the Star Cinema, Lahore (vol. 2).

In his written testimony, S. D. Puri states that his theater has been in business since 1912 and primarily hires out films for public shows, though they also produce topicals on wrestling matches (*ICCR*, vol. 2, 143–49). Puri mentions how the percentage of viewers from the educated class in Lahore is double those from the illiterate class, and that fighting serials and Wild West dramas, along with big spectacular dramas, are popular among Indians. While Bombay is described as the major film-production center, there are "only a couple of films which were popular with both the Hindus and the Mohammadans [Muslims]." The list of popular films, for both Hindu and Muslim elites, according to Puri's testimony, include *Light of Asia*, *Krishna janma*, *Laila Majnu*, *Shirin Farhad*, and *Gulhakavli*, while "legends, kisses, adventure, detective, and fast action films" are popular among "illiterate" classes (*ICCR*, vol. 2, 143–49).

Importantly, Puri's and Marwa's oral testimonies also explain the ways in which cinema halls developed in Lahore. As evident from their interviews, Star Cinema in Lahore was rebuilt after Madan Theatres in Calcutta (one of the pioneering production-distribution-exhibition companies of the period) gave up proprietorship, which indicates emerging shifts within the industry (see also Govil and Hoyt 2014). Previously, Madan had four theaters in Lahore, but by 1927 they had just two. Star Cinema showed both Indian and American films, and sourced Indian films primarily from Sharda Film Company, Kohinoor Film Company, and Krishna Company (Bombay). According to Puri, while Anglicized Indians of Lahore apparently did not appreciate Indian films (such as social dramas), regarding screenings in Srinagar, Kashmir, he said:

> A. I remember having shown two pictures in Kashmir this year [1927]. One was "The Light of Asia" and the other was "A Thousand and One Nights." I showed both these picture [*sic*] there and there was a packed house every time. The audience included all the European[s] in the station, and they appreciated both the dramas. . . .
>
> Q. How many cinemas are there in Lahore?
>
> A. There are six cinemas in Lahore. . . .
>
> COLONEL CRAWFORD [committee member]. I am very much interested in your evidence. *I gather that you said that, so far as Lahore is concerned, Indian and Western [American] films are of about equal popularity to an Indian audience.*
>
> A. Provided the Western films are fight serials, wild west dramas with plenty of action or very high class comics [comedy]. (*ICCR*, vol. 2, 153, italics added)

The shifting and dissolving matter of taste across Indian territories shows how a decidedly hybrid film culture was evolving via screenings of certain types of American films, alongside the circulation of Phalke's films and the wide acceptance of *The Light of Asia* among the Indian bourgeoisie, which was located in disparate regions of British India.

Moreover, N. C. Laharry, secretary of Globe Cinema, Calcutta, explained to the Indian Cinematograph Committee:

> Q. If according to your computation only 200 [cinemas] are used regularly, the other 150 may be used by these travelling people [cinemas].
>
> A. That's quite possible. . . .
>
> Q. So there are in India only 4 distributing agencies for foreign films, are there not? Madans, Yourself, Pathe and Universal?
>
> A. In Karachi I think there is the Capital Bioscope Company. (*ICCR*, vol. 2, 770–801)

Besides the above evidence, the popular magazines of the early 1930s, such as *Filmland*, *Varieties Weekly*, and *The Cinema*, also illustrate how the distribution networks between Bombay, Calcutta, Lahore, and Karachi were active and operational. In addition, Laharry provides a range of information regarding rapidly transforming cultural spaces:

> Q. Have they [viewers] not started any cabarets in Calcutta?
>
> A. No not to my knowledge.
>
> Q. Have you heard of any clubs or cabarets started in Calcutta at all where they could imitate the drinking scenes [and] other things that they see on the screen?
>
> A. No.
>
> *MR. GREEN* [committee member]. Are there no nautch parties in Calcutta?
>
> A. There are in certain parts of the town.
>
> *CHAIRMAN*. You don't think that there is risk that sons of rich zemindars [landed gentry], members of the permanently settled estates, and scions of rich families having seen the cinemas, are likely to start such night clubs for enjoyment if they don't exist already?
>
> A. Westernised Indians who desire to do so can just as well go the Grand Hotel or to Fipros [Hotel and Market] and enjoy themselves, there is nothing to Prevent them from doing so. (*ICCR*, vol. 2, 779)

While this account brings forth a rich pool of data, allowing us to understand the viewing cultures of the 1920s (which differ from watching films in permanent houses or in temporary tents outside the city), it also illustrates how Hollywood films were circulated in India and informs us of the specific viewing conditions in Calcutta. Calcutta appears to have been pulsating with multiple crosscurrents, including nautch parties and parties in big hotels, cabarets, jazz music halls, and clubs—an entire panoply of new cultures of consumption and various other widely held markers of a modern world (Prakash 2010). In fact, while there have been many studies on modernity and cities, there are fewer studies of the cities of British India involving research on locations, architecture, and public culture (see Chattopadhyay 2005). Thus, I propose that a systematic study of cinema practices vis-à-vis *places and spaces* presents a far more pointed history of the period, which is dotted with multifarious and sometimes contradictory developments, and may therefore put in doubt any proposition of definitive and singular change in the subcontinent.[6]

The eminent historian of modern India Sumit Sarkar (1984) argues that the 1920s indicated diverse political trends. Such manifold trends may be effectually explained through narratives of cinemas, in which many types of people gathered to celebrate this marvel of modernity and its varied accounts of changing life.

"COMING TO YOUR NEAREST THEATRE": GENRE AND CINEMAS

While S. D. Puri discusses the circulation and wide acceptance of *The Thief of Baghdad*, Anupama Kapse (2014) shows how American stunt films and their multiple adaptations in India during the late 1920s and early 1930s generated space for active exchanges between colonial contexts and international forms. A range of stunt films produced by companies such as Imperial Film Company, Kohinoor, explored what Kapse describes as "new social, psychic, and artistic possibilities" (224; see also Vitali 2010). In *Diler Jigar* (dir. G. P. Pawar, 1931), the heroine goes through "Douglasization," after Douglas Fairbanks, and performs stunts with great physical energy (Kapse 2014). The style of the narration (including the shots, use of close-ups, and editing) underscores a passionate struggle over developing cinematic forms and new cultures of cinema.

Neepa Majumdar (2010) shows how physicality and movement were fundamental to action films. Majumdar discusses how in *Diler Jigar* "the acrobats who are the main characters put on a show that is merely tableau like display of bodybuilding and gymnastic exercises" (118). This display of the body and its agility became the main features of stunt films. Hence, stunt films may be read as evidence of "new body cultures" and also a mode of presenting the body as spectacle. Majumdar further argues that "the replay of film stunts is in the experience of moviegoing, from buying tickets, to finding seats, to vocally responding to the screen, encompasses the entire spectrum of film culture in a form of embodied spectatorship" (118). In effect, the sight/site of the cinema was both an object and a means through which the multilayered courses of modernization could be lived and realized.

The *ICCR* testimonies present accounts of the inflows and outflows of a range of films, which became a significant aspect of the early phases of Indian cinema. In their article "Thieves of Bombay," Nitin Govil and Eric Hoyt (2014) show how the film *The Thief of Bagdad* became hugely successful across Indian territories, largely due to United Artists' (USA) new distribution networks throughout Asia. Moreover, the Hollywood studios functioned across British India in association with the colossal distribution-exhibition system established by Madan Theatres in Calcutta. In fact, several ICC interviewees described how the Madans controlled distribution and exhibition circuits, enjoying a monopoly of sorts.

Because of such industrial arrangements, the Indian film scene was teeming with Hollywood films. In addition, research on early and silent films, such as that done by Valentina Vitali (2008) and Anupama Kapse (2014), draws attention to the vibrant presence of action and stunt films across Indian regions. Nevertheless, such Western films were probably not as popular in Bombay's Parel area and among the mill workers of the vicinity, though the masses in Calcutta, Bhawanipore area, preferred them. Moreover, in Lahore, films such as *Light of Asia*, *Krishna janma*, *Laila Majnu*, *Shirin Farhad*, and *Gulhakavli* were popular among both Hindus and Muslims, although the release of Phalke's film seemingly caused huge losses to Wellington Cinema's business in Bombay.

Ashish Rajadhyaksha's 1987 landmark essay, "The Phalke Era," not only laid the groundwork for new approaches to studying Indian cinema, but it also addressed the larger networks of visual practices and analyzed the ways in which notions of modernity were reconstituted via D. G. Phalke's mythological films. In his 1994 essay "India's Silent Cinema: A 'Viewer's View,'" he elaborated on the subjects of early films in the public domain and issues of iconicity and recognition:

> *Shri Krishna Janma* constitutes a series of highly familiar episodes in the young Krishna's life: . . . to evoke wonder and awe, a highly coded, strongly *erotic* identification with the benevolent play of the young god.

> The film seeks to make no intervention other than bringing that wonder cinematically alive . . . the wish-fulfillment in the mythical "coming alive." (Rajadhyaksha 1994, 69)

Such spectacular encounters with modernity become evident in an oral interview with the pioneering filmmaker D. G. Phalke, illuminating that while Western films were circulated throughout British India, Indian productions also traveled to the West. For instance, when asked by the committee about the standards of Indian films, Phalke stated:

> Q. Do you think if you improve the quality of Indian film you will have a wider market abroad? Do you think well made Indian film will command a good audience if shown in England?
> A. Not the present ones produced in India, but well made ones may command a good audience, I have exhibited some of my own films in England in London such as "Savitri," "Harishchandra," and other films and the press in London remarked "From the technical point of view Phalke's films are excellent."
> . . .
> Q. Who actually distributed your films?
> A. I did it myself.
> . . .
> Q. But you have no agents in other parts of India?
> A. Yes—there are some.
> Q. You said you sent your films to Singapore. Had you success there?
> A. Yes, it was a success. We have sent films to Singapore, Rangoon and other places.
> Q. Have you ever tried to send your films to West Africa?
> A. Yes, we have sent some of our films to Zanzibar. (*ICCR*, 869–85)

Phalke's films were shown in English in Asian and African cities, demonstrating the transnational reach of Indian films. Additionally, the eminent Indian filmmaker Himanshu Rai, who initiated several Indo-German productions during the silent era, describes how profits from *The Light of Asia* were shared by three parties—one German interest, along with the Great Eastern Corporation Limited, as well as between himself and Niranjan Pal (later his screenwriter). He describes how Niranjan Pal contracted with Emelka Studios and got the exhibition rights to show the film in Great Britain. In his interview with the ICC, Rai explained:

Q. The finance was found by the Great Eastern Corporation, I mean the whole finance for the production?

A. Yes. But services were rendered by the German Syndicate. They supplied cameras, etc. The German interest was by their supplying the technicians and the equipment required for camera work.

. . .

Q. Even that is not really oriental, because the technicians, etc. were all Germans?

A. It [*The Light of Asia*] is an International art. (*ICCR*, vol. 3, 998–1015)

The above interviews highlight the international framework in which Indian filmmakers produced and distributed their films during the 1920s. In fact, the making of "international art" for Indian and international audiences, as well as the wide circulation of Phalke's mythological films, and the vast popularity of *The Light of Asia* and *The Thief of Baghdad* in British India, shows the diverse composition of the public, and the densities of public preferences and economic-political intensities, alongside the wide networks of cinema and culture that transpired through boundaries of localities, cities, provinces, states, and national circuits.[7]

The *ICCR* reveals the wide variety of films that were circulating in Indian circuits and their wide acceptance among the public. However, considering that films like *Broken Blossoms* (dir. D. W. Griffith, 1919) were banned, this provokes us to reflect on how the colonial state monitored and controlled public preferences. Volume 4 of the *ICCR* includes "miscellaneous papers," which provide a list of cinemas across British India. For instance, while the Bombay Presidency had more than one hundred permanent cinemas by 1928, Bengal had twenty-six permanent cinemas and three seasonal cinemas in the hill towns (like Darjeeling). Similarly, Punjab had twenty-two permanent cinemas in the plains and fourteen seasonal cinemas across important hill stations like Shimla, Solon, and Dalhousie. The miscellaneous papers also include a long list of films that were not certified for screenings. For example, three reels of *Six Wonderful Nights in Paris* (1925) were not issued a certificate because "women were exhibited almost in a state of nudity posing and dancing" (*ICCR*, vol. 4, 369). *The Triumph of the Rat* (dir. Graham Cutts, 1926) was censored, and *Orphans of the Storm* (dir. D. W. Griffith, 1921) was restricted from screening because of its political content. The Indian film *Bhakt Vidhur* (dir. Kanjibhai Rathod, 1921) was not allowed to be screened because it was deemed a "veiled resume of the political events [involving] Mr. Gandhi" (*ICCR*, vol. 4, 375). Similarly, films such as *Veer*

Durgadas (1924) and *Razia Begum* (1925) were not issued certificates on "religious" grounds. The testimony casts light on these issues and shows how geographies and people were imagined and framed, and how public tastes nonetheless remained heterogeneous.

CONCLUSION

With regard to contestations over public tastes and opinion, one may argue that cinema captured the excitement and eclecticism of the bazaar as well as the entire span of concerns pertaining to modernity, politics, cultural movements, and technological developments. Films and film-viewing cultures translated, to evoke Kaushik Bhaumik (2001, 139), the "dynamic transformation of social relations in Indian society under the impact of market and technology," and "the *bazaar* was where this transformation was taking place." In fact, manifold political, economic, and cultural trends and multiple ideas about modernity flowed across the wide map of the subcontinent. Conjuring Arjun Appadurai's (1991) crucial formulation regarding "parallel modernities," one may stress that there existed, *or exists*, heterogeneous spaces and social realities, cultures, communities, practices, and economic conditions that may not be covered by the blanket term *modernity* or even by analyzing social histories of the subcontinent as alternative modernity.

It can be meaningful to examine what Appadurai describes as "social reality of imagination" and how fantasy "enters in a host of ways into the fabrication of social lives" (198), thereby studying the *varying and altering modernities* with regard to the complex circumstances of social life on the Indian subcontinent. I propose that cinema became a potent carrier of such complexities. Additionally, Bhaumik (2001, 130) makes a crucial point while suggesting that the "immediate cultural context for cosmopolitan [and modern] cinema was provided by the efflorescence of Urduised popular culture in Bombay and north India, most notably in Lahore." Circuits of cinema through British India, in the bazaars and *mahallas* (neighborhoods), as evident from *ICCR*, hint at the possibility of rereading the plurality of what Partha Chatterjee (1997) refers to as "our" modernization, forceful struggles over it, and the effervescent cultures of cosmopolitanism that were a definitive aspect of pre-independence cinema. The *ICCR* offers a rich pool of data showing how cities such as Bombay, Calcutta, and Lahore were pulsating with a variety of crosscurrents and comprised a wide spectrum of crowds who gathered in and around the cinemas.

Contrary to the purpose for which the committee was established, the ICC eventually rejected a proposal to give preferential treatment to British propaganda films; instead, it demanded a program to support Indian filmmakers and producers. Similarly, as far as the subject of good cinema was concerned, Western films (with kissing, etc.) were accepted, though censorship was encouraged. The report also proposed that cinema should be used as a means of mass education. Likewise, cinema was described as both an art form and a thriving industry that supported hundreds of technicians and workers. Barring a few critics, cinema was recognized as a positive and effective agent of change. By and large, the *ICCR* provided a multifaceted picture of British India that not only featured disparate types of films in different languages and genres, but also demonstrated the fashion in which cinema halls became a channel via which the byzantine pathways of modernity could be traversed, and perhaps even appreciated. Furthermore, such readings indicate a different approach to studying the history of cinema by considering the "archaeology" of cinema and foregrounding the material history of a cultural form, which involves celluloid, old and new machines, workers, locations, grease, sweat, dust, heat, light, aroma, movement, and an entire range of engagements evoked in and by the physical places of cinematic transactions.

Moreover, this chapter showed the links between Bombay, Calcutta, and undivided Punjab. In fact, the *ICCR* records how Punjab, especially Lahore, was considerably anglicized.[8] Cosmopolitism became the key feature of such cities, owing to the prevalence of colleges, offices, clubhouses, bazaars, army cantonments, British soldiers, as well as the varying processes of modernization, which began during the Mughal period. Likewise, many genres of film—including action, comedy, romance, Arabian Nights narratives, fantasy, and adventure—coexisted side-by-side and sometimes merged into one another. Indeed, many temporalities and topos or places exist and thrive in parallel zones in the contexts of "our modernity."

Furthermore, skilled and semiskilled workers from Punjab, as well as writers, performers, and other technical personnel, steadily migrated to Bombay and Calcutta as the sector grew during the late 1920s and early 1930s. The traffic of films, personnel, and capital between Punjab, Bombay, and Bengal, as reflected through the *ICCR*, was fervent. I argue that such connections eventually produced particular types of popular cinema, which included traces of multiple genres and cultures. Additionally, a number of artists from Lahore and Calcutta migrated to Bombay following the Second World War, a time when industrial conditions weakened in these sectors following riots and Partition. Despite this decline in the industry, Bombay experienced phenomenal economic and geographic growth. Indeed, post independence Bombay drew heavily from the styles and techniques of so-called regional centers like Calcutta and Lahore.[9] Therefore, it is not a surprise that several decades after independence and the formation of India and Pakistan, films scripts and song lyrics were commonly written in Perso-Arabic script, considering that many of the writers were educated in undivided Punjab. Likewise, certain well-known actors, performers, and composers came to Bombay from Bengal and Punjab (or returned to their hometowns after independence). Clearly there was a dynamic dialogue among Bombay, Bengal, and Punjab that has remained somewhat unfinished—or continues in hushed tones—following independence and Partition.

NOTES

1 For instance, some of the early and seminal works by Sumita Chakravarty and Jyotika Virdi.

2 For information on how Bombay cinema became synonymous with Indian cinema following war, independence, and Partition, see Manto (2014) and M. Mukherjee (2018).

3 See the extensive work of Ravi Vasudevan and S. V. Srinivas on 1930s Indian cinema.

4 Especially see Manto and Ḥasan (1998) on Bombay and the film industry. See also D. Mukherjee (2013b).

5 On issues of women and work, see M. Mukherjee (2017b).

6 See "Unsettling Cinema: A Symposium on the Place of Cinema in India," special issue, *Seminar* 525 (May 2003), for a comprehensive debate on history of cinema and city through accounts of cinema-halls and its public.

7 The careers of both Devika Rani and Rai had an international beginning. While Rai began as an actor with a theater group in London, *The Light of Asia* was directed by his long-term associate (in Bombay Talkies) Franz Osten and was coproduced by Peter Ostermayer, Osten's brother. The film was shown in Berlin, Brussels, Budapest, Genoa, Venice, and Vienna. Rai's next two films, *Prapancha Pash* (1928–29) and *Shiraz* (1928), were presold to UFA (Germany) and British Instructional films. Moreover, *Karma* (1933, English), starring Devika Rani, was an international success and established Rani as a star of international repute.

8 Actor Kamini Kaushal spoke about her life in Lahore during a personal communication (November 16, 2016):

> We used to cycle around [in Lahore]. But I grew up much later. . . . I was interested in doing things. Like whether it is drawing or painting or elocution or making films . . . we were given complete freedom in our home.

That was the most important element I think I imbibed. . . . That was the norm in our home. . . . Let them explore the world, let them discover. My brother would take us with him everywhere. Us, three sisters. . . . I learnt Kathak and Bharat Natyam in Lahore, before Partition. . . . There were no restrictions as such. I went cycling, I went swimming, I played all the games. But it was not anything that I was doing anything extra special.

9 On the subject of Bombay film styles, see Prasad (1998).

REFERENCES

Appadurai, Arjun. 1991. "Global Ethnoscapes: Notes and Queries for a Transitional Anthropology." In *Recapturing Anthropology: Working in the Present*, edited by Richard Fox, 191–210. Santa Fe, NM: School for Advanced Research Press.

Bhaumik, Kuashik. 2001. "The Emergence of the Bombay Film Industry 1913–1936." PhD diss., University of Oxford.

———. 2011. "Cinematograph to Cinema Bombay, 1896–1928." *BioScope: South Asian Screen Studies* 2, no. 1: 41–67.

Chakravarty, Sumita S.1993. *National Identity in Indian Popular Cinema, 1947–87*. Delhi: Oxford University Press.

Chatterjee, Partha. 1997. "Our Modernity." In *The Present History of West Bengal: Essays in Political Criticism*, edited by Partha Chatterjee, 193–210. Delhi: Oxford University Press.

Chattopadhyay, Swati. 2005. *Representing Calcutta: Modernity, Nationalism, and the Colonial Uncanny*. Abingdon, UK: Routledge.

Chaudhuri, Sukanta. 1995. *Calcutta: The Living City*. Oxford: Oxford University Press.

Dass, Manishita. 2009. "The Crowd outside the Lettered City: Imagining the Mass Audience in 1920s India." *Cinema Journal* 48, no. 4: 77–98.

———. 2015. *Outside the Lettered City: Cinema, Modernity and the Public Sphere in Late Colonial India*. New York: Oxford University Press.

Dharamsey, Virchand. "The Early World of Cinema: Bombay/Mumbai Theatres." Unpublished manuscript.

Govil, Nitin, and Eric Hoyt. 2014. "Thieves of Bombay: United Artists, Colonial Copyright, and Film Piracy in the 1920s." *BioScope* 5, no. 1: 5–27.

Hughes, S. P. 2010. "What Is Tamil about Tamil Cinema?" *South Asian Popular Culture* 8, no. 3: 213–29.

Huhtamo, Erkki, and Jussi Parikka. 2011. *Media Archaeology: Approaches, Applications, and Implications*. Berkeley: University of California Press.

Indian Cinematograph Committee Report, 1927–28 (ICCR). 1928. Madras: Government of India, Central Publication Branch.

Jaikumar, Priya. 2003. "More Than Morality: The Indian Cinematograph Committee Interviews (1927)." *Moving Image* 3, no. 1: 82–109.

———. 2017. *Cinema at the End of Empire: A Politics of Transition in Britain and India*. Durham: Duke University Press.

Kapse, Anupama. 2014. "Around the World in Eighty Minutes: Douglas Fairbanks and Indian Stunt Films." In *Silent Cinema and the Politics of Space,* edited by J. Bean, A. Kapse, and L. Horak. Bloomington: Indiana University Press.

Majumdar, Neepa. 2010. *Wanted Cultured Ladies Only! Female Stardom and Cinema in India, 1930s–1950s.* Champaign: University of Illinois Press.

Manto, Sa'ādat Ḥasan. 2014. "Pakistani Film." *BioScope: South Asian Screen Studies* 5, no. 2: 163–66.

Manṭo, Sa'ādat Ḥasan, and Khālid Ḥasan.1998. *Stars from Another Sky: The Bombay Film World in the 1940s.* London: Penguin Books.

Mukherjee, Debashree. 2013a. "Creating Cinema's Reading Publics: The Emergence of Film Journalism in Bombay." In *No Limits: Media Studies from India*, edited by Ravi Sundaram, 165–98. Oxford: Oxford University Press.

———. 2013b. "Notes on a Scandal: Writing Women's Film History against an Absent Archive." *BioScope: South Asian Screen Studies* 4, no. 1: 9–30.

———. 2015. "Bombay Modern: A History of Film Production in Late Colonial India (1930s–1940s)." PhD diss., New York University.

Mukherjee, Madhuja. 2008. "The New Theatres Ltd.: 'The Cathedral of Culture' and the House of the Popular." PhD diss., Jadavpur University.

———, ed. 2012. *Aural Films, Oral Cultures: Essays on Cinema From the Early Sound Era.* Kolkata: Jadavpur University Press.

———. 2013. "House of Images, Sealdah: A Photo-Essay on Chhabighar Cinema." *SEPHIS e-Magazine* 9, no. 2 (April): 68–81.

———. 2016. "Toward a New Frame for Regional Films: Manbhum Videos and the Other Side of (Indian) Cinema." *Bioscope: South Asia Screen Studies* 7, no. 1: 58–79.

———. 2017a. "Inside a Dark Hall: Space, Place, and Accounts of Some Single-Theatres in Kolkata." *South Asian History and Culture* 8, no. 2: 269–83.

———, ed. 2017b. *Voices of the Talking Stars: The Women of Indian Cinema and Beyond.* Delhi: Sage Publications.

———. 2018. "Forking Paths of Indian Cinema: Revisiting Hindi Films through Regional Networks." In *The Routledge Companion to World Cinema*, edited by Rob Stone, Paul Cooke, Stephanie Dennison, and Alex Marlow-Mann, 213–24. London: Routledge.

Nowell-Smith, Geoffrey. 1997. *The Oxford History of World Cinema.* Oxford: Oxford University Press.

Prakash, Gyan. 2010. *Mumbai Fables.* Princeton, NJ: Princeton University Press.

Prasad, Madhava. 1998. *Ideology of Hindi Film: A Historical Construction.* Delhi: Oxford University Press.

———. 2003. "The Natives Are Looking: Cinema and Censorship in Colonial India." In *Law's Moving Image*, edited by Leslie Moran et al., 161–72. London: Cavendish.

Radhakrishnan, Ratheesh. 2015. "Thiruvithamkoor, Malabar, Kerala: Speculations on the Regions in 'Regional Cinema.'" *BioScope: South Asian Screen Studies* 6, no. 2: 126–44.

Rajadhyaksha, Ashish. 1987. "The Phalke Era: Conflict of Traditional Form and Modern Technology." *Journal of Arts and Ideas* 14–15: 47–78.

———. 1994. "India's Silent Cinema: A 'Viewer's View.'" In *Light of Asia: India's Silent Cinema, 1912–1934*, edited by Suresh Chabria, 25–40. New Delhi: Wiley Eastern.

Sarkar, Sumit. 1984. *Modern India, 1885–1947.* Delhi: Macmillan India.

Vasudevan, Ravi. 1995. "Addressing the Spectre of a 'Third World' National Cinema: The Bombay 'Social' Film of the 1940s and 1950s." *Screen* 36, no. 4: 305–324

Vitali, Valentina. 2008. "Not a Biography of 'Indian Cinema': Historiography and the Question of National Cinema in India." In *Theorising National Cinema*, edited by Valentina Vitali and Paul Willemen. London: British Film Institute.

———. 2010. *Hindi Action Cinema: Industries, Narratives, Bodies*. Bloomington: Indiana University Press.

7 CROSS-WING FILMMAKING

East Pakistani Urdu Films and Their Traces in the Bangladesh Film Archive

LOTTE HOEK

AN EXTRAORDINARY IMAGE SAT ON A DESK IN THE CRAMPED quarters of the Bangladesh Film Archive (figure 7.1). Framed behind glass, the painted image shows a boy, face lifted to the sun, his eyes closed. In the clouds painted behind him, Bengali lines proclaim, "I do not fear injustice and untruth, let my *iman* be known by a hundred tests." It is a film poster, with the title *Son of Pakistan* printed along the bottom. The tagline "My country, my love, Pakistan" is wrapped around the image of a globe highlighting the shapes of East and West Pakistan. An additional English text identifies the film as the "first film for children filmed all over Pakistan." Though the name of the director, Fazlul Huq, is printed along the bottom of the image, the archive's librarian shrugged his shoulders: neither he nor his assistants had any idea where the image had come from or what the film *Son of Pakistan* was about. "It's an old film," said the librarian, and with that, the discussion ended.

The small map of Pakistan on the *Son of Pakistan* poster illustrates a country that no longer exists: Pakistan made up of West *and* East Pakistan. What was once the eastern wing of Pakistan is today Bangladesh. The country has emerged from two bloody sets of liberation struggles against exploitation and political repression: first as East Bengal was liberated from British imperial rule to become East Pakistan in 1947 and subsequently as the population of East Pakistan fought the Liberation War of 1971 for the independence of East Pakistan, which became the sovereign nation-state of Bangladesh (van Schendel 2009). The liberatory potential of the Bengali nationalism that had helped fuel the struggle against repression during the

This chapter has been extensively abridged from its original: Lotte Hoek, "Cross-Wing Filmmaking: East Pakistani Urdu Films and Their Traces in the Bangladesh Film Archive," *Bioscope: South Asian Screen Studies* 5, no. 2 (2015): 99–118.

FIGURE 7.1. Poster for *Son of Pakistan* (dir. Fazlul Huq, 1966). (Courtesy of the Bangladesh Film Archive)

Pakistan period took on new guises within the new nation-state of Bangladesh (Murshid 1993). Here, nationalism became a tool for consolidating the dominance of particular classes and communities to the exclusion of others (Jahangir 2002; Mohsin [1997] 2002), as well as producing well-established and orthodox accounts of the pre-Bangladesh past (Feldman 1999; Mohaiemen 2011). Within such a nationalist perspective, the prominent display of the *Son of Pakistan* poster, with its explicit visualization of eastern Bengal as Pakistan, in a government institution such as the Bangladesh Film Archive, was more surprising to me than the librarian's reticence.

This chapter is based on my attempt to find out more about *Son of Pakistan.* My spectacular failure to do so, despite tracking the boy in the picture, sheds some light on the place of Urdu cinema from East Pakistan within contemporary Bangladeshi film historiography. Going through the collection of the Bangladesh Film Archive, I came across other accounts and images that hinted at the shared cinematic history of what was once Pakistan, stretching from Sylhet to Quetta. Posters, stills, and journal articles recounted in unexpected ways the translations, adaptations, and collaborations between filmmakers, producers, and actors across what used to be East and West Pakistan. Where contemporary narratives of cinema history in Bangladesh often focus on a nationalist genealogy that posits the past as an inevitable run-up to the present (Nasreen and Haq 2008; Raju 2002), these archival traces tell other stories of aesthetic and creative synergies among filmmakers that continued right up until the war that tore the two wings of the country apart for good. These stories not only present a new perspective on the history of the cinema in Pakistan between 1947 and 1971; they equally allow a rethinking of contemporary practices and debates in Bangladeshi and Pakistani cinema.

Recognizing that the archive presents an opportunity to explore "the ongoing connections or disjunctures of futures and pasts in heterogeneous presents" (Axel 2002, 3), in this chapter I open up the tensions that exist between the contemporary accounts of Bangladeshi film historiography on the one hand, and traces of filmmaking activities across East and West Pakistan that remain in the Bangladesh Film Archive on the other hand. In particular, I focus on the archival traces of Urdu-language films made in East Pakistan. I argue that the cross-wing nature of Pakistani filmmaking and viewing in the 1960s is evident from archival material, particularly when looking at Urdu films from East Pakistan, but it has become difficult to account for such cross-wing filmmaking and spectatorship within contemporary accounts of cinema in Bangladesh, to the point of being forgotten even by its protagonists. I use my search for *Son of Pakistan* to ask what shape its forgetting has taken and how the political watershed of 1971 limits the possibilities for excavating the past of Bangladeshi cinema. The peculiar opacities around this film direct us to pay attention to those fragments of visual culture that refer not just to a disappeared past but an actively forgotten world of everyday pleasures and aspirations.

NATIONALIST FILM HISTORIOGRAPHY AND THE LEAKY ARCHIVE

The largest part of the collection of the Bangladesh Film Archive consists of old celluloid reels stacked up in film tins kept in cooled storage, back issues of film magazines bound together into heavy volumes by year, and similar volumes of newspaper and magazine clippings. While the librarian busied himself with cutting film news from a dozen or so daily newspapers, I rummaged through volumes of Bengali film journals that sat heavily on the shelves of the small library. Trying to trace some sort of genealogy for the contemporary outcry over film obscenity that I was studying, I imagined the archive might contain historical traces or comparatives from the longer history of filmmaking in East Bengal. As I plucked the dusty volumes off their shelves and leafed through the first few, the uneven historical depth of the collection was evident. Some international English language texts and a few scattered volumes of Bengali magazines from the 1960s punctuated the many volumes of magazines and clippings from the 1980s, 1990s, and 2000s. Bengali language magazines from before 1975 were largely absent from the collections.

"We don't have them," said the librarian when I asked to see back issues of magazines from before the 1970s. His colleague with the alluring job title "film investigator" said that while efforts had been made to retrieve journals from reluctant editors and private collectors, they had not been able to add many volumes from before 1978, the year in which the archive was set up. While private individuals had old reels and magazines in their possession, few were willing to entrust these (often personally significant and potentially lucrative) objects to the Bangladeshi state for safekeeping.

The uneven historical records and the attendant lack of clarity about film history should not have surprised me. During the course of my research, I was on more than one occasion told a version of the following story. After the breakup of East and West Pakistan, a decision was made, perhaps by the Film Censor Board of what was now Bangladesh, to recensor films that had been made and released in East Pakistan. All traces of Pakistan had to be erased from the visual record of the cinema of Bangladesh. And thus the picture of Jinnah that had adorned so many film sets had to be removed from the endless reels of celluloid released over the twenty-four years of East Pakistan. "It is true," said a friend, "you watch these old films and you see a scratchy blur on the image, and with a shock you realise it must have been Jinnah on the wall of that scene!" I imagine a single bureaucrat tasked with the duty to remove the Quaid-e-Azam from all those reels. Sitting in a small office among piles of celluloid, he goes through every single frame, razor blade at the ready, scratching out the picture of Jinnah from each frame, tirelessly.

Whether the story is true and whether such a bureaucratic position was ever really called into existence I can't be sure. To me, the telling of the tale is more relevant than its veracity. It illustrates well what we know of regime changes, in which the taken-for-granted nature of a new political order must be immediately instantiated and the going-without-saying of the accounts of its own making continually reinscribed in public. The change of political regime is made tangible through its media.

Under the combined influence of a war-torn country and the active production of the new nation-state of Bangladesh, the details of the film history of East Pakistan have become somewhat blurred. The data about the film industry in East Pakistan presented in secondary sources is contradictory, and statistics about the industry were considered unreliable even by contemporaneous observers (Kabir 1969, preface). The "facts" of Pakistani cinema between 1947 and 1971 are contested.

The forgetting of Urdu films from East Pakistan in Bangladesh coincides with their uncomfortable position alongside better-rehearsed lines of analysis and historical narrative in Pakistani cinema history. Those films and directors who moved between what are now two nation-states are especially prone to being forgotten. Take director Nazrul Islam. Born in Calcutta and having worked in Bombay before Partition, Nazrul Islam moved fluidly between making films in Urdu (*Kajal*, 1965) and Bengali (*Kaar bou*, 1967) in Dhaka before opting for Pakistan after the independence of Bangladesh. Presumably on account of the latter, Alamgir Kabir does not list his films in the directory at the back of *Film in Bangladesh* (1979). Nonetheless, a production still from *Kaar bou* is included in the picture section of the book, accompanied by the caption "Scene from delightful slapstick comedy *Kaar bou* (1967 Subhas Dutta, Nasima Khan) directed by Nazrul Islam (now settled in Pakistan)." Similarly, Gazdar (1997, 150) suggests that Nazrul Islam "made notable movies there [in East Pakistan] but at the time of the dismemberment of the country opted for Pakistan." Nazrul Islam's East Pakistani films disappear from either record.

The lack of clarity within the written historical record of filmmaking in East Pakistan has definite effects on the ways Bangladeshi film history is written today. This effect can be demonstrated by looking at the place of East Pakistani Urdu films in recent academic and journalistic accounts of Bangladesh film history.

The Urdu language has become one of the central and undisputed symbols of alterity within Bangladeshi nationalism. The Bengali nationalism that emerged in the course of the 1950s found its point of origin in the language movement of 1952, in which students protested and died to resist Urdu as the only state language of Pakistan. The Bengali language galvanized political resistance in East Pakistan, with Bengali cultural forms providing a crucial affective pull for the movement for independence (Ahmed 2012). Today Bangladeshi nationalism simply sets apart "us" and "them" through the marker of Bengali. If you don't speak Bengali, you are not really part of "us." While other languages indigenous to the territory of Bangladesh struggle for recognition during major national events focused on Bengali as the mother tongue (such as February 21st and the attendant book fair), the Urdu language is the constitutive outsider to these events. It remains the mark of the Other, a clear indicator of what side you are on, in a way religion was not.

Given the thoroughly symbolic nature of the Urdu language in contemporary Bangladesh, accounts of the place and appeal of Urdu films in East Pakistan in scholarly accounts and journalistic write-ups are inflected in particular ways. Nasreen and Haq (2008) write about the "assault" by the Urdu language on the film industry in Dhaka: "Cinema emerged as a cultural institution as a consequence of the cultural identity that developed among Bengalis due to the language movement; but before that institution could gain shape, the assault [*akronto*] by the Urdu language can be considered a historical catastrophe [*biporyoy*]" (Nasreen and Haq 2008, 45, my translation). Linking the language movement to the cultural identity of Bengalis in a moment of national awakening, Urdu films made in East Pakistan are considered catastrophic for the development of the film industry in East Bengal. Nasreen and Haq do not articulate what the catastrophe consists of exactly, but it can be inferred that a "proper" development would consist of films in Bengali rather than Urdu being made at the new film studio in Dhaka and audiences interested in those Bengali films rather than their Urdu counterparts. That this is not the case is a puzzle to Zakir Hossain Raju, who admits that "we do not know . . . why even the so-called Bengali nationalist filmmakers had to make entertainment films in Urdu" (Raju 2002, 13).

These authors find the solution to the paradox in a financial logic. Rather than *wanting* to make such films, it is regularly suggested that filmmakers in East Pakistan were financially compelled to do so. "Making films in Urdu expands the financial market up to West Pakistan. Which is why some films became a hit initially" (Nasreen and Haq 2008, 46, my translation). Similarly, Ahmed Aminul Islam (2009, 24) suggests in a review of Zahir Raihan's films that his Urdu features were made only because this allowed him to survive financially (figure 7.2). The continual suggestion in these accounts is that films made in Urdu in East Pakistan by Bengali-speaking filmmakers was merely a financial necessity, generating income from the distant West Pakistani market—not a choice but a hand forced by the vulgar logic of capital. While this financial logic surely played a part in the production of Urdu films, as an *analytical* perspective such arguments effectively neglect any consideration of the style, form, circulation, or reception of these films in favor of the one-size-fits-all analysis and assumption that all Urdu films made in East Pakistan were just commercial vehicles to fund the true passion of these directors: the making of Bengali-language films.

FIGURE 7.2. Promotional image for Zahir Raihan's Urdu film *Bahana* (1965). (Courtesy of the Bangladesh Film Archive)

Accounts of the history of Bangladeshi cinema since the 1950s are instead framed in terms of a larger Bengali cultural universe reaching across the border into Indian West Bengal and are focused on art, socially minded, and TV films (Haq 2011; Kabir 1979; Raju 2002). Such accounts strongly suggest that the appropriate unit for analysis of Bangladeshi cinema is the art cinema of greater Bengal, often tinted with a somewhat undefined concern about Islam. Given the explicitly commercial and popular appeal of Urdu films made in East Pakistan, these films are doubly prone to being excluded from Bangladeshi film histories.

The combination of inconclusive film records with a nationalist film historiography focused on Bengal and "good" films creates not so much a distortion in film history, which is always a contingent narrative (Ali 1999). Rather, it has created the conditions under which contemporary Bangladeshi cinema comes to be understood and interpreted. Urdu films from East Pakistan themselves are not otherwise studied. And so I only found brief references to *Son of Pakistan* in the two key surveys of Bangladesh cinema: both Hayat (1987, 133) and Qader (1993, 276) mention the film's title only in historically undefined sections on "children's films" in their respective histories of Bangladeshi cinema.

CROSS-WING FILMMAKING IN AND BEYOND THE ARCHIVE

In 1970, Nadeem and Bobita graced the silver screens of Pakistan in the Urdu film *Jaltey suraj ke neeche*. It was among the last Urdu films to be both made and released across East and West Pakistan. Directed by Zahir Raihan (though in places credited to his assistant director, Nurul Hoque) with music direction by Subal Das, cinematography by Afzal Chowdhury, and playback singing by Irene Parveen, the film was an all-Pakistan venture drawing on well-established talent. Between 1958 and 1971 the film industry of Pakistan straddled Lahore, Karachi, and Dhaka in a cross-wing love affair between stars and audiences, producers and profit, directors and fame that could not always be assigned exclusively to either East or West, Urdu or Bengali. This story emerges out of bits and pieces of archival material from the 1960s in the Bangladesh Film Archive, through which can be discerned a series of translations, collaborations, and movements across and between East and West Pakistan, Urdu and Bengali. The few 1960s magazines in the Archive present a rather different image of East Pakistani Bengali filmmakers, their audiences, and their relation to Urdu cinema than what is found in subsequent history books. There are four interventions that emerge from the material in these magazines.

First, the magazines speak elaborately of the continuous going and coming of film personnel between East and West in the 1960s. They present Dhaka as part of a national film industry straddling East and West Pakistan. In the few scattered Bengali-language film journals from the 1960s in the collection of the Bangladesh Film Archive, the movement of actors, directors, and films between the film studios and labs in East and West Pakistan is evident. Columns such as Studio News (Studio Khobor) in the film magazine *Jhinuk* or In the Dhaka Studio (Dhaka Studiote) in *Chalontika* bring news of ongoing film work, not only in Dhaka but also in Karachi and Lahore.

The self-evidence in these Bengali-language magazines of a cross-Pakistan cinematic world is not surprising. There were many cross-wing collaborations and partnerships in cinema during the 1960s, and the actors, musicians, technicians, and craftspeople who participated in them can't be easily positioned on one side of the country. They were also created through a geographically dispersed cinematic infrastructure. For example, the film

Daagh (1969, Ehtesham) was produced and processed at the Film Development Corporation in Dhaka, but all songs were recorded in Lahore. Similarly, the distribution of Urdu films from East Pakistan relied on interlocking distributors plying East and West markets, with *Daagh* distributed by Eveready Pictures in West Pakistan and Anis Films Corporation in East Pakistan. The careers and reputations of artists still at work today in Bangladesh were established in such cross-wing collaborations. One of the brightest stars that shone over both halves of the country, yet possibly the most readily forgotten actor in contemporary accounts of Bangladeshi cinema, was Nadeem.

Nadeem was a superstar, a favorite of audiences across Pakistan. The "Amitabh Bachchan of Pakistan" (Ahmed 1992, 303; Gazdar 1997, 106), Nadeem started his acting career in Dhaka. Born in South India, Nadeem's family moved to West Pakistan after Partition, where he tried his luck in the film world (Gazdar 1997, 106). When he failed to get ahead, a chance encounter in Karachi with crooner Firdausi Begum of East Pakistan motivated him to seek work in Dhaka. There he came in contact with Ehtesham, and that proved to be a milestone in his life both on and off the screen. *Chakori* won him instant popularity and the heart of Ehtesham's daughter, Farzana (the art director on *Chakori*), who became his lifelong companion (Gazdar 1997, 106).

Here was a cross-wing love affair that went well beyond personal companionship. Nadeem took in the hearts of fans and followers across East and West Pakistan. After two films from Dhaka in quick succession, *Chakori* (1967, dir. Ehtesham) and *Chotey saheb* (1967, dir. Mustafiz), he was seen the next year in *Sangdil* (1968, dir. Zafar Shabab) made in West Pakistan. It was the start of a flourishing career, with at least another six films made in Dhaka during the four remaining years of East Pakistan. Like his East Pakistani colleagues, the actresses Shabana, Shabnam, and Sultana Zaman, Nadeem moved between film studios across the country in the 1960s. Nonetheless, he received only one mention in the more than four-hundred-page-long, thoroughly researched, *Bangladesher cholochitro shilpo* (Bangladesh film art), and this in the section "Foreign Artists in Bangladeshi Films and Bangladeshi Artists in Foreign Films" (1993, 178–79, my translation).

From the contemporary moment it seems obvious why Nadeem is not the hero of the history of Bangladeshi cinema. Besides already being cast in that role in Pakistan, all Nadeem's films were in Urdu. There seems to be no way to admit Nadeem's films in any meaningful way to the canon of Bangladeshi film history. But from the various traces in the Bangladesh film archive as well as Alamgir Kabir's contemporary account, it quickly becomes clear that Urdu films played an important role in East Pakistan, both for filmmakers and for audiences.

The records of the Bangladesh Film Archive suggest that of the 207 films recorded as having been made and released in East Pakistan between 1956 and 1971, 63 were in Urdu. Alamgir Kabir posits 206 films in total, of which 48 were in Urdu. Even as ballpark figures these numbers suggest that between a quarter and one-third of all films made in East Pakistan would have been in Urdu. These films were made at the East Pakistan Film Development Corporation, notably by the brothers Ehtesham and Mustafiz, who directed and produced mainly Urdu films. Even directors retrospectively placed at the heart of the nationalist narrative of Bangladeshi cinema, such as Adbul Jabbar Khan and Zahir Raihan, made both Urdu- and Bengali-language films in the 1960s.

Implicit in some of the historical accounts of Bangladeshi cinema cited above is the assumption that these Urdu films were aimed at non-Bengali speakers. The film *Sangam* (1964, Zahir Raihan) was hyped in film magazines even before its successful release. An issue of *Shajghor* from the early 1960s has a section "Some Songs from the Film *Talash*" (my translation), and prints the Urdu lyrics from Mustafiz's 1963 film, transliterated into Bengali script. From these magazines it is clear that there was an audience for Urdu films in East Pakistan that was at ease reading Bengali. Urdu films made in East Pakistan, that is to say, were not aimed solely at local Urdu speakers or more distant West Pakistani cinema halls.

Indeed, there was a Bengali market for Urdu films. This is evident from the third facet that emerges from the journals: the debates in the 1960s among Bengali filmmakers themselves about the reasons why Bengali audiences weren't interested in Bengali films. The financial logic that so many point at to explain the making of Urdu films in East Pakistan is unlikely to have been predicated exclusively on audiences in faraway, multilingual but much less densely populated West Pakistan or non-Bengali Urdu speakers in the East. The dimensions of the market are hinted at by the fact that the large profits for East Pakistani films in densely populated East Bengal were not in Bengali films but in Urdu films. As Kabir observes in 1969, "The [film] industry [in East Pakistan] was fast heading for a disaster when a director dared to go a little bit further and made an Urdu language film. The film was 'Chanda' (1962) directed by Ehtesham. It proved a money-spinner in both East and West Pakistan. 'Chanda's' performance *naturally* encouraged a trend of Urdu filmmaking in East Pakistan" (44, my emphasis).

This "natural" trend occurred despite the fact that according to Kabir (1969, 49) it was a good Rs. 100,000 more expensive to make an Urdu feature in Dhaka than it was to make a Bengali movie. Khan Ataur Rahman suggested caustically in a 1963 issue of *Chitrali* that "those among our cinema audience who really want to see Bengali films are so few in numbers that Bengali films cannot even recoup their costs" (quoted in Hayat 1987, 116, my translation). It was initially difficult for Bengali films in East Pakistan to make a profit (Misir 1962, 11), and the unnamed author of In the Dhaka Studio in a 1962 issue of *Chalontika* is told by an industry insider of "the crisis of Bengali films. Up until now, besides one or two producers, no one has been able to make a profit off a Bengali film; therefore, to escape from the crisis, to make a profit, they are all scrambling to make Urdu films" (*Chalontika* 1962, 62, my translation). The obvious conclusion, rarely drawn, was that a significant part of those profits for East Pakistani Urdu films was coming from within East Pakistan, where a Bengali-speaking

FIGURE 7.3. Advertisement in Bengali for the Urdu film *Aur gam nahi* in a 1961 issue of *Shajghor*. (Courtesy of the Bangladesh Film Archive)

audience would have enjoyed these films alongside those who didn't speak Bengali.

Finally and self-evidently, until 1965 all Urdu and Bengali films from East Pakistan were part of a larger space of film distribution in which audiences had their pick of English films, Indian films in Hindi, Urdu, and Bengali, as well as West Pakistani films. The overwhelming force of the 1952 language movement and the subsequent events of the liberation struggle make it increasingly hard to imagine the multilingual public space of East Bengal that antedated the now increasingly monolingual Bangladesh. But a glance at the film industry illustrates linguistic diversity. From the early days of cinema in South Asia until 1965, the cinema halls of East Bengal and East Pakistan were open to films of all sorts of provenance (Chatterjee 2012). In the Pakistan period, Indian films in Hindi, Urdu, and Bengali were screened alongside English features in its cinemas. From before Partition and until the 1965 India-Pakistan war, cinema audiences in East Bengal / East Pakistan would have been familiar with non-Bengali films, especially those in Hindi/Urdu. The fearsome state imposition of Urdu existed alongside the long-standing presence of everyday entertainments in Hindi/Urdu provided by Bombay and Lahore film studios in East Bengal and subsequently East Pakistan.

Of course, this doesn't mean the language movement, the political repression and conflict, and the inequalities between Urdu and Bengali, between East and West Pakistan, are entirely absent from the film journals of the 1960s. Some authors express frustration with the preeminence of Urdu in the East Pakistani studios.

The deteriorating political situation starts to appear explicitly in film news from 1970. In the Studio News column of the January 1971 issue of *Jhinuk*, the author describes how in between their work, the cast and crew of films are discussing politics and "Bhashani shaheb's historic announcement of the independence of East Pakistan" (*Jhinuk* 1971, 159). Zahir Raihan is quoted as saying that "the slogan 'Joy Bangla' was really disrupting work on set. Lightmen would suddenly yell 'Joy Bangla.' But that day I told them, 'You are the proletariat [*sorbohara*], you don't have anything,' from that day they have been yelling the slogan 'Joy Sorbo'" (*Jhinuk* 1971, 159–60, my translation). Leaving a line break after this, the article continues over the next six pages to give studio news. This produces a clear division between the political turbulence on the first page of the article and the stardust-filled film world on the following pages. It includes a welcome to "newcomer, actor Omar Chisthi. Omar Chisthi spent half his life in West Pakistan. He didn't know Bengali well. But seeing him speak Bengali dialogues, I was amazed" (*Jhinuk* 1971, 161, my translation). Even as the struggle for equality and the independence of East Pakistan is on the lips of those in the industry, the movement between East and West Pakistan continued, at least within the world of film.

IMAGES FROM THE EAST PAKISTANI URDU FILM

The archival material suggests that Bengali filmmakers were reflective about making Urdu films and that Bengali reading audiences had an interest in all sorts of Urdu films. Taking a closer look at the Urdu films made in Dhaka suggests further that they featured technological and aesthetic innovations: director Zahir Raihan and his cinematographer, Afzal Chowdhury, were experimenting with color and cinemascope in *Sangam* and *Bahana*; cinematographer Baby Islam was making his aesthetic mark as a director in *Tanha*; and Khan Atta and Robin Ghosh were writing and composing across languages and genres. In part this was facilitated by the extraordinary institution of the East Pakistan Film Development Corporation (EPFDC), a highly equipped state-funded institution ran by the visionary Nazir Ahmed, in which both technology and a certain level of goodwill were available. The EPFDC had no counterpart in West Pakistan, which had no state-run and -equipped national studio and where films were made through private studios. If there was any governmental incentive to produce Urdu films in East Pakistan (of which until now I have found no evidence, but which may have existed), then it was the extraordinary institution of the EPFDC, called for originally by then industries minister Sheikh Mujibur Rahman in 1957 through the East Pakistan Film Development Corporation Bill (Hayat 1987, 58). Whether due to individual creative energies or the facilitating environment of the EPFDC, Urdu films from East Pakistan provided a ground for formal and technological cinematic experimentation and innovation.

A closer look at the films, however, allows the context of their forgetting to come more sharply into view. East Pakistani Urdu films from this period present the image of a modern, youthful, and ambitious Pakistan on screen, represented by actors such as Nadeem, Rahman, Rajjak, and Harun, alongside Shabnam, Shabana, and Sultana Zaman. In films such as *Akheri station* (1962), *Sangam* (1964), *Chand aur chandni* (1968), or *Darshan* (1967) we see them confidently pursue their love interests in Urdu, the landscape of Bengal a comfortable backdrop to exploits in shiny cars, new hotels, and fancy bungalows, often at the all-Pakistan tourist destinations of Cox's

Bazaar and Kaptai Lake. These films integrate Chittagong division, and particularly the Hill Tracts, into the national landscape of Pakistan: visually through its images of heroes on boats, dancing tribal girls and pans across the hills; aurally through the Urdu language and songs. It illustrates how these East Pakistani Urdu films from the 1960s participated in the production of a singular national space in which a young and modern audience could be addressed in Urdu as Pakistani.

The cinematic sleight of hand of montaging these sights and sounds into a convincing cinematic vision of a unified nation-state would soon run into the reality of the increasingly untenable Pakistan experiment of a state stretched over miles of foreign territory and across different communities, regions, and classes. With hindsight that foresees the bloodshed soon to visit East Pakistan, it becomes difficult to suspend disbelief when watching the beautiful young actors and actresses frolic at Cox's Bazaar resorts in a film such as *Chand aur chandni*. It is this dissonance between the idealized cinematic imagination of Pakistan in 1960s East Pakistani Urdu films, the knowledge of the subsequent violence and destruction, and the subsequent image of East Pakistan as an era of darkness, and Urdu as a language solely of repression, that makes it difficult to understand, analyze, or even remember these films. An encounter with the protagonist of the film *Son of Pakistan* brought this home to me.

SON OF PAKISTAN

The film *Son of Pakistan* does reappear in the Bangladesh Film Archive. A 1966 *Studio News* report suggests that *Son of Pakistan* was released "in Dhaka and other places of the province [*prodesh*]" (*Jhinuk* 1966, 167). Among the stacks of laminated production stills, I also found a promotional image for the film *President* (figure 7.4). It says, "First film filmed all over Pakistan and dedicated to the children of our country," produced and directed by Fazlul Huq. Of course, it is the same film: the promotional image of *President* from before the film's censorship and the poster as it was released under the Censor Board–approved but rather uncreative title *Son of Pakistan*. The *Jhinuk* reporter also notes that the film had a number of objectives, one of which was "to increase children's knowledge about the geographic characteristics of their own country [*swadesher bhougolika boishishto*]" and "to create a sound understanding of both parts of Pakistan among boys and girls" (1966, 167, my translation). Alamgir Kabir does not mention the film in his 1969 *The Cinema in Pakistan* but lists it in the film index at the back of his

FIGURE 7.4. Lobby card for the film *President* (*Son of Pakistan*, dir. Fazlul Huq, 1966). (Courtesy of the Bangladesh Film Archive)

1979 *Film in Bangladesh*. He also adds a clue as to why opacity now surrounds the film: it was in Urdu. Alongside *Sangam* and *Chand aur chandni*, *Son of Pakistan* is a pedagogic project entirely out of sync with contemporary Bangladesh, and in Urdu on top of that. With that, it has become part of a series of now nigh-illegible East Pakistani films.

Determined to find out more about *Son of Pakistan*, I sought out the one person I imagined would be able to tell me about the film, its narratives, making, language, and fate. This was the boy in the poster, his eyes lifted to the sky. Qader (1993, 276) reports that the little boy and girl who played the main roles in *Son of Pakistan* were director Fazlul Huq's children Sagar and Keka. The small boy in the poster had grown into a Bangladeshi media mogul. Faridur Reza Sagar, son of Fazlul Huq, is today the managing director of the private Bangladeshi television channel Channel i and a key player in the contemporary world of Bangladeshi telefilms. He had donated the framed poster of *Son of Pakistan* to the Bangladesh Film Archive.

In luck when I arrived at the Channel i offices, I found both Faridur Reza Sagar and his paternal uncle, Fazlul Huq's younger brother, Dr. Fazlul Alam. I talked to them about the film. They described their enterprising father and brother, founder of the magazine *Cinema*. The details of the making of *Son of Pakistan*, however, were slightly less clear.

Faridur Reza Sagar, who would have been about ten years old at the time of shooting, remembered very little of the actual filmmaking process. He did recount how his entire nuclear family, he himself, his father—the director Fazlul Huq—his mother and noted author Rabeya Khatun, whose novel *Dushahoshik obhiyan* (Courageous adventure) was the basis of the script, and his little sister Keka had traveled all the way to and across West Pakistan to shoot the film. He describes the journey in an essay titled "The Actor of *President* Speaking," part of a collection of children's tales. "For the needs of the story, we went to Karachi, Lahore, Pindi, Islamabad, Peshawar, Swat" (Sagar 2006, 226, my translation). Throughout the short memoir that is the essay, the author consistently uses the title *President*, though he mentions at the end that the film was released as *Son of Pakistan* (228).

With some trepidation I asked about the Urdu that Sagar and Keka must have spoken to make this film. But rather than discomfort or explanation, the quicksand of recollection produced confusion:

LOTTE: The film was originally made in Urdu, is that right?

SAGAR: No, no, no, no.

LOTTE: Is that not right?

SAGAR: The film, yes . . . [hesitates, turns to his uncle]. Did we shoot the film in Urdu?

FAZLUL ALAM: What film?

SAGAR: Made in Urdu?

FAZLUL ALAM: What happened?

SAGAR: The film was in Bangla or in Urdu?

FAZLUL ALAM: In Bengali.

SAGAR: In Bengali?

FAZLUL ALAM: It was in Bangla. Yes, Bangla.

SAGAR: No, I don't think so.

FAZLUL ALAM: But with lots of Urdu dialogue. Because when they [the crew] went to West Pakistan, they were not speaking in Bangla.

LOTTE: Right.

FAZLUL ALAM: They were speaking in Urdu, their local language. So it became mixed. Linguistically it was double.

SAGAR: I don't remember.

LOTTE: You forgot.

SAGAR (LAUGHS): I forgot.

FAZLUL ALAM: Because how would they communicate?

LOTTE: Because in the history books it is marked as Urdu.

SAGAR: It should be Urdu. Because it was made for that time. In that time, it should be Urdu. It was for the whole Pakistan, so it should be Urdu.

To encounter this level of genuine confusion was not what I had expected. But it illustrates well the contemporary place of East Pakistani Urdu films in Bangladesh. Mildly surprising, sometimes confusing, mostly forgotten, these films have left little trace in contemporary understandings of Bangladeshi cinema. The very possibility of Urdu films cannot be clearly recalled.

But my meeting with Sagar was not the end of the story. I subsequently met two men who remembered seeing *Son of Pakistan* as children when it was released in East Pakistan. The first, a filmmaker now based in Dhaka, saw the film in a cinema in Chittagong and was fascinated by the child protagonist. When I asked him what language the film was in, he unhesitatingly said it was in Urdu. However, when I presented an earlier draft of this paper at a conference, a colleague intervened. He said he had seen *Son of Pakistan* as a boy in a Dhaka cinema. "My mother took us to see the film," he recounted, "because it was a children's film in English." Leaving me bewildered, he also generously gave me a stash of *Eastern Films* to plow through. There, in a 1964 issue, a letter from Sagar to future viewers is printed, in English, announcing that "*President* is releasing very soon & it is in English and Urdu also." Never mind Bengali, this film was *in English*, and Urdu also.

The reels of *Son of Pakistan* can no longer be found, despite's Faridur Reza Sagar's efforts. He has tried to trace both the film and his father, both having disappeared from his life at some point. While Sagar sent out a party to look for the film reels at Lahore's Shahnur Studio in vain, he himself traveled to Kolkata to find his father's grave. Having left East Pakistan in 1970 or '71 under unclear circumstances, Fazlul Huq never returned to independent Bangladesh. He stayed on in India and continued to try to make films in Calcutta until he died a mysterious death there. He thus slips from the record altogether, impossible to amalgamate into any nationalist historiography but true to the creative and labor movements that stretch across borders which are continually drawn and redrawn.

CONCLUSION

The details of the film *Son of Pakistan* are blurred, nowhere solidly recorded. And in that sense, the librarian at the Bangladesh Film Archive was absolutely right: it is an old film about which we don't know much. Why might a film like *Son of Pakistan* nonetheless be relevant to the understanding of contemporary Pakistani and Bangladeshi cinema? Looking through the Bangladesh Film Archive presents a series of images of Pakistani cinema that trouble some of the better-established historical narratives that the nation-state imposes upon itself. It presents oblique angles and alternative readings of that narrative. I have shown in this chapter that there was a continuous interaction among film personnel between East and West Pakistan in the 1960s; that there was a Bengali-reading audience for East and West Pakistani Urdu films; and that Bengali filmmakers avidly debated the question of the Urdu film. Engaging with this material allows an appreciation of the complex flow of both national and international films in a range of languages through both sides of Pakistan until 1965.

But this material is not merely informative about what cinema and film culture were like once upon a time. Looking back through the archive presents a series of opportunities to reimagine the questions before the industry as well as its audiences, scholars, and practitioners.

In particular, the shared history of Pakistani cinema, East and West, brings new avenues to approach the study of the cinema across South Asia. Sifting through contemporary primary sources from the 1950s and '60s to find cross-wing romance narratives and collaborations is a prerequisite to making sense of the shared histories of Bangladeshi and Pakistani cinema. These shared histories can help us understand the present forms, modes, and appeals of cinema in South Asia, which have never been rigorously confined to the borders of current nation-states.

REFERENCES

Ahmed, Akbar S. 1992. "Bombay Films: The Cinema as Metaphor for Indian Society and Politics." *Modern Asian Studies* 26, no. 2: 289–320.

Ahmed, Nazneen. 2012. "The Poetics of Nationalism: Cultural Resistance and Poetry in East Pakistan/Bangladesh, 1952–71." *Journal of Postcolonial Writing*, iFirst Article: 1–13.

Ali, Daud, ed. 1999. *Invoking the Past: The Uses of History in South Asia*. Delhi: Oxford University Press.

Axel, Brian Keith, ed. 2002. *From the Margins: Historical Anthropology and Its Futures*. Durham: Duke University Press.

Chalontika. 1962 [1369]. *Dhaka studio-te* (In the Dhaka studio). *Kharthik* 4, no. 2: 61–64. Available at the Bangladesh Film Archive.

Chatterjee, Ranita. 2012. "Cinema in the Colonial City: Early Film Audiences in Calcutta." In *Audiences: Defining and Researching Screen Entertainment Reception*, edited by Ian Christie, 66–80. Amsterdam: Amsterdam University Press.

Feldman, Shelley. 1999. "Feminist Interruptions: The Silence of East Bengal in the Story of Partition." *Interventions: International Journal of Postcolonial Studies* 1, no. 2: 167–82.

Gazdar, Mushtaq. 1997. *Pakistan Cinema, 1947–1997*. Oxford: Oxford University Press.

Haq, Fahmidul. 2011. *Digital Film in Bangladesh: Call for a New Cinema?* Saarbrücken: Lambert Academic Publishing.

Hayat, Anupam. 1987. *Bangladesher Chalachitro Itihash* (The history of Bangladeshi cinema). Dhaka: Bangladesh Film Development Corporation.

Islam, Ahmed Aminul. 2009. "Zahir Raihaner Cholocchitre somaj o rastroproshongo" (State and society in the films of Zahir Raihan). *Bangladesh Film Archive Journal* 2:23–30.

Jahangir, B. K. 2002. *Nationalism, Fundamentalism and Democracy in Bangladesh*. Dhaka: International Centre for Bengal Studies.

Jhinuk. 1966. *Studio Khobor* (Studio news). *Jhinuk*, November 1, 1966, 165–73. Available at the Bangladesh Film Archive.

———. 1971. *Studio Khobor* (Studio news). *Jhinuk*, January 2, 1971, 159–65. Available at the Bangladesh Film Archive.

Jonaki. 1969. *Tarka Porichito: Kobori* (Star introduction: Kobori). *Jonaki*, November 1969, 131–34. Available at the Bangladesh Film Archive.

Kabir, Alamgir. 1969. *The Cinema of Pakistan*. Dhaka: Sandhani Publications.

———. 1979. *Film in Bangladesh*. Dhaka: Bangla Academy.

Misir, Aziz. 1962. "Purbo Pakistaner Cholocchitro Prosonghe" (About the cinema of East Pakistan). *Chalontika* (October): 9–14. Available at the Bangladesh Film Archive.

Mohaiemen, Naeem. 2011. "Flying Blind: Waiting for a Real Reckoning on 1971." *Economic and Political Weekly*, September 3, 2011, 40–52.

Mohsin, Amena. (1997) 2002. *The Politics of Nationalism: The Case of the Chittagong Hill Tracts Bangladesh*. Dhaka: University Press.

Murshid, Tazeen M. 1993. "Bangladesh: The Challenge of Democracy—Language, Culture and Political Identity." *Contemporary South Asia* 2, no. 1: 67–73.

Nasreen, Gitiara, and Fahmidul Haq. 2008. *Bangladesher Chalochchitra Shilpo: Sangkote Janosangskriti* (The film industry of Bangladesh: Popular culture in crisis). Dhaka: Shrabon Prokashoni.

Qader, Mirza Tarekul. 1993. *Bangladesher Chalachitra Shipla* (The cinema of Bangladesh). Dhaka: Bangla Academy.

Raju, Zakir Hossain. 2000. "National Cinema and the Beginning of Film History in/of Bangladesh." *Screening the Past* 11. www.latrobe.edu.au/screeningthepast/firstrelease/fr1100/rzfr11d.htm.

———. 2002. "Bangladesh: A Defiant Survivor." In *Being and Becoming: The Cinemas of Asia*, edited by Aruna Vasudev, Latika Padgaonkar, and Rashmi Doraiswamy, 1–25. Delhi: Macmillan.

Reza, Hafiz. 1963. "Studio Prodikhon" (Studio tour). *Shajghor* 6: 112–14.

Sagar, Faridur Reza. 2006. *Kishorshomogro* (Children's collection). Dhaka: Shomoy.

van Schendel, Willem. 2009. *A History of Bangladesh*. Cambridge: Cambridge University Press.

8 ACTION HEROINES AND REGIONAL GIFTS

Authorship Crossing Pakistan

ESHA NIYOGI DE

SHAMIM ARA PRODUCTIONS, LED BY THE EPONYMOUS FEMALE star, director, and producer of the Pakistani Urdu screen, released a series of action-adventure heroine narratives (among others) from the late 1970s through the 1980s. These include *Miss Hong Kong* (1979), *Miss Colombo* (1984), *Miss Singapore* (1985), *Lady Smuggler* (1987), and *Lady Commando* (1989). A number of these titles suggest the travels of the production company. The films indeed were shot on location throughout South and Southeast Asia. These productions arose from collaborations between small-scale film and tourism entrepreneurs who were moving across the regions and forging word-of-mouth connections. The entrepreneurs not only moved beyond national borders, but they collaborated across religious, linguistic, and ethnic differences. Collaborations between South Asian entrepreneurs often meant that the films were released in several countries and dubbed in the local languages (Ahmed 2015), even though the primary frame of reference was Pakistan. While this traveling film production process perfectly exemplifies Sumita Chakravarty's (1993, 13) observation that "hybridity [can well be] a fact of cinematic life" in industrial contexts, it also begs the cautionary question raised by Chakravarty: Should we discern a ready correspondence between the hybrid "devil" of resource and capital and the "deep sea of representation and signification"?

Mushtaq Gazdar, for one, implicitly refuses any such correspondence between filmic signification and the mobility of resources, images, and people characterizing the Pakistani film industry in the 1980s. The Urdu industry, in particular, was depleted at the time both by waning state support and by intensified economic competition, in this video age, from a big-budget and fast-gentrifying Hindi film industry (Vitali 2008, 203), with which Urdu shares a linguistic register. Diagnosing an instrumental logic behind industrial mobility, Gazdar (1998, 205) maintains that small-scale film entrepreneurs from Lahore were aiming for such spectacles as multi-location shoots and cross-regional stars in order to stem a decline in the film business and manage rising production costs through incorporating the "freshness . . . of new locations and faces." Collaborative productions also opened new regional markets (Sri Lanka and Nepal) and helped reclaim markets lost to geopolitical liberation (Bangladesh). This chapter demonstrates to the contrary that figurations of dissident hybridity—contesting the rise of an Islamist patriarchal regime in Pakistan—emerged on the Shamim Ara Action screen precisely out of the industrial drive for heterogeneous locations, collaborations, and audiences.

Considering *Miss Hong Kong* and *Miss Colombo*, I discuss the cultivation of a paradoxical aesthetic. Locating cross-dressed martial artists and gunfighters in glamorous settings, these films certainly estrange the female body from the everyday Pakistan of the era, where women were empirically perceived and policed. Yet the aesthetic simultaneously rehabilitates feminine forms (body types and actions) in a familial comfort zone. This familial telos, while retaining a patriarchal commitment, not only upends masculinist aggression but also grows defiant of the religious and ethnic divides ascendant in an Islamizing state powered by Cold War flows. Scholars of Urdu cinema such as Kamran Asdar Ali (in this volume) and Iftikhar Dadi argue that the Urdu social film tended to internalize "contestation and conflict around questions of difference" (Dadi 2016b, 90) riddling nation-state formation in Pakistan. I extend these insights on the entwining of formal and social politics to a consideration of production culture. Turning to the women's Urdu action film, emergent from the late 1970s, I maintain that its politics of form is grounded not only in social transformations but also in the mobile infrastructures of the Urdu industry. Shamim Ara's conventional films are best described in the words of Jane Gaines (2012, 17, 20, 27), as an "unlikely . . . locus" for innovation that comprises a vast "storage" both of performative practices and of the "socioemotional raw materials" upholding the practices across diverse contexts of production and reception. This industrial locus of creativity must be seen as collecting emotional knowledge and fostering interactions among the woman director/entrepreneur herself, collaborators spread across cultural differences and national borders, and target audiences bringing along conventional ways of consuming desires and fears. In these interactive choices of conventions and locales, supported by the intimacies of an informal production community, we find a seedbed of the paradoxically familial arts of being with difference outlined above.

Shamim Ara's location shoots at first glance appear to be amassing marketable spectacles taken from the images of sensational action and exotic setting flowing into urban Pakistan through widespread video trade or piracy—be they spectacles of Hong Kong and Singapore tourist sites or Tarzan's animals reanimated in Sri Lanka or Singapore (see fig. 8.1). What deters me from settling on the notion of an instrumental pile of sensations abstracted from their historical contexts is the way both locations and associated figurations (Hong Kong streets, kung fu fighters, tropical forests, She-Tarzans) are made to interact with the prevailing Pakistani sensorium. The topoi and their moving forms alike, called out from their cultural lineages, as Priya Jaikumar (2017, 224, 239) puts it, into the "vagaries of dynamic, historical time," are made to perform a "second act" of hybridity. This ambivalent act corresponds with the hopes and horrors being experienced in the here and now by creators and audiences. Seen in the light of interactive knowledge, Shamim Ara's familial production networks also cannot be

FIGURE 8.1. Film poster for *Miss Singapore* (dir. Shamim Ara, 1985). (Courtesy of Salman Carim, son of the late Shamim Ara)

dissociated from the aesthetic products. Forged through cultural commonalities (of languages, sensory inclinations, and attitudes) that bridged national and religious differences, these networks were sustained by a gift-type system of obligatory exchange. Michael Taussig (1992, 68, 70) reminds us that economies of exchange exceeding the capital logic of accumulation and ownership forge a bond between the spirit of giving or trading things and the spirit of miming another's sensory aura (sights, sounds, motions, speech forms) in order to be with the other on an even footing. In this vein Catholic piety, for example, is mimicked on location in *Miss Colombo* as if to embrace as a gift the emotional knowledge of crew members and target audiences influenced by missionaries in Sri Lanka and Pakistan. As elaborated in this chapter, the gendered imagery of action locales and border-crossing kin-makers in the Shamim Ara films carries a *polycentric archive of authorship*. It bears the imprint of an economy that functioned to an extent as a gift-type system processing sensory auras and associated geographies. This reflexive process was led by a female star-author/entrepreneur in ways meaningful to target audiences under divisive historical conditions.

AUTHORSHIP AND FEMALE ACTION: STAR-DIRECTOR SHAMIM ARA IN A CHANGING PAKISTAN

Shamim Ara implicitly claimed authorial agency by rebutting the charge of escapism leveled against her kind of cinema and instead asserting the relevance of her productions to the times. The Urdu action/travel genre was facing allegations from the popular press of always being elsewhere, forsaking native soil and normative commitment. For example, "Why Don't Our Film Heroes Have a Goal?" published in the Urdu periodical *Film Asia* in 1989, accuses the film industry of failing to recognize "which world is its own world and which characters are the sons of its own soil" (*kaun si dunya us ki apni dunya hai aur kaun sai kirdar us ki apni dharti kai betai hain*). The writer maintains that producers and directors of the day are "devoid of any political responsibility" (*kisi siyasi zimmadari*) insofar as they roam around Singapore, Hong Kong, and Nepal and throw together a "topsy-turvy" (*ulat pulat*) mishmash of image, music, and movement. Especially troubling for this reporter is a gender-norm confusion stemming from the putative irresponsibility. As described by the article itself, "Here, the hero is dancing, and there the heroine has got hold of a rifle or a Kalashnikov" (*Film Asia* 1989, 21). In the same vein, Shamim Ara (1993) faced derisive queries from the press about the gender trouble caused by the line of heroines she was producing—women who roamed around and got into fights and threw punches (*mardhar*)—as against the appropriate femininity she herself had embodied (in the "golden era" Urdu Social of the 1960s). Contradicting the anachronistic nostalgia attached to her star iconography, Shamim Ara invariably claimed authorship of her productions while she emphasized the pertinence of their gender imagery to contemporary Pakistan. Available accounts of the ways Shamim Ara Productions chose (or rejected) conventions suggest that the meanings of found images, locations, and support structures were being processed and comprehended anew within the temporal "vagaries" of Zia's Cold War Pakistan (Jaikumar 2017, 226). In this section, I contextualize the authorial process in relation to social and aesthetic transformations in Pakistan. The next section, which turns to Shamim Ara's polycentric creativity, situates the production process in relation to contemporary historical concerns.

In promoting her new heroine line, Shamim Ara (1993) herself maintained that wanting to change what she had disliked about her own roles as voiceless and tyrannized women (facing *zulm*) singing sad songs, she was configuring female characters who fought for their rights or prerogatives (*haq*), her goal being to make "family subject" films for Pakistani girls of a new epoch (*naya daur*). In making the claim that she produced family films for a new Pakistani epoch, Shamim Ara was, of course, reauthoring an earlier Urdu bourgeois family genre (discussed by Kamran Asdar Ali and Nasreen Rehman in this volume) in order to open space for altering industrial conditions and audience tastes. Censor reports of the day note that not only imports but also Pakistani films were "flooding" the video market (Rashid 1987, 61). Bringing films into urban homes at a time when a pall of obscenity hung over theaters, video trade and piracy may well have enabled this female-focused line of action cinema: made with an explicit female address by an authority on gendered pleasures such as the renowned female star and director Shamim Ara. At the same time, the Urdu family narrative was being adapted to a local and global boom in this era of what Tom Gunning calls the new "cinema of effects," a film form whose primary appeal and meaning are "rooted in stimulus" rather than in the narrative (quoted in Tasker 1993, 7). In the action film, social conflict comes to be exteriorized in spectacular excitation, stimulated at once by fighting bodies and by surprising or adventurous locations. Shamim Ara Productions accordingly developed the action aesthetic by shooting on locations that evoked "grandeur," according to Syed Hafeez Ahmed (2015), the late associate director for Shamin Ara. Neither these grand landscapes nor the stimulated bodies populating them, however, should be seen as disembedded from pressing social concerns.

Scholars of action cinema in 1980s Pakistan situate the proliferation of confrontational stimuli on popular screens in relation to the culture of gun violence and militarizing Islam upheld by the US-backed regime of Zia-ul-Haq. Ali Khan and Ali Nobil Ahmad (2016, 124, 126) delineate the rise of an influential Punjabi action hero cinema, addressing the everyday oppressions of peasant and working-class men under a parallel gun-and-drug economy; this genre dramatized the purity of violent anger "against an oppressive state [embodied in a] monstrously impure society." Gwendolyn Kirk (in this volume) demonstrates how a translocal siting of the angry Punjabi action hero further stimulates the aesthetic of confrontation. While this insurgent Punjabi aesthetic of pure anger influenced the Pakistani film market of the time, its impact on the Shamim Ara repertoire necessarily was mediated by its own Urdu legacy: a cinema made in the national language, submitting to censorship (Shamim 1987), and addressing the urban middle classes (Khan 2016, 255). Shamim Ara's fighter heroine imagery, reaching urban women even at home, must be studied both for how it was repurposed for women's desires and fears under current local conditions and for how it spoke to the globalizing tastes of regional audiences in this age of flows.

Studying the earliest Hollywood action heroines, Ben Singer (2001, 114, 124) discerns "eustress," a euphoric and "curiosity-inducing" excitation that prepares the female body to keep pace with the "rapid stimuli" of urban change. Readings of action heroines, such as Yvonne Tasker's (1993, 148), argue that the stimulating spectacles of active women typically cross the line of traditional gender behavior. Across historical contexts, these spectacles of female action stage responses to women's aspirations for independent agency and accompanying contestations over the female body born of both increased urban mobility and feminist movements. Social changes of the time likewise made urban Pakistan a hospitable context for an action heroine imagery combining these appeals. Women's workforce participation was fast expanding under what Saadia Toor (2011, 154) describes as a Cold War–fueled "macro-economic revival." Hand in hand arose a groundswell of the Pakistani women's movement against Zia's brutally censorious Islamist dictatorship (Toor 2011, 138–49). In the public mobility and the technological independence of the Shamim Ara heroines (driving cars and wielding guns) we find, on the one hand, an eustressful celebration of women's freedom under urban change. The combative cross-gender action, on the other hand, combines insurgent local imaginations with global forms to produce a practice that is well characterized by Lalitha Gopalan (2002, 51) as a practice "throw[ing] up the aggressive strands of feminism."

Shamim Ara's promotion of aggressive new womanhood, quoted above, certainly displays her energetic interaction with the liberal discourse of women's independence and the fight for rights, taken from local and global sources. Her repeated insistence that she makes only "family subject" dramas, at the same time circumscribes the aspirational urge within the customary pleasures of community life immanent to women's mainstream entertainment in Pakistan. Such vernacular entertainment cultures as Shamim Ara's Urdu cinema appealed to tastes across urban class divides. In these vernacular domains of Pakistani women's entertainment, liberal representations of "individualized agency," argues Kamran Asdar Ali (2004, 140), could well be "tempered with other visions of the self . . . [such as] the desire to be . . . modest" and therewith to fulfill familial obligations. As explained by Hamid Naficy (2012, 102), with reference to post-Revolution Iranian cinema, feminine modesty rests on a premodern supposition that the self is "more collective, communal, familial and hierarchical [such that] . . . women are a constitutive part of the males to whom they are related." While such pieties of family and community life were habitual both in women's daily practices and in the vernacular entertainment cultures of the middle classes in Pakistan, Zia's Islamization program imposed a new set of divisions.

Addressing the specificity of Pakistani women's modest familial habits, Shahnaz Rouse (2004, 98) makes a distinction between practices prior to and during Zia's regime of religious censorship. Whereas Pakistani women's somatic practices of modesty had always been both voluntary and (fashionably) fluid, Zia's Islamist state imposed a brutal proscription precisely of the fluidity of women's familial modern worlds, in the name of obscenity. The sphere of obscene exposure necessarily included the cinema, such that the revised Motion Picture Ordinance of 1979 banned no less than three hundred Pakistani films on "grounds of immorality" (Gazdar 1997, 167). In a similar vein, the gender ideals of the pious (Sunni) Muslim family came to mark the standard of a morally elevated Islamic civilization against which the putative licentiousness of westernized consumerism was measured. Whereas religious minorities, including Western-dressed Christians, had coexisted with Muslims in earlier eras (Rouse 2004, 98), they were increasingly separated and policed. All in all, the immediate frames of reference for the action genres were such contradictions of the Zia era as sexual censorship and state-incited religious extremism in parallel with Pakistani customs of familial lives and cohabitation with difference.

Shamim Ara's heroine aesthetic comprehends in paradoxical ways these intense vagaries surrounding the changing body politics in Pakistan. On the one hand, the films stage the righteous anger of invincible fighting bodies—an anger seeming to surge up against violent censorship (on and off the screen) even as the latter is written onto female bodies. On the other hand, customary female pleasures of committing to the (patriarchal) family and to caring for the vulnerable across social divides contain the glamour of individualized prowess. While later sections of this chapter detail these paradoxical performances of genre, the next section explores how a polycentric, implicitly polyvocal, production process could have been a seedbed of familial affect.

POLYCENTRIC AUTHORSHIP AND REGIONAL GIFTS: THE PRODUCTION ARCHIVE

Let me begin my consideration of production practice with the choice of location for the inaugural film of the action series, *Miss Hong Kong* (1979). Available records suggest that the collective desire for familial yet invincible female action—a desire implicitly shared by the director and her target audiences—is what prompted the turn to the legacy of Chinese women fighters and its associated geography, Hong Kong. The archive discussed here has been gathered in bits and pieces from both private and public collections, since no official film archive exists in Pakistan. My attempt has been to "follow" the mobility of the Shamim Ara aesthetic as a socioemotional "thing" (Marcus 1995, 106–7) through multiple sites of production, reception (off-screen), and reanimation (on-screen). My conversations with Shamim Ara's family and crew members have constituted a valuable assemblage of memories and insights, alongside print and visual records (scattered and scant as these are).

On this research route, I expressed my intrigue with Shamim Ara's action heroines to the late filmmaker's brother Irshad Ahmad Khan and son Salman Carim; I had the privilege of meeting both at the latter's London home in late 2014. In a flash of memory, marked by what Alessandro Portelli ([1998] 2006, 34) would describe as meaningfully heightened "velocity" of speech, Irshad Ahmad Khan responded that Shamim Ara had been inspired by what "women could do" upon watching the 1973 Bruce Lee film *Enter the Dragon* (dir. Robert Clouse). Coproduced by Warner Brothers and the Hong Kong–based Golden Harvest Company, *Enter the Dragon* features the kung fu artist of Taiwanese descent Angela Mao fighting a gang of potential rapists to the death. Following the trail of Khan's recollection through records of exhibition in late 1970s urban Pakistan, I did note *Enter the Dragon* in the list of films with "a ten and more weeks" run (Slote 1987, 57). Perhaps my words had triggered Khan's memory of a moviegoing experience with Shamim Ara. Yet I could not but observe that Shamim Ara's *Miss Hong Kong* crucially differs from Angela Mao's Hollywoodized performance in that it rejects both the latter's self-defeat and also the patriarchal narrative pretext this provides for action *hero* Bruce Lee (her brother) to enact revenge. In the place of Mao's conclusive act of suicide, an act encoding anxieties about the active female body in 1970s Hollywood (Tasker 1993, 24), we find in *Miss Hong Kong* a gender-reversed spectacle of *invincible* female chivalry *leading the battle for family and honor.* It seems that on the Shamim Ara screen Hollywood's version of the martial heroine was being jostled out by the Chinese *nuxia* heroine imagery. Based on Chinese *wuxia pian* mythology, the classic *nuxia* tradition configures the heroine's indomitable "martial spirituality . . . [in which] personal struggles symbolise social struggles; women [are] able to fight while remaining within dominant gender paradigms" (Driscoll 2007, 163–64). Magazines from the era report that the influx of big-budget Hollywood action cinema into Pakistan was complemented by a steady stream of kung fu films (SHE 1984, 8). Very likely, these included the popular "Jane Bond" genre (Fonoroff 2008) of martial heroine spawned by increased female public mobility in 1960s Hong Kong and related Chinese histories of New Womanhood (Hunt 2007, 153).

Shamim Ara's reported thrill with "what women could do" may well have been illuminating an interactive process of choosing knowledge on female fighting aesthetics from multiple cultural soils. In this light, the selection of Hong Kong as the debut location for the action heroine series seems meaningful. It suggests not simply an instrumental drive but more a journey for contact with the materiality of an authentic soil of familial female valor. In touching this soil while interacting with local actors and martial artists, the Shamim Ara production was receiving these motion arts as both compatible trading material and a cultural gift to Pakistani practices. The familial energies of *nuxia* fighters becoming legible to contemporary Pakistani body politics are made to interact with indigenous traditions in *Miss Hong Kong.*

Moving on to the second film of the series, I find that *Miss Colombo* (1984) forges an even clearer mimetic bond with the multiple religious and ethnic identities populating the reception and production circuit of Shamim Ara films. To begin with, images of Catholic or Sikh piety in this film seem to become "sociocultural trigger points" (Jaikumar 2017, 226) for the distress with Islamist separatism harbored by urban Pakistani audiences. As a film shot and distributed in Sri Lanka, the country with the highest percentage of Catholics and Protestants in South Asia, *Miss Colombo* could have been addressing as well similar inclinations among Sri Lankan audiences. Beyond this, the film costarred Sri Lankan actress/entrepreneur Sabita, a consistent collaborator with Shamim Ara Productions. A small-scale collaboration such as this, between the female star entrepreneurs Shamim Ara and Sabita, exemplifies the interdependent practices of filmmaking and distribution linking the small industries of South Asia in this period. Upheld by familial trust, these "soft infrastructures" (Larkin 2008, 6) may also have left their mark on the cross-border energies in *Miss Colombo*.

Associate director Syed Hafeez Ahmed (2015) explained to me that although contracts were signed "for tax purposes" (affirming the legal status of Urdu film companies), they frequently came after a bridge had been built via oral or face-to-face contact based on familiarity. These tenuous infrastructures were sustained by kinship rituals of obligatory gift exchange. As meticulously delineated by Gwendolyn Kirk (2016, 91), to this day, the Lahore industry survives on kin relations, be they based on blood ties or on cultivated "fictive kinship ties." The fact that the obligatory kinship practices sustaining the film business extended across cultural and geopolitical borders in the 1980s is well illustrated by a captivating account published in the Urdu periodical *Film Asia* (1987, 25). The article describes at length the Islamic ritual of giving gifts of sacrificial meat on the occasion of Eid al-Adha in order to cement family ties and kin-like relations with close friends. We learn that industry stalwarts such as Shamim Ara distributed packets of sacrificial meat to film personalities located not only in Lahore or Karachi but also in neighboring countries such as Nepal. These active "investment[s] into sociality" (Larkin 2013, 338) were meant to sustain a web of economic interdependence *and* sociomoral commitments. The precise logic of mutual commitment and aid, across difference, comes to aesthetic life in *Miss Colombo*. Indeed, the striking feature of this film is that it seems to assemble onscreen the heterogeneous identities cohabiting Shamim Ara's production team. As described by crew members (R. Khan 2016; Ahmed 2015), the team included at different times Pakistani Muslims, Indian Sikhs, Catholics, Sri Lankans, Bangladeshis, Filipinas, Hong Kong Chinese, and Malaysians (figure 8.2).

FIGURE 8.2. On location in the Philippines. Left to right: coproducer Mary (Philippines; surname unknown); director-producer Shamim Ara; associate director Syed Hafeez Ahmed (Pakistan); and other crew members. (Courtesy of Salman Carim, son of the late Shamim Ara)

We glimpse a similar gift-type logic animating the creative process in an account given by Shamim Ara herself. She was responding to a pointed question from a talk show host, who asked how she had been able to portray a Hindu girl and perform the requisite religious rites in the Pakistani Partition narrative *Lakhon mein ek* (1967, dir. Raza Mir). Shamim Ara (1993) readily responded that she had learned to do *pujapath* (Hindu rites) from living with Hindus in a close-knit neighborhood in pre-Partition India, and that she could show her interlocutor by doing puja (*puja karke*) right there. Two points are noteworthy. First, Shamim Ara draws a ready parallel between *trading* in religious resemblances and *producing corresponding religious behavior* as a palpable investment in social exchanges (in subcontinental contexts, where religion mattered). Her words suggest a gift-type economy of artistry in which, to recall Taussig's formulation, the spirit of miming another's religious aura is coterminous with the spirit of trading images in a multireligious region. Beyond this, Shamim Ara sees image making not only nor necessarily as a system for representing prefabricated knowledge. Instead, it is viewed as something of a mimetic process of perception wherein images forge correspondences with everyday bodies and habits. Such mimetic energies of image making in fact could conflict with instrumental logic both in making choices and in rejecting marketable conventions. Interactions with the Hindi action hero plots flooding the Pakistani market, for example, reveal the politics of rejection underneath superficial parasitism. Hindi action cinema's patriarchal idealism seems to have been incompatible with a Pakistani circuit such as Shamim Ara's, where women were mobile on both sides of the camera.

PAKISTAN TO HONG KONG: FEMALE FIGHTERS AND A SUPERFLUOUS PATRIARCHAL DRAMA

Miss Hong Kong (1979) tells the story of martial arts champion Tina, a young Pakistani woman raised in Hong Kong, who is on a mission to rescue her brutalized scientist father from the clutches of an international Pakistani gang of drug dealers headed by the self-anointed "Black Business" magnate Black Jack. While the plot relates to the (state-supported) rise of drug-related crimes in Pakistan, it borrows obvious narrative devices from the influential Hindi film *Amar, Akbar, Anthony* (1977), an ensemble narrative centering the iconic Indian action hero Amitabh Bachchan. Scripted by the veteran Urdu screenwriter Syed Noor, *Miss Hong Kong* retains such marketable Hindi action narrative devices as "the dismemberment of the family . . . the failure of the patriarch," and a narrative resolution reinstating a new heteropatriarchal family order centering romantic couples (Vitali 2008, 208). The striking Pakistani innovation, of course, is the rejection of male heroism in favor of action heroines mobilizing against masculine violence to become preservers of the family. The Bachchan-style patriarchal paradigm of "calling women back into the house" (Vitali 2008, 211) is made curiously superfluous to the dramatic stimulus of female action.

As the opening credits roll in *Miss Hong Kong*, we see a montage of city lights by night crosscut with close-ups of the heroine (Babra Sharif) at the wheel, cruising along with a Chinese girlfriend by her side. This transregional image of women's friendship across ethnic and geographic divides is not simply a pretext for a narrative set in Hong Kong; it is both a literal record of local participation and a metaphor of how interpersonal relations were sustained in these informal industries. As explained to me by Fokrul Alam (2014), Bangladesh Film Archive research officer, small-scale region-crossing collaborations in this era required and assumed participation by "local talent" and their resource networks, the latter frequently foregrounding women. Processed on-screen by a conventional narrative, the aura of female bonding, however, is laid open to masculine intrusion. The arts through which female action and women's concerns regain centrality in this film at the same time as familial norms are sustained are provocative.

To begin with, the euphoric female mobility showcased in the opening scenes is soon to be censored. The heroine, Tina, is assaulted by drunken men while she sits in her parked car awaiting her girlfriend's return. Thus provoked, female mobility turns out to be aggressively cross-gender, such that phallic intrusion is angrily confronted and reversed. A series of rapid cuts at medium to long range capture the woman leaping out of her car and overpowering the harassers. These fight scenes, embracing and mimicking a 1970s style of Hong Kong martial arts cinematography, balance rapid edits with legible sequencing (Bordwell 2003, 11) so as to clarify the female fighter's dexterity. Another euphoric scene of the heroine bonding with her girlfriend likewise turns into a battleground of male invasion and combative female triumph. Beyond this is a more lasting form of male intrusion—by no less than the romantic hero. Despite the fact that the man is a comic and feeble sidekick to the invincible heroine, the stock romance develops. Expatriate Pakistani Tina (Babra Sharif) grows enamored of a ship captain named Aved Ali (Asif Raza Mir) from Pakistan. Featuring song-and-dance interludes set in Hong Kong tourist sites, the romantic scenes capitalize on couple glamour from a transnational Hindi screen. Along these lines, a familiar South Asian filmic tableau concludes the plot by restoring patriarchal order. Yet this tableau is what Iftikhar Dadi (2016a, 486) calls a "hollow" formation of gender hierarchy insofar as it assumes men's displacement from the center of familial power and preservation. In their place we find the familial action heroine—a figuration that draws on the Chinese *nuxia* tradition while making female kung fu motion meaningful to Pakistani feminine practices.

Tina finds her way into the cell where Black Jack is brutalizing her father. Fighting for her father's cause and under his eyes, the cross-dressed woman gains control of frames. Through a series of exhilarating moves, the female body bypasses aggressive contact and mocks (the men's) phallic aggression. This choreography takes kinesthetic vocabularies from different screen traditions and makes them mutually hospitable. Tina's magical multiplanar agility (slides, jumps, and scurries), for example, draws on the dance-fight moves of a "soft" kung fu style of avoiding brutal contact (Anderson 2009 194). Her ludic acrobatics, folding into a song and dance staged high above the predatory men, encode the Pakistani-style celluloid *mujra* (courtesan) dance. Combined, the antirealistic screen arts are heightened by fudgy edits such that the moving female body keeps deferring predatory contact. The martial-arts-inspired magical movements dodge invasive contact on-screen, while the sheer implausibility of her movements by comparison to everyday motion avoids circumscription by the gaze of men off-screen. This magical agility of the female body is particularly suggestive in this context of cinema since the Islamicate male gaze, according to Hamid Naficy (2012, 106–7), among others, is considered to be physically invasive rather than voyeuristic.

Duriya Kazi (2012, 4) maintains that popular Pakistani films bypass Islamist censorship precisely by portraying a "supramundane space" wherein the "rules of politics and society" are temporarily suspended. Her point is that nonrealistic entertainment (whether magical screen arts or exotic location shoots) tactically bypass historical realities. While building on Kazi's insight, I argue instead that the politics of estrangement in the Shamim Ara action series constitutes an oblique engagement with a violent sphere of gendered action. The very next film of the series clarifies this dissident engagement by pitting the telos of the family film against separatism.

PAKISTAN TO SRI LANKA: MULTIRELIGIOUS FAMILIES AND PARENTAL GIFTS

Whereas *Miss Hong Kong* portrays an imperiled and debilitated Pakistani patriarch, *Miss Colombo* (1984) begins with the death of the birth father and the destruction of an ideal Pakistani family, living in Sri Lanka, at the hands of yet another Pakistani villain. The orphaned Pakistani children, who manage to escape from the clutches of the villainous drug dealer Black Eagle, find nurturance from a strikingly heterogeneous cast of other-parents. Salman, the son, is adopted by a bumbling restaurant owner, a traditional turban-wearing Sikh man who speaks largely in a rustic Punjabi. The young daughter is raised as "Bela" by the Mother Superior and inhabitants of a Catholic mission. There she finds a parental companion in the shape of the gigantic Sabu. An elephant who belongs to the convent, Sabu embodies the Catholic community's commitment to care work—a way of giving to the orphaned and the vulnerable that is depicted by this narrative as calling forth obligatory loyalty.

Religious, ethnic, and geographic divides seem at first glance to be easily overcome through fluid mimicries and shifting allegiances. Brother Salman lapses into slapstick imitations of his adoptive Sikh father, invoking tropes from a Punjabi Sikh comedy common to Pakistani television and theater, or indulges in prolonged interludes of song and dance through the picturesque Sri Lankan countryside with his girlfriend, Rosie (played by Sri Lankan star/entrepreneur Sabita). Growing up as a cross-dressing Christianized She-Tarzan, action heroine Bela (Babra Sharif) swings from trees and rides Sabu until she encounters a handsome Pakistani backpacker who kindles erotic adulthood in her. Therewith, the freewheeling and publicly mobile woman takes a step toward bourgeois Pakistani domesticity. The complexity in *Miss Colombo*, however, is that the predictable family subject drama refuses to stay suspended in these euphoric border-transcendent spaces. Growing legible in relation to the oppressive sensorium unfolding both in the public culture and on the popular screens of Zia's Pakistan, it attempts to confront and transform devastating conditions.

First, the kinesthetics of avoidance we find in *Miss Hong Kong* is relatively infrequent in action heroine Bela's fights. Instead, Bela's single-handed battle against five or six hulky men involves phallic whips. Second, the woman's body is overpowered by the attackers, flogged and maligned nearly to death. Annette Kuhn (1998, 4–6) reminds us that film censorship, being "activated . . . in the interrelations of various practices," extends beyond legal proscriptions into text production. In this vein, the corporeal freedom generic to Bela as a cross-dressed She-Tarzan is severely punished. The audiovisual performance of Bela's brutal humiliation at the hands of phallic men—resounding with the relentless lash of whips—mimics the sonic agitation experienced by Pakistani women in this context. It evokes women's fears about the practice of flogging and public degrading of the female body for alleged sexual offenses that was sanctioned by the Zia state (*SHE* 1984, 11). Third, the film gestures also at the escalation of violence toward Christians that accompanied state-level measures against blasphemy (Toor 2011, 156). We see the Mother Superior who had adopted Bela being captured and the mission taken over by Black Eagle (depicted with an Islamic beard) and his gang. Drawing on scenic constructions of the Crucifixion found in Hollywood biblical cinema, the climax of *Miss Colombo* shows the Mother Superior mounted side by side on the gallows with Bela, her brother Salman, and Salman's fiancée Rosie, with Black Eagle holding the ropes.

The compelling appeal of *Miss Colombo* lies in the fact that other-parental care surges against these images of violence and eventually reinstates an order of familial relations going against the grain of ethnoreligious brutality. Embodying an androgynous familial spirit, the mission's elephant, Sabu, charges into the scene of the flogging to rescue Bela and then tenderly carry her limp body to a haven of tranquil rehabilitation (figure 8.3). Soon a medium- to close-range camera is tracking the elephant as it hastens back and forth to nurse Bela's wounds with therapeutic fruits and twigs. Slowly, she revives and begins to await the return of Sabu's unfailing touch. This reciprocal motion—of a nurturing touch and the clinging dependent—is best described in the words of Laura Marks (2000, 92) as a "fetish": a volatile image corresponding to "the materiality of its original scene" of care work.

We are soon to realize that Sabu's protective volatility is divinely motivated insofar as it responds to supplication by the pious. Sabu reappears at the head of a herd of warring elephants to invade the enclosure of the gallows and rescue the captives, including action heroine and hero Bela and Salman, for the final fight against Black Eagle and gang. This melodramatic battle of the virtuous Pakistani action figures against predatory Pakistani masculinity embodied by Black Eagle is catalyzed by the Mother Superior's (Nayyar Sultana) desperate prayer to Jesus Christ. Evoking the "close-up's

FIGURE 8.3. The elephant Sabu rescuing wounded Bela. (Source: *Miss Colombo*, dir. Shamim Ara, 1984)

FIGURE 8.4. The Mother Superior's prayer. (Source: *Miss Colombo*, dir. Shamim Ara, 1984)

fetishlike ability" (Marks 2000, 93) to enliven face and voice, the camera zooms in on the nun in prayer (fig. 8.4). She is ardently calling on Christ to "save the children," the youths Bela, Salman, and Rosie. The palpable quality of this supplication evokes many a material scene of Christian missionaries working as caregivers and educators of children and orphans both in Pakistan and elsewhere across the region.

The series of close-ups jump-cuts to a rapid montage of objects and icons in and around the mission's church. We see these coming to violent life and whirling around on screen. Crucifixes fall from walls, a Virgin Mary figurine slides from the pedestal, and a cacophonic church bell refuses to come to rest. The tension building up through this montage of supernatural motion comes to a climax as a bolt of lightning strikes down Black Eagle, who is cringing with momentary blindness. The camera once again jump-cuts to Sabu at the head of a charging herd. As Sabu crashes into Black Eagle's enclosure, we see Bela turn toward her parental protector with utter childlike dependency. Soon thereafter, it is Bela's turn to fulfill her filial obligation by tending to her wounded parental figure and crying over the gigantic suffering body. The resolution of the melodramatic conflict, marked by the defeat of evil forces, is preceded, moreover, by one more intervention, tellingly spearheaded by yet another pious parental figure. The Sikh man who had adopted Salman appears with the police at the scene of battle, and then runs to grab his *kirpan* (dagger) and join the fray.[1] We see here the dual appeal of minority stereotypes (caregiving missionary and bumbling Sikh), both as prefabricated commodities and as gifts of emotional knowledge about multireligious community exchanged between filmmakers and audiences across the subcontinent.

CONCLUSION

It is useful to return to Sumita Chakravarty's (1993, 13) important question about the implication for aesthetic politics of the hybrid assemblages of peoples and locations that so often are a "fact of cinematic life" in the industries. Scholarship on the hybrid economies of large-scale industries such as Hollywood (replete as these are with exotic locations and forms) demonstrates that transnational exchanges typically inscribe "categories of difference" into systems of cross-cultural contact (Govil 2015, 154, 159). The archive studied in this chapter reveals, to the contrary, that transnational cinematic economies can differ in scale and leadership. A small-scale Urdu film industry that sought new sources of economic collaboration and commodity material within and across the national borders of Pakistan spawned a border-crossing aesthetic inspired by multiple regional influences. The artistry on the Shamim Ara screen was reclaiming female bodies from impending phallic violence and also rehabilitating women-centered practices of multireligious cohabitation against the grain of militarized religious hierarchy. This cinematic tradition illuminates how specific conditions of industrial hybridity—in this instance, familial exchanges led by professional women entertainers and creators—could yield an *authorial process of creating correspondences across division and difference*. Such polycentric images as these at one and the same time can be conventionally entertaining and legible to multiple audiences while criticizing separatist norms.

NOTE

1 The *kirpan*, or ritual dagger, is an essential article of faith worn on the body by practicing Sikhs. See "Kirpan," *Sikhi Wiki: Encyclopedia of the Sikhs*, www.sikhiwiki.org/index.php/Kirpan.

REFERENCES

Ahmed, Syed Hafeez. 2015. Skype interview, March 14, 2015.

Akhbar-e-Jahan Weekly, March 10, 1987, 55.

Alam, Fokrul. 2014. Personal interview, Bangladesh Film Archive, Dhaka, March 29.

Ali, Kamran Asdar. 2004. "Pulp Fictions: Reading Pakistani Domesticity." *Social Text* 22, no. 1 (Spring): 123–45.

Anderson, Aaron. 2009. "Asian Martial-Arts Cinema, Dance, and the Cultural Languages of Gender." In *Chinese Connections: Critical Perspectives on Film, Identity, and Diaspora*, edited by Tan See-Kam, Peter X. Feng, and Gina Marchetti, 190–202. Philadelphia: Temple University Press.

Bordwell, David. 2003. "How to Watch a Martial Arts Movie." In *Heroic Grace: Chinese Martial Arts Film*, edited by Cheng-Sim Lim and David Chute, 9–12. Los Angeles: UCLA Film and Television Archive.

Chakravarty, Sumita S. 1993. *National Identity in Indian Cinema, 1947–1987*. Austin: University of Texas Press.

Dadi, Iftikhar. 2016a. "Lineages of Pakistan's Urdu Cinema: Mode, Mood and Genre in *Zehr-e-ishq* / Poison of Love (1958)." *Screen* 57, no. 4: 480–87.

———. 2016b. "Modernity and Its Vernacular Remainders in Pakistani Cinema." In *Cinema and Society: Film and Social Change in Pakistan*, edited by Ali Khan and Ali Nobil Ahmad, 77–100. Karachi: Oxford University Press.

Driscoll, Catherine. 2007. "Superheroine: Women as Martial Artists in Early Twenty-First Century Cinema." In *Women Willing to Fight: The Fighting Woman in Film*, edited by Andris Silke and Ursula Frederick, 161–77. Newcastle: Cambridge Scholars Publishing.

Film Asia. 1987. "Eid Mubarak." Translated by Lubna Saira. *Film Asia* 2, no. 8 (August).

———. 1989."Why Don't Our Film Heroes Have a Goal?" Translated by Lubna Saira. *Film Asia* 4, no. 11 (November).

Fonoroff, Paul. 2008. "Film Studies: Jane Bond," *South China Morning Post*, January 31, 2008. https://www.scmp.com/article/624985/film-studies-jane-bond.

Gaines, Jane. 2012. "The Genius of Genre and the Ingenuity of Women." In *Gender Meets Genre in Postwar Cinemas*, edited by Christine Gledhill, 15–28. Urbana: University of Illinois Press.

Gazdar, Mushtaq.1997. *Pakistan Cinema, 1947–1997*. Karachi: Oxford University Press.

Gopalan, Lalitha. 2002. *Cinema of Interruptions: Action Genres in Contemporary India Cinema*. London: British Film Institute.

Govil, Nitin. 2015. *Orienting Hollywood: A Century of Film Culture between Los Angeles and Bombay*. New York: New York University Press.

Hunt, Leon, 2007. "Zhang Ziyi, 'Martial Arthouse' and the Transnational *Nuxia*." In *Women Willing to Fight: The Fighting Woman in Film*, edited by Andris Silke and Ursula Frederick, 144–60. Newcastle: Cambridge Scholars Publishing:

Jaikumar, Priya. 2017. "*Haveli:* A Cinematic Topos." *Positions* 25, no. 1: 223–48.

Kazi, Duriya. 2012. "Portrayal of Women in Pakistani Cinema." *Meethapani*, March 14, 2012. http://durriyakazi.blogspot.com/2012/03/portrayal-of-women-in-pakistani-cinema.html.

Khan, Ali. 2016. "Film Posters: Reflections of Change in the Pakistani Industry." In *Cinema and Society: Film and Social Change in Pakistan*, edited by Ali Khan and Ali Nobil Ahmad,209–61. Karachi: Oxford University Press.

Khan, Ali, and Ali Nobil Ahmad. 2016. "Violence and Horror in Pakistani Cinema." In *Cinema and Society: Film and Social Change in Pakistan*, edited by Ali Khan and Ali Nobil Ahmad, 115–36. Karachi: Oxford University Press.

Khan, Irshad Ahmad. 2014. Personal interview, London, November 12, 2014.

Khan, Raja Riaz. 2016. Personal interview, Lahore, Pakistan, September 7, 2016.

Kirk, Gwendolyn. 2016. "Uncivilized Language and Aesthetic Exclusion: Language, Power and Film Production in Pakistan." PhD diss., University of Texas at Austin.

Kuhn, Annette. 1998. *Cinema, Censorship and Sexuality, 1909–1925*. New York: Routledge.

Larkin, Brian. 2008. *Signal and Noise: Media, Infrastructure, and Urban Culture in Nigeria*. Durham: Duke University Press.

———. 2013. "The Politics and Poetics of Infrastructure." *Annual Review of Anthropology* 42: 327–43.

Marcus, George E. 1995. "Ethnography in/of the World System: The Emergence of Multi-Sited Ethnography." *Annual Review of Anthropology* 24: 95–117.

Marks, Laura. 2000. *The Skin of Film: Intercultural Cinema, Embodiment, and the Senses*. Durham: Duke University Press.

Naficy, Hamid. 2012. *A Social History of Iranian Cinema*, vol. 4, *The Globalizing Era, 1984–2010*. Durham: Duke University Press.

Portelli, Alessandro. (1998) 2006. "What Makes Oral History Different." In *The Oral History Reader*, 2nd ed., edited by Robert Perks and Alistair Thomson. New York: Routledge.

Rashid, Abdur. 1987. "Censor Chief's Report on Film." In *Platinum Jubilee Film Directory, 1913–1987: From Colorless to Colorful*, edited by A. R. Slote, 61–70. Karachi: Hamdard Press.

Rouse, Shahnaz. 2004. *Shifting Body Politics: Gender, Nation, and State in Pakistan*. New Delhi: Women Unlimited.

Shamim Ara. 1987. Interview. *Film Asia*, March. Translated by Lubna Saira.

———. 1993. Exclusive interview. *BBC Urdu*. https://www.youtube.com/watch?v=yfiUUbPBvzI&t=429s.

SHE: The Newsmagazine for Women. 1984. Karachi: Zeeday Publications.

Singer, Ben. 2001. *Melodrama and Modernity: Early Sensational Cinema and Its Contexts*. New York: Columbia University Press.

Slote, A. R. 1987. "Import of Foreign Films." In *Platinum Jubilee Film Directory, 1913–1987: From Colorless to Colorful*, edited by A. R. Slote, 61–70. Karachi: Hamdard Press.

Tasker, Yvonne.1993. *Spectacular Bodies: Gender, Genre, and the Action Cinema*. London: Routledge.

Taussig, Michael. 1992. *Mimesis and Alterity: A Particular History of the Senses*. Reprint, New York: Routledge, 2018.

Toor, Saadia. 2011. *The State of Islam: Culture and Cold War Politics in Pakistan*. London: Pluto Press.

Vitali, Valentina. 2008. *Hindi Action Cinema: Industries, Narratives, Bodies*. New Delhi: Oxford University Press.

9 REALISM AND REGION IN SOUTH INDIAN CINEMAS, 1947–1977

HARIPRASAD ATHANICKAL

THIS CHAPTER USES THE THEORETICAL FRAMEWORK OF REALISM to explore the issue of why there are not many auteurs in South Indian cinema. In the history of post-independence cinema, it is possible to mark the steps toward a peculiar kind of realism that culminates in the so-called parallel cinema movements spearheaded by Adoor Gopalakrishnan, Aravindan, Girish Karnad, Balu Mahendra, and Girish Kasaravalli—filmmakers who were exposed to classics of world cinema through their film-school training or through some other means, like their involvement in film society activities. This trajectory of South Indian new wave directors and auteurs has more to do with the development of realist aesthetics from the embryonic forms available within mainstream cinema. A lack of cerebral engagement with the underlying reality in India is a major hallmark of mainstream cinema. According to some historians of Indian cinema (Das Gupta 1991), popular films tend to be escapist and rely on devotional and mythical content; they do not concern themselves with being realistic. With the peculiar organization of the narrative and the compromises the cinema makes with larger political and social systems, the criticism has always been that the mainstream cinema will never be able to venture into higher forms of realism. This chapter attempts to situate new wave South Indian directors in relation to mainstream South Indian cinematic traditions. I argue that even though, at first glance, new wave cinema appears to be quite disconnected from mainstream cinema, on closer reading, we find that the new wave builds on the realistic aesthetics that were already burgeoning in the mainstream films. What the new wave directors provide is a much more nuanced, reflexive, and analytical approach in their work than what is found in popular cinema.

More than any idea of realism, Siegfried Kracauer's notion helps us understand the popular and mainstream cinemas' realist tendencies in South India. Kracauer (1997, 155), connecting photography and cinema, defines how "films may claim aesthetic validity if they build from their basic properties; like photographs, that is, they must record and reveal physical reality." He calls this tendency of recording and revealing physical reality "basic realism." He goes on to say that "a film is realistic because it correctly reproduces that part of the real world to which it refers" (299). Moreover, Kracauer draws a distinction between the "basic" and the "technical": if a film with all kinds of technical imperfections records interesting aspects of physical reality, this realistic record defines its cinematic quality rather than its technical perfection (29–30). I argue that South Indian cinemas' engagement with realism has been to discover the landscape, space, native place, and narrative principles in cinema to suit real-world anxieties.

This chapter analyzes several representative films from Malayalam and Tamil with occasional references to Kannada and Telugu films made in the three decades after independence, arguing that the literary aesthetics of realism prevalent during this period did not necessarily morph into a cinematic realist tradition in the 1950s and 1960s. What is surprising about this fact is that some of the same writers who are known for a harsh style in their literary endeavors did not follow the same style while engaged in filmmaking. It should also be pointed out that the picturization of film songs, a necessary evil in South Indian popular cinema, showed a disconnect between the lyrics (sometimes describing landscapes) and the pictures themselves, which could well have been shot within the confines of the studios. Adding to the complexity is the idea of region, village, and landscape, and what in Tamil is referred to as "ur," a sociological term denoting one's identification with place (Daniel 1984). Such categories are to be part of the inquiry, below, for a nuanced and reflexive understanding of the production of realism in South Indian cinemas.

My position is that realistic aesthetics were already present in mainstream cinema, but the new wave filmmakers of the 1960s and 1970s brought a reflective approach that previously had been missing from the films. Such an argument has to be contrasted with existing discourses on Indian cinema. Indian cinematic history has primarily been analyzed within a postcolonial framework.[1]

Among other engagements with cinema, the important ones are as follows: the development of censorship from colonial times constituting certain narrative tropes (Prasad 1998, 88–99); the close reading of narrative styles (Vasudevan 1993); and the analyses of mythic elements and value systems embedded in iconic films from both the preindependence and postindependence eras (Kapur 1987, 79–108). All these approaches acknowledged the development of national cinema. Indeed, nationalist and statist paradigms have been the most popular approaches in Indian cinema studies. My attempt differs considerably from these approaches since it tries to locate the progress of an aesthetic—rather than an allegorical reading of the nation and state—which moved through aspirations for an independent nation toward a fruitful creative attempt at realism in the 1970s. Several movements in mainstream Indian cinema had direct or indirect affiliations with the nation's political history. I am particularly interested in the movement of these aesthetics into basic realism based in regional languages rather than into the plastic realism one finds in Hindi-based nationalist endeavors.[2]

MATERIAL CULTURE OF MAINSTREAM SOUTH INDIAN CINEMAS: STATE, INDUSTRY, AND LOCATIONS

The three decades after independence were the most politically active in the history of South Indian cinema. Multiple factors contributed to the piecemeal growth of basic realistic elements in mainstream South Indian cinema, including the emergence of outdoor shooting, the use of landscape for song-and-dance shoots, linguistic reorganizations,[3] and regional government incentives—such as tax incentives. This created a populist and propagandist emphasis on what were perceived as the "real" (especially for the political leadership) issues influencing cinema during this period. Also of importance were factors such as the industry's treatment of the director as manager rather than artist, the influence of the theater and its social role, and interventions by political parties (whose agendas also led to populist and propagandist uses of popular realism). This section endeavors to connect these various factors of material and state culture in order to explain how they work together to produce heterogeneous and fragmented forms of basic realist aesthetics in mainstream films.

Foremost among the many significant political events is the linguistic reorientation of states in India. Whereas this had no significant impact on Bombay or Calcutta—two of the three major film industries in India—South Indian cinema, located in and around Madras, had to be reimagined in the appropriateness of continuing in the same city. Also the thematic, stylistic, and formal orientation of the films in these languages—namely Kannada, Telugu, and Malayalam—had to be reconfigured. Films in all of the four regional languages in South India were made in the studios of Madras. Madras's status as a significant port and the capital of the Madras presidency during British rule helped the industry to grow. Even so, the linguistic reorientation of states changed the importance of the city considerably. Some regional governments even provided incentives if films were shot in the respective regions. For example, the Andhra Pradesh government gave land to construct studios and a colony for film workers, whereas the Kannada government announced tax sops for Kannada films made in Karnataka. In contrast to this statist drive for regionalism was the fact that many of the film production and postproduction activities continued to be centered in Madras. Also, most of the producers and financiers belonged to Madras, which, many of the commentators believed, indirectly controlled the content and style of these films.

Rather than a national style, what emerged in South Indian cinema is a style that is in line with regional linguistic identities, which could be understood in terms of the subnational vision essentially projected by several political formations in the region. The reason one never finds the rise of coherent realistic styles in mainstream South Indian traditions is because of heterogeneous factors contributing to the material cultures of film production in these industries. South Indian cinema, known for its excess, forges certain principles of narrative, which, for an unfamiliar observer, might appear completely unrealistic. Accepting that cinematic realism is not the only method of narration in cinema, we attempt to trace the modes of realist aesthetics in South Indian cinema in the three decades from India's independence to the end of emergency (1947–77). The idea of a particular culture being properly represented became an artistic tour de force for many a filmmaker in South Indian regional languages. In such an endeavor the mere fact that the characters in the films spoke the language of the region entailed virtually no authenticity. Speaking of the concept of national cinema, as well as film studies from the perspective of multiculturalism, Paul Willemen comments, "In this way, such [ethnic] groups are condemned to repeat the rituals of ethnic authenticity, regardless of how uncomfortable many members of the so-called communities may feel with them" (1994, 207). The easier formulation would be to name these inquiries and searches for authenticity of culture in the use of language. But the filmmakers soon realized that the mere use of local language does not immediately speak to the quest for authenticity. There were popular demands to depict lifestyle and landscapes more accurately.[4]

If cinema is to be considered outside of its formal and thematic constraints, it has to be viewed as material culture as well. An aspect usually neglected in the discussion of cinema is advances in the instruments and paraphernalia used in filmmaking. For example, developments in the chemicals used to make the negative more sensitive to light had a large impact on altering cinematic culture. Likewise with the use of trollies and cranes, which went hand in hand with a reduction in the weight of cameras. All these had a positive impact on the maverick technicians and directors who sought, in the 1960s, to bring filmmaking out of the confines and comforts of the studio in the language films of South India. Thus, many films of the 1960s were shot both outdoors and in studios. Getting out of the studio is essentially a path toward realism. Especially germane is the fact that song sequences first began to show glimpses of the actual landscape. Even such minimal inclusion of regional landscapes within the three-hour run of the film began to be celebrated for its veracity. This interest in veracity demonstrates that authentic landscape was considered an important aspect of realism. As such, the 1960s represent an intermediate period in the aesthetic history of realism—a forerunner of the decade in which the contours of full-blown and avant-garde realism were fully actualized. What is clear in the predominantly melodramatic culture of the 1960s, then, is the emergence of realist basic fragments by way of landscapes and actual outdoor locations. I now look at specific linguistic traditions of mainstream South Indian cinema to further illustrate my points about the fragmented realist aesthetics produced by the heterogeneous industries.

POLITICS OF SPACE IN THE SOUTH: TELUGU AND KANNADA CINEMA

The consolidation of realist aesthetics in mainstream South Indian cinema happens toward the beginning of the 1970s. This section situates the anxieties born out of the linguistic reorientation of states in the industrial contexts of Telugu and Kannada cinema. Also of interest is the way space and language contribute to realist aesthetics. Prior to this period several films dealt with crucial issues and themes that might have benefited from a realistic style. Despite demonstrating occasional glimpses of a realist plot and camera work, films made before the 1970s did not sustain constant engagement or reflexivity. We find glimpses of realistic plot and camera work, especially when films moved outdoors. Themes of poverty, hardship, and postwar devastation—the standard leitmotifs of neorealism—were part of South Indian cinema of this period too, but the style of filmmaking characteristically lacked the documentary realist style that such attempts elsewhere characteristically flaunted. Since this was the case with popular cinema, the fact that many film shoots started moving out into the open from the confines of the studio by the late 1950s has to be understood in some perspective beyond the obvious features of basic realist aesthetics. We will have to look beyond the industry to make sense of such an urge.

This is the period when the linguistic reorganization of states took place. But that in effect does not impinge on the style of cinema. From its inception, Indian regional cinema always used regional languages, and characters spoke in their native tongues. More importantly, the state supported regional language cinema. In the changing political climate, cinema was to have the patronage of the regional powers. Hence, the popular film industry was hoping to have some support. Since this was the most popular medium of entertainment in all regions, regional governments were more than happy to extend their support to the film industry. The Andhra Pradesh government, for example, had taken measures to move the Telugu industry to its capital, Hyderabad, immediately after the state was formed. The fact that the actual shift took almost thirty years is another matter altogether. The government was more than willing to give large pieces of land to studios in Hyderabad. Srinivas (2006) notes, "Movement of the film industry meant, among other things, acquisition of vast tracts of land for the construction of cinema halls, studios and production and post-production facilities." They also gave land for a colony to be built for the industrial workers employed in Hyderabad cinema. Both Prasad and Annapurna studios were established as a result of such initiatives on the part of the government.

Kannada cinema's history prior to Indian independence was almost the same as Telugu cinema. Occasional original films were made in the language. Films made in this region also had distinct identities. The two major hubs of production were Mysore and Kolhapur, where several studios were built. Bangalore gained prominence as the center of Kannada cinema after the linguistic reorientation of the states. Kolhapur was known for producing films in multiple languages, including Kannada, Marathi, Hindi, and Tamil. But eventually these studios relocated to Pune and then to Bombay. Mysore catered to Kannada cinema and some Tamil and Telugu films. Once the industry was completely rooted in Bangalore, filmmaking concentrated only on the production of Kannada cinema.

Karnataka's dependence on the Kannada language to tie together regions that had distinct histories of their own eventually led to a staunch linguistic nationalism (Nair 1996, 2814). Certain parts of Karnataka, like Shimoga, had a majority-Marathi population, whereas regions adjacent to present-day Andhra Pradesh had a Telugu-speaking population. Kannada cinema rode on this wave of Kannada nationalism for its own popularity. Bidar and Gulbarga, regions that were under the Nizam's rule, had an Urdu-speaking community. The southern districts in and around Mangalore had Konkani- and Tulu-speaking majorities.

Accepting Kannada as a thread to bind these distinct languages required a consistent and concerted effort at various levels. Cinema's acceptance of several mythological and historical stories to suit this purpose is clear in films such as *Bedara Kannamma* (dir. H. L. N. Simha, 1954) and others. The story of *Bedara Kannamma* revolves around Kanna, a hunter and devotee of Lord Shiva. In the folktale popular across Karnataka, Kanna gouges out his eyes and offers them to the lord to show his extreme devotion. The character of Kanna was played by Rajkumar, who went on to become an emblem of Kannada nationalism (Prasad 2000, 4140). The industry had long realized that intense Kannada nationalism in cinema could only be sustained if the filmmaking process was shifted completely to Karnataka.

In 1961, the Karnataka government declared that additional tax rebates would be given to films made in Kannada if they were shot in Karnataka. It was not enough that films were made in the Kannada language; the government insisted also on the space where they were made. Beyond political motives and the market-driven popular cinema's populist engagements with Karnataka's landscape and space, the 1970s brought a group of young directors to the fore who wanted to look beyond propagandist representations of space. Girish Kasaravalli, among several others of this generation, drew inspiration from modernist literature. Kasaravalli's adaptation of Ananthamurthy's acclaimed novel *Samskara* is an example of this influence (the novel was published in 1965 and the film produced in 1970). Kannada life is not etched in the film as part of any sloganeering; rather, it has to do with the customs, practices, and lifestyles typical of village life in Karnataka. The film also has a staunch anticaste sentiment, which made the certification process difficult.

TAMIL CINEMA: ROOTS OF REALISM IN POPULAR CINEMA

As the most significant film industry in South India, Tamil cinema merits extensive discussion. Outsiders always call out Tamil cinema for its "excess." Non-Tamilians also point to Tamil cinema's distinct presence in the daily life of Tamilians. To be fair to such scoffers, Tamil politics from the 1960s onward had been dominated by film stars who were far from being career politicians. By the time M. G. Ramachandran, the most famous film star of the 1960s and 1970s, formed Anna Dravida Munnetra Kazhagam (ADMK) and became the chief minister of the state, the influence was felt even in other regions.[5] For a star to become a politician overnight and transform him- or herself as a leader and then become the head of the state administration without much experience was baffling. The activity surrounding film exhibition, like the celebratory gestures when a film star's film was released, the intense adulation of fan clubs toward the stars, the huge publicity cutouts, and the fans' physical proclamations of loyalty (such as etching the star's image on their bodies) demonstrate just how excessive both the fan culture and the cinema culture were.

Several commentators have attributed the excesses of Tamil cinema to the long history of folk tradition and performances. Most of these performance traditions included very colorful attire, loud rhythmic music, and exaggerated dance movements. The local folk culture that still exists in the rural areas of Tamil Nadu has several artistic and popular culture ingredients to contribute to Tamil cinema's practices. However, equally important is the fact that the cinema of Tamil Nadu has not always been entwined in such extremes. There have been several inquiries regarding the style and content of cinema practiced according to the spirit of the times. Burning political and social issues were correspondingly represented in films of the time. Tamil cinema in the 1940s—immediately after independence—began to include stories of poverty, class conflict, and ill treatment of those belonging to lower castes. The stories—if we just look at the plot line—could be considered fit for socialist realism; however, these films remained predominantly oriented toward entertainment, relying on the formula of songs, comedy scenes, dances, and fights. Most films from this period also contained a love story, a trope and angle to be construed in suggestions of a marriage by the end of the narrative. Films like *Velaikaari* (The maid, dir. A. S. A. Sami, 1949), *Nalla thambi* (dir. Krishnan-Panju, 1949), *Chandralekha* (dir. S. S. Vasan, 1948), and *Ezhai padum padu* (Plights of the poor, dir. K. Ramnoth, 1950) are cases in point.

However, the ensuing period saw the dominance of the studio system, constraining the larger directions taken by South Indian cinema. Easy access to background scenery and manageable lighting within the studios impacted the treatment of the story and style of these films. The love interests were left mostly undeveloped so as to bring in the notion of secular love as a climax. There were explosive outbursts over social inequality too. The Dravida Munnetra Kazhagam (DMK) was pushed to depict its ideology in films (M. Pandian 1991, 759). Prolific public speakers and writers were roped in to give the ideology mass appeal through the screenplays. As is evident in the films *Velaikkari* and *Parasakthi* (Goddess Parasakthi, dir. Krishnan-Panju, 1952), the DMK was largely successful in its attempt to spread its ideology. Both films contained graphic narrations of the goddess being challenged and verbally abused. C. N. Anna Durai, DMK's ideologue whose play was remade into *Velaikkari*, wrote the dialogue for *Velaikkari*, and M. Karunanidhi wrote the gripping script for *Parasakthi*. It is worth noting that other experiments in Tamil cinema, like eliminating songs and stunts from films, also took place during this time period. While these could be viewed as formal changes, they were understood as hampering the aesthetic. *Andha naal* (That day, 1954) directed by Sundaram Balachander, tried to get rid of songs altogether (Dhananjayan 2011, 138). This film had no stunt scenes. In some senses, this can be interpreted as Tamil cinema negotiating with realist aesthetics.

Several waves of depicting villages have been part of the history of Tamil cinema. What are called nativity films (for their realistic portrayal of rural life in Tamil Nadu) in the 1970s and the neo-nativity films in the 2010s presented village life in detail (A. Pandian 2008). *Makkalai petra maharasi* (Blessed mother, dir. K. Somu, 1959) apparently inaugurated this trend in Tamil (Dhananjayan 2011, 161). In the following decades, several filmmakers in Tamil went on to explore various facets of village life in Tamil Nadu. These ranged from bleak sketches of hardship and poverty to gruesome renderings of family feuds. The village, as Prasad contends, "is a concrete settlement with social relations unleavened by the virtual resources of modernity" (Prasad 2010, 260). In the Tamil cinema of the 1970s, the village is a trope to evoke stark human feeling and an occasion to proclaim the inherent innocence of people.

What is interesting about Tamil cinema from the period 1947 to 1975 is that unlike the Hindi Popular Cinema, the filmmakers were open to new ideas and themes and interested in experimentation, at least in certain aspects of filmic art. Many Tamil filmmakers were not completely ready to bring in large-scale experimentation. One cannot perceive a paradigm shift in Tamil cinema of this time. If "realism"—not just as a style but also as a project—bore the weight of this shift, in the case of Tamil cinema's history, it was a slow process. The suggestion here is not to be confused with a teleological process of cinema developing into a completely realistic endeavor. The argument could be oversimplified as cinema progressing from the commercial or popular variety to meaningful and appropriate realistic aesthetics. However, I am skeptical of categories such as commercial, popular, mainstream, and parallel cinemas. Beyond that, a trajectory of progress is inappropriate for a completely different reason as well. The history of Tamil cinema proves that styles keep changing. No style sticks for long. In this light, I emphasize that there were several waves of realism in Tamil cinema.

As I have argued so far—in reference not only to Tamil cinema but to South Indian cinema in general—the exploration of realism has not occurred as a sudden shift in narrative style nor as a complete overhaul of accepted styles. In stating this, I am not denying the existence of a group of new wave filmmakers, including Adoor Gopalakrishnan, G. Aravindan, and Girish Kasaravalli. Nor do I deny their deliberate attempt to break away from the shackles of popular cinema and to shake off the excesses of existing conventions. Having said that, I maintain that popular cinema also used realism as a trope when the plot required it. We can see glimpses of this trope as early as 1950.

MALAYALAM CINEMA: AUTHENTICITY OF SPACE AS REALISM

This section discusses the engagement with space in cinema as a matter of realistic aesthetics. This idea is exemplified by the Malayalam film *Thiramala* (The wave), directed by Vimar Kumar and P. R. S. Pillai and released in 1953. Because the film has not survived in its entirety, it is impossible to analyze the movie as a whole. However, from what survives, *Thiramala* comes across as a quintessential film of its age, a period when a debate raged within film circles as to whether the studio or the outdoors was preferable. The film apparently had two different endings. The unsubstantiated claim is that these two different climaxes were meant for different regions in Kerala. How these regions contributed to the conceptualization of two climaxes cannot be determined. What is available by way of journalistic accounts, however, is only speculative. *Thiramala* can also be seen as a precursor to another historically important 1954 Malayalam film, *Neelakkuyil* (The blue cuckoo), directed by P. Bhaskaran and Ramu Kariat, as both share similar themes.

The basic story line was typical of the period, revolving around a love story between the daughter of a rich man and a poor boy. The class conflict found in other Tamil and Telugu films of the same period was depicted vividly. The heroine, Lakshmi, played by Kumari Thangam, is the beautiful, wealthy, educated daughter of the landlord Kurup (a name marking caste in Kerala). She grows up with the ferryman's son, Venu, played by Thomas Berleigh. Since her father opposes their relationship, they cannot marry each other. When Kurup arranges for Lakshmi to marry Vijayan, played by Sathyan, Venu leaves the village for the city, where he finds a job as a waiter at a hotel. Vijayan's lavish lifestyle eventually leads to his doom. He drinks and gambles and visits women other than his wife. He also starts to abuse Lakshmi. Eventually they end up fighting at the same hotel where Venu works as a waiter. When Venu returns to the village, he encounters Lakshmi in difficult circumstances. During a flood, Lakshmi falls into the river but is saved by Venu. The story ends with Venu dying in the same river after saving Lakshmi from drowning. On the other side of the river, Vijayan, now a changed man, accepts her back into his life. However, an alternative climax had Venu escaping from the river. The surviving print at the National Film Archives of India, Pune, has the tragic ending, which is allegedly accepted by the people of Travancore. However, popular lore states that the Malabar audience did not accept the tragic ending; hence, a new ending was shot and substituted for the original version. More than realism, this film had to do with the use of location, which contributed to the concept of realism in this period.

The film has thirteen songs. Except for a few original scores, the songs are note-for-note adaptations of popular Hindi songs. Bhaskaran, who wrote the lyrics and played Venu's father, was associated with the Communist Party and penned several songs for party functions as well. While the film was hailed as the first musical hit in the history of Malayalam cinema, the most relevant aspect of the film to this analysis is the picturization of the songs. Most of the songs are shot in the studio. One love song, which describes a river, is filmed outside. However, the filmmaker's nervousness is visible in the handling of the landscape as the background to the songs. The film's climax, either the tragic one or the happy one, interestingly is on location. Like many other films of this generation, *Thiramala* is also a verbal film, in the sense that the dialogue pushes the story forward, more than the cinematography or physicality of the actors.

Film is not explored to its full potential as a visual medium in these movies, since films were often considered equivalent to the theater, a popular form of entertainment at the time. The fact that most of the technicians and actors had their initial training in the theater also contributed to the similarity. However, *Thiramala* can be interpreted as a transitional film in the cinematic history of South India. Here landscapes and interiors are given equal importance. However, by setting some songs and the climax in the actual landscapes, *Thiramala* points to a future where film will depend on location shoots to lend realistic atmosphere.

Although part of the film is shot outdoors and the story involves class conflict, *Thiramala* cannot be considered realistic. The stylized dialogue and acting, which borders on overdramatic, make it difficult for it to be considered realistic. But this film paved the way for many films that came after it: the same ambiguity and complexity of indoors and outdoors are present in a much more intense way in the film *Neelakkuyil.* Another complexity is the dual climax and its association with the two regions Malabar and Travancore. There has been a popular perception that Malabar is not up to national standards in terms of education and social awareness, and hence, the region's aesthetic taste is much inferior when compared to the culturally superior Travancore. The filmmakers of *Thiramala* would have envisaged the tragic end to the film as an aesthetically appealing and realistic ending to the class conflict story. And the lukewarm response to the ending in Malabar would have resulted in such an interpretation. The suggestion, then, is that certain parts of Kerala were not ready for aesthetically challenging realism in cinema. Even then, cinema was viewed primarily as a form of entertainment where aesthetic challenges were not well received.

Jeevitha nouka (The boat of life, 1951), directed by Vembu, is an interesting example of the easy course that cinema undertakes even after the independence. The film was released in three southern languages—Malayalam, Tamil, and Telugu—and tells a story of village life. It includes several outdoor shots, some of them documentary-style shots of folk performances and temple festivals. True to the period, this film deals with class conflict: the love between an upper-caste moneyed gentleman and a girl from a comparatively poor background and lower caste. As in the case of *Thiramala*, most of the songs are remakes of popular Hindi songs. The camera wanders a little bit in the songs, but most of the film is shot in studio. In its overenthusiasm to narrate the story, the film clearly underplays the significance of the milieu or styles such as overdramatic dialogue delivery or stylised movements of the actors. The peculiar way *Jeevitha nouka* uses outdoor shoots is specific to the age. Close-up and middle-range shots are invariably shot in the studio, though it has to be said that the mixing of outdoor and studio shots is intelligently done. The message of the meaninglessness of caste and class difference is articulated through the songs. Sophisticated and stylized language used throughout the film also hampers the film from tackling the gravity of the complex social equations at work.

As we see from the specific examples discussed above, the themes have always been structured along serious issues in the society in the specific period discussed in this essay. The class and caste conflicts hampering the hero and heroine from uniting in marriage were a consistent theme for all three decades analyzed in this chapter. Progressive ideas are articulated much too verbally than is needed in a film. The verbosity of the characters is another common trait of films of the era, so often the main theme is told frontally by way of a speech or a piece of dialogue. It is as if the director fears that the film's message will be lost if it is not articulated in such a way. This narrative device was very common in almost all the regional language cinema in South India during this period. Cinema needed to find its own narrative style and a visually organic method to add to the complex themes most of these films tackled. For such an organic existence, apart from exposure to several films from various styles and approaches, a thorough understanding of one's own capabilities is required. A certain reflexivity regarding the medium and one's own position as against the theme dealt with in the respective films is another trait that could add to choosing the required and appropriate style. It is this search that eventually took cinema to basic realism.

The director was viewed as a manager by the industry, especially by the producers and the financiers. They were supposed to handle the investment so that backers did not lose money. Hence, choosing to shoot on location was viewed as unnecessarily extravagant and a practice to be avoided. More than a creative genius, the director was viewed as a scene arranger. It was not important that directors possess skills in cinematography or editing, and formal training was very limited. Most directors learned the trade by apprenticing with an established director. People only needed to be assistant directors on a few films before they were considered expert filmmakers. During this period, creativity was not a measure of excellence, and it wasn't considered as such until a new generation of filmmakers ushered in a new concept of the director. The director as an auteur of his work was an alien idea in the popular cinema. I am not suggesting here that auteur cinema is the ideal kind of filmmaking, only that there was very little directorial variety in this era.

THE NEW WAVE: REFLEXIVE, SELF-CONSCIOUS REALISM

It took several decades for the director to emerge as an artist and a creative force of filmmaking in popular cinema. Two important Malayalam filmmakers who had made their debut films in the early 1970s showed glimpses of such potential. Adoor's first film, *Swayamvaram*, was made in 1972, and G. Aravindan's *Utharayanam* in 1974. These two films showed a tendency to move beyond the conventional practices of filmmaking prevalent during that time on several fronts. They were hailed as the arrival of new wave Indian cinema. They also inaugurated what is now called parallel cinema down south. Notably, both directors avoided common embellishments, such as the songs, comedy skits, and fights that were seemingly ubiquitous at the time. While there were songs in *Utharayanam*, they were shot in a way that diverged from conventional methods.

Swayamvaram followed a plot that had been used and abused in popular cinema for decades: a couple getting married against the wishes of their parents. *Swayamvaram* was a reaction to rampant unemployment, poverty, and the problems of unplanned urbanization. While the film's story line cannot claim a major departure from popular films, *Swayamvaram* examines what happens when an unprepared couple is pushed into the real world, a world bereft of values or morals. This bleak worldview is quite antithetical to the rosy picture that popular cinema always painted. The characters in *Swayamvaram*, while going through hardships, act as if they are feeling the hardship presented at the urban space where they find themselves. The first of such careful juxtapositions is when the couple undertakes a journey from the hotel to the house, and eventually to the slum. Sharing their living space with a prostitute is another instance. They merge with the locale and the happenings in the city (Vishvam even attends a public meeting that deliberates on poverty and unemployment). Most of the action takes place outdoors, and the characters are very closely followed by the camera. The camera is more of an observer of the action here and mingles with the environs in a way not seen in popular cinema at the time.

Along with the movement, acting, and camera work, the fact that *Swayamvaram* pauses for the audience to take note of each sequence, along with its environs, could be interpreted as an attempt on the director's part to try an innovative new technique. This could be said of G. Aravindan as well. His first film, *Utharayanam*, in spite of being a journey to find inner truths, also externalizes this journey. The slow, unhurried evolution of the narrative is deliberate. The characters are given much time to develop through their interaction with the environs. This use of the mise-en-scène makes Aravindan unique when compared to contemporaries such as Adoor. However, it is not just the use of the camera or the mise-en-scène—the technical aspects of filmmaking—that distinguishes these two filmmakers. They both were inclined toward a style or philosophy of filmmaking that was intense, deliberate, and reflexive. The two filmmakers perfected their styles only toward the end of the 1970s, Adoor with *Kodiyettam* (1977) and Aravindan with *Thampu* (1978) and *Kummatti* (1979). These films showed the paradigm shift in terms of the use of space and the complicated internal landscape of the region they wanted to showcase.

Utharayanam is set in two distinct times: the present, in which the protagonist reminisces over his father, and the father's revolutionary past. True to the literary tradition of Malayalam of the time, the film's hero feels insecure. The political implications of this period twenty years after independence are etched deep within the film and reflected in the thought processes of the disillusioned youth. The protagonist is similar to modernist, existentialist heroes found in European literature. Though the camera and the style are a bit amateurish, what Aravindan does in *Utharayanam* in terms of narrative style is quite extraordinary. He would follow this same pattern of slow exposition in all of his later films too. The brooding hero is another quintessential Aravindan motif. We come across the same kind of exposition and brooding in *Pokkuveyil* (1982). Most significant of all the elements in the films is the very specific space Arvindan uses in *Utharayanam*. The story is based on the bombing of a bridge in Kozlikode district in Kerala during the freedom struggle. The hero's father was one among the few freedom fighters behind that daring act, and he deeply reveres his fellow revolutionaries. However, he comes to slowly realize that such heroic deeds cannot be sustained in the present day, as is proven harshly by his father's friend, a partner in the act of valor, who later becomes a corrupt businessman. The film is set in such a way that the very specific story is articulated as a universal one that could occur at any place or time. The questions of morality the film raises are relevant, and they touch a chord. The beauty of *Utharayanam* is not technical or stylistic; on the contrary, it lies in the realism of the interiors. The film is made in an allegoric way so as to create a reflexivity in the audience. This interiority pushes *Utharayanam*'s very locally rooted story to be universal and realistic.

Calling the new wave directors' style the most authentic realism in the cinema of South India would be a grave mistake. Several attempts were made to engage with the realistic style in mainstream cinema as well. No doubt, some popular film directors were hard pressed not to try anything extravagant in shooting style, since the popular cinema always restricted the cost of shooting with stringent measures. However, even within the strict budgetary restrictions and conventions, popular filmmakers tried their hand at cinematic realism, which, in hindsight, can be said was not fully developed or reflexive enough. Sometimes these attempts are limited to a single scene or a song sequence; at other times, they are restricted to the initial stages of the film. All in all, the attempts at realism are found in embryonic form in mainstream South Indian cinema. A complete film following such a style was never attempted due to the constraints of the industry, where box-office returns settled and restricted most creative ambition.

NOTES

1 See Prasad (1998). Unlike many earlier scholars of Indian cinema, Prasad approaches the cinema as emblematic of India's complicated transition to a yet-to-be-arrived-at capitalist state.

2 I borrow the term *plastic* from André Bazin. Bazin alludes to the mechanical means that freed plastic arts like painting and sculpting to pursue the impossible goal of likeness or verisimilitude. He asserts that plastic realism does not add anything "to reality, it does not deform it, it forces it to reveal its structural depth, to bring out the preexisting relations which become constitutive of the drama" ([1967] 2005, 12).

3 Through the State Reorganisation Act of 1956, the Indian state's boundaries were organized along linguistic lines. British administrative boundaries of the provinces were deemed arbitrary and the language spoken in the region was considered for this reorganization. The British province of Madras was divided into four states, where Tamil, Kannada, Malayalam, and Telugu were spoken.

4 Several such articulations are recorded in the dossier on Telugu cinema *Workshop on Telugu Cinema: History, Culture, Theory*, organized by Anveshi Research Centre for Women's Studies and Centre for the Study of Culture and Society, Hyderabad, August 13–16, 1999.

5 Anna Dravida Munnetra Kazhagam was founded by Ramachandran in 1972. In fact, the party's name is a spinoff of the Dravida Munnetra Kazhagam (Dravidian Progress Federation) to which *Anna*, the Tamil word for "big brother," was added. *Anna* was also a reference to the big brother roles that Ramachandran played in many of the films. The party became AIDMK with the prefix *All India* added later on.

REFERENCES

Bazin, André. (1967) 2005. *What Is Cinema? Essays Selected and Translated by Hugh Gray.* Vol. 1. Berkeley: University of California Press.

Daniel, E. Valentine. 1984. *Fluid Signs: Being a Person the Tamil Way.* Berkeley: University of California Press.

Das Gupta, Chidananda. 1991. *The Painted Face: Studies in India's Popular Cinema.* New Delhi: Roli Books.

Dhananjayan, G. 2011. *The Best of Tamil Cinema, 1931–2010.* Galatta Media.

Jacob, Preminda. 2009. *Celluloid Dieties: The Visual Culture of Cinema and Politics in South India.* Lanham, MD: Lexington Books.

Kapur, Geeta. 1987. "Mythic Material in Indian Cinema." *Journal of Arts and Ideas*, nos. 14–15: 79–108.

Kracauer, Siegfried. 1997. *Theory of Film: Redemption of Physical Reality*. Princeton, NJ: Princeton University Press.

Nair, Janaki. 1996. "'Memories of Underdevelopment': Language and Its Identities in Contemporary Karnataka." *Economic and Political Weekly*, October 12–19, 1996, 2809–16.

Pandian, Anand. 2008. "Cinema in the Countryside: Popular Tamil Film and the Remaking of Rural Life." In *Tamil Cinema: The Cultural Politics of India's Other Film Industry*, edited by Selvaraj Velayudham, 124–38. London: Routledge.

Pandian, M. S. S. 1991. "Life and Times of a DMK film." *Economic and Political Weekly* 26, nos. 11–12 (March): 759–70.

Prasad, M. Madhava. 1998. *Ideology of the Hindi Film: A Historical Construction*. Oxford: Oxford University Press.

———. 2000. "Where Does the Forest Begin?" *Economic and Political Weekly* 35, no. 47: 4138–40.

———. 2010. "The Imagined Village: Representations of Rural Life in Indian Cinema." In *Village Matters: Relocating Villages in the Contemporary Anthropology of India*, edited by Diane P. Mines and Nicolas Yazgi, 256–71. Oxford: Oxford University Press.

Rajadhyaksha, Ashish. 1993. "The Phalke Era: Conflict of Traditional Form and Modern Technology." In *Interrogating Modernity: Culture and Colonialism in India*, edited by Tejaswini Niranjana, P. Sudhir, and Vivek Dhareshwar, 47–82. Kolkata: Seagull Books.

Srinivas, S. V. 2006. "Persistence of the Feudal: Star and Film Form in Post 1970s Telugu Cinema." http://jmionline.org/articles/2006/persistence_of_the_feudal_star_and_film_form_in_post_1970s_telugu_cinema.pdf.

Vasudevan, Ravi S. 1993. "Shifting Codes, Dissolving Identities: The Hindi Social Film of the 1950s as Popular Culture." *Journal of Arts and Ideas*, nos. 23–24: 51–84.

Willemen, Paul. 1994. *Looks and Frictions: Essays in Cultural Studies and Film Theory*. Bloomington: Indiana University Press.

10 "THIS IS LONDON, NOT PAKISTAN!"

Articulations of the Diaspora in Pakistani Punjabi Film

GWENDOLYN S. KIRK

"*I SAY DON'T SPEAK SO LOUD!* THIS IS *LONDON*, NOT PAKISTAN!" Arguing heatedly with her husband, the heroine's mother in *Pehlwanji in London* (Chaudhry 1971), while standing up for her daughter's right to choose her own husband, reveals a key set of linked dichotomies on which the film's narrative pivots: loud and soft, barbaric and civilized, traditional and modern, conservative and liberal, Punjab and London. She goes on to tell her husband:

> ایسٹ ایسٹ اے تے ویسٹ ویسٹ۔ انّاں دوواں دا ملاپ ہرگز نئیں ہو سکدا۔
>
> *East east ai te west west. InnāN dowāN da milāp hargiz naīN ho sakdā.*
>
> East is east and west is west. These two can never meet.

This chapter analyzes the Pakistani Punjabi films *Pehlwanji in London* and *Jatt in London* (Malik 1981) in and against the analytical frames commonly used to discuss the portrayal of foreignness and diaspora in South Asian cinemas. Although both of these films ostensibly embrace the classic East-West binary present in so many South Asian films set in Europe or North America, I argue that Pakistani Punjabi films show a distinct ambivalence toward this dichotomy, and that these films actively construct a Punjabi identity that not only contrasts with the West, but at times clashes with the Pakistani nation-state itself. Moreover, these relationships are changing in concord with other sociopolitical shifts, as reflected in the narratives of the two films, which were both made at critical moments in the history of Pakistan.

Although Punjabi films have often held the largest market share in Pakistan and have a loyal fan base, they have typically been perceived by the cultural elite as unimaginative and repetitive, crudely made, overly vulgar, and violent, and have generally been disparaged by the aesthetic and moral hegemony of the Pakistani bourgeoisie. It is important to note that although the Punjabi language is marginalized in important ways in Pakistan, and Punjabi literature and to a great extent film are also given less social capital, Punjabis themselves are not as a whole a marginalized ethnic group. They are the largest ethnolinguistic group in the country and make up more than half of the Pakistani population; yet to a large extent Punjabis themselves associate Punjabi language and culture with lower socioeconomic status, less education, lower social mobility, and rural/hyperlocal, rather than urban/national/globalizing, socialities.[1]

The association of the Punjabi language with a working-class and often rural identity, along with a discourse that constructs the Punjabi language as fundamentally loud, vulgar, and inherently violent, is key to understanding the ways *panjābiyat* (Punjabiness) is depicted and mobilized on-screen. The focus of this chapter is on how Punjabi cinema in Pakistan strategically deploys a Western setting as the foreign "other" in order to assert national identity and Islamic morality versus the West, but also to highlight the way subregional cinema in Pakistan resists what Kamran Ali has describes as "nationalism of one language (Urdu), one religion (Islam), and one people (Pakistani)" (Ali 2015, 391) by using the state as a foil for *panjābiyat*. This paper examines the valences of Punjabi identity and its markers across cinematic contexts, asking how differences in the relationships between postcolonial national and regional identities inhere in filmic representations.

PAKISTANI CINEMA'S DIASPORIC GAZE

Many scholars have written on South Asian films made by and for the diasporic community (Desai 2004; Gopinath 2005), analyzing the use of European landscapes as the exotic moral antithesis of South Asia. These visualizations are distillations of postcolonial cultural encounters, which provide viewers with tantalizing images of the West, as well as offering spaces to assert regional and national identities.[2] Scholarly work on these films has focused primarily on Hindi popular cinema or English-language films made in the West by South Asian diaspora filmmakers. Kaur and Sinha (2005, 16) propose the term *Bollyworld*, which not only refers to the hybridity of Hindi popular cinema and its global distribution, but also serves "as a means of negotiating both Indianness and its transformation, particularly when representing and being received by diasporic populations." Pakistani cinema, while markedly different from Hindi popular cinema, has undergone its own transformations over the past seventy years, some of them similar to Hindi cinema and some markedly different. Pakistani cinema has not developed as extensive a subgenre of diaspora films; this is perhaps due in large part to the decline in film production since the mid-1990s, the exact moment when Indian cinema began looking to its diaspora on a much larger scale, with Bollywood actors performing stage shows in Europe, North America, and other centers of diaspora population, and with films starting to be released internationally and circulated widely. Most notable of these are the slew of Western-set Hindi popular films that began with 1995's superhit *Dilwale dulhaniya le jayenge* (Chopra 1995). Films that deal with the lives and experiences of Indians living overseas became enormously popular, and hundreds of such films were made, and continue to be produced, in mainstream Hindi as well as regional popular cinemas.

Although Pakistani cinema perhaps did not deal as extensively with themes of diaspora and transnational identities as Indian films, such films do exist, punctuating the canon of Pakistani cinema at significant times. The record of Pakistani films is not as complete nor as detailed as that of other cinemas, and many films exist only in sketchy details with prints impossible to find, but according to my research the first Pakistani film set abroad seems to have been 1970's *Love in Europe* (Akhtar 1990), a gangster thriller and romance. Set primarily in mod London with some scenes shot in Italy and Lebanon, the film stars Rozina and Kamal, whose characters are thrown together when he mistakes her for a member of the gang he is investigating. Stylistically and thematically, the film bears a close resemblance to several Hindi-language films of the era, notably *An Evening in Paris* (Samanta 1967) and *Love in Tokyo* (Chakravorty 1966), which center on romance between South Asian tourists in other, "exotic," parts of the world.

Ranjani Mazumdar (2011) ties these films directly to upward mobility, innovations in air travel technology and infrastructure, and developments in tourism and advertising. She points out that "travel to foreign locations in *An Evening in Paris* was tinged with a particular kind of desire and boldness not common in the films of the time" (139). *Love in Europe* follows this pattern, with its depiction of mod gambling dens, international crime rings, and sultry molls in sequins and fringe. However, this relatively one-dimensional portrayal of the West as a land of worldly desires, technology, and modernism was to change significantly over the following decades. As Kaur (2005, 311) argues, "Representations of the 'foreign' in Bollywood have also accelerated in leaps and bounds—from sporadic 'travels' through Euro-America . . . to its almost normative inclusion in virtually all contemporary Indian film plots." Although such representations are still relatively few and far between in Punjabi cinema, *Love in Europe* and many other regional or subnational South Asian films do make use of evocative foreign locations and visuals, and even use foreign (usually white) faces and bodies for a variety of narrative strategies and visual effects. In outlining two films' representations both of the West and of the Pakistani diaspora settled there, this chapter seeks to understand how these representations have shifted and changed within Punjabi Pakistani cinema, and what they can tell us not only about political and cultural tensions between East and West, but also within the Pakistani nation-state.

THE SEXUAL POLITICS OF SUCCESS: *PEHLWANJI IN LONDON*

Pehlwanji in London, directed by Haidar Chaudhry in 1971, tells the story of Aslam, a *pehlwān* (traditional wrestler) from the old city of Lahore who must travel to London to earn money for his sister Salma's dowry. Aslam was engaged to his uncle's daughter Ruby in childhood, but her mother is dead set against the marriage, arguing that the two are not equally matched. She tells her husband, "An uncivilized, uneducated idiot absolutely cannot become a companion to my well-mannered and well-educated daughter!" Meanwhile, Aslam is busy defending his neighborhood from the encroachment of a gang of gamblers and drug dealers, who take revenge on him by threatening to reveal that his sister has been meeting a boy named Iqbal in the park, thereby dishonoring his family. Aslam goes to Iqbal's father to request that he consent to the marriage of Iqbal and Salma, but the father, who is wealthy, demands a large dowry.

Aslam decides he must go to London to earn money in order to afford the demanded dowry, and he sets off to find his uncle, who lives there. However, once in London, he loses the uncle's address, and after a series of struggles and hardships eventually earns the money for the dowry by defeating a British champion wrestler. He also manages to rescue his cousin Ruby from being kidnapped by gangsters, thus preserving his family's honor, and is able to secure her marriage to her boyfriend, Jaidi. Aslam returns to Lahore to deliver the dowry money just in time, as Iqbal's father is about to marry him off to someone else. There is a confrontation at the wedding, and finally, chastized, Iqbal's father recognizes the evils of demanding large dowries and consents to Salma and Iqbal's marriage.

The *pehlwān* is an important cultural symbol of masculinity and strength, as well as particular practices of morality, purity, and asceticism. Wrestlers across South Asia follow highly specific dietary and exercise regimens, and adhere to a strict moral code, particularly as pertains to expending sexual energy (cf. Alter 1992). Additionally, many wrestling practices involve spiritual and religious components, whether the practitioners are Hindu, Muslim, or Sikh. *Pehlwānī*, also known as *(desi) kushtī*, is often listed among those practices that are thought to be dying out or irretrievably corrupted by globalization and migration to urban centers. Mohammad Ahsan Shakoor (2016, 220), for instance, writes, "Since the ancient period, Pehalwani encouraged a large number of following in Punjabi culture as a national sport. At present, the admiration of this cultural tradition is in sharp decline owing to varying tastes, modern way of life, and values adopted from the West. Traditional *akharas*[3] of *Pehalwani* are dying out, along with their perfect ethos of discipline, interactions, and patience." *Pehlwānī* thus has become one of those elements of Punjabi culture (along with, for example, Sufi poetry, folk music, kite flying, and traditional arts and crafts) that are frequently invoked as symbols of traditional, local Punjabi values that are perceived to be under threat by an urbanizing, globalizing, Urdu- and English-speaking hegemony aligned with the Pakistani nation-state.

The year 1971, when *Pehlwanji in London* was released, rocked the identity of the Pakistani nation-state to its core. Ostensibly created as a homeland for the Muslims of South Asia, tensions between its western wing, dominated by Punjabis and coalesced around Islam and Urdu, and the Bengali-dominated eastern wing, had been brewing since the country's inception. As Ayesha Jalal (2014, 153) writes, "Bengali outrage at the [central government's] Urdu-only language policy was just the tip of the iceberg, concealing a deep-seated resentment at the marginalization of their culture in the emerging narratives of the Pakistani nation." After ten months of fighting, Bangladesh was officially recognized as a separate and independent state in December 1971. This political rupture also impacted Pakistani cinema; Bengali filmmakers and artists largely chose to stay in Bangladesh after its independence. Moreover, a quarter of Pakistani cinemas had been located in its eastern wing, significantly truncating the overall film circuit (Noorani 2016). These events prompted a reorganization of film production, enabling "a turning point for the development of regional cinema as the producers looked into the financial viability of making more films in the provincial languages—Punjabi, Pushto [*sic*], and Sindhi" (Gazdar 1997, 124). The 1970s saw Urdu cinema gradually lose the lion's share of the film market to

TABLE 10.1. Films released in Pakistan, 1961, 1971, and 1981

Year	Urdu films released	Punjabi films released	Other languages	Total films released
1961	30 (88%)	4 (12%)	0	34
1971	34 (43%)	39 (49%)	6 (8%)	79
1981	24 (28%)	45 (52%)	18 (20%)	87

Source: Pakistan Film Magazine, https://pakmag.net/film.

Punjabi films. To illustrate, in 1961, only a few films were released in Punjabi; by 1971, Punjabi had begun to overtake Urdu in terms of film production, and in 1981 the number of Punjabi films released was nearly double that of Urdu films, as shown in table 10.1. It is also notable that the number of films made in other regional languages (mostly Pashto, but others such as Siraiki) grew significantly during these years, further showing the destabilization of Urdu's dominance as the language of cinema, and the general increase in the linguistic diversity of film production during these decades. *Pehlwanji in London* heralded the beginning of one of the key historical currents of Pakistani cinema, presaging later films by its emphasis on the main character's *panjābiyat* and the linkage between patriarchal morality and ethnic identity in the face of threats from national and transnational others.

Manoj Kumar's noted 1970 film *Purab aur Paschim*, made during the same period as *Pehlwanji in London,* squarely positions a nationalist Indian/Hindu identity in opposition to an immoral, even depraved, Western one. In contrast, *Pehlwanji in London* actually has a remarkably ambivalent relationship with the West and with Pakistanis settled there, although the same stereotypes that construct it as other to Pakistan, more specifically to Punjab, exist throughout the film. In fact, the film provides a more exotic, voyeuristic view of London and Britain than the later *Jatt in London*. There are, of course, extended montages of London scenery throughout the film, perhaps most notably during the segment when Aslam first arrives in London. Beginning in Heathrow Airport, the camera lingers on the modernist architecture and bustling crowds filled with European faces. We see Aslam leave the airport, conspicuous in his colorful *lācā-kurtā* and *pagṛī*.[4] He walks through the crowded airport, craning his neck and conspicuously taking in the sights; even this body language separates him from the other pedestrians, who are going about their business. Exiting the airport, he crosses a busy street and, disoriented, almost stumbles into traffic. He shows a piece of paper (on which his uncle's address is written) to a white woman, who shakes her head that she does not know where it is located. As Aslam walks off, the camera zooms to the ground to show that he has dropped the paper. The next few shots show him wandering past various London landmarks: Piccadilly Circus, the Tower Bridge, and Parliament. Eventually he ends up on a double-decker bus, and the camera cuts between shots of his face, somewhat distressed, in the bus window and then the bus passing more famous landmarks: the Marble Arch, Trafalgar Square, and again Parliament. Finally, he ends up seated on the ground at the feet of the statue of Cupid in Regent's Park, mournfully eating a snack out of a paper envelope. In a voice-over, his internal monologue speaks to the alienation he feels:

> سیانیاں نے نٹھیک ہی آکھیا اے: انسان نوں اپنے دیس دی قدرپردیس جا کے معلوم ہندی اے۔ جس دن دا ایس ملک اچ آیا آں، نا ہی کھوہ دا تازہ پاٹی نصیب ہویا اے، تے نا ہی بداماں دی سردائی ملی اے، تے نا ہی لسی پیتی اے۔ کجھ سمجھ نئیں اوندی، گورے ایتھے کیویں زندہ لگے پھردے نے!
>
> *SiāniāN ne ṭhīk hī ākhiyā ai. Insān nūN apṇe desh dī kadar pardes jā ke mālūm hundī ai. Jes din dā es mulk ich āyā, nā khū dā tāzā pāṇī nasīb hoyā ai, te nā hī badāmāN dī sardāī milī ai, te nā hī lassī pītī ai. Kujjh samajh naīN aundī, gore etthe kiweN zindā lage phirde ne!*
>
> The wise ones were right: A person discovers the value of his own country when he goes to a foreign land. Since I came to this country, I haven't been blessed with fresh well water, nor have I found any chilled sweet almond milk, nor have I had any *lassi*.[5] I can't understand how white people survive here!

Unlike many depictions of the diaspora in South Asian cinema, the film portrays diasporic Pakistanis in a relatively complex manner. For example, Aslam's uncle critiques his wife's and daughter's westernized ways (staying out late with a man, wanting to choose one's own spouse). Although he himself has settled in Britain and done well for himself financially, he wants the women in his family to conform to Pakistani sexual mores.[6] Additionally, the minor character Hashmat provides another positive example of a foreign-settled Pakistani character. Although he has settled in London and been financially successful, he brings his daughter Nasreen back to Pakistan to be married, thus securing an honorable match with his friend's son Iqbal. When it is revealed that the friend has also promised to marry his daughter to Aslam, provided that Aslam can come up with a dowry of twenty-five thousand rupees, Hashmat roundly criticizes his friend for his dishonorable behavior. Both of the foreign-settled characters show that it is possible for Pakistanis to assimilate to a certain extent to Western culture (for example, unlike Aslam, both wear Western clothes), but they must still maintain their honor by controlling the sexuality of their wives and daughters.[7] That control, however, is equivocal; ultimately a paternal blessing legitimizes the love match, and the mother's desire for her daughter to have the right to choose her life partner is fulfilled.

Again, a useful comparison can be drawn here with *Purab aur paschim*, which was released just a year before *Pehlwanji in London*. The character of Ruby is somewhat analogous with Preeti in *Purab Aur Paschim*. Both are shown as thoroughly westernized children of South Asian immigrants to Britain, who associate much more strongly with the country where they grew up than with that of their heritage. Kumar's film frames this more explicitly as moral decay compared to *Pehlwanji*, but both women are depicted as transgressing traditional Eastern ideals of modesty and femininity. Both wear Western clothes and even have dyed blond hair; Ruby stays out late with her boyfriend and raises her voice to her father when he objects, and Preeti drinks and smokes and hangs out with hippies. Ultimately both do end up married to matches with parental blessing, after initial objections. However, Preeti's filmic destiny is to leave London, return to India, marry the not-so-subtly-named hero Bharat,[8] and conform to ideals of Indian (Hindu, upper-caste) womanhood.

Ruby's story is slightly less predictable. From the beginning of the film she insists, with the support of her mother, that she be allowed to marry her boyfriend, Jaidi. However, when she meets him and asks him to elope with her, he refuses on the grounds that she is too "modern" and *āzād khayāl* (free-thinking) for him. He tells her, "Every free-thinking man in the world can be friends with a girl who runs away from home, but he can't accept her as his wife."[9] Further, he tells her that her actions are motivated by selfishness rather than love. It is only when the supremacy both of Punjabi masculinity and also of the patriarchal system of control over marriage are reasserted that their union can go ahead. First, Jaidi attempts to save Ruby from gangsters who attack her, even though he has ostensibly left her; it is his duty as a Punjabi man to defend her honor. Aslam arrives to help just in the nick of time and remarks, "This means that in Jaidi's chest too that very same blood is flowing that has been made red by the water of Punjab." Next, Aslam relinquishes his claim on her as his fiancée (they were engaged as children) by calling her his sister and thereby reframing their relationship into one that cannot be sexual. Finally, Aslam intercedes with her father, his uncle, on Jaidi and Ruby's behalf. Once the nephew convinces his uncle (never mind that his wife had been arguing for the same thing for the duration of the film), Ruby and Jaidi are reunited, and their family formally accepts them as a couple. Unlike Preeti, Ruby did not have to be redeemed by rediscovering her Eastern morality, and she is able (once the structures of the patriarchy are also on board) to choose her own life partner and remain in the West.

Partha Chatterjee has famously argued that as part of a gendered postcolonial nationalism, women are relegated to the domestic sphere, and only men are able to access the public sphere. Women are entrusted with piety and tradition, and they "must not lose their essentially spiritual (that is, feminine) virtues; they must not, in other words, become *essentially* Westernized" (Chatterjee 2001, 159). Ruby stands in stark contrast to this pattern, eventually bowing to one patriarchal norm that says she can only marry with her father's blessing but contradicting others that would not allow her to choose her own partner or spend a great deal of time alone with him before marriage. Scholars such as Gayatri Gopinath (2005) and Jigna Desai (2004) note that transnational cinema, along with confronting and confounding physical and geographic borders, also generates new possibilities for reconfigurations of race, gender, and sexuality. Subnational and regional cinemas such as Punjabi cinema provide fertile ground for these possibilities to develop and for the frequent portrayal of alternative relationships, moralities, and objects of desire that do not necessarily conform to a simplistic nation-Other, inside-outside dichotomy.

MAULA JATT AND THE PROXY STATE

The 1981 *Jatt in London*,[10] sometimes referred to as *Maula Jatt in London*,[11] directed by Yunus Malik, is a sequel to the 1979 genre-defining blockbuster *Maula Jatt*.[12] The titular character of *Maula Jatt* is a rural strongman whose arch nemesis is Nuri Natt, an equally strong member of a rival clan who roams Punjab causing trouble and looking for a worthy adversary. At the end of *Maula Jatt*'s epic battle between the Jatts and the Natts, Nuri surrenders to Maula by chopping off his own leg. *Jatt in London* picks up not long after these events; Maula is on trial for murdering fifty of the Natt clan, but nobody will testify against him. Still, he is considered too dangerous to keep in Pakistan, so he is sentenced to be exiled. However, no country seems willing to take him; Britain, India, Russia, and the United States all refuse, but Maula decides to go to London anyway. Upon his arrival, however, they imprison Maula and confiscate his *gaṇḍāsā* (long-handled ax),[13] which is put in Madam Tussaud's Wax Museum. Eventually Maula tangles with Nuri's older brother Dara, who has settled in London and become a gangster, and the feud resumes. In the final confrontation, Maula is unarmed and somewhat handicapped against Dara, who has an ax, a submachine gun, and a gang of armed men, but manages to hold out until his fiancée Mukho restores his *gaṇḍāsā* to him. Ultimately, Maula's former enemy Nuri arrives from Pakistan in the nick of time, taking sides with Maula against his own brother and gunning down Dara just as Dara is about to shoot Maula. Nuri tells the police, who (as ever) have arrived just as the fight is ending, that instead of the *gaṇḍāsā*, they should put Dara's dead body in the museum, with a sign that repeats the famous dialogue: "Maula won't die until Maula [also an epithet of God] himself kills him."

As in most Punjabi films of this genre, which Ali Khan and Ali Nobil Ahmad have referred to as Pakistani "natural horror" (Ahmed and Khan 2010), the apparati of the Pakistani state are generally portrayed as weak, ineffective, and even irrelevant to the concerns of the main characters. Police in particular, but also elements of the larger legal and political system, are corrupt, dishonorable, and easily fooled or evaded by both heroes and villains alike. They have little impact, positive or negative, on the outcome of conflicts, and always seem to arrive too late to break up a fight. Even when they do manage to stop a conflict, rather than turning to the police for support or justice, the characters in conflict choose to get rid of them as quickly as possible. For instance, in *Jatt in London*, Dara and Maula have encountered each other and begun fighting on the sidewalk of a residential street; Maula has been wounded. The police arrive and ask him (in English translated simply, perhaps so Punjabi-speaking audience members can more easily understand), "Who kill you?"[14] This is the exchange that follows:

POLICEMAN: Who kill you?

DARA (TAUNTINGLY TRANSLATES FOR MAULA):

اوئے پچھدا ای تینوں کِنّےِ ماریا اے؛ (ایہنوں دس) کہ تینوں میں ماریا اے۔

Oye pucchdā ī tainūN kinne māriyā ai; (ohnūN das) ki tainūN maiN māriyā ai.

He is asking who has struck you; [tell him][15] that I struck you.

MAULA (TO POLICEMAN):

اوئے کُبّے نوں کھارے چڑھنا کدوں نصیب ہویا فرنگیا! ایہنے تے صرف میری جان بچائی اے!

Oye kubbe nūN khāre caṛhṇā kadoN nasīb hoyā firangiyā! Ehne te sirf merī jāṇ bachāyī ai!

Hey whitey, a hunchback never gets a chance to get married![16] He has just saved my life!

POLICEMAN (TO A SUBORDINATE): Mr. Mike, bring the stretcher!

MAULA (TO DARA):

ایہ جٹّ دا پنڈا اے نتّا! ایہنے کُہاڑی دے ڈکاں نال نیّو ڈگنا!

Eh Jaṭṭ dā piṇḍā ai Nattā! Ehne kuhāṛī de dakkāN nāḷ nayyo ḍigṇā!

This is the body of a Jatt, you Natt! It's not going to fall just with the blows of an ax!

DARA:

اوئے حالے پھٹ گرم نے، ٹھنڈے ہوئے تے تینوں دارا یاد آوے گا۔

Oye hāle phaṭ garam ne, ṭhaṇḍe hoye te tainūN Dārā yād āwegā.

Right now your wounds are still warm. When they cool down you'll remember Dara.

MAULA (the policemen bring the stretcher; Maula knocks it to the ground)

مینوں کسے قبرستان دا راہ وی وخا دے نتّا! تھوڑے دناں تک اکّ مردہ دفنان دی مینوں لوڑ پینی وا!

MainūN kise kabristān dā rāh wī wikhā de Nattā! Thoṛe dināN tak ikk murdā dafnāṇ dī mainūN loṛ paiṇī ū!

Show me the way to some graveyard too Natta! In a few days I'll be needing to bury a corpse!

DARA:

چل صدقے جاواں اوہ قبرستان تینوں میں آپ وخانا آں۔

Chaḷ sadke jāwāN oh kabristān tainūN maiN āp wikhāṇā āN.

Come on, my darling, I'll show you that graveyard myself.

(To policemen)

Okay, officer, thank you, you go. Thank you!

The two then walk off arm in arm as though they were friends, leaving the befuddled police behind. Rather than rely on state-supported systems of law and order, the two actively and purposefully choose to keep their conflict in their own moral and juridical sphere. Ahmad and Khan (2010, 154) write, "The action film is generally regarded as reflective of the brutality of the Zia years. . . . [W]hat is perhaps most striking is its deeply ambiguous relationship with the Pakistani nation-state." This ambiguity was perhaps not an entirely new development of the reign of the dictator Zia-ul-Haq, but this period certainly saw heightened tensions between cinema and state (Ahmad and Khan 2010, 154).[17] *Maula Jatt* was actually banned by the new Zia government shortly after it was released, as it was seen as violent and subversive, though the ban was eventually lifted, and the film went on to run for five years (Ahmad and Khan 2010). Overtly, the Pakistani state barely makes an appearance in *Jatt in London*, as most of the action takes place in London, and no Pakistani officials or police are seen after the first few minutes of the film, when Maula is exiled. However, I argue that in London, the British police and legal system can easily be read as a proxy for their Pakistani equivalents. This manifests in a few different ways.

Similar to criminal justice agents in Pakistan-set Punjabi films, the British law enforcement characters in *Jatt in London* play a marginal role in the film's central conflicts. Like their Pakistani counterparts, the police and courts in *Jatt in London* almost exclusively speak Urdu. When Maula is first brought up before a British court, the judge requests that the proceedings be conducted in Urdu so the accused may understand. This makes it easier for the audience to understand as well; most Punjabi speakers in Pakistan understand Urdu fairly well, since it is generally taught in schools and is the national language of government, bureaucracy, and business. The Urdu used in this courtroom is noticeably foreign-accented, in the way that English speakers' accents are generally parodied in South Asian films, here performing the Otherness of the foreign state. When English is used in a few instances in the film, it is simplified to the point where it is almost ungrammatical—"Who kill you?"—in ways that seem to make it easier for viewers with limited fluency in English to understand. However, the filmmakers could just as easily had the police and courts speak Punjabi, which would have been perfectly understandable to the audience; why, then, have they chosen Urdu? In Pakistan, Urdu is closely associated with government, education, and domains of power—domains that exclude Punjabi. Thus, the choice of Urdu not merely serves to make this dialogue intelligible but also positions the British police and courts in a sociolinguistic hierarchical domain echoing that of their Pakistani counterparts. This differentiates them from the Punjabi-speaking characters and reinforces the linguistic hierarchies experienced by the film's viewers in their daily lives.

More so than in *Pehlwanji in London*, the characters in *Maula Jatt* are portrayed as irrevocably and essentially different from their Western surroundings. Even Dara Natt, who has supposedly been settled in Britain for many years and has made a great deal of money with his illegal operations, is never shown wearing Western clothes (although he does sport a pair of shiny aviators). Like Maula, he always appears wearing *lācā-kurtā*, a style of dress that was becoming much less common in urban Pakistan at that time. To the extent that the surroundings are discussed by the film's characters, the attitude seems to be that London is exotic and foreign, and somewhat morally suspect, but even its modern delights pale in comparison with the wholesome traditional life of Punjab. There are a few montages of London scenery, particularly in the songs, which are shot not only in London but also in Brighton and Blackpool, and many key scenes are also shot outside in various residential and commercial neighborhoods. Several of the songs use these exotic European backdrops to celebrate the superiority of Punjab and Punjabis. Wandering along the beach at Brighton and on the streets of central London, surrounded by Western onlookers, the heroine Mukho sings:

ولایتی سڑکاں تے اسّیں پیار پنجابی کرنا
Wilaitī saṛkāN te assīN pyār Panjābī karṇā
On European streets we are going to make Punjabi love.[18]

Later in the film she further praises Maula's prowess, noting that Londoners bow down and pay respect to him:

سارے لندن نے جھک کے سلام کیتا اے، اوہ مولے جٹ نے کھڑاک سرے عام کیتا اے
Sāre Landan ne jhukk ke salām kītā ai oh maule jaṭṭ ne khaṛāk sare ām kītā ai
All of London has bowed and saluted him, Maula Jatt has roared out in the open.[19]

Finally, alone in the middle of a nightclub, having had the Western music shut off and pushed the Londoners[20] to the side, she warbles:

> جہڑے کہندے لندن سارے دنیا کولوں سوہنا، پنڈی لہور کراچی اوہنے اجے نئیں تکیا ہونا۔۔۔پنج دریاواں ورگا کوئی دیس نظر نئیں آیا!
>
> *Jehṛe kehnde London sāre duniyā koḷoN sohṇā Piṇḍī Laur Karāchī ohne aje naīN takiyā hoṇā . . . panj daryāwāN wargā koī des nazar naīN āyā!*
>
> Those who say London is the most beautiful place in the world / Must not yet have seen Pindi, Lahore, and Karachi. . . . I've never seen a land like that of the five rivers![21]

Throughout the film there are references to the lax sexual morality of Westerners, but unlike in *Pehlwanji in London*, there are almost no visual representations of, for example, women in skimpy clothing or couples touching in public. This is likely due to the stricter censorship practices that had come about since Zia's rise to power. The absence of these images is replaced by verbal description: Maula comments as he sits on a beach that "even the water here is shameless," hinting at the specter of scantily clad bathers that cannot be shown on screen. As far as the Punjabi women are concerned, they are as concerned with upholding their own unquestioned moral order as the men are—in fact, perhaps even more so. It is the thought of Maula surrounded by desirous white women that impels Mukho to go find him in London, where she sings the praises of the chaste Punjabi way of loving. In general, the East-West tensions are markedly less pronounced in *Maula Jatt in London,* with London merely serving as a change in backdrop for the continuation of the original Jatt-Natt feud, rather than representing competing ideologies that have the potential to alter the characters' very identities. There are no characters who face any sort of internal identity crisis, or indeed who show more than the smallest amount of hybridity in identity markers such as language, dress, discourse, or attitude.

The seeming lack of concern for the diasporic and transnational experiences of cultural conflict and alienation is perhaps the most striking aspect of the film and sets it apart from a host of other foreign-set South Asian films. To better understand why this may be so, it can be useful to look at the Pakistani political context at the time. First, through the repeated assertion of the superiority of *panjābiyat,* Punjabi masculinity, and morality centered around very specific Punjabi notions of honor and vengeance, the film strikes an overt postcolonial blow against notions of Western, and specifically British, supremacy. Maula is so powerful and dangerous that when he is exiled at the beginning of the film, he is denied entry by a host of powerful Western countries, including the United States. His likeness and *gaṇḍāsā* are said to be world famous; they are housed with great ceremony in Madame Tussaud's Wax Museum, which here is conflated with the Tower of London. Ultimately, it is Maula's *gaṇḍāsā*, that rich Punjabi symbol of masculine violence, which defeats even Dara's submachine gun, a more technologically sophisticated, "modern" weapon. Throughout, the supremacy of Punjab—a rural, hypermasculine, and perhaps premodern Punjab—is never challenged, even by Westerners and by UK-settled Pakistanis, which leads one to believe that the real foil for Punjab here is not Britain or the West at all. Rather, it seems that this display of *panjābiyat*—of the dominance, masculinity, and power of a *lācā*-clad rural figure such as Maula Jatt—speaks to a populism that had been long suppressed by the Pakistani state and had recently been dealt another blow by the ousting and execution of Zulfikar Ali Bhutto and the takeover by Zia's right-wing regime.

CONCLUSION: SUBNATIONAL CINEMATIC ARTICULATIONS OF TRANSNATIONALISM

In this chapter, I have offered analyses of the ways that *Pehlwanji in London* and *Jatt in London* incorporate and subvert popular understandings of diasporic identities and experiences. During the ten years between the two films, a series of events occurred that destabilized internal and external politics, most notably the breakup of East and West Pakistan and Zia's violent coup, which significantly altered Pakistan's relationship with the West as well as the political situation within the country. This change is evident in the different ways the two films deal with moral, ideological, and political conflicts between the West, Punjab, and the Pakistani nation-state. Its relationship to the last of these is perhaps the most remarkable, as it stands in contrast to most analyses of the diasporic films of Hindi popular cinema, which tend to emphasize the moral supremacy of the nation-state. Although a larger regional survey may be necessary, it is possible and perhaps unsurprising that this would be a common feature of subnational diasporic films. For instance, as Gill (2012) describes, Punjabi cinema in India boasts a large subgenre of what he refers to as NRI (Non-Resident Indian) films. Although the relationship of Punjab the province to the larger nation-state is completely different in India than it is in Pakistan, Gill notes that "the popular cinematic articulations of diaspora seem to be exclusively invested in reproducing regional culture and reinforcing its tradition within the diaspora. . . . [T]he diasporic circulation of Punjabi films seems to more closely resemble its 'glocalization' under which highly localized representation[s] are further accentuated and projected into transnational geographical and cultural spaces" (124). As in the two films I have discussed, ultimately the supremacy of Punjabi culture and *panjābiyat* is upheld, even where its relationship to the postcolonial nation-state remains somewhat ambiguous.

In recent years, Pakistani cinema has moved into what is frequently framed as a phase of revival or renaissance, with films taking new directions to explore both transnationalism (such as *Zinda bhaag* [Gaur and Nabi 2013] or *Janaan* [Jafri 2016]) as well as interregional relationships within Pakistan (*Karachi to Lahore* [Rauf 2015] and *Lahore se aagey* [Rauf 2016]). Significantly, the recent film revival has largely excluded Punjabi and Pashto cinema; most of the new films are being made in Karachi (not Lahore or Peshawar), and they are produced in Urdu rather than in regional languages. Although the exact ramifications of these developments remain to be seen, such changes within the film industry have clear implications for the way it will deal with transnational imaginings and diasporic identities. The relationships of homeland to the diaspora, the familiar to the strange, the local to the global, are constantly in flux, emergent and mutable. Moreover, as Stuart Hall (1990, 235) famously pointed out, diasporic identities themselves are "those which are constantly producing and reproducing themselves anew, through transformation and difference." There is a definite filmic pleasure that lies in the bombastically exaggerated differences between Pakistan and the West that are portrayed in *Pehlwanji in London* and *Jatt in London*, but they also must be read as products of a *subnational* rather than a national cinema (moreover, one that has had a historically complex and ambivalent relationship with the postcolonial nation-state), and thus offer a subnational and perhaps even subaltern perspective on transnationalism and globalization.

NOTES

1 Cf. Shackle 1970; Mansoor 1993; Rahman 1996; Kirk 2014, 2016.

2 Cf., for instance, Mishra 2002; Kaur 2002; Kaur and Sinha 2005; Rao 2010; Mazumdar 2011; Gill 2012.

3 *Akhāṛā* (Punjabi: اکھاڑا) can refer to either the actual wrestling ring or the training center of a given group or school of wrestlers.

4 *Lācā* (Punjabi: لاچا) is a floor-length unstitched loincloth that serves as a visual marker of Punjabi, and in later representations, specifically *rural*, identity. *Kurtā* (کرتا) is a long tunic-like shirt worn over it, and *pag* or *pagṛī* (پگ/پگڑی) is a turban, generally elaborately wrapped from a single length of colorful cloth.

5 A traditional South Asian yogurt drink.

6 Although, significantly, his wife criticizes this as hypocrisy, pointing out that he used to dance arm in arm with her in pubs and clubs. This tension is never completely resolved.

7 Honor: *izzat*, *ğairat*; Punjabi: عزت، غیرت

8 Bharat is another name for India.

9 Friendship here implies not just a platonic but potentially a sexual relationship.

10 Jaṭṭ is an agricultural caste (Punjabi: جٹ), alternatively rendered in English as Jut, Jutt, or Jat. For an excellent and detailed analysis of caste and masculinity in Punjabi films, see Sevea 2014.

11 Interestingly, my copy of the film as well as the versions available online show a black smear on the title card that because of its placement appears to be covering the word *Maula* in the title *Maula Jatt in London*. This could either be an accident, some kind of general degradation of the already poor print, or an intentional edit of the name. Some sources do refer to the film as *Maula Jatt in London*, but the sources I take as most authoritative (Mushtaq Gazdar and pakfilms.net) use the shorter version.

12 This film itself is a sequel to Hassan Askari's 1975 hit *Wehshi Jatt*, based on Ahmad Nadeem Qasmi's Urdu short story "Gaṇḍāsa."

13 Punjabi: گنڈاسا

14 The Punjabi verb *mārṇā*/مارنا can mean either to strike or to kill.

15 This section is slightly cut off in my copy of the film.

16 I.e., you aren't even worthy to fight with us.

17 After a 1977 coup, right-wing Islamist dictator General Zia-ul-Haq controlled the government until his suspicious death in a plane crash in 1988.

18 I have translated the verb *pyār karṇā* as literally as possible here, rendering it as "make love"; however, the verb in Punjabi (as historically in English) does not necessarily imply sexual contact, but rather more generally to be romantic with someone. A less literal but perhaps more accurate translation would read, "We will love in the Punjabi way," which when juxtaposed with European streets implies a certain degree of chastity and discretion, avoiding public displays of affection or open touching.

19 For a discussion of roaring (*khaṛāk*) and its relationship to gender, violence, and power, see Kirk 2014; Kirk 2016; and Sevea 2014.

20 One of whom, interestingly, speaks to her in Urdu.

21 I.e., Punjab, the name of which literally translates to five (*panj*/پنج) waters (*āb*/آب), referring to the five major rivers that flow through the region.

REFERENCES

Ahmad, Ali Nobil, and Ali Khan. 2010. "From Zinda Laash to Zibahkhana: Horror and Violence in Pakistani Cinema." *Third Text* 24, no. 1: 149–63.

Akhtar, Jameel, dir. 1970. *Love in Europe*. Lahore: Aurlga Pictures.

Ali, Kamran. 2015. "Cinema and Karachi in the 1960s: Cultural Wounds and National Cohesion." In *Handbook of Religion and the Asian City: Aspiration and Urbanization in the Twenty-First Century*, edited by Peter Van der Veer, 387–402. Oakland: University of California Press.

Alter, Joseph. 1992. *The Wrestler's Body: Identity and Ideology in North India*. Berkeley: University of California Press.

Chakravorty, Pramod, dir. 1966. *Love in Tokyo*. India: Pramod Films.

Chatterjee, Partha. 2001. "The Nationalist Resolution of the Women's Question." In *Post-colonial Discourses: An Anthology*, edited by Gregory Castle, 152–66. New York: Wiley-Blackwell.

Chaudhry, Haider, dir. 1971. *Pehlwanji in London*. Pakistan.

Chopra, Yash, dir. 1995. *Dilwale Dulhaniya Le Jayenge*. India: Yash Raj Films.

Desai, Jigna. 2004. *Beyond Bollywood: The Cultural Politics of South Asian Diasporic Film*. New York: Routledge.

Gaur, Meenu, and Farjad Nabi, dirs. 2013. *Zinda Bhaag*. Pakistan: Matteela Films.

Gazdar, Mushtaq. 1997. *Pakistan Cinema, 1947–1997*. Karachi: Oxford University Press.

Gill, Harjant S. 2012. "Masculinity, Mobility and Transformation in Punjabi Cinema: From *Putt Jattan De* (Sons of Jat Farmers) to *Munde UK De* (Boys of UK)." *South Asian Popular Culture* 10, no. 2: 109–22.

Gopinath, Gayatri. 2005. *Impossible Desires: Queer Diasporas and South Asian Public Cultures*. Durham: Duke University Press.

Hall, Stuart. 1990. "Cultural Identity and Diaspora." In *Identity: Community, Culture, Difference*, edited by Bill Ashcroft, Gareth Griffiths, and Helen Tiffin, 222–37. London: Lawrence and Wishart.

Jafri, Azfar, dir. 2016. *Janaan*. Pakistan: IRK Films.

Jalal, Ayesha. 2014. *The Struggle for Pakistan: A Muslim Homeland and Global Politics*. Cambridge, MA: Harvard University Press.

Kaur, Raminder. 2005. "Cruising on the Vilayeti Bandwagon: Diasporic Representations and Reception of Popular Indian Movies." In *Bollyworld: Popular Indian Cinema through a Transnational Lens*, edited by Raminder Kaur and Ajay Sinha, 309–29. Los Angeles: Sage.

Kaur, Raminder, and Ajay Sinha. 2005. "Bollyworld: An Introduction to Popular Indian Cinema through a Transnational Lens." In *Bollywood: Popular Indian Cinema through a Transnational Lens*, edited by Raminder Kaur and Ajay Sinha, 11–32. Los Angeles: Sage.

Kaur, Ravinder. 2002. "Viewing the West through Bollywood: A Celluloid Occident in the Making." *Contemporary South Asia* 11, no. 2: 199–209.

Kirk, Gwendolyn. 2014. "Language Ideologies and Verbal Art in Pakistani Cinema: The Punjabi Barhak." *Texas Linguistic Forum* 57: 76–85.

———. 2016. "Uncivilized Language and Aesthetic Exclusion: Language, Power and Film Production in Pakistan." PhD diss., University of Texas at Austin.

Kumar, Manoj, dir. 1970. *Purab aur Paschim*. India: VIP Films.

Malik, Yunus, dir. 1981. *Jatt in London*. Lahore, Pakistan.

Mansoor, Sabiha. 1993. *Punjabi, Urdu, English in Pakistan: A Sociolinguistic Study*. Lahore: Vanguard.

Mazumdar, Ranjani. 2011. "Aviation, Tourism and Dreaming in 1960s Bombay Cinema." *BioScope* 2, no. 2: 129–55.

Mishra, Vijay. 2002. *Bollywood Cinema: Temples of Desire*. New York: Routledge.

Noorani, Asif. 2016. "What Pakistan's Film Industry Lost in 1971." *Dawn*, December 11, 2016. https://www.dawn.com/news/1301644.

Rahman, Tariq. 1996. *Language and Politics in Pakistan*. Karachi: Oxford University Press.

Rao, Shakuntala. 2010. "'I Need an Indian Touch': Glocalization and Bollywood Films." *Journal of International and Intercultural Communication* 3, no. 1: 1–19.

Rauf, Wajahat, dir. 2015. *Karachi Se Lahore*. Pakistan: Showcase Films.

———, dir. 2016. *Lahore Se Aagey*. Pakistan: Showcase Films.

Samanta, Shakti, dir. 1967. *An Evening in Paris*. India: Shakti Films.

Sevea, Iqbal. 2014. "'Kharaak Kita Oi!': Masculinity, Caste, and Gender in Punjabi Films." *BioScope* 5, no. 2: 129–40.

Shackle, Christopher. 1970. "Punjabi in Lahore." *Modern Asian Studies* 4, no. 3: 239–67.

Shakoor, Mohammad Ahsan. 2016. "Basant and Pahalwani: Dying Cultural Traditions of Punjab (a Case Study of Lahore)." *Thaap Journal*, 216–31.

11 THE BIRTH OF A CINEMA IN POST-9/11 PAKISTAN

ZEBUNNISA HAMID

OVER THE LAST TWENTY YEARS, PAKISTAN HAS WITNESSED CONtinuous political, social, and economic change. Despite some of the chaos and turmoil experienced in the country during this time, there have also been several new developments. Among them is the emergence of what I refer to as New Pakistani Cinema, or NPC (Hamid 2017). Rather than a revival of cinema in the country, NPC is both the product and a reflection of modern-day Pakistan, and consequently of rapid urbanization, a new cinema audience, the introduction of new cinema technology, the growth of the multiplex, and the resulting evolution of cinema culture. While the first NPC films were not released till 2013, the factors behind the cinema's development began to take root much earlier on, soon after the attacks of September 11, 2001, a defining moment that would also significantly shape the future of Pakistan.

CINEMA IN THE INTERSECTIONS OF LOCAL, TRANSREGIONAL, AND GLOBAL FORCES

Immediately following 9/11, Pakistan was forced to choose a side and either support the war on terror and become a frontline state or risk being isolated from the world community and labeled a pariah. Despite Pakistan's support for and subsequent role in the war on terror, or perhaps more aptly, *because* of it, the country suffered tremendously from internal terrorism in the face of pressure from external actors to do more in the new global fight against terrorism (Puri 2012, 38). However, even while fighting numerous literal and figurative wars, various economic and political initiatives by the government led to a period of growth and development. These included the liberalization of the media and small but significant changes in policy that also had an impact on film—a sector that had often been ignored, if not outright suppressed, in the past. These developments had significant social implications as well, because they created the space for nonradical voices to be heard for the first time since the silencing of such elements in society, especially in the 1980s. Liberal thought clashed with fundamentalism and authoritarianism, illustrating the multiple divides in Pakistani society.

General Pervez Musharraf, who took control of the country two years prior to 9/11 in a bloodless coup and presented himself as more liberal in thought and less authoritative in nature than previous dictators, emphasized the need to promote Pakistan's "soft" image. Realizing the potential in the television sector and pushing a neoliberal philosophy, President Musharraf's government began to deregulate the media in 2002 and issued licenses for private local channels. This can also be seen as an attempt to counter local audiences' continual access to global and Indian media and discourse by promoting local media with local perspectives, and to present an alternative view of Pakistani progress (Khan 2011). This alternative picture was exactly the kind of narrative that the government was keen to promote in order to counter the negative image of the country being shown in the international media following 9/11.

The number of local channels grew exponentially over the next ten years. Urdu television dramas, which had previously been replaced by Indian soap operas as the preferred viewing choice, started to make a comeback. Indian channels, however, continued to be popular among Pakistani audiences, as were the Indian movies and soap operas shown (mostly illegally) on local channels. To stem this, the government banned the broadcasting of Indian channels and content by local cable operators in 2006 (Mir 2006), which cable operators protested, ignored, or briefly complied with before bringing back the banned content due to popular demand. This back-and-forth between regulators and cable (and then Dish TV) operators still exists today. This friction is most pronounced when there is heightened tension between Pakistan and India (at the time of writing this chapter, for example, Indian content is not available in Pakistan, and Pakistani content is not shown in India).

Despite the ban on Indian television programming, the government took a softer approach to Indian films on Pakistani screens. By this point, Pakistan's audiovisual audience had primarily become a television audience, as film studios and cinemas shut down, depleted of their former glory (for more on cinema in Pakistan prior to the 2000s, see chapters by Asdar Ali, Niyogi De, and Kirk in this volume). However, having allowed the screening of three Indian films in the previous year (*BBC News* 2008), Musharraf lifted the ban on Indian films in 2007 (Zaidi 2016). This was a major shift from previous policy regarding Bollywood films in the country.

Many film veterans opposed the screening of Indian films in Pakistani cinemas, which had been banned following the 1965 war between the two countries, arguing that the return of these films would cripple an already struggling industry. India had also banned Pakistani films since 1965, though more recently popular Pakistani television dramas had aired on an Indian channel. Another group, however, took the position that lifting the ban on Indian films was the only way to bring new audiences to local cinemas. Bollywood's popularity in Pakistan had much to do with shared historical, cultural, and linguistic links between the two countries. This group, therefore, lobbied the government for the release of Indian films, claiming that audiences would return, having grown up watching them and being familiar with the music and actors of the industry. This, they argued, would help rebuild the nation's cinemas and local infrastructure. The return of Bollywood films to Pakistani cinemas did what its advocates predicted. When Bollywood films were regularly screened, the demand increased, and new and upgraded cinemas followed (Hamid 2017).

Hollywood, like Bollywood, remained popular in Pakistan, and foreign content held a monopoly in the ever-increasing new cinemas, suggesting the future potential for a viable film culture in the country. Still, the image of a country disintegrating and falling into the hands of radicals was further perpetuated through Hollywood films and television shows that depicted Pakistan as a safe haven for terrorists. In *Thor* (dir. Kenneth Branagh, 2011), the superhero is asked if he has received combat training in Pakistan (among other terror-linked countries). *Zero Dark Thirty* (dir. Kathryn Bigelow, 2012) follows the capture of Osama Bin Laden from a compound in Abbottabad, Pakistan, where locals speak Arabic, a language not spoken in Pakistan (Boone 2013). In *G.I. Joe: Retaliation* (dir. Jon M. Chu, 2013), Pakistan's nuclear weapons are under threat. Similarly, on television, popular shows like *Homeland* (Showtime, season 4, 2014) presented Pakistan as explosive, violent, and on the brink of chaos and anarchy.

Prior to 2013, a handful of local films, produced and released outside of existing systems, led the way for the new cinema that has emerged. In 2007, Pakistani director Shoaib Mansoor, who himself had come from television, released *Khude kay liye* (*KKL*; In the name of God). The film provided a strong critique of fundamentalism and radical Islam in Pakistan, while simultaneously criticizing the racial profiling and extreme interrogation of

Muslims in the United States following 9/11. *KKL* proved to be very popular among local audiences and presented an alternative image of the country through a more liberal or moderate stance and a rejection of radical elements and the attributes that had become associated with Pakistan in the foreign media. Other films included *Khamosh pani* (Silent water, dir. Sabiha Sumar, 2003), *Ramchand Pakistani* (dir. Mehreen Jabbar, 2008), and *Bol* (Speak up, dir. Shoaib Mansoor, 2011). Touching on important social issues, these films introduced Pakistani cinema to different types of storytelling. For example, Mansoor's second film, *Bol*—released around the time digital cinema technology was being introduced in the country—addressed many social issues in Pakistan, including women's rights, and broke local box office records previously set by Indian films.

Beyond their subject matter, these films are important to New Pakistani Cinema for several reasons. *KKL* is a rare example of a local film competing against Bollywood and Hollywood films at a time when foreign content dominated the local box office. The film starred the Indian actor Naseeruddin Shah and was one of the first Pakistan films to get a commercial release in India after 1965 (Schifrin 2008), creating links between Pakistani and Indian cinemas that went beyond the return of Bollywood films to Pakistani screens. New filmmakers were encouraged by the success of films like *KKL* and *Bol*, despite the fact that these were big-budget films, with the former supported by Inter-Services Public Relations (ISPR) of the Pakistani Army (Ahmad 2016). Still, the six NPC films released in 2013 were the first group of films to compete with foreign films for audiences and screen time. Over the next few years, the number of NPC films increased, though Bollywood films often received more favorable screening times because of greater expected box office returns.

New Pakistani Cinema does not, however, produce enough films to keep local cinemas running. Therefore, without being completely dependent on local films, a diverse cinema culture emerged, one that comprised Bollywood, Hollywood, and local films. As a result, this foreign and local content came together to form a new national digital cinema circuit. The films, along with the screening of foreign content, growing demand for the exhibition sector, the introduction of digital cinemas, and the expansion of the local media landscape, all contributed to the emergence of a new cinema and cinema culture in Pakistan. This new screen culture and the various factors discussed here are linked to urbanization and the growth of the middle-class audience.

THE URBAN, MIDDLE-CLASS AUDIENCE AND A NEW VIEWING CULTURE

NPC is a digital, urban cinema that caters to a growing middle class. Conversely, the government's neoliberal agenda accelerated the pace of urbanization and the rise of the middle class, which in turn contributed to the emergence of a new cinema culture in Pakistan. While both hold true, the key is in rapid urbanization and growth, seen especially in the last few decades. Migration from rural areas to cities has increased significantly, reflecting a trend seen worldwide in developing countries. Pakistan's urban population grew from 33 percent (or 44 million) in 1999 to 39 percent (or 73 million) in 2015 (World Bank, "Urban Population"). Concurrently, the per capita income increased from US$465 to US$1,428 (World Bank, "GDP per Capita").

As suggested, while these statistics illustrate the changes taking place in Pakistan, they are also significant for understanding the recent emergence of a new cinema in the country. The middle class in Pakistan is the fifth fastest-growing middle class in Asia (Chun 2010, 13–14), and the rate of urbanization is among the fastest in the world (Runde 2015). Approximately 60 percent of the upper middle class lives in urban areas, representing 20 percent of all urban households in the country (Ghani 2014, 15). Many of those who are a part of this growing middle class are also first- or second-generation migrants from rural areas to the cities. This has resulted in a more socially conservative middle class. Yet many of their actions—such as sending daughters to universities or families going to the cinema—may not always suggest an obviously conservative outlook. As a result, contradictions, tensions, and changing social dynamics that challenge the existing status quo are at play in Pakistan's growing and often overpopulated cities, as internal migration continues to put pressure on infrastructure, capacity, and resources.

One of the most evident challenges to the status quo is the place of women in society. While more women can be seen in public and have joined the workforce, a more conservative society is also on display, further highlighting the existing contradictions. Traditionally confined to the home, more women in urban centers in Pakistan are moving beyond their prescribed roles as wife and mother. As the cost of living goes up, women are frequently required to contribute to the family income, either as the sole provider or as an earning member of the family. As a result, many are moving away from housework and leaving the home to join the workforce, oftentimes to do work that is no longer attractive to men, who are looking to move up the economic and social ladder.

Education has also been a factor behind the changing social dynamics in Pakistan. Under Musharraf, education—like television—was privatized as the government opened institutions of higher education to the private sector. The government was liberal in granting charters for higher education during this time, also allocating funds for public universities. This resulted in a boom in private education at all levels, especially in the Punjab, extending out to the rural areas. Therefore, while financial necessity and economics are contributing factors in bringing women out of the home and into the job market, the growth in education has also contributed to their changing roles. These shifts in society and challenges to the status quo have not gone unnoticed—especially by ultra-conservative elements. These changes, in conjunction with the recent passage of laws for the protection of women's rights, have further highlighted the friction and at times even violent reactions within society, and reflect the transition that modern Pakistan finds itself in today. Such developments and the changing social dynamics discussed here are not only apparent in the audience of New Pakistani Cinema and the growing screen culture but also in the themes and narratives of these contemporary local films.

One of the demands of a growing middle class is for different forms of entertainment suitable for women and families. This can be particularly challenging in countries like Pakistan, where public spaces are limited and extremely gendered, with men largely dominating existing spaces. Thus, cinemas play a significant role in the development of suitable public spaces for families. Since the 1970s and especially the 1980s, cinemas in Pakistan had been perceived as masculine venues, where the presence of women (whether in the audience or on screen) would elicit excitement, stares, and comments. However, with traditional cinemas unable to support the sound and picture quality newer Bollywood and, in particular, Hollywood films required (especially 3-D films, whose popularity was quickly rising), digital cinema technology become a necessity, with the bulk of the national digital circuit box-office revenue coming from cinemas in Lahore, Karachi, and Rawalpindi/Islamabad. This also pushed distributors to choose the larger cities as the main target for new films and further suggests the multiple divides that fractured film audiences in Pakistan as a result of geography, class, and access to technology (Hamid 2017).

The number of digital cinemas in Pakistan has grown exponentially, with over ninety screens operating across the country as a result of the reintroduction of Indian films to Pakistani screens and the spread of new cinema technology. Within the current scenario, the differences between the more urban, middle-class, digital-cinema audience and those of traditional cinemas, especially in smaller towns and rural areas, have become even more evident. Many multiplexes are located in shopping malls in more affluent parts of cities with American-style concession stands and ticket prices almost twice that in traditional cinemas. The new digital screens, contained within secure and clean premises, provide an alternative space for families of a particular class that had left the cinema halls and turned to television and home entertainment. Therefore, the growing urban middle class is particularly important for Pakistan's new cinema, as they form the bulk of the multiplex audience, given the locations of many of these new cinemas, the facilities available, and the cost of tickets (Hamid 2017).

NPC IMAGINARIES AND NARRATIVES

As the exhibition sector grew, private television channels saw the potential for the development of this new film industry in Pakistan and began to set up their own film production and distribution wings. The first example of this was Geo Films, which ran under the banner of "the revival of Pakistani cinema" and was behind such earlier films as *KKL* and *Bol*. Other networks followed suit, and the links between the television industry and film became more pronounced. At the same time, the opening of new screens and the steady import of foreign films provided new opportunities for people who aspired to work in film but previously had seen no other option than to turn to television. As a result, much of the support for the new film industry in the country—financial, technical, and personnel—came from television (Hamid 2017).

Many filmmakers, for example, have links with television, including Shoaib Mansoor and Mehreen Jabbar (*Ramchand Pakistani* and *Dobara phir se* [Again once again, 2016]). Other first-time filmmakers worked as ad and music video directors before they moved into film. While Pakistan's new cinema industry was able to grow rapidly with the support of television, this posed other problems, as television networks had begun to function as large media houses, bringing a particular corporate culture with them. At the same time, television is a technically different medium of storytelling, and NPC films have been criticized as large-screen versions of Pakistani television dramas.

Despite such criticisms, NPC filmmakers have their own stories to tell and counternarratives to present. Often global and regional in nature yet local in perspective, and representing the social, political, and economic worlds the filmmakers find themselves in, these films bring a transnational element of storytelling to Pakistani cinema. For example, the films of the emerging years of this cinema, between 2013 and 2015, often reacted and responded to socioeconomic and political changes in the country over the last fifteen years. These films explored various themes and issues. While a few touch on religion and terrorism, most address concerns of personal security and survival—both physical and financial. Through stories centered on love, family, friendship, and individual struggle, NPC filmmakers have dealt with issues ranging from migration to the clash between modernity and traditional ways of life. These various narratives reflect both the imaginaries and preoccupations of today's filmmakers and modern-day Pakistan.

These films also feature a diverse range of female characters, many of which are strong, independent women, often working and, like their male counterparts, dreaming of a better life. Yet, unlike some of the men in these films, the women are empowered by their freedom, take pride in their work, and confront the obstacles they face more pragmatically. Two female characters that bring these qualities to life are Rubina (Amna Illyas) in *Zinda bhaag* (Run for your life, dir. Meenu Gaur and Farjad Nabi, 2013) and Amber (Soniya Hussain) in *Moor* (Mother, dir. Jami, 2015). Rubina runs her own soap business in Lahore and finds creative ways to promote it. She has her own aspirations and desires but approaches them practically, an approach she encourages in her love interest, Khaldi (Khurram Pataras). However, his obsession with leaving the country in the hope of working abroad consumes him to the point that he is willing to pursue illegal means and give up everything, including Rubina, to reach his goal.

In *Moor*, Amber is shown working in an office in Karachi, caring for her father, and moving around the city freely on her own. Ehsaan (Shaz Khan), the man Amber was in a relationship with, however, is spiraling into despair as he negotiates the death of his mother while struggling to make a life for himself in a city that is not his home. As Ehsaan also turns to illegal means of making money, Amber encourages him to find an honest living. Ehsaan, however, sees no other way and rejects Amber's advice and her attempts to help him. The image of the struggling young man in these two films, as well as other NPC films, is a shift away from the hypermasculinity on display in many Pakistani films of earlier eras. The strong female leads in many NPC films today are also a departure from the damsel-in-distress notion perpetuated in film as well as Pakistani television dramas, despite criticism of the similarities between the two mediums.

These films reflect not only changing social dynamics and shifts in traditional gender roles, but also the impact of urbanization and migration on the youth of the country through increased competition for jobs and limited prospects of upward mobility. For example, in the dark comedy and surprise box office success *Na maloom afraad* (Unknown persons, dir. Nabeel Qureshi, 2014), Moon (Mohsin Abbas Haider), while attempting to leave the country for Dubai, ends up in Karachi, where he remains, struggling to pay rent from his salary at the electricity company. With his two companions, also out of luck and struggling to make ends meet, he pursues an elaborate scam to make money, which includes taking advantage of chaos and unrest in the city.

Rather than being simply a motif, the city is perhaps one of the most prominent elements in NPC films, and a construct through which NPC and other cinemas of the developing world can be compared. With both undertones and overt depictions of violence, the widening gap between the rich and the poor, and the growing uncertainty and insecurity felt by its inhabitants, the city in NPC films is also representative of global urban developing centers such as Mexico City, Mumbai, and Manila, and thus lends itself to the idea of a transnational cinematic city. As a site where stories of hope and fear, love and loss, unfold, the transnational cinematic city serves as both the backdrop and impetus for some of today's most pressing issues, such as migration.

At the same time, the city is also a shared element between different types of NPC films, which can loosely be divided into two categories: social realism, or issue-driven films, and commercial, or entertainment-driven, films. While genres sometimes overlap in terms of themes and techniques, social realist films deal with the prevalent social, political, and economic issues in the country and take more of an art-house approach in their storytelling and art direction. These films have received critical acclaim and been screened at international film festivals, as well as received local recognition as Pakistan's official Oscar submissions. Commercial, or entertainment-driven, cinema tends to be much louder and closer to the song-and-dance tradition of Indian melodrama. The popularity of these films at the local box office is not surprising, given the links between Indian and Pakistani cinemas and audiences.

However, even commercial films marketed as pure entertainment have addressed social issues and stereotypes. For example, though *Karachi se Lahore* (From Karachi to Lahore, dir. Wajahat Rauf, 2015) is a comedy, it breaks stereotypes by showing the female lead as the only girl among boys on a road trip. This type of interaction between men and women would not be considered the norm in Pakistan. In *Ho mann jahaan* (Be where your heart is, dir. Asim Raza, 2016), a film about love and friendship, a woman rebels against her conservative husband, who disapproves of the life she has made for herself and their daughter as an artist. Their daughter wants to pursue her music, and rather than give into her father's demands, she asks him to accept her as she is. Here the clash between tradition and modernity, between conservative and liberal values, is highlighted. The film also hints at the possibility of a relationship between an older woman and a younger man. Such commercial films respond to pressure on local content to be successful in the box office and sustain the exhibition sector, and suggest that as New Pakistani Cinema evolves it may continue to take on commercial characteristics. As a result, more filmmakers may forsake social realism and issue-driven narratives for conventional entertainment films. However, recent films suggest that even as commercial cinema takes precedence over other factors, like cinema all over the world, some realist elements will remain as filmmakers continue to respond to their environment.

BORDER-ENFORCING POLITICS AND NPC GROWTH

The continued growth of New Pakistani Cinema is in many ways a hostage to the state of India-Pakistan politics and relations. Before films can be released on local screens, distributors must get the approval of the censor boards. The censor boards may order certain cuts before the film can be certified for release or deny the certificate for a film they find to contain "objectionable" content. Further confusion can arise from the fact that there are currently three censor boards in Pakistan—the Central Board of Film Censors (CBFC), the Sindh Board of Film Censors (SBFC), and the Punjab Film Censor Board (PFBC). While technically individual boards can approve the screening of films in their provinces regardless of the action taken by the other censor boards, they often follow the decision of the Central Board, especially when a Bollywood film has been deemed "anti-Pakistani" or "anti-Muslim" and thus does not get the required certification.

Indian films have often come under greater scrutiny from the censor boards, and the fate of these films on Pakistani screens can be determined by issues of religion and politics, as in times of crisis or rising tension it is the arts that suffer first on both sides of the border. For example, the Indian film *Raees* (Baron, dir. Rahul Dholakia, 2017), starring Pakistani actress Mahira Khan and Indian superstar Shah Rukh Khan, was banned in Pakistan for what the censors found to be a negative portrayal of Muslims (Boone 2017). Yet audiences in Pakistan tend to react differently from policy makers and politicians, often expressing disappointment when a particularly anticipated film is not screened in local cinemas or when both countries decide to close the door on the movement of films, television shows, or actors, which has become more frequent since 2016.

While most Pakistani films have not been distributed in India, the flow of foreign content has not only always been one way across the border from India to Pakistan. Pakistani music, from traditional musicians to Coke Studio Pakistan, and television dramas, including the Urdu dramas of the 1980s as well as more recent ones, have found receptive audiences in India. This is despite the fact that Pakistani channels are not available in India. In 2014, the launch of Zee Zindagi officially brought Pakistani television dramas to Indian audiences for the first time. Dramas such as *Humsafar* (Companion, Hum TV, 2011) and *Zindagi gulzar hai* (Life is a rose garden, Hum TV, 2012), already hugely popular in Pakistan, were very successful in India. The stars of these dramas became household names, which translated into work on the big screen in India. Two such stars were Mahira Khan (*Humsafar*) and Fawad Khan (*Humsafar* and *Zindagi gulzar hai*), who, already having worked in television and film in Pakistan, became involved in big-budget Bollywood films. Though Fawad Khan's first two Indian films, *Khoobsurat* (Beautiful, dir. Shashanka Ghosh, 2014) and *Kapoor and Sons* (dir. Shakun Batra, 2016), were well received in both India and Pakistan, his more recent Bollywood venture, *Ae dil hai mushkil* (This heart is complicated, dir. Karan Johar, 2016), has been controversial.

Following an attack on Indian soldiers in Kashmir in September 2016, tensions between the neighbors rose, as India blamed Pakistan for the deaths of the soldiers. The film and television industries of both countries were immediately affected. The Indian Motion Picture Producers' Association (IMPPA) decided to ban Pakistani artists from working on Indian films. Zee Zindagi also announced it would stop airing Pakistani dramas (Shekhar 2016). Maharashtra Navnirman Sena (MNS), a right-wing political party in India, pushed the issue farther by declaring that Indian films with Pakistani actors should also be banned and warned all Pakistani artists to leave India (Shoard 2016). As a result, with a Pakistani actor cast in the film, the release of *Ae dil hai mushkil* came under threat. The director, while agreeing to conditions set by the MNS for the release of his film, also released a video in which he paid respect to the Indian Army and said he would not work with talent from Pakistan under the current scenario, but asked viewers to support the film because of the hard work of fellow Indians who were part of the project (Ramachandran 2016).

For their part, the Pakistan Exhibitors' Association responded to the ban on Pakistani artists in India and the rising tensions between the two countries by halting the screening of Indian films in Pakistani cinemas. The Pakistan Electronic Media Regulatory Authority (PEMRA) also banned all Indian channels and content from being broadcast in Pakistan (Ramachandran 2016). While these actions did not include a ban on Indian artists working on Pakistani films, the environment created by heightened political tension and the reciprocal bans on television and film could act as a future deterrent for Indian actors as well. Like Naseeruddin Shah in *KKL*, Indian actors have appeared in Pakistani films in the past. Indian or Pakistani films starring actors from both countries generate a lot of interest in the press and among audiences, even when politics between the two countries prevent the official or legal flow of art and cultural goods. Though such actions may hurt the industries involved and jeopardize future collaborations between the two countries, cultural and linguistic links, growing interconnectivity, advancements in technology, piracy, and easy access to YouTube and Netflix mean that existing goods are still easily transferable, especially if there is a demand.

While the new cinema culture in Pakistan has emerged within a relatively short time, its dependence on Bollywood films has become clear, especially given the recent freeze on the screening of Indian films. The impact on the local exhibition sector has been immense, and viewership has fallen dramatically. As a result, all parties invested in Pakistan's new cinema culture now have something at stake, given the rapidly changing political environment. Even when (or if) Bollywood films return to Pakistani screens, there always remains a chance that this could change again (especially while the status of the ban on Pakistani artists in Indian films remains unclear). This poses a problem, not only for local filmmakers but also for exhibitors and distributors, and represents a very serious and real challenge to Pakistani cinema. While different forms of distribution are now available to filmmakers, including Netflix, iTunes, and other nontraditional mediums such as inflight entertainment on airlines, the recent developments in local cinema culture are under threat if cinemas have to shut down because of a lack of content and cinemagoers.

The foundation for a small, new local cinema has been laid with the introduction of the latest cinema technology, the building of new cinemas, and the growth of a multiplex audience. At the same time, the growth of regional-language films and the import of foreign films are just as important for a diverse cinema culture. By seeking the support of the government, industry members have tried to reduce the uncertainty by doing away with arbitrary regulations and giving the import of Indian films greater legal cover, though this comes second to the rise in nationalist sentiment. The onus now falls on the local industry to support and significantly increase film production in order to have a more independent and sustainable industry.

CONCLUSION

The development of New Pakistani Cinema serves as a unique case study, not just because it points to the kinds of factors that led to the emergence of such a cinema, but also because of the different issues that small cinema cultures may face, which can simultaneously support and impede its development. As seen with the example of Pakistani cinema, many of these issues are often based on geographical location. This cinema has grown up in a time of changing global politics, which Pakistan often finds itself at the center of. The focus on terrorism and the Pakistani connection, which has served as a backdrop for some of the foreign content coming from outside, has also created the desire for counternarratives.

The growth of the local media industry and the screening of Bollywood films were a result of neoliberal policies introduced over fifteen years ago. This in turn helped bolster the exhibition sector, which created space for a new local cinema to develop. However, this resulted not only in the new cinema's dependence on Bollywood films but also in a need for positive border politics. Rising tensions lend themselves to kneejerk reactions, often leading to the freezing of ties between the two countries and slowing growth and development in fields that most benefit from mutual cooperation.

At the same time, the growth of Pakistani cities through increased urbanization led to the emergence of a new Pakistani cinema audience and greater demand for more entertainment. This deepened the urban-rural and class divides, together with the technological divide due to the introduction of digital technology and multiplexes to cities and big towns. However, the new digital screens and multiplexes in Pakistan also opened up a public space in which women and families, especially those belonging to the growing middle class, could participate. This brought in a part of the population, namely women, who are frequently excluded from most public spaces in Pakistan. The new urban middle-class audience in Pakistan also shared viewing practices and preferences with transregional and global audiences, rather than local audiences of a different class or those living in rural areas of the same country.

While the films of the new cinema may share transregional and global themes, with an emphasis on the transnational cinematic city, the stories are localized and focus on some of the interconnected issues and events that have directly affected the development of the New Pakistani Cinema. This serves as an example of the changing social dynamics evident in Pakistan, as well as the contradictory relationships between various factors brought in by a new cinema culture. In this way, NPC culture is not only a product of modern-day Pakistan but a reflection of it as well.

These scenarios and examples make it difficult to predict the future of this cinema, as it continues to evolve in an environment of contradictory influences with varied implications. This uncertainty is further compounded through the understanding that internal and external elements play an extensive role in shaping Pakistani cinema. It remains to be seen if the divides and contradictions highlighted here will eventually lessen as the exhibition sector grows, but examples of other cinema cultures and countries suggest this is unlikely. However, changes in technology, falling prices of communication and growing interconnectivity have made the future of cinema difficult to predict. This is especially true during the Covid-19 pandemic era, the impact of which will be felt for years. This makes the study of new cinema cultures, as they evolve in real time, even more fascinating and important.

REFERENCES

Ahmad, Ali Nobil. 2016. "New Cinema from Pakistan: Film, Technology and Media in Transition." In *Cinema and Society: Film and Social Change in Pakistan*, edited by Ali Khan and Ali Nobil Ahmad. Karachi: Oxford University Press.

BBC News. 2008. "India Opens up to Pakistan Film." April 4, 2008.

Boone, Jon. 2013. "*Zero Dark Thirty*: The View from Pakistan." *Guardian*, January 27, 2013.

———. 2017. "Pakistan Bans Hit Bollywood Film *Raees*." *Guardian*, February 7, 2017.

Chun, Natalie. 2010. "Middle Class in the Past, Present and Future: A Description of Trends in Asia." Asian Development Bank Economics Working Paper Series, no. 217. Manila: Asian Development Bank.

Ghani, Jawaid Abdul. 2014. "The Emerging Middle Class in Pakistan: How It Consumes, Earns and Saves." Karachi School for Business and Leadership Working Paper Series, no. 2014-11.

Hamid, Zebunnisa. 2017. "New Pakistani Cinema—Emerging Processes and Imaginaries." PhD diss., SOAS, University of London.

Khan, Hamid Raza. 2011. "Impact of Transnational Media on Broadcasting in Pakistan." *Criterion Quarterly* 5, no. 2. www.criterion-quarterly.com/impact-of-transnational-media-on-broadcastng-in-pakistan.

Mir, Amir. 2006. "Remote Switch-Off." *Outlook Magazine*, February 27, 2006. http://www.outlookindia.com/magazine/story/remote-switch-off/230349.

Puri, Samir. 2012. *Pakistan's War on Terrorism: Strategies for Combating Jihadist Armed Groups since 9/11*. New York: Routledge.

Ramachandran, Naman. 2016. "Karan Johar's 'Ae Dil Hai Mushkil' to Get Release after Political Compromise." *Variety*, October 24, 2016. http://variety.com/2016/film/asia/karan-johar-ae-dil-hai-mushkil-to-get-release-1201898487.

Runde, Daniel. 2015. "Pakistan: The Next Colombia Success Story?" *Forbes*, August 3, 2015.

Schifrin, Nick. 2008. "'Lollywood' Hits Bollywood." *ABC News*, April 4, 2008.

Shekhar, Mimansa. 2016. "Zindagi Channel Not to Have Pakistani Shows, Zee Announces Revamp." *Indian Express*, September 27, 2016. http://indianexpress.com/article/entertainment/television/zee-no-pakistani-shows-zindagi-channel-mns-fawad-mahira-3049325.

Shoard, Catherine. 2016. "Indian Film Producers Ban Pakistani Actors 'For Ever' over Kashmir Crisis." *Guardian*, September 30, 2016.

World Bank. N.d. "Urban Population (% of Total)." Accessed February 5, 2017. http://data.worldbank.org/indicator/SP.URB.TOTL.IN.ZS?locations=PK.

———. N.d. "GDP per Capita (Current US$)." Accessed February 5, 2017. http://data.worldbank.org/indicator/NY.GDP.PCAP.CD?start=1999&view=chart.

Zaidi, Hasan. 2016. "Cutting the Nose to Spite the Face, Again: How the Bollywood Ban Is a Mistake Pakistan Has Made Before." *DAWN Images*, October 16, 2016. http://images.dawn.com/news/1176423.

PART III

FRACTURED GEOGRAPHIES, SOUTH CONNECTIVITIES

12 ZAHIR RAIHAN'S *STOP GENOCIDE* (1971)

A Dialectical Cinematic Message to the World

FAHMIDA AKHTER

THIS CHAPTER PROVIDES A CLOSE ANALYSIS OF THE DOCUMENTARY film *Stop Genocide* (1971), made during the Liberation War of Bangladesh (*Muktijuddho* in Bangla) by the Bangladeshi film director, Zahir Rihan. This chapter also considers examining how this wartime film tackled and negotiated issues of atrocity, memory, and witness. *Stop Genocide* (1971) is widely considered to be the most authentic, artistic, and positive treatment of the Liberation War of Bangladesh (Shahaduzzaman 2009, 31; Qader 1993, 225; Hayat 2011, 40; Mutsuddi 1987, 58; Hasan 2011, 114). As a documentary film, it not only records the events of the war in order to bring the trauma of Bangladeshis to global attention, thereby provoking collective action from the world community to stop the genocide, but it also unmasks the conditions and complexities of the war, in part through a dialectical visual style. By focusing on the inert response of the United Nations (UN) to the barbarous acts committed by Pakistani forces in Bangladesh, the film, to some extent, criticizes the United States for indirectly sponsoring the atrocities of the war by providing arms and ammunition to Pakistan. By foregrounding a series of radical ideas and questions, *Stop Genocide* opposes the narrative articulated by those responsible for maintaining international peace, such as the UN. The film exposed the UN pledge to support peace and human rights as little more than empty rhetoric, through its juxtaposition of horrific scenes from the Liberation War and the Vietnam War. In both cases, the UN failed to protect civilians, contrary to the stated aims of its charter. Consequently, *Stop Genocide* can be

This chapter is a revised version of my previously published article "Framing Pain as Spectacle: The Aesthetics of the Wartime Films of Bangladesh," *Bangladesh Film Archive Journal*, issue 7 (December 2014): 38–50.

interpreted as a plea for justice on the part of subjugated people worldwide and also a representative of the *testimonio* genre, in which "the cry against oppression" is recorded (Peters 2009, 31).

Mahmudul Hossain points out that this short-length film has an "epic wideness" that transforms the film into a visual document of oppressed people beyond its immediate time and place (quoted in Hayat 2007, 146). Chinmoy Mutsuddi (1987, 58) asserts that Raihan perceives and portrays the Liberation War as representative of a broader struggle for freedom that extends beyond Bangladesh and encapsulates the struggles of people around the globe. While agreeing with their views, I would suggest that *Stop Genocide* is an ethical cinematic appeal for humanity and justice that also creates a dialectical cinematic language opposing dominant cinema practices and follows the aesthetics of Third Cinema. I also look at the film's reinscription of the gender stereotypes of nationalist struggle.

LOCATING *STOP GENOCIDE* IN THE FRAMEWORK OF THIRD CINEMA

The "revolutionary conjuncture" from which Third Cinema emerges is the nucleus of *Stop Genocide* (Wayne 2001, 8). The term *Third Cinema* was coined by the Argentinian film directors Fernando Solanas and Octavio Getino (1976) to describe a countercinema voicing a revolutionary spirit and perception during a time of political upheaval. The authors contend that Third Cinema "recognizes in that struggle the most gigantic cultural, scientific, and artistic manifestation of our time, the great possibility of constructing a liberated personality with each people as the starting point—in a word, the decolonization of culture" (47).

This cinematic form is similar to the conception of revolutionized documentary articulated by another Argentinian filmmaker, Fernando Birri. Birri (1997, 86) calls for a cinema that troubles, worries, shocks, and diminishes reactionary consciousness, is antibourgeois at a national level, and at the international level is anticolonial and anti-imperialist. Similarly, at the national level, *Stop Genocide* records the struggle for freedom of a colonized nation, while at the international level it participates in an anti-imperialist struggle by highlighting the contradictory attitudes and actions of the United States and the UN. Ultimately, the film aims to bring about a new society free from all kinds of oppression.

I also argue that by combining the conventions of both realism and a relatively stylized approach, the film is able to register a more complex historical truth than would otherwise have been possible. In echoing the dialectics of Third Cinema, *Stop Genocide* depicts both the genocide that took place in Bangladesh in 1971, and its causes and consequences. The film in this way enables the viewer to engage critically with a point of time in history. Mike Wayne (2001, 8) describes such moments as "a time of reaction and [modern] barbarism," which fosters the emergence of Third Cinema, intervening into the main political process of the epoch. Noting *Stop Genocide*'s revolutionary impetus in calling for change and for a new world, Alamgir Kabir (1979, 49) states that this documentary is an expression of "the relentless struggle for better life being waged all around the world by working men and women," as well as providing evidence of "genocidal crimes" committed against the Bangladeshi people.

Although the film targets mainly the international community and highlights a humanitarian crisis within a larger context, *Stop Genocide* nevertheless also appeals to the national concerns and cultural context of Bangladesh. In spite of its revolutionary impulses, I argue that in its depictions of women, *Stop Genocide* could not throw off the problematic and conventional notion of femininity in which the female body is symbolized in terms of a nationalistic discourse. As I elaborate below, women's sufferings were made to represent both the individual trauma of a vulnerable victim group as well as the collective trauma of Bengalis by symbolizing the subjugation of the "mother nation" brought about by the Pakistani forces. The film also highlights the responsibilities and heroic acts of the *muktijoddha*s (Bengali freedom fighters), portraying them as the brave sons of Bengal fighting valiantly to free the mother nation.

A FEW UNFRAMED FACTS

Made in black and white, the twenty-minute *Stop Genocide* is the first documentary film on the Liberation War to be both made and shown during the war. The director, Zahir Raihan, wrote the screenplay, while Alamgir Kabir wrote and read its English voice-over. Arun Roy did the cinematography, and the editing was done by Debabrata Sengupta. The film was coproduced by the Bangladesh Chalachitra Shilpi-O-Kushali Swahayak Samity (Bangladesh Film Artist-Performers Support Union) and Bangladesh Liberation Council of the Intelligentsia (Kabir 1979, 48). Raihan did not receive support or financial assistance for the film from the Department of Film and Publication of the provisional government of the People's Republic of Bangladesh (Qader 1993, 223).[1] Instead, a number of Bangladeshi film producers and intellectuals who, like Raihan himself, had taken refuge in Kolkata during the war tried to persuade the provisional government to ban *Stop Genocide*. One of these film personalities was Fazlul Haque, who "sent a letter to Syed Nazrul Islam," the acting president of the provisional government in the absence of Shiekh Mujibur Rahman, the first president of Bangladesh and the supreme leader of the Liberation War (Hayat 2007, 143). The letter highlighted that the film did not include a single shot of Sheikh Mujib, that it starts with a speech and image of V. I. Lenin and ends with the playing of the international marching song of the revolutionary proletariat, which, in their view, misconstrued the nature of the conflict (Hayat 2007, 143). However, the members of the government in exile reviewed the film and certified it for exhibition, recognizing its clear historical significance. Concurrently, the film provoked a strong reaction from the then Indian prime minister, Indira Gandhi, who saw the film's potential to engage audiences with the issues it addressed, in part by shocking them through its depiction of the casualties and consequences of the war. Moreover, the film persuaded her to order the Films Division of India to purchase it and circulate it worldwide (Qader 1993, 224; Leahy 2002).

Shortly afterward, the provisional government commissioned Raihan to produce three more documentary films on the subject of the Liberation War. This resulted in *Liberation Fighters* by Alamgir Kabir, *A State Is Born* by Zahir Raihan, and *Innocent Millions* by Babul Choudhury, all of which were produced under Raihan's direct supervision and recorded different aspects of the war. These three films, along with *Stop Genocide*, convey Raihan's distinctive creative and critical views, leading to their characterization as unique "first-hand filmic documents" of the Liberation War (Kabir 1979, 49).

THE EMERGENCE OF A GUERRILLA FILMMAKER IN RAIHAN

Being a revolutionary leftist activist and writer, Raihan initially expressed his political views in writing before turning to cinema. In his film *Jibon Thekey Neya* (Glimpses of Life, 1970), he utilized the medium of cinema as a symbolic means of expressing the voices of the oppressed people of Bangladesh under Pakistani colonial exploitation. He was the first revolutionary filmmaker in Bangladesh to take up the camera as a rifle (to borrow a metaphor from Solanas and Getino) and shoot the anticolonial struggle of an exploited people. This combination of political commitment and political aesthetic earned Raihan the epithet "the guerrilla filmmaker of Bangladesh" (Rebeiro 2010).

On the night of March 25, 1971, the Pakistani army initiated a hostile military crackdown in East Pakistan known as Operation Searchlight. They engaged in indiscriminate mass killings, first in Dhaka and then across other major cities in an attempt to crush Bengali nationalism and the political power of the Awami League (AL), which had overwhelmingly won the 1970s Pakistan parliamentary election and was thus due to form a government. AL's decisive victory in the election represented an overpowering triumph of the Bengalis at the state level in Pakistani politics. However, instead of transferring power to the elected party, West Pakistani rulers launched a systematic military attack on the night of March 25, 1971, to eliminate the political authority of the AL. Raihan was deeply shocked by the contemporary political ambience. On April 21, 1971, he escaped to Kolkata via the Comilla border and began to explore opportunities for filming the horrors of the war and the people's struggle in the border zones (Hayat 2007, 43–44). This risky and secret voyage to arrange resources to document the war on film reflects his effort to create "guerrilla cinema." Raihan traveled fearlessly across the borders and liberated zones to shoot the processions of displaced refugees, their plight and suffering, and the training and combative actions of the Bengali guerrillas. Even though he was "handicapped by the paucity of filmic documents," he went to the battlefield to shoot with whatever pieces of equipment he had on hand (Kabir 1979, 48).

Alamgir Kabir, one of the crew members of *Stop Genocide*, describes Raihan's desperate zeal in recording the reality of the battlefield, even to the extent of disregarding threats to his own life: "Zahir was a revolutionary, and when revolutionaries go to war, they know that their chance of death or life is fifty-fifty. Either to die or live. At the time of the shooting of *Stop Genocide*, we went to the Maldah border area. There was a Pakistani camp very near the place where we were traveling, and they [the Pakistani army] could have blown us up. We could have died there. Foolishly, we went through a minefield and crossed it. Whoever went before us, they died—we're alive."[2]

The conditions—the "revolutionary conjunctures"—under which *Stop Genocide* was made show its status as both Third Cinema and guerrilla cinema. Although guerrilla cinema and Third Cinema are two distinct film genres, they also have similarities. Wayne (2001, 8) identifies this period as the "dark times of neo-liberalism's hegemony," when Third Cinema made many attempts to intervene in political situations. Regarding guerrilla cinema, Wayne mentions that "when filmmakers are working in conditions of political danger and state authoritarianism, when their work may be seized, censored, or when they themselves might be imprisoned, the only way they can film is by using secrecy and subterfuge" (57). The features of the critical period from which guerrilla cinema and Third Cinema emerge are evident in the context and conditions of *Stop Genocide*. This is reinforced by the film's specific content—that is, its representations of guerrilla warfare and the atrocious treatment of an imperialist power. Here imperialist power represents the Pakistan government, run mostly by the West Pakistanis, which exploited the populace of East Pakistan. However, Raihan's commitment to the techniques of filmmaking, similar to those of Third Cinema or guerrilla cinema with their distinctive purpose of intervening in the political system, were, in fact, in evidence even before the war, in fiction films such as *Jibon Thekey Neya* and *Let There Be Light* directed by him. He could not complete the latter project due to the outbreak of the war, and he lived for only two months after the independence of Bangladesh.[3]

THE PROLOGUE WITH A CALL FOR FREEDOM

Stop Genocide begins with the voice-over of a quotation from V. I. Lenin, accompanied by the triumphant music of "The Internationale."[4]

> To accuse those who
> Support freedom of
> Self determination i.e.,
> freedom to Secede,
> of encouraging Separatism,
> is foolish and hypocritical
> as accusing those who advocate
> freedom of Divorce
> of encouraging the
> destruction of family ties. (Lenin [1914] 1964, 422)

The quotation, read and shown in the film, condemns the imperialistic tendency of the developed world to confuse freedom-seeking people's demand for freedom with the activities of separatists. This tendency is described as foolish and hypocritical. The quotation ultimately suggests that the Bangladeshis' demand for freedom cannot be seen as the work of secessionists or terrorists. In a fixed frame, the reading of the quotation plays out over Lenin's profile. Thus, the film, from its very first frame, clearly conveys its central meaning: a call for the oppressed to rise up against all forms of exploitation and demand their freedom from their oppressors.

The next sequence fades in with a long shot of a village girl and a woman, revealing them working a husking pedal. Then a mid-close shot of the innocent smile of the girl, working on the pedal, reveals the beauty and simplicity of the Bengali village women. However, the monotonous sound and movement of the pedal, and its operators' fixed postures, also create a collective image of Bengalis as an exploited working class: their exploitation is constant, like the motion of the pedal. Then, after a dissolve transition, still images of village life appear on the screen, foregrounding some of the film's credits on them. By juxtaposing images of women and nature, Raihan illustrates a common Bengali theme—the notion of the "mother nation" that is synonymous with nature. Drawing on the writing of Rebecca Grant, Nira Yuval-Davis (1997, 6) points out that equating women with nature excludes women from the "'civilized' public political domain" since nature is perceived to be the antithesis to civilization. She adds that this mechanism is evident in all cultures, and despite its apparent adoration of women as nature, it undervalues women socially in comparison to men.

In Bengali literature and art, the construction of woman as nature is mainly derived from the concept that both mother and nature can create new things, thus nature becomes a mother-like figure. However, being a leftist and having adopted a more critical approach, Raihan purposely lessens the sentimentality of traditional depictions of nature as "beautiful mother" by overlaying images of natural scenery with the monotonous sound of the husking pedal. Afterward, sound effects of marching, bombing, and dogs barking accompany a blank frame, connoting a colonial attack on the mother nation and the inability of the cinematic medium to convey the ravishing of the mother. Raihan employs this empty space as "a vision without image" (Emmanuel Levinas quoted in Saxton 2010b, 96), which has been created to awaken the imaginative and intellectual sensitivities of viewers to the full horror of the war. The blank frame, held for a full twenty seconds, is intended to provoke ethical engagement on the part of the film's audience by signaling the inexpressible trauma of the war.

Horrifying images of anonymous dead bodies then appear in still images one after another, offering a montage of the genocide—anonymous shattered bodies in a field, a series of decomposing dead bodies floating in a river, dogs feasting on human corpses, the wounded dead body of a child, half-naked and rotting bodies of women—slowly displaying evidence of the atrocities and brutalities against Bengalis. As Susan Sontag (2003, 42) contends, images of atrocities or bodies in pain both shock us and provoke shame in us as we see close-up the reality of the war. The images in

Raihan's film elicit both of these emotions. They jolt the critical faculty within us into seeking an ethical engagement to stop the brutality, which is even displayed by the insertion of the graphic "Stop Genocide," accompanied by the sounds of explosions and gunfire. "The Internationale" also recurs, suggesting a revolutionary spirit breaking with the shocking mood previously created. Then the rest of the film's credits appear. By referring to Wayne's words on Third Cinema, we can say that the opening of the film achieves a "synthesis between the spectator's emotional and intellectual capacities" (2001, 42), preparing the viewer to interrogate and comprehend the causes behind the genocide and the political struggle of Bengalis for national liberation.

CREATION OF THE V-EFFECTS AND COLLABORATIVE PRACTICES OF THIRD CINEMA

Next a *Dateline News* teleprinter appears in the frame, a symbolic apparatus for recording history. It reveals the UN Declaration of Human Rights, cited in the Charter of the United Nations, which is arguably one of the most significant historical documents in the history of mankind. The words continuously emerge from the teleprinter while the voice-over confidently quotes the preamble of the UN Charter explaining that the organization was intended to create hope in the international community and determined "to reaffirm faith in fundamental human rights, in the dignity and worth of the human person, in the equal rights of men and women." This teleprinter's news is then followed by two newscasts from two different places: one is Saigon, Vietnam; the other is Bongaon, India. Still images depict the brutal attacks of US gunships and jet fighters, discharging explosives and bombs on the villages of Vietnam. Still images of wounded and dead Vietnamese testify to the mass killings in Vietnam. Then we see moving images from Bongaon: endless lines of malnourished Bengali refugees running across the Indian border, haunted by the fear of losing their lives, fleeing the attack by the Pakistani army. Some are carrying with them their few remaining possessions and holding the hands of their near ones, in search of a safer place. These civilians appear as the visible victims of the turmoil and torture inflicted by the West Pakistani army. Thus, by juxtaposing these three realities—the UN Declaration of Human Rights, the violation of human rights in Vietnam, and the suffering of displaced Bangladeshis escaping across the Indian border—Raihan reveals the contradictory values and promises of the world's authorities. This evocation of the contradictory nature of history gives rise to a *Verfremdungseffekte* (V-effect or alienation effect), the central device of German dramatist-director Bertolt Brecht's epic theater. The *Verfremdungs* effect does not appeal to the audience's capacity for empathy, but rather arouses its astonishment. This effect "consists in turning the object of which one is to be made aware, to which one's attention is to be drawn, from something ordinary, familiar, immediately accessible, into something peculiar, striking and unexpected" (Brecht 1964, 143). In a similar fashion to the V-effect, Raihan also reveals historic conditions as strange. He introduces history in this way so that the spectator can identify the limitations of received history or ideology. This arouses a higher consciousness in the audience, which is able to reposition itself in relation to history. In this way, the film seeks to awaken collective political action among the audience in order to confront the contradictory nature of history (driven by the world's leading authorities).

Nearly all the fragments of the film are constructed in a similar fashion, with the inclusion of dialectical effects intended to interrupt the movement of history or time. For example, most sequences conclude with a freeze-frame prolonging the image for a few seconds, with the word "stop" imposed by the voice-over narration. Through antirealist effects of this sort, Raihan surprises the audience by disrupting narrative continuity. These effects create distance between film and audience, drawing viewers' attention to the conditions behind the injustices and human rights violations taking place before them. They are also charged with the responsibility of seeking justice to stop the suffering of others. Drawing on Luc Boltanski's views on the obligation effect created in viewers by images that portray the suffering of others, Libby Saxton (2010a, 65) notes that "watching suffering from a distance can act as a spur to ethical thought and action." Likewise, *Stop Genocide*, by employing a series of "stop"s in the voice-over and freeze-frames, generates distance between the audience and the images of suffering people in the film, and provokes an urgent obligation in the audience to find ways to stop the genocide.

Many filmmakers have anticipated this aesthetic strategy, which is a characteristic of Third Cinema, by involving their audience in a dialectical mode of critical thinking employed in pursuit of social change. This is also evident in *Stop Genocide*, in what critics identify as the influences Raihan takes from the films of Eastern Europe and Cuba. James Leahy (2002), a film historian and screenwriter, claims that *Stop Genocide* would not have been possible "without the filmmaker's exposure to the exemplary work of [Santiago] Alvarez," during his exile in Kolkata in 1971. However, Leahy's observation somewhat overstates the influence of Cuban films on Raihan's work. I want to emphasize that Raihan's leftist engagement from his early life and the political awareness that emerged from the colonial repression that he, as a Bengali, experienced firsthand, made him desperate to explore a new cinematic language. The aim of this new cinematic language was to depict the anticolonial struggle of Bengalis. Consequently, his earlier movie, *Jibon Thekey Neya*, made in 1970, before his exile in Kolkata, also contains techniques that mirror the thrust of the Bengalis' progressing political struggle in a metaphorical manner. As a leftist activist, Raihan was involved in a range of political movements and took an active part in the Language Movement (Rebeiro 2010). He also became involved in the activities of the Communist Party, for which he worked as a courier secretly transporting messages and letters (Hasan 2011, 120). Originally named Abu Abdar Mohammad Zahirullah, he was given the pseudonym Raihan by the underground leaders of the party. Later, he became known as Zahir Raihan. In 1965, while organizing the Pakistan Film Festival in Dhaka, Raihan pledged to reject mainstream cinema; this was the moment in which he first gave public voice to his desire for a new cinematic language: "The star system is a weapon of profit hunting for the capitalist. Greedy businessmen imported this system from America. By destroying this system, we may foil the insidious plot of the imperialist. Let us create the right mental attitude for collective work" (Raihan quoted in Hayat 2007, 30; translation mine).

Clearly, Raihan's commitment to creating a working practice in the collective interest of his group, the Bengalis, developed long before his exposure to Cuban film. The collaborative/collective working aspect of the cinema format that Raihan dreamed of, mentioned in this quotation, is also an integral part of Third Cinema. Wayne (2001, 3) defines this attribute of Third Cinema as "democratic working practices." By denying dominant cinema practices dependent on the star system and capital accumulation, which strategically cultivate individuality, *Stop Genocide* is able to articulate the collective experience of the Bengalis. Like other wartime films, *Stop Genocide* does not highlight the individual role of Sheikh Mujibur Rahman; indeed, it does not even refer to him, though he was arguably the central figure behind the Liberation War and has been hailed as the "Father of the Nation" since the independence of Bangladesh. Instead, Raihan highlights the national crisis: the atrocious sufferings of Bengalis, their collective longing for freedom, and above all, a revolutionary consciousness of justice and a deep desire to stop the genocide. It is, therefore, the "revolutionary conjuncture" that provides the central characteristic of Third Cinema and brings together *Stop Genocide* and Third Cinema, whether the latter is from Cuba, Argentina, or any other region where such cinema is produced.

DIFFERENT DEPICTION STRATEGIES FOR MEN AND WOMEN

Stop Genocide gives rise to an understanding of the nation as a form of collective belonging; in the war it is the Bengali nation *as a whole* that suffers and fights. Nonetheless, the collective wholeness created in the film is not fully gender neutral. The nationalist discourse of *Stop Genocide* assigns different roles to men and women according to their culturally constructed positions. Men are mainly depicted as active freedom fighters and protectors of the nation; women appear as survivors, victims, and bearers of the nation. Although Raihan captures images of women of different ages, from teenagers to old age, he represents them collectively as a body of tortured victims who are passive, voiceless, and noncombative.

Even when women become the focus in images of dutiful mothers, running breathlessly while holding children in their arms, their portrayals signify the notion of "endangered motherhood," an iconic depiction of victimization of the mother. In fact, the image of endangered motherhood is a common trope in works by Bengali writers and artists created during the national crisis period. This common motif in the narratives of motherhood reflects a patriarchal notion of femininity. Zainul Abedin, a pioneering painter of Bangladesh, who was given the honorific title Shilpacharya (Great Teacher of the Arts), portrayed endangered motherhood with deep pathos and sympathy by highlighting the starving, gaunt mother feeding her child in his *Famine* series. He drew this series during the Bengal famine of 1943; it is still considered to be among the most powerful visuals in Bengal art history.

The motivation, composition, and contents of Abedin's sketches are reflected in Raihan's framing of women as devoted mothers in *Stop Genocide*. Indeed, both Abedin and Raihan have valorized motherhood to assign to women childbearing roles, which, until their last breath, lock them into service as devoted mothers. However, this valorization of women in artworks through a depiction of endangered motherhood indirectly exposes the ideological functions of patriarchy. It reveals the power relations between the two genders, whereby women are situated in the private sphere of reproduction but not in the productive sphere, regarded as the male domain.

Most significantly, through this motif of endangered motherhood, Raihan represents the nation as mother/female to evoke nationalism in a nation that does not have its own independent state free from Pakistani colonial exploitation. As Ernest Gellner (1983, 55–56) has argued, the nation is invented by nationalism where it does not exist. In *Stop Genocide*, the nationalist discourse of the endangered "mother nation" stimulates nationalist sentiment and reinforces the need to free the nation from its enemies. Historically, however, this discourse of nationalism "typically has sprung from masculinized memory, masculinized humiliation and masculinized hope" (Enloe 1990, 44), as can be seen in the way Raihan glorifies the images of the *Mukti Bahini* (Bengali guerrillas) as *mukti pagol torun shingho* (freedom-snatching young lions), who are determined to free the motherland at any cost. Although they are dressed in *lungi* (a traditional Bangladeshi skirt-like garment for males) and *genzi* (undershirts and vests), their spirit and actions in the second half of the film make them appear as the saviors of the Bengali nation. When Raihan portrays the activities at the guerrilla training camp, the dialectical effect of "stops" are not employed. Instead, by playing "The Internationale" on the soundtrack, he instills the sequence with a lofty emotional force and elicits empathy from the audience by highlighting the spirit and strength of the *Mukti Bahini,* similar to the Aristotelian hero. Here, I mention the Aristotelian hero in order to relate the tragic hero's ability to stir the emotions to the characteristics of the *muktijoddhas*. The audience's emotional engagement and catharsis are important in plays and films that follow the Aristotelian theory of tragedy. Although from the beginning of *Stop Genocide*, Raihan purposefully breaks both the narrative continuity and the audience's emotional involvement, in a move similar to the Brechtian technique of alienation, he does not bring the alienation technique to bear in the portrayal of *muktijoddhas*. They, rather, are projected as Aristotelian heroes, seen as stimulating empathy and nationalist spirit. They are adorned with the virtue of pride for their service to the motherland.

By contrast, women are typically represented as care-worn and almost entirely lacking in nationalist sentiment; their sole concern is shown to be for the lives of their children. In this way they are turned into passive, mute victims of the war. Although Raihan's intention is to highlight the horror of the war by framing the suffering of women, he cannot avoid re-creating the patriarchal view of women as inferior. This inferiority is sometimes exoticized, notably in the representation of a woman who has been raped. A sixteen-year-old girl who has been raped by six Pakistani soldiers is depicted as silent. The voice-over, redeeming her unspeakable history, articulates her violent experience of being raped. The girl, we learn, was also witness to the army's killing of her father, uncle, and two brothers. Close-up shots of her muted profile, taken from different angles without her directly looking toward the camera, make her into a spectacle and a passive object. The visuals and voice-over come together to construct the culturally repressed dimension of a raped woman, one who is burdened physically and mentally with shame. Nayanika Mookherjee (2006, 80) has suggested that the portrayal of this raped girl is "representative of that invisible 'shamed' group" of raped women. The girl is paradoxically threatened with silence.

The male voice-over authoritatively recounts the girl's brutal personal history, as if it "knew best." According to Kaja Silverman (1988, 48), the convention of voice-over in classic narrative cinema acts as "a voice which speaks from a position of superior knowledge, and which superimposes itself 'on top' of the diegesis"; it is also "an exclusively male voice." In *Stop Genocide*, the authority of the male voice-over also indicates the cultural code of Bangladesh, where, according to Islamic law, a man is counted as a full person and a woman as half. From the ownership of family property to education, in most spheres, discrimination toward women is evident at home and in public institutions. Perhaps, being informed about the social system, Raihan employs a male voice-over to lend credibility to the rape victim's suffering, while erasing her subjectivity by removing her voice from the narrative. Although in some cases the silence of such women is explained as resulting either from a wish not to speak or from post-traumatic stress syndrome, their muteness ultimately serves to perpetuate a masculinized ideological framework of language that associates women with lack.

Women are silenced in *Stop Genocide* despite the fact that the resistance of the Bengalis entailed a war of existence for the whole nation, regardless of class, caste, or gender. Men, by contrast, are depicted exclusively as heroic fighters, indirectly revealing the film's limitations as a historical document and drawing attention to its selective approach to the event. The direct and indirect participation of women on the battlefield and their various contributions to the fighting are absent from the film. Of course, we cannot demand exhaustive, ideally impartial coverage of the war from a film produced under such volatile and dangerous circumstances. The camera could only capture the phenomena that the filmmaker (Raihan) was able to shoot during the gruesome situation of the war. At the same time, he had to collect footage from different sources. Inevitably, *Stop Genocide* cannot, strictly speaking, be interpreted as an *inaccurate* narrative of the war for not being able to capture every last aspect of the conflict, including the active roles played by women in the war. However, we do not find any reference to that missing evidence of women's active participation in the war.

THE FINAL APPEAL

In the concluding fragment of the film, while Raihan appeals to all mankind to come forward and stop this genocide, he mentions that the Liberation War is a collective resistance by Bengalis and an integral part of the ongoing struggle by working men and women of the world for a better life. Here we see the political commitment with which Raihan desperately aspires to engage both men and women in creating a better world free from injustice, reflected in the aesthetic strategy and consciousness of Third Cinema. Conversely, the ways in which female images have been constructed in this narrative through their subject positions and the operation of certain codes of framing, camera angles, voice-over use, and editing do not manifest revolutionary motivation or imagery. Women are deployed as symbols to represent the traumatized other.

THE FILM'S RECEPTION: THEN AND BEYOND

At the time of its release *Stop Genocide* deeply moved the world's spectators with humanitarian sentiment that includes both emotion and logic to stop the genocide that took place in East Pakistan. It was possible for its dialectical cinematic technique to unmask the causes and consequences of the war. It became a creative document of the Liberation War, depicting the suffering of the oppressed people of East Pakistan by connecting them with the broader struggle for freedom and justice around the world. The film won the SIDLOC award at the Delhi Film Festival and also received an award at Tashkent Film Festival (Hayat 2007, 144) in 1972. After the war, the producers of the film donated the film with its negative print to the government of Bangladesh (Qader 1993, 225). Still today, after nearly forty-nine years of the Liberation War, *Stop Genocide* is regarded by Bangladeshis as a great documentary film on the Liberation War of Bangladesh. The film, with its combination of sound and images, both preserves the past and is able to place that past into a vivid present. Thus, it became a key agent for maintaining the collective memory of Bangladeshis and shaping their imagination of the Liberation War through subsequent decades.

CONCLUSION

In the process of making sense of the experience of the Liberation War in the collective imagination of Bangladeshis, *Stop Genocide* is acclaimed as the most authentic and influential visual text. However, the collective trust that has been invested in this documentary needs to be reexamined and contested from different perspectives. In saying this, I do not wish to deny the evidential or factual basis of the film. Drawing on John Grierson's (1946, 11) definition of documentary as a "creative treatment of actuality," I would like to stress that, even as a historically grounded piece of filmmaking, *Stop Genocide* nevertheless moves us imaginatively beyond the available evidence. However, in the representation of women, the film forever links our imagination to victimized images by focusing on them again and again, making a spectacle of their suffering. Men are also revealed in the film as spectacle—not always as pitiful but usually glorified as heroes who fight bravely in the war. Overall, despite having the impulses of a Third Cinema structure that emerged in a revolutionary context such as the Liberation War, *Stop Genocide* reconstructs gender stereotypes within the nationalist struggle.

ACKNOWLEDGMENTS

This chapter is based on the second chapter of my PhD thesis, titled "Fragmented Memory, Incomplete History: Women and Nation in War Films of Bangladesh," completed at the University of Essex in 2017. My heartfelt thanks to my supervisors Professor Shohini Chaudhuri, Dr. John Haynes, and Professor John Gillies for their valuable comments on earlier versions of this chapter. My research was supported by the Commonwealth Scholarship Commission in the UK and also received further grants from the FfWG Trust, Charles Wallace Bangladesh Trust, and Snowdon Trust. My sincere appreciation goes to the funding bodies. I am grateful to the two anonymous reviewers of this book and its editors, Professor Elora Halim Chowdhury and Dr. Esha De, for their insightful comments.

NOTES

1 The provisional government of the People's Republic of Bangladesh was initially known as the Mujibnagar government, formed on April 10, 1971, by the leaders of the Awami League at Mujibnagar. After the mass killing of the people of East Pakistan (now Bangladesh) by the Pakistani army on the night of March 25, 1971, the populace of this land started resistance. Their revolt against the Pakistani attack was sudden and took place without any prior preparation. In order to lead the Liberation War in a well-organized structure, the Mujibnagar government was formed. The headquarters

of this short-term official government of Bangladesh was shifted to Kolkata, India, due to a bomb attack by the Pakistan Air Force just two hours after its formation.

2 Alamgir Kabir's interviews in the documentary film *Proikuler Jatree (Counter Image)*; my translation.

3 After the Pakistani army surrendered on December 16, 1971, the Liberation War came to an end and Bangladesh achieved victory. Raihan immediately returned to Bangladesh. On January 30, 1972, he visited Mirpur to search for his brother Shahidullah Kaiser, an eminent writer and intellectual, who had been seized by collaborators during the war. The collaborators were helping the Pakistani forces in the mass killing of the Bengali people, and it is thought that, with their help, the Pakistani army killed Kaiser during the war, as he never returned. Raihan also disappeared following his visit to Mirpur, and his body was never found.

4 "The Internationale" is widely sung as the anthem of socialist parties. It expresses the thriving movement for social change, justice, and freedom for oppressed people. It was written by Eugène Pottier, a transport worker of Paris, in June 1871, after the demolition of the Paris Commune by French troops. It also served as the national anthem of the Soviet Union from 1918 to 1944.

REFERENCES

Birri, Fernando. 1997. "Cinema and Underdevelopment." In *New Latin American Cinema: Theory, Practices, and Transcontinental Articulations*, vol. 1, edited by Michael T. Martin, translated by Malcolm Coad, 86–94. Detroit: Wayne State University Press.

Brecht, Bertolt. 1964. *Brecht on Theatre: The Development of an Aesthetic*. Edited and translated by John Willett. New York: Hill and Wang.

Enloe, Cynthia. 1990. *Bananas, Beaches and Bases: Making Feminist Sense of International Politics*. Berkeley: University of California Press.

Gellner, Ernest. 1983. *Nations and Nationalism*. Oxford: Blackwell.

Grierson, John. 1946. *Grierson on Documentary*. Edited by Forsyth Hardy. London: Collins.

Hasan, Khondokar Mahmudul. 2011. *Muktijuddher Chalachchitro* (Films on the Liberation War). Dhaka: Kathaprokash.

Hayat, Anupam. 2007. *Zahir Raihaner Chalachitra: Patabhumi, Bishoy O Boishistaya* (Films by Zahir Raihan: Context, contents and characteristics). Dhaka: Dibyaprokash.

———. 2011. *Bangladesher Muktijudha Bhittik Chalachitra (A book on film of Liberation War of Bangladesh)*. Dhaka: Bangladesh Film Archive.

Kabir, Alamgir. 1979. *Film in Bangladesh*. Dhaka: Bangla Academy.

Leahy, James. 2002. "Films that Make a Difference . . . Santiago Alvarez and the Politics of Bengal: *Ciclon*." *Senses of Cinema*, December 12, 2002. http://sensesofcinema.com/2002/cteq/alvarez_ciclon/ (accessed December 15, 2012).

Lenin, V. I. (1914) 1964. "The Right of Nations to Self-Determination." In *Collected Works*, vol. 20, *December 1913–August 1914*, translated by Bernard Isaacs and Joe Fineberg, edited by Julius Katzer, 393–454. Moscow: Progress Publishers.

Mookherjee, Nayanika. 2006. "Muktir Gaan, the Raped Woman and the Migrant Identities of the Bangladesh War." In *Gender, Conflict and Migration*, edited by Navnita Chadha Behera, 72–96. New Delhi: Sage Publications.

Mutsuddi, Chinmoy. 1987. *Bangladesher Chalachittre Samajik Ongikar* (A critical study of Bangladeshi cinema). Dhaka: Bangladesh Shilpakala Academy.

Peters, John Durham. 2009. "Witnessing." In *Media Witnessing: Testimony in the Age of Mass Communication*, edited by Paul Frosh and Amit Pinchevski, 23–41. Basingstoke: Palgrave Macmillan.

Qader, Mirza Tarequl. 1993. *Bangladesher Chalachitra Shilpa* (The cinema of Bangladesh). Dhaka: Bangla Academy.

Rebeiro, Bidhan. 2010. "Zahir Raihan: Ekatturer Guerilla Nirmata" (Zahir Raihan: The guerrilla filmmaker of 1971). *Banglanews24.com*, December 13, 2010. https://www.banglanews24.com/art-literature/news/bd/20455.details (accessed December 4, 2019).

Saxton, Libby. 2010a. "Ethics, Spectatorship and the Spectacle of Suffering." In *Film and Ethics: Foreclosed Encounters*, by Lisa Downing and Libby Saxton, 62–75. Abingdon, UK: Routledge.

———. 2010b. "Blinding Visions: Levinas, Ethics, Faciality." In *Film and Ethics: Foreclosed Encounters*, by Lisa Downing and Libby Saxton, 95–106. Abingdon, UK: Routledge.

Shahaduzzaman. 2009. *Bioscope, Cholochchitro Provity* (Bioscope, cinema, *provity*). Dhaka: Banglayan.

Silverman, Kaja. 1988. *The Acoustic Mirror: The Female Voice in Psychoanalysis and Cinema*. Bloomington: Indiana University Press.

Solanas, Fernando, and Octavio Getino. 1976. "Towards a Third Cinema." In *Movies and Methods: An Anthology*, vol. 1, edited by Bill Nichols, 44–66. Berkeley: University of California Press.

Sontag, Susan. 2003. *Regarding the Pain of Others*. New York: Picador.

Wayne, Mike. 2001. *Political Film: The Dialectics of Third Cinema*. London: Pluto Press.

Yuval-Davis, Nira. 1997. *Gender and Nation*. London: Sage Publications.

FILMS CITED

Choudhury, Babul. 1971. *Innocent Millions*. Bangladesh: Bangladesh Government.

Chowdhury, Kawsar. n.d. *Proikuler Jatree (Counter Image)*. Bangladesh: Prova-Sruti-Obolokon.

Kabir, Alamgir. 1971. *Liberation Fighters*. Bangladesh: Bangladesh Government.

Raihan, Zahir. 1970. *Jibon thekey neya* (Glimpses of life). Pakistan: Zahir Raihan.

———. 1971a. *Stop Genocide*. Bangladesh: Bangladesh Chalachitra Shilpi-O-Kushali Swahayak Samity and Bangladesh Liberation Council of the Intelligentsia.

———. 1971b. *A State Is Born*. Bangladesh: Bangladesh Government.

13 GENDER, WAR, AND RESISTANCE

The Case of Kashmir

ALKA KURIAN

IN AREAS RIDDLED BY POLITICAL CONFLICT, WOMEN'S NARRATIVES tend to go unreported. What gets highlighted is their victimization. However, an increasing number of women use art as a tool to resist this narrative undergirded by systemic and interlocking structures of oppression. To unravel moments of "resistance in subaltern historiography" (Sunder Rajan 1993, 3), this chapter analyzes the political embeddedness in art made by women, which is implicitly defiant and contestatory, and is articulated against statist, militaristic, political, legal, and social injustices in South Asia. I see this as a bold gendered engagement with the postcolonial nation-state, marked by forces of new orientalist regressive cultures, neoliberalism, indigenism, dispossession, and anti-Enlightenment rhetoric. I define a specific kind of women's creative work—subversive, revolutionary, and dissident—as "uprising textualities" that have the power to decolonize received knowledge and statist authority and move us "from postcoloniality and the state of 'postness' or 'afterness' . . . into a more radical consciousness of our creativity" (Boyce-Davis 1994, 81).

To substantiate my argument, I examine a range of documentary films that form part of women's resistance movements in South Asia. I analyze films set in Kashmir, one of South Asia's most troubled spots, that explore the gendered fallout of brutal state-led, militarized repression. An exploration of these films is accompanied by an investigation into the following questions: In what way do these films constitute a political force? How do they decolonize received knowledge and subvert oppression? How does raising awareness, sharing hope, and coping with trauma help reconstitute identities? Are these films undergirded by a genuine humanitarian appeal, or are they simply rescue narratives of humanity at risk? Given the material exigencies of filmmakers, would these films always be considered progressive and transformative?

KASHMIR: A LEGACY SHAPED BY VIOLENCE

Soon after the 1947 Partition of the Indian subcontinent, the Muslim-majority state of Kashmir joined India, much against the will of its population, which preferred to be part of Pakistan. Kashmir's Hindu leader, Maharaja Hari Singh, had sought India's help to push back Pashtun tribesmen sent by Pakistan to support the first Kashmiri Muslim uprising. India agreed to support Kashmir on condition that Kashmir join its territory, and the conflict was temporarily settled by drawing a cease-fire line (now called the "Line of Control") that divided the state into Indian Kashmir and Pakistani Azad Kashmir. Kashmir's accession to India was meant to be decided by a plebiscite to determine the will of the people; however, this referendum was never held.[1] India and Pakistan have had three full-scale wars over this thorny issue. Armed resistance groups in Kashmir have been fighting for decades for the Kashmiri people's right to self-determination. India blames Pakistan for sponsoring terrorism in the state and has responded with brutal militarized repression, resulting in substantial human rights violations in the state. The 2014 Human Rights Watch report claims that over the course of this five-decade-long conflict, nearly one hundred thousand people have lost their lives, more than ten thousand have become refugees, and nearly seven thousand have sought asylum (Asia Watch and Physicians for Human Rights 1993). Referred to by Amnesty International as a crime against international law, this state-led practice has resulted in eight thousand disappearances since the late 1990s, with the disappearances peaking in the early stages of the militant movement in the 1990s and early 2000s (Essa 2011). Despite India being a signatory to the International Convention for the Protection of All Persons from Enforced Disappearances, perpetrators of this crime are not held accountable in Kashmir. Since it is difficult to tell militants from civilians, people are randomly abducted, tortured, threatened, or killed, and their whereabouts and fates are never disclosed to their families. Survivors live with permanent physical and psychological wounds, and their families are scarred for life, especially women, given that most of the disappeared are men.

While much has been written on this volatile region, most of the scholarship tends to focus on the political and territorial conflict between Pakistan and India. What gets left out of this discourse is its impact on the people—the ways in which people experience this conflict daily and the lived reality of the loss and grief that results. This chapter explores some key documentary films that deal with the physical and emotional fallout of the conflict in Kashmir—represented as a site of pain, trauma, and resistance to brutal state repression. It also examines the consequences of disappearances carried out by members of the Indian Security Forces, who remain protected by the draconian Armed Forces (Special Powers) Act (AFSPA), enforced in Kashmir since the 1990s. Due to the limitations of space, I focus on the Indian part of Kashmir and not Azad Kashmir.

"CINEMA OF CONFLICT" AND FEMALE AUTHORSHIP

A content and formal analysis of women's films reveals a specific perspective that is different from that of men's films. French filmmaker Agnès Varda celebrates the feminist politics of women filmmakers whose world, shaped by their gendered lived experience, refuses to dilute female subjectivity by being colonized by a gaze other than female. This is because "gender causes an inflection which might be described as an awareness of 'otherness' or difference, and women share this and recognize it as a factor of the experience of patriarchal culture" (French 2018, 10–11).

Drawing on psychoanalysis, structuralism, and poststructuralism, feminist film scholarship in the 1970s and 1980s had relegated the film's "author" to the margins. Feminist realist debates, particularly on realist documentary films focused on women, derided representation of women's experiences as unreal, biased, and therefore unreliable. However, bringing the "author back into focus . . . and . . . placing the female director squarely on the agenda" (Modleski 2002), other feminist film scholars reject such antirealist positionalities. Not only does the realist form of documentary cinema help the audience identify with marginalized groups, but for those with inadequate background in filmmaking, it is frequently the only method available (Waldman and Walker 1999, 12).

Kashmiri documentary filmmaker Iffat Fatima's *Khoon diy baarav (Blood Leaves Its Trail)* (2015) and *Where Have You Hidden My New Moon Crescent* (2009) and Uzma Falak's *'Till Then the Roads Carry Her* (2015) are powerful femalecentric resistance documentaries challenging the state-led oppressive policies in Kashmir.[2] Their "cinema of conflict" stems from filmmaking practices entrenched in and shaped by the conflict within which they operate, measuring from up close its impact on the everyday life of people around them, on themselves, and on their political positionality vis-à-vis the conflict (Smets 2015). Their cinematic practices place them in a "shared-goal filmmaking" model (Waldman and Walker 1995, 18), understood as films made by people inhabiting the milieu of their subjects, overcoming in the process the ethical issues related to the filmmaker/subject divide (Hankin 2007, 78). Their work is pathbreaking since women—let alone those from Kashmir—are rarely offered filmmaking opportunities in a field that has historically been dominated by non-Kashmiri men. Examples of mainstream commercial filmmakers include Mani Ratnam (*Roja*, 1992), Vidu Vinod Chopra (*Mission Kashmir*, 2000), Soojit Sarkar (*Yahaan*, 2005), and Kunal Kohli (*Fanaa*, 2006), whose blockbusters, set in an imaginary Kashmir, offer simplistic narratives typically centering Muslim male radicalization, with female characters organized to serve the majoritarian nationalist agenda (Khan 2009; Kabir 2010; Haider 2014; Rabindranath, Kashyap, and Nazir 2016). Faced with this propagandist onslaught are independent and documentary filmmakers such as Sanjay Kak (*Jashn-e-azadi*, 2007), Amir Bashir (*Harud*, 2012), or Sheikh Adnan and Furkan Khurshid (*The Tales of Siege*, 2016), whose stories depict the historical brutalization of the Kashmiri people and the resulting armed uprising. While these male documentarians are able to offer a sustained challenge to the mainstream commercial Kashmiri fantasies, their films end up reproducing a masculinist response to the Kashmir crisis.

Focusing on women-centered narratives, female documentarians make an important intervention and take the shared-goal filmmaking tradition farther by enabling marginalized women to voice the commonality of their experiences, grounded in their collectivist grief and rage. Being women, they do not make films about women as a political decision. They do so because being women, they can engage with the world through their eyes, tell women's stories from their gendered point of view, and focus on women's personal stories, their private and domestic spheres, their families and community, their interiority and psychology, and their emotional and economic struggles. As pointed out by Lisa French, their narratives are shaped by the female gaze: the "communication or expression of female subjectivity—a gaze shaped by a female 'look,' voice and perspective—the subjective experience of someone who lives in a female body. The knowledge of gender difference, of living as a woman, is what connects women and the reason they often claim to identify with films made by women and recognize the gendered experience each variously captures in their 'female gaze.' Part of this recognition is due to visible female aesthetic approaches, world views, and treatment of subjects, themes and the overall privileging of female subjectivity" (French 2018, 19).

MEMORIES AND COUNTERMEMORIES

Iffat Fatima constructs her films as a space to explore the narrative from below—the daily struggles and challenges suffered by the families of the disappeared—using their memory and recall as a feminist lens to critique the oppressive Indian state.[3] Her 2015 film *Khoon diy baarav* builds on her 2009 narrative *Where Have You Hidden My New Moon Crescent*, both of which outline the despair that comes with the loss of loved ones. Structured around the lives of lonely and grieving mothers, the films offer interviews with family members, still photography of the disappeared, and live footage of protests and demonstrations for justice and freedom. They draw upon the "vox populi" documentary style of filmmaking, juxtaposing a multiplicity of women's voices to make the larger argument about their oppression, belying in the process any accusations of possible absolutist claims on the subject (Rabiger 1998, 224–27).

Fatima calls her films a testimony, "a consequence of [her] bearing witness" (quoted in Ramnath 2015), through which the audience observes the grotesque violation of human rights in a brutalized Kashmir, a valley in the Himalayas that looks more like a space besieged by death, a graveyard rather than the tourist destination fantasized in the country's popular imagination. Memory strengthens the resolve of the families of the disappeared and propels them into seeking redress through political action. Memory is a political weapon, claims Fatima, as "they live and relive every moment . . . [of the disappeared who] are not dead for them but alive. . . . Theirs is a very active hope and it is a political act on their part" (quoted in Ramnath 2015).

Fatima enters the complex situation in Kashmir through the female relatives of the disappeared, who, faced with the most brutal forms of violence, can do nothing but remember. This shared memory is their final act of resistance and "defiance against powerful instruments of the state that try to erase their individuality" (Film Southasia 2015). Rather than obscuring their memories, the excess of grief and despair strengthens their recall of the event: they remember the time of the abduction, the names of the soldiers and officers, the visceral reactions of the families and neighbors, and the shared grieving of their loss. Each family's loss is suffered both individually and collectively. Their personal testimonials turn into political articulations, and their individual lives into part of a collective, so that the personal becomes political, and the political, personal. Nancy C. M. Hartsock (1998, 35) reminds us that feminism is a "mode of analysis, a method of approaching life and politics, rather than a set of political conclusions about the oppression of women." Accordingly, women's location on the margins affords them a feminist standpoint, enabling them to have a critical understanding of the world as they figure out strategies to work around and challenge their oppression. Privileging women's perspectives and experience that challenge misrepresentations of marginalized women, women's documentary cinema acts as an important feminist activist media and a "tactical tool" for social justice (Hankin 2007, 62), or what Clare Johnson calls a "counter cinema."

The film *Where Have You Hidden My New Moon Crescent* is structured around the commanding figure of Mughal Mase, one of the cofounders in 1984 of the Association of the Parents of Disappeared Persons (APDP). With the goal of holding the Indian Army accountable for its role in the violation of human rights in the Kashmir Valley, the APDP is seen as representing the human face of the conflict. It provides a collective space to seek justice by documenting and commemorating the lives of the disappeared, obtaining information on their whereabouts, and organizing national and international public protests and campaigns to put an end to this practice. For the past twenty-two years, on the tenth day of every month, members of the APDP participate in a sit-in at Srinagar's Pratap Park. There, they perform a ritual of grief surrounded by photographs of the disappeared, offering public visibility of the crimes and constructing a public "postmemory" for younger Kashmiris who have forgotten the human rights violations of the 1990s (Misri 2014). The film follows Mase's journey as a single mother, juxtaposing memories of her disappeared son with interviews about her personal life, her estranged husband, and her fearless disregard for the occupying forces of the Indian Army. Interspersed through her grief are images of her joie de vivre and sense of humor as she supports a community of grieving mothers who cook, clean, and reminisce together. In a photograph that is emblematic of Mase's resistance, with her upper body and face shrouded in darkness, we see her hands holding her son's photograph, asserting the body of her son, who has been invisiblized, both figuratively and literally, by the Islamophobic machinery of oppression. Long after being abandoned by her husband, and twenty years after her son disappeared in 1990s, Mughal Mase passed away, becoming the first member of the APDP to die without getting justice.

In *Khoon diy baarav* Fatima takes her cinematic narrative farther by focusing on the other cofounder of APDP, Parveena Ahangar, as she journeys across Kashmir to unravel the anguish of the families of the disappeared, tracing their deeply networked collective, which began at Srinagar's

Batamaloo Sahib Shrine in early 1990s. Made over a span of nine years in the interiors of Kashmir, *Khoon diy baarav* is a personal "act of active citizenship," for the filmmaker, who privileges women's lived experiences over gender-neutral or masculinist-centric grand narratives on militarization, communalism, insurgency, and war (Jayashankar and Monteiro 2016, 98). By collating women's testimonies in this film, Fatima opens an important conversation on and troubles the meaning of citizenship, rights, and belonging in this explosive geopolitical region. This countercinema takes as its subject women who are hypervisiblized by media, the state, and policy makers, but since their voices don't count, they are devalued, objectified, and dehumanized. This cinema turns this imbalance on its head by encouraging its women subjects to shape the storytelling process, affording them a chance to counteract hegemonic portrayals and fill in gaps of representation by taking ownership of their own narratives, self-portraits, and images from their own perspectives.

Ahangar's activism stems from an unambiguously Muslim feminist standpoint precisely because of her focus on Muslim women's gendered human rights, which are imperiled in a militarized, misogynistic, Islamophobic, and nationalist state (Khan 2016, 21). Since her son's disappearance, Ahangar has been giving speeches, reaching out to hundreds of families of the disappeared, mobilizing them to protest, organizing sit-ins, urging government officials in Delhi to sanction prosecution, and holding the army to account while challenging its occupation of Kashmir. She is desperate to see her son, or at least his dead body. Without closure, the mothers' wounds will never heal. "Where did they disappear?" she asks in the film. "Has the sky devoured them or has the earth swallowed them? Have they become ether?"

Khoon diy baarav also follows similar stories of other women in the region. Using cinema as an activist tool, the filmmaker documents and interrogates the specific human rights challenges in the society they live in. Panning across the lake, her camera takes in images of sandbags, guns, and barbed wire, revealing this as a state of normalcy in Kashmir—a spectacular and ubiquitous presence of the army and its apparatus of control and death that exemplifies Kashmir's colonization and facilitates disappearances. Her female gaze unfolds in a circular manner. It twists and turns, crisscrosses between space, time, and characters, and builds layers upon layers of stories, relinquishing narrative linearity. What we see is a series of short narratives sutured together to form the larger story. With an iterative absence of closure, the audience doesn't see what became of each woman, nor does it know why some people willy-nilly become leaders to mobilize others and make sense of the collective tragedy. Instead, we see the day-to-day lived experience of despair and hope of women crushed and yet resistant. Using a web of feminine symbols, the filmmaker takes us along a journey that is fluid, silent, maternal, patient, empathetic, embodied, vivid, poetic, lyrical, and autobiographical (Probyn 2002; Barrett 2000).

Shunning bribes offered by the army, Halima Begum in Handwara refuses to testify against her militant husband, who has disappeared. He crossed the border in 1989 for training, as his way of resisting Kashmir's occupation by the Indian military. Begum's friends sing songs in the fields, beckoning the mujahideens to come down from the mountains and "burst upon them bullet spray." Kupwara district's Jana Begum has lost two sons, one martyred and the other disappeared. At a wedding in a nearby house, women are shown in a domestic space cooking and organizing, doing little things that women do because they come to them "more easily" and "more naturally" (Jain 2014). Intersecting these little female gestures, the women also sing songs about their imprisoned heroes bringing them newspapers so that their truth can sing. Hajra Begum's son was blindfolded, stripped naked, drenched in water, given electric shocks, and returned after eleven days, leaving him practically blind. After losing four sons, this old widow from Bandipore suffers from survivor's guilt and is harassed by the army in the same way as the mujahideens who used to come to her house.

Reminiscing on the lay of the land before the violence escalated, Subhan Tantray from Pattan misses the Battas (Hindus) who fled Kashmir when they began to increasingly be targeted by Kashmiri insurgents. As doctors and engineers, the Battas were good neighbors, he says. The army has usurped the homes vacated by the Hindus, converting them into detention camps and using their land to bury unidentified bodies. Accidentally coming across a shallow grave, Tantray pulls out the body of a young boy, who, he was told, had run away along with Tantray's son. The narrative takes us to a run-down former army base in Pattan, where members of a counterinsurgency militia known as Ikhwans—the "eyes and ears" of the Indian Army—are trained to abduct, torture, rape, or disappear people and are rewarded with jobs for exemplary social service. Indian troops, too, are regularly given medals, promotions, and money for killing Kashmiris (whom they refer to as terrorists) in encounters.

The camera pans over to mass graves with unidentified bodies where people recognize their children through birthmarks, clothes, and shoes.[4] Mass graves constitute particularly distressing sites because they represent a "contiguous display of death," the state's arrogance in killing with impunity and its flaunting of its power to those who are forced to witness this drama of terror (Chatterji et al. 2009). When some of the bodies are exhumed for DNA testing—on the insistence of family members—violence erupts in the valley, where thousands of men and women, unmindful of gunfire, chant slogans for freedom, pelt the army with stones, and beat its vans with sticks. A group of women push and shove the soldiers, screaming at them. The soldiers back off, for they do not know how to deal with women. As a procession of army trucks and vans leaves, women and men, young and old, jeer and clap. As many as 800,000 people gather in Eidgah (an open-air enclosure used for Islamic prayers) in Srinagar, chanting slogans of *azaadi* (freedom). Separate newspaper reports reveal how, in 2012, nearly 130 unarmed protesters were killed, most of them teenagers, inflaming rage among people who swell the number of freedom-chanting crowds.

The film comes full circle with Ahangar warning that it is time the rule of law be used to account for the disappearance of nearly ten thousand men in Kashmir. The blood of the dead is leaving a trail, says Ahangar, and angry young Kashmiris are risking their lives by throwing themselves into a situation that has become uncontrollable. How many more lives must be lost? Going beyond active recall of violence, within these final scenes of the film's diegesis is a feminist challenge to the militaristic solution to a political problem that has destroyed the lives, dreams, and hopes of five generations of people in the Kashmir Valley. The film fulfills the purpose of consciousness-raising, promoting social change through women's empowerment. It spotlights crimes perpetrated by the Indian Army, such as the torture of abducted men at the detention centers, the terror unleashed by the Ikhwans, and the young graffiti artist asked to wipe the wall clean with his tongue, while highlighting the slogans of freedom (*Go India*, *Drub India*, *Scrub India*) and outlining the extent to which Kashmiri dissidence came at a price. The film's screening at various locations across India was accompanied by highly passionate patriotic responses by the audience, most of whom were suspicious of Kashmiri people's desire for political self-determination (Kramer 2017, 3).

Kashmiri feminist, writer, artist, and human rights activist Uzma Falak also uses film, in addition to poetry, essays, narratives, and political commentary, to disrupt stereotypes of Kashmiri women as ill-fated victims of the repressive statist militarist politics. Her 2015 debut documentary short, *Till Then the Roads Carry Her*, subverts mainstream narratives of Kashmiri women's victimhood by contextualizing the lived experiences of the survivors of violence and offering resistant "counter-histories and counter-memories" (Jha 2017). In this manner, she performs the role of what film scholar Michel Renov might call a "historiographer who brings out oral histories and submerged accounts of people . . . to public notice" (Khan 2016, 19). She offers a poetic homage to women's vulnerabilities, struggles, strength, and activism in the face of militarized repression in the Kashmir Valley.

Through a creative intersection of poetry, photographs, songs, calligraphy, and interviews, the images and sounds in the film's diegesis are offered as strands that are separate and yet intertwined. Each lingering length of the shot, each carefully planned detail and its movement within each frame, and each circularity of the narrative reveals the gentle presence of the female gaze. Stitching the narrative with her voice-over and helping us make sense of the horror, never once does Falak appear in the film. Voices clamoring for freedom are set against the ultrasound image of a fetus, its heart throbbing, as though beating to the sound of people chanting slogans amid the crackling of gunfire. Falak's poem "When They Burned My Grandma's House" accompanies the shot of a slowly moving potter's wheel, still photographs of rooms destroyed by war, and police checkpoints. Set against this drama of loss and fear are women praying, weeping, agitating, and resisting, with their testimonials superimposed onto images of daily life. Images of grieving mothers holding pictures of the disappeared are juxtaposed with a collage of paintings and a song from Bollywood's blockbuster *Kashmir ki kali*.[5] Still photographs of women protesting shown inside broken homes or on the streets accompany Falak's poem: "Our feet breathe journeys . . . memory is not a victim, memory is a survivor . . . the dead will speak someday, till then the roads carry her."

Women filmmakers in Kashmir were among the first to choose documentary film "as their activist medium" to examine and document the ramifications of human rights violations despite a repressive political environment that challenges their creative process as Muslim women (Khan 2016, 20). Embedded within this feminist politics is the feminist (not only female) gaze, trying to make sense of the history of masculine film production and representation that has resulted in women's lives being colonized by men at the level of looks, assumptions, and portrayal. Having seized the Kashmir narrative from the clutches of mainstream elitist Bollywood cinema that promotes a regressive brand of masculinist nationalism, Kashmiri women filmmakers' "imperfect cinema" (Espinoza 1983) offers a "cinema of accountability that questions and challenges state policies, laws and official versions of history, and engages with crucial social and political developments" (Khan 2016, 17). It offers a "different voice, a different psychology and a different experience of love, work and the family from men . . . that is valued as not better, nor worse, nor inferior (French 2018, 16). Moreover, taking a cue from Ella Shohat's (2003) idea of the new post–Third Worldist feminist work that sets out Third World women's "difference" in their resistance against oppression, one would argue that Kashmiri women are uniquely positioned to challenge their abuse, located as they are inside Kashmir.

GENDER, MILITARIZATION, AND DISSENT

While men undergo disproportionate suffering in the face of direct violence (illegal confinement, torture, disappearances, and extrajudicial killings), women's experience of violence is in the realm of the social, cultural, sexual, and economic. Loss of male members of the family because of military conflict further heightens women's economic, social, political, and sexual vulnerability, reinforcing traditional gender hierarchies. This multilayered nature of oppression clearly has had the power to muzzle dissent among women, who have traditionally relied on a strategy of silence, given that "militarized environments empower both public and private patriarchy" and heighten their victimization (Manecksha 2014, 3). Further, they have learned to sanitize their speech by weeding out expressions such as *human rights violations*, *freedom of speech*, *rape*, *sexual molestation*, or *conflict*, speaking as a result in the "state-sanctioned language." This self-censorship is further exacerbated by loss of academic freedom, where in the name of their protection and for the sake of "national integration," women are urged to choose "safe" topics of investigation in state-controlled universities and kept away from the reality of atrocities committed on Kashmiris.

This facade of silence, however, has been crumbling over time. Unlike women in other parts of the Muslim world and despite being entrenched in patriarchy, Kashmiri women have enjoyed relative freedom, which comes from a culture of gendered integration rather than segregation within the cultural and religious spheres, as well as equal participation in traditional forms of labor such as agriculture. Having faced the brunt of the conflict in Kashmir—with their sons and husbands illegally and systemically arrested, tortured, disappeared, or murdered—in ways that are urgent, women are fighting back, making "the language of resistance their mother tongue" (Hariharan 2014, 6). As pointed out by Sanjay Kak (2010), "Until the other day, Kashmiri women were little more than a convenient set of clichés . . .

cast as victims, wailing mourners . . . but now an unfamiliar new photograph of the Kashmiri woman has begun to take its place on newspaper front pages. She's dressed in ordinary *salwar-kameez* . . . her head is usually covered with a *duppatta* and she is unconcerned about being recognized. She is often middle aged, and could be even middle class. And she is carrying a stone."

Challenging the mediatized stereotypes of disempowered, veiled victims, using ordinary weapons at their disposal, women in Kashmir are coming out against tyranny: tossing the *kangris* at a stalking soldier, participating in stone pelting, street demonstrations, and mass funerals, and intervening in public, cultural, and social spaces. For example, to contest the arrival of militarized bodies in Srinagar in 1990–91, many school- and college-age female students took to the streets, engaged in a battle with the police, and marched to the United Nations Military Observer's office, urging the world at large to help resolve the Kashmir problem (*The Hindu* 1990). Others expressed their solidarity with the movement for *azaadi*—seeing it as inseparable from their own safety—through a commemoration of the lives of the local mujahideens, articulating in the process their political liberation and self-expression.

Utilizing their cultural roles as mothers, wives, and sisters and "heavily swathed in burqas or in voluminous head scarves [women] came pouring out into the streets, their voices joining those of men in the cry for *azaadi* . . . [and] singing . . . (oh, you holy fighters, rise and awake! The time of your martyrdom has come)" (Manchanda 2001, 139–40). By offering medical care, shelter, and food, as well as transporting arms and information, many women expressed political solidarity and kept their families going, gendering and politicizing survival and domesticity in the process.

CONCLUSION

In this chapter I have examined the ways in which, despite their vulnerability to sexual violence and in spite of experiencing some of the worst human rights violations, Muslim Kashmiri women have gone beyond their cultural symbolism as widows, half-widows, or grieving mothers. Their resistant narratives help us understand the profoundly subversive role they play not only through a deliberate reinscription of gender within the masculinist process of militarization, highlighting questions of state culpability and legitimacy, but also in the struggle for independence from the Indian state.

Further, I have explored the medium of documentary films as an artistic corollary of women speaking out, helping to sustain the public memory of a crime and attempting to force the state to take responsibility both for its acts of violence and for the victims. The filmic narratives are articulated with the goal of ensuring social recognition of the hurt and making the case that those who were hurt deserve justice. When one recognizes suffering, one begins to understand impunity as an act of the state dehumanizing itself, justifying its criminality on the basis of lies and untruths. While social recognition does not always lead to justice or legal victories, it does mobilize what V. Geetha (2016, xxv) refers to as an "ethical effect," which means a lot to the victim:

> Bearing legal and social witness in the cause of those who have suffered affirms a horrific reality that the victim imagines only she can really ever know or understand. In turn, such affirmation implicates in a common humanity those who have suffered as well as those who do not want such suffering to go unacknowledged. . . . Therefore those who listen [social activists, filmmakers, audience], acknowledge and are prepared to bear witness on behalf of victims, help lighten and even dissolve the latter's burdened memory. The 'alone'ness of suffering is somewhat mitigated as pain finds a hearer—and if that in turn finds a legal resonance, the chances of securing justice are that much higher. . . . Speaking on behalf of the victims . . . [underlines] a civil responsibility of a particular kind: it stands testimony to citizens' efforts to not only heed but also represent the grievances of the disenfranchised and bear witness to their salience. (xxvi–xxvii)

NOTES

1 As of this writing, the Indian central government has removed the special status of Kashmir by abrogating Article 370 and has demoted the state by dividing it into two Union Territories—Jammu and Kashmir, and Ladakh—which are now directly under the central government's rule.

2 Shilpi Gupta's 2003 film *When the Storm Came* focuses on one of the worst cases of sexual violence in Kashmir. In February 1991 members of the Indian Army gang-raped a large number of women in Kunan Poshpora (KP), twin villages of the Kupwara district, known to be the most militarized space in Indian Kashmir. Despite Gupta's attempts at an authentic reproduction of the incident, her film fails to humanize its female subjects and instead constructs them as victims. Further, several

historical inaccuracies, a jumbled narrative, and editorial errors detract from the film's accuracy. For example, the 1947 Partition is referred to as a division of South Asia, and Kashmiri militants are conflated with members of the Indian Army. Moreover, the presence in the film of Dr. Zook, a specialist on Kashmir with unspecified university affiliations, is puzzling. The use of a white professor reinforces a colonialist attitude toward knowledge production. His analysis is suspect in the way he simplifies the Kashmir problem as mere ideological competition between India and Pakistan, completely glossing over the history of Kashmir's accession to India and side-stepping the question of the referendum. In *When the Storm Came*, his claim that in 1987 "it was no longer a conflict between India and Pakistan. Now you see the rise of militant/paramilitary groups" has a flattening effect and is, therefore, misleading.

3 A well-known filmmaker, Iffat Fatima's films include *Lanka—the Other Side of War and Peace*, a biographical film on the artist Dashrath Patel titled *In the Realm of the Visual*, and *Boojh sakey to boojh*, which explores the poetry of Amir Khusro.

4 In 2011, the State Human Rights Commission confirmed the burial of 2,156 unidentified bodies in unmarked graves across North Kashmir.

5 Taken from a series titled "Kashmir: A Metaphor of Pain: Stories through Painting and Poetry," it contains Falak's poems and Rollie Mukherjee's paintings and is organized around the themes "Reclaiming the Self," "Topography of Oppression," "Embellished Museum of Annihilation," and "The Tapestry of Sacrifice."

REFERENCES

Asia Watch and Physicians for Human Rights. 1993. "Rape in Kashmir: A Crime of War." *Human Rights Watch* 5, no. 9: 1–5. https://www.hrw.org/sites/default/files/reports/INDIA935.PDF.

Barrett, Terry. 2000. *Criticizing Art: Understanding the Contemporary.* 2nd ed. Mountain View, CA: Mayfield Publishing.

Boyce-Davis, Carole. 1994. *Black Women, Writing and Identity: Migration of the Subject.* London: Routledge

Chatterji, Angana P., Parvez Imroz, Gautam Navlakha, Zahir-Ud-Din, Mihir Desai, and Khurram Parvez. 2009. *Buried Evidence: Unnamed, Unmarked, and Mass Graved in Indian-Administered Kashmir, a Preliminary Report.* India: International People's Tribunal on Human Rights and Justice in Indian-administered Kashmir (IPTK).

Espinoza, Julio Garcia. 1983. "For an Imperfect Cinema." In *Twenty Five Years of the New Latin American Cinema*, edited by Michael Chanan. London: BFI Books.

Essa, Azad. 2011. "The Disappeared of Kashmir." *Al Jazeera*, April 18, 2011.

Falak, Uzma, dir. 2015. *Till Then the Roads Carry Her.*

———. 2016. "Kashmir: A Metaphor of Pain: Stories through Painting and Poetry." *Himal South Asia*, June 28, 2016. http://immersive.himalmag.com/kashmir-a-metaphor-of-pain7vtyc.

Fatima, Iffat, dir. 2009. *Where Have You Hidden My New Moon Crescent?*

———. 2015. *Khoon diy baarav* (Blood leaves its trail).

Film Southasia. 2015. "Blood Leaves Its Trail (Khoon Diy Baarav)." www.filmsouthasia.org/film/blood-leaves-its-trail-khoon-diy-baarav/.

French, Lisa. 2018. "Women in the Director's Chair: The 'Female Gaze' in Documentary Film." In *Female Authorship and the Documentary Image: Theory. Practice, and Aesthetics*, edited by Boel Ulfsdotter and Anna Backman Rogers, 9–21. Edinburgh: Edinburgh University Press.

Geetha, V. 2016. *Undoing Impunity: Speech after Sexual Violence*. New Delhi: Zubaan.

Haider, Nishat. 2014. "Exploration in History, Film and the Nation: A Study of the Representation of Kashmir Insurgency in the Hindi Mainstream Cinema. *South Asian Review* 35, no. 3: 95–115.

Hankin, Kelly. 2007. "And Introducing . . . the Female Director: Documentaries about Women Filmmakers as Feminist Activism." *NWSA Journal, Feminist Activist Art* 19, no. 1: 59–88.

Hariharan, Geeta. 2014. "The Place Kashmiri Women Live In." www.githahariharan.com/the-place-kashmiri-women-live-in.html.

Hartsock, Nancy C. M. 1998. *The Feminist Standpoint Revisited and Other Essays*. Boulder, CO: Westview Press.

The Hindu. 1990. "More Kashmiri Women Turning Militant." September 3, 1990.

Jain, Nishta. 2014. Interview with Lisa French, Amsterdam, November 20, 2014.

Jayaskankar, K. P., and Anjali Monteiro. 2016. *A Fly in the Curry: Independent Documentary Film in India*. New Delhi: Sage Publications.

Jha, Abhishek. 2017. "Beyond 'Victimhood': Uzma Falak's Film on the Role of Kashmiri Women in Resistance." *Youth Ki Awaz*. https://www.youthkiawaaz.com/2015/09/psbt-film-festival-2015-interview-uzma-falak/.

Johnson, Clare. 2004. "Women's Cinema as Counter-Cinema." In *Film Theory: Critical Concepts in Media and Cultural Studies*, vol 3, edited by Philip Simson, Andrew Utterson, and K. J. Shepherdson, 183–92. New York: Routledge.

Joshi, Namrata. 2016. "Are they Dead, Alive, or Have They Turned into Ether?" *The Hindu*, February 13, 2016.

Kabir, Ananya Jahanara. 2010. "The Kashmiri as Muslim in Bollywood's 'New Kashmir Films.'" *Contemporary South Asia* 18, no. 4: 375–85.

Kak, Sanjay. 2010. "The Last Option: A Stone in Her Hand." *Times of India*, August 8, 2010. http://timesofindia.indiatimes.com/home/sunday-times/deep-focus/The-last-option-A-stone-in-her-hand/articleshow/6272689.cms..

Khan, Rahat. 2016. *Activist Documentary Film in Pakistan: The Emergence of a Cinema of Accountability*. New York: Routledge

Khan, Shahnaz. 2009. "Nationalism and Hindi Cinema: Narrative Strategies in *Fanaa*." *Studies in South Asian Film and Media* 1, no. 1: 85–99.

Kramer, Max. 2017. "Mobilizing Conflict Testimony: A Lens of Mobility for the Study of Documentary Practices in Kashmir Conflict." *Social Sciences* 6, no. 3: 1–21.

Manchanda, Rita. 1999. "Empowerment with a Twist" *The Hindu*, November 21, 1999.

———. 2001. "Guns and *Burqa*: Women in the Kashmir Conflict." In *Women, War and Peace in South Asia: Beyond Victimhood to Agency*, edited by Rita Manchanda, 42–101. New Delhi: Sage Publications.

Manecksha, F. 2014. "Autonomy under Siege." *Himal Magazine*, January 7, 2014. http://old.himalmag.com/component/content/article/5218-autonomy-under-siege.html.

Misri, Deepti. 2014. *Beyond Partition: Gender, Violence, and Representation in Postcolonial India*. Champaign: University of Illinois Press.

Modleski, Tania. 2002. "On the Existence of Women: A Brief History of the Relations between Women's Studies and Film Studies." *Women's Studies Quarterly* 30, nos. 1–2: 15–24.

Probyn. Fiona. 2002. "J. M. Coetzee: Writing with/out Authority." *Jouvert* 7, no. 1: 1–12.

Rabiger, Michael. 1998. *Directing the Documentary*. 3rd ed. Boston: Focal Press.

Rabindranath, M., Geeta Kashyap, and Arif Nazir. 2016. "Portrayal of Kashmir Terrorism in Bollywood Films: A Critical Analysis of Films: Roja, Mission Kashmir and Haider." *Journal of Innovations* 10, no. 2.

Ramnath, Nandini. 2015. "Film on Kashmir Disappearance Reminds Us of the Cruelty of Forgetting, the Power of Memory," *Scroll.in*, October 12, 2015. https://scroll.in/article/760147/film-on-kashmir-disappearances-reminds-us-of-the-cruelty-of-forgetting-the-power-of-memory.

Ranjan, Amit. 2015. "A Gender Critique of AFSPA: Security for Whom?" *Social Change* 45, no. 3: 440–57.

Sarkar, Urvashi. 2016. "Kashmir: A Look at the Kunan Poshpora Rapes." *Al Jazeera*, December 24, 2016.

Shohat, Ella. 2003. "Post-Third Worldist Culture: Gender, Nation, and the Cinema." In *Rethiinking Third Cinema*, edited by Anthony R. Guneratne and Wimal Dissanayak. New York: Routledge.

Shohat, Ella, and Robert Stam. 2014. *Unthinking Eurocentrism: Multiculturalism and the Media*. 2nd ed. New York: Routledge.

Smets, Kevin. 2015. "Cinemas of Conflict: A Framework of Cinematic Engagement with Violent Conflict Illustrated with Kurdish Cinema." *International Journal of Communication* 9: 2435–55.

Sunder Rajan, Rajeswari. 1993. *Real and Imagined Woman: Gender, Culture and Postcolonialism*. New York: Routledge

Waldman, Diane, and Janet Walker. 1999. "Introduction." In *Feminism and Documentary*, edited by Diane Waldman and Janet Walker, 1–35. Minneapolis: University of Minnesota Press.

14 CINEMA THAT RAISES A CRITICAL CONSCIOUSNESS

The Films of Alamgir Kabir

NAADIR JUNAID

THE CONSCIOUS ATTEMPT TO DISPENSE WITH FORMULAIC audience-pleasing elements makes politically aware films depart from the aesthetics of profit-driven cinema. Instead of immersing the spectators in escapist entertainment, politically critical films attempt to expose the underlying causes of urgent social and political problems. The disclosure of social injustice unsettles and disturbs the viewers. Such films also provide scathing criticisms of contemporary problems. Experimentation with the filmic form is another important trait of political cinema. Thus, such films subvert the stereotypical conventions of commercially motivated films both thematically and stylistically. In a political film, raising revolutionary and critical consciousness is given precedence over commercial interest. Political cinema marks a radical departure from the clichéd entertainment-based films produced to maximize profit. Instead of deploying trite filmic techniques and sentimental slush, politically conscious films experiment with the film form and come to grips with social and political issues.

The Bangladeshi filmmaker Alamgir Kabir, who died in a car accident in 1989, believed that a good film should make people aware of contemporary problems. It should illustrate the actual condition of society. To become a good film, he said, a film should have social value (Atikuzzaman and Paul 2018, 223). According to this director, a film that does not deal with social reality would not be useful to the people. In 1971, during the Liberation War between Bangladesh and Pakistan, Kabir went into exile in India and actively took part in the cultural activities organized to strengthen Bangladesh's struggle for independence. At that time in India, Kabir worked closely with Zahir Raihan, the renowned Bengali filmmaker whose films achieved commercial and critical success during Pakistani rule. In 1970, Zahir Raihan made *Jibon thekey neya* (Glimpses from life, 1970), in which for the first time the spectators of East Pakistan saw in a Bangla film the conscious attempt to tackle contemporary political problems head-on. Through a metaphorical narrative, Raihan provides angry denunciations of the dictatorial regime and political repression that tormented Bengalis of East Pakistan.

Jibon thekey neya is not experimental in style. It has a linear narrative, and in the film the director uses certain ingredients typical of commercial cinema such as songs, humor, and romantic relationships. However, instead of utilizing them to provide entertainment, Raihan effectively conveys political statements through these elements. Political criticisms of *Jibon thekey neya* certainly disturbed the military establishment, and the government tried to ban the film at the production stage. The director had to make a few changes to get official permission for its release. But due to the hostility of the establishment toward this film, Raihan experienced difficulty securing official permission for release in cinemas. The situation angered the people of Dhaka and other nearby towns, as they were eagerly awaiting this film. Then, for the first time, East Pakistan witnessed moviegoers demonstrating in the streets to protest the administration's attempt to prevent the Bengalis of East Pakistan from watching a politically conscious Bangla film made by a Bengali director (Hayat 2007, 107).

In the 1960s, East Pakistan was often politically turbulent. However, Bengali directors in East Pakistan at that time rarely confronted contemporary reality in their films. We may assume that because of the restrictions imposed by military rule, Bengali filmmakers were reluctant to make overt political statements in their films. In *Jibon thekey neya*, Zahir Raihan condemns an oppressive regime through allegorical narrative. Until that time, few Bangla films produced in East Pakistan attempted to provide political critiques. Bengali filmmakers of East Pakistan did not demonstrate much interest in experimenting with film language. Thus, when Bangla films did address social problems, their critiques seemed ineffective because these films did not break with the traditional way of depicting reality suggested by Jean-Louis Comolli and Jean Narboni (1993) in their influential essay "Cinema/Ideology/Criticism." For Comolli and Narboni, in order for a film to be considered oppositional or politically effective it has to be unconventional both in form and content (Nichols 1993, 26). Despite the political oppression and people's courageous protest in the 1960s, Bangla films made in East Pakistan did not incorporate piercing political critiques to denounce the system. Nor were Bangla films formally innovative. Alamgir Kabir observes:

> Sentiments of all kinds used to reign supreme in the Bengali Cinema's 'realism' from pre-Independence days. A lot of tears, exaggerated and sentimentalized depiction of the plight of the lower middle-class that appeared more like a complaint than a social protest; simple, adolescent romance between handsome boys and beautiful girls etc were the typical ingredients that Dacca film-makers of the early period easily inherited and assimilated. . . . By the end of 1969 the film scene looked really dismal. Majority of the productions were either plagiarized versions of third rate but popular Indian movies or were simply uninspired hack-work. (Kabir 1979, 38, 44)

Zahir Raihan's seminal political feature *Jibon thekey neya* brought a much-needed breakthrough in the realm of socially meaningful Bangla cinema made in East Pakistan. During the Liberation War in 1971, Zahir Raihan made an aesthetically innovative documentary, *Stop Genocide*, that exposes and denounces the atrocities and genocide committed by the Pakistani army in Bangladesh. Alamgir Kabir made a documentary titled *Liberation Fighters*. These political documentaries demonstrated these directors' interest in making films that depart from the conventions of entertainment-based mainstream cinema. Bangladesh was liberated in December 1971. In January 1972, Zahir Raihan disappeared from Mirpur in the city of Dhaka when Bangladeshi army and police personnel came under attack in this area by armed pro-Pakistani Biharis. Zahir Raihan has not been seen since that day, and his body was not recovered along with the bodies of Bengali soldiers killed on that day in Mirpur (Manik 2002, 13, 57). Raihan's disappearance certainly came as a serious blow to politically conscious filmmaking in Bangladesh. After the unfortunate disappearance of Zahir Raihan in 1972, Alamgir Kabir played a key role in making socially meaningful and aesthetically innovative films in Bangladesh.

In one of his articles Kabir opines that a truly gifted artist does not lack political consciousness. A talented artist may possess a progressive or reactionary ideology, but s/he does not remain indifferent to social and political issues (Atikuzzaman and Paul 2018, 150). Before embarking on filmmaking, Kabir worked as a journalist in London and Dhaka. He was also a film critic in various magazines. In these years, Kabir did not remain detached from political activities. He became involved in revolutionary politics. During his stay in Europe in the 1960s, Kabir became a member of FLN, a nationalist political party of Algeria that fought against the French colonizers from 1954 to 1962 and achieved Algeria's independence from

French colonial rule. He also showed an interest in taking part in activities to liberate Palestine. In England, he took part in the Campaign against Racial Discrimination. Once, Kabir, along with a few of his companions, was arrested by French authorities on the border between France and Switzerland. French authorities found some secret documents in their possession, and three of Kabir's companions were executed. Kabir, fortunately, was only sent to prison. After eight months, he was released from jail and returned to London (Atikuzzaman and Paul 2018, 216–17).

In 1963, with a view to working to liberate East Pakistan from Pakistani rule, Kabir and others formed a secret organization, the East Bengal Liberation Front. They wanted to organize an armed struggle in East Pakistan. Kabir learned to use light firearms at that time. Soon, he returned to Dhaka and contacted the leaders of certain far-left political parties. But Bengali far-left leaders did not support armed insurrection in East Pakistan (Atikuzzaman and Paul 2018, 217). In the meantime, the Pakistani establishment learned of Kabir's opposition to the government. He was arrested and sent to prison, where he was interrogated by the Special Branch.

At that time, Bangabandhu Sheikh Mujibur Rahman was in jail, and he and Kabir became close. Kabir was released after three months in jail on condition that he would not travel outside the Dhaka metropolitan area. In 1971, when the Liberation War began in Bangladesh, Kabir went to India to work as the chief reporter for the Bangladesh government in exile. He also became the chief of the English news section of Swadhin Bangla Betar Kendra, the radio broadcasting center established by the Bangladesh government. Using a pseudonym, Kabir read English news at Swadhin Bangla Betar Kendra until November 1971. In December 1971, when Pakistani troops were surrendering to the Bangladeshi liberation forces and the Indian Army, Kabir entered Bangladesh with Bengali liberation fighters and captured images of the surrender of Pakistani forces. He returned to independent Bangladesh from India in January 1972.

Kabir's opposition to colonial and undemocratic rule indicates that he was strongly critical of political oppression and injustice. For him, a true artist has to be politically conscious. Kabir's films were informed by his politically aware temperament. From 1973 to 1979, Kabir made four features. Because of their unconventional form and politically critical subject matter, his films were significantly different from most other films made in Bangladesh in the 1970s. Formal innovation was not commonplace in Bangladeshi alternative films even in the post-independence period. From the 1970s to the present, only a handful of Bangladeshi films have used unorthodox and innovative film techniques, and they rarely provide direct political statements. Kabir's films thus stand in sharp contrast to many alternative films made in Bangladesh thus far. In London, when Kabir was working in a British firm, he watched Ingmar Bergman's influential film *The Seventh Seal* (1957). The Swedish film made a profound impact on Kabir. He writes, "After watching this film, I realized for the first time that cinema is such a powerful and promising medium. I was so deeply moved. I gave up my job. Following the suggestion of my friends, I did a course on cinema theory in an academy in London. I achieved some ideas about filmmaking in that academy" (Atikuzzaman and Paul 2018, 216).

Kabir also studied film history, film direction, and film aesthetics at the British Film Institute. He wrote on cinema in various magazines, including the well-known film journal *Sight and Sound*. In Dhaka, he was the editor of the film magazine *Sequence*. Given his preference for political awareness, his taste for thought-provoking films such as *The Seventh Seal*, and his knowledge of filmmaking, it was obvious that he would not produce formulaic, showy, entertainment-based films. This chapter examines three films made by Alamgir Kabir in the 1970s to understand how these films depart from the aesthetics of profit-driven mainstream cinema and how the director provides criticisms of social and political problems in these films.

DHEEREY BOHE MEGHNA: A CONSCIOUS ATTEMPT TO BREAK WITH TRADITION

Kabir's debut full-length feature, *Dheerey bohe Meghna* (Quiet flows the River Meghna, 1973), was the first film produced in post-independence Bangladesh that made a radical departure from the language of Bangladeshi conventional and alternative cinema. Kabir was aware of the lack of formal experimentation in Bangladeshi films, and in his maiden feature he used filmic devices not often seen in films made in Bangladesh. In his book on Bangladeshi cinema, Kabir writes, "When I opted for film-making during Liberation War I had felt that my foremost task would be to try and usher in a simple cinematic language and make it acceptable to an audience who have been thoroughly brainwashed for decades by what may be termed as *camera-theatre*" (Kabir 1979, 70). Keeping this in mind, in *Dheerey bohe Meghna* Kabir dispensed with theatricality, which was a common feature of Bangladeshi cinema drawing on a realist aesthetic. The film is set just two years after the Liberation War, when people's minds were still haunted by painful memories of the death and destruction they had witnessed. Kabir portrays the confusion and ambivalence of people, including freedom fighters, in the newly liberated society.

Lyle Pearson (1977, 28) says, "*Meghna*, as Kracauer would have film, resembles Italian neo-realism, structured in episodes, as if Dhaka has become Rossellini's *Open City*." Kabir uses extensive documentary footage of genocide and carnage that he captured during the war. The use of documentary material in a drama was disliked in Bangladeshi cinema, but Kabir (1979, 71) avers, "Despite pressure, I stubbornly resisted surrender to the conventional format." Flashbacks appear frequently in the film, disrupting the linear progression of the narrative. The film also uses other complicated devices, such as voice-over narration and internal monologue. Sometimes the characters are seen talking about contemporary issues, conveying the director's stance on particular political issues.

In newly independent Bangladesh, many people were confused about the relationship between Bangladesh and India. In 1971, thousands of Bangladeshi refugees took shelter in India, Bangladeshi political leaders conducted their activities from India, and Bangladeshi freedom fighters received military training from the Indian Army to fight the Pakistani forces. From December 1971, the Indian Army officially started confronting Pakistani forces. Many Indian soldiers died in 1971 during battles with the Pakistani army. However, after independence some people in Bangladesh were hesitant about a close relationship with India, fearing that a powerful neighbor such as India would dominate Bangladesh. Kabir expresses his view on this issue in a scene showing a discussion between two journalists. Rahimullah asks Sumit the freedom fighter whether it is necessary to admire India in order to be considered a patriot. Sumit replies that the term *patriotism* is very complex, but for him, the issue about the relationship between Bangladesh and India is quite simple. Sumit points out that without India's help it would have been very difficult for Bangladesh to achieve independence in such a short time, because in 1971 some powerful nations opposed the emergence of Bangladesh as an independent country.

When Rahimullah shows his anxiety by saying that Bangladesh might become a weak nation by being very thankful to its powerful neighbor, Sumit says that Bangladesh will only become weak if it fails to keep its dignity and self-respect. Such dialogues reveal the director's political position, and the technique resembles the explicit teaching method. Explicit teaching takes place when the director conveys a message through direct audience address or two persons conversing, where the dialogues are actually directed at the audience (Campbell and Cortes 1979, 385). The scene demonstrates that the director is using cinema to provide political statements and to make people think about contemporary problems instead of offering an escape from social reality. Another scene showing two freedom fighters in Dhaka after two years of independence illustrates Kabir's intention to confront the tensions of post-independence Bangladesh. A car has been hijacked by two armed young men in a city street in broad daylight. The following scene shows the hijackers in a quiet place. Soon we hear one hijacker's internal monologue and realize that this man, Ujjol, had been a freedom fighter, but after the war he received no recognition or job, so he became a hijacker. He seems disgruntled that he did not get anything from the country even though he took part in the war, risking his life to free Bangladesh from the occupation of the Pakistani army. But soon he starts thinking rationally: Can I expect a reward for saving my mother? Can I become so mean-spirited? When he has this realization, he smiles faintly.

Ujjol now decides to return the hijacked car to its owner. His accomplice is surprised and asks if Ujjol has gone mad. But Ujjol replies that he acted like a madman in becoming a hijacker, but now he is sane again. Ujjol remains adamant about returning the car. The other young man shoots him point-blank in the back, but before dying, Ujjol manages to shoot and kill his companion. Thus two young men die in the independent country where they were supposed to live happily and work for the development of society. The scene shows that the young freedom fighters are getting neither recognition nor an opportunity to make a decent living in the newly independent society. Out of frustration, insecurity, and anger, some of them become hijackers because they keep firearms with them. Through the character of Ujjol, the director shows that not all of the young men involved in crime in today's society are morally debased.

We may surmise that Kabir condemns the social and political structure of the new society. Due to the failure of the political system, a patriotic and courageous young man such as Ujjol, who took part in the Liberation War, is now tormented by feelings of despair and dissatisfaction in a society that was liberated through the fearless struggle of freedom fighters against brutal military aggression. Kabir surely encourages the spectator to think critically as to why a freedom fighter with a conscience would turn into a hijacker in the newly independent society. However, Kabir does not show the causes of such a negative situation nor does he expose the people who are responsible. But he draws attention to one of the major problems of contemporary society.

The director said he had two major aims in this film: the story of the film would not include any imaginary events, and the film would reject the traditional storytelling style of Bangladeshi films. *Dheerey bohe Meghna* shows various incidents that took place during the Liberation War—the rape and torture of Bangladeshi women by Pakistani army personnel, the killing of a Bengali military officer by a Pakistani army officer, and the boat journey of frightened Bangladeshis toward a safe place. The film begins with a voice-over. This strategy is used in some other scenes as well. The linear progression of the narrative is often interrupted by flashbacks. The inclusion of real footage captured in 1971 makes two sequences similar to scenes of a documentary. In one of the sequences, Sumit and a family friend, Anita, are sitting in a projection room watching some film footage. On the projection screen before them, real footage of carnage and destruction committed by the Pakistani army appear. This sequence calls attention to the film medium and reminds people of the barbaric acts of the army and its local collaborators.

At one point in the screening, Sumit says that now images appear of dead bodies of Bengali intellectuals who were murdered in Dhaka in December 1971. Decomposed dead bodies are seen floating on the water and lying in the ditch. The hands are still tied on some of these bodies. Grim and gloomy background music is heard on the soundtrack when such real images are shown. Just a few days before the surrender of the Pakistani army, local collaborators abducted many Bengali intellectuals from their houses. Later, the dead bodies of some were found in certain areas in the city. Others were never found. In 1971, a group named Al-Badar was formed with Bengali collaborators of the Pakistani army. The members of Al-Badar were Islamist fanatics. When Pakistani soldiers and Al-Badar members realized that the army was on the verge of defeat, Al-Badar started abducting Bengali secular intellectuals. They brutally murdered Bengali intellectuals so that these knowledgeable, enlightened, and cultured persons could not impart their wisdom and provide people with guidance in independent Bangladesh. The use of such documentary footage disturbs viewers and serves to disrupt their passive involvement with the film's narrative. At the end of the film, the director uses documentary footage again to show Bangladesh after the surrender of the Pakistani army. Images show the jubilation of Bengali freedom fighters, the movement of Indian tanks, and Bangladeshi national leaders addressing the people. Through the use of filmic devices such as voice-over, flashbacks, and documentary footage, *Dheerey bohe Meghna* departs from the traditional storytelling pattern of Bangladeshi cinema.

In this film, we see the romantic relationship between a Muslim man and a Hindu woman and close relationships between Muslim and Hindu families. Religious conflict is a long-standing problem in the Indian subcontinent, but in 1971, the Bangladeshis maintained religious harmony and secularist principles when they fought the Pakistani aggressors. By showing the strong attachment and close friendship between Muslims and Hindus, *Dheerey bohe Meghna* advocates a noncommunal spirit. During the conversation between Sumit and Rahimullah in the newspaper office, Sumit says: "By going through agonizing oppression, peace-loving people of Bengal continued their struggle against exploitation, superstition, and communalism for centuries. Today's independent Bangladesh is just the first step toward real victory. The next phase would be to establish an exploitation-free society. And Bangladesh needs to inspire millions of oppressed people throughout the world who are struggling against imperialism, racism, and exploitation." We understand that through these dialogues the director conveys his own ideas. Kabir's first feature strongly denounces political oppression and exploitation. He highlights the courage and determination of the people of Bangladesh to resist and fight the oppressors. At the same time, the film also encourages people to embrace noncommunal values.

SURJOKANNYA: CRITICISM OF PATRIARCHY THROUGH FANTASY

Whereas *Dhirey bohe Meghna* makes extensive use of documentary footage to establish realism, Kabir's second feature, *Surjokannya* (Daughter of the sun, 1976), revolves around fantasy, dream, and illusion. Instead of footage of real events, imaginative and unrealistic scenes appear frequently in *Surjokannya*. A young artist named Lenin is the protagonist of the film. He has a tendency to fantasize about becoming a hero. He often imagines that he becomes a powerful political leader, or a successful cricket player, or a strong individual who helps people by punishing criminals. But in reality, Lenin is jobless, and most of the time he only wanders aimlessly around the city streets.

At one point, he is employed as an interior designer in the shop of his affluent friend Russell. One night, to Lenin's utter surprise, a female mannequin in the shop turns into a human being. When the light of day appears, she changes back into a mannequin, but every night at midnight she becomes a beautiful woman and starts talking with Lenin. They even leave the shop and go to other places, and they enjoy each other's company. Lenin starts calling the woman Labannya. The spectator may think that because of his habit of immersing himself in fantasy and daydream, Lenin is imagining talking to a beautiful woman like Labannya. At the end of the film, Lenin meets a friend of his younger sister, and to his surprise he finds out that the young lady is Labannya.

Despite the director's use of fantasy, *Surjokannya* remains far from an escapist film. Through the conversations between Lenin and Labannya, the director criticizes the domination and maltreatment of women in patriarchal society. In one scene, they are sitting on a boat in the river, and Lenin asks Labannya about her true identity. Then, through a jump-cut, Labannya is seen in a long shot on the deserted balcony of a very old palace from a low angle. She speaks about an ancient time when women were free, and they considered the sun to be their father. The women raised their male children lovingly. But when the males grew up, they used their strength to imprison the daughters of the sun. From that moment onward, the men started treating the women as slaves, mere commodities to satisfy their lust. The women lost their independence. Giving birth to babies turned into their primary duty.

Labannya walks slowly on the balcony. The huge pillars of the palace are seen beside her. The row of huge pillars conveys a sense of confinement, suggesting Labannya's lack of freedom. In the film, the mannequin metaphorically indicates the state of women in a male-dominated society. The mannequin of a woman is used in a shop to display clothes and attract customers. Just as people tend to look at a mannequin kept in the display window, women are subjected to the male gaze in a patriarchal society. It is often claimed in feminist critiques that in patriarchal society women are treated as objects for achieving pleasure. In her influential essay "Visual Pleasure and Narrative Cinema," Laura Mulvey states, "In a world ordered by sexual imbalance, pleasure in looking has been split between active/male and passive/female. The determining male gaze projects its fantasy onto the female figure, which is styled accordingly" (quoted in Rushton and Bettinson 2010, 72). In patriarchal society men get pleasure from looking, and women are objects to be looked at.

By showing the mannequin in *Surjokannya*, the filmmaker points at the objectification of women in the patriarchal society. Kabir also uses a cartoon animation sequence depicting the maltreatment of women by men, the first use of animation in Bangladeshi cinema. Other unorthodox cinematic devices, such as internal monologue, shot in negative, freeze shot, and dream sequences, are used in the film. The director also uses contrasting shots and elements. In one sequence, city streets are shown through a rapid tracking shot. The shot cuts to the scenic beauty of a calm river. On the soundtrack we hear the music of indigenous instruments as well as a track by the Beatles. Local artistic objects are shown, while in another scene a character recites dialogue from Shakespeare's *Richard III*. Like Kabir's first feature, *Surjokannya* is also formally innovative.

Dheerey bohe Meghna ends with optimism. Although Kabir draws people's attention to the long-lasting problem of the domination of women, *Surjokannya* also ends on a happy note. A friend of his younger sister comes to meet Lenin. To his great surprise, she looks exactly like Labannya. Lenin's friend Russell returns to his girlfriend, Monica, and they seem very happy. The question can be raised whether it is possible to raise consciousness about a social problem such as the domination of women without disturbing viewers. In this film, two male characters, Lenin and Russell, seem to have decent dispositions. They do not seem like men who abuse women. But by showing their caring attitudes toward women, the director makes men aware of the importance of taking responsibility in society as refined and reasonable individuals.

RUPALI SHOIKAT E: A FILM'S RESEMBLANCE TO A POLITICAL PAMPHLET

The form of Kabir's film becomes more adventurous in his fourth feature, *Rupali shoikat e* (On the silvery beach, 1979). Kabir also provides overt political condemnations of the autocratic regime in this film. The film is set in former East Pakistan, and it depicts the period from 1966 to 1970. In those years, East Pakistan witnessed the growing discontent of Bengalis with the Pakistani military government. As in *Surjokannya*, the protagonist's name is Lenin (actor Bulbul Ahmed plays the role of Lenin both in *Surjokannya* and *Rupali shoikat e*). Unlike *Surjokannya*'s protagonist, who has a predilection for pleasant contemplation, the protagonist of *Rupali shoikat e* is a courageous young journalist who belongs to an underground socialist party. Lenin is very critical of the military regime. In *Rupali shoikat e*, the director uses this protagonist with a revolutionary bent to provide strong denunciations of authoritarian rule. In independent Bangladesh, from 1975 onward military generals became most powerful figures in the government. We may assume that *Rupali shoikat e* intends to draw people's attention to the harmful effects of military rule in Bangladesh by denouncing the military regime of the Pakistani period.

The director incorporates real events in the fictional narrative of *Rupali shoikat e*. At times, the film seems autobiographical. The narrative is loosely structured, and the film is often interrupted by documentary footage, interview sequences, or scenes from the shooting of a film. The film bears a resemblance to direct cinema, a documentary film genre that emphasizes authentic depiction of real events. Kabir's camera does not go to the streets often, but the repeated use of footage of real events and specific dialogues that seem more like political discussions lend the film a documentary-like quality. *Rupali shoikat e* becomes self-reflexive by showing the shooting of films. By foregrounding aspects of the filmmaking process, a self-reflexive scene disrupts the spectator's passive immersion in the film's fictional world. Thus, self-reflexivity within a film serves to ensure the spectator's active engagement with the film's events.

In one sequence, Lenin is seen capturing images using a movie camera. He points his camera directly at the viewer. The scene is followed by real footage captured during the shooting of *Jibon thekey neya*. Zahir Raihan is seen directing the performers. The scene of Lenin pointing the movie camera at the spectator and the real images of the shooting of an important Bangla film draw attention to the filmmaking process. Until that time Bangladeshi film viewers did not see such complicated techniques in a local film. In fact, self-reflexive strategies are still rarely used in Bangladeshi films. Kabir's strong interest in using unorthodox cinematic means serves to distinguish his films from those made by his contemporaries and successors.

Lenin is a member of a left-wing political party and is sometimes seen attending clandestine meetings organized by the party. In these sequences we hear discussions among party activists about various initiatives and strategies taken by their party to resist the Pakistani government. Such scenes containing political messages distinguish *Rupali shoikat e* from an entertainment-based film. But Kabir was aware of the difference between a political film and a propaganda film. Although Kabir's preference for leftist politics is obvious in the film, he does not uncritically support the leftists.

The film is critical of the tendency of left-wing parties to become engaged in factional conflict rather than initiating organized movements against an oppressive regime. Criticizing intraparty conflict during a conversation with a left-wing leader, Lenin says, "All of you claim to be revolutionaries. But do you respect democratic centralism for the sake of party discipline? Every time some members tend to disagree with the others, the party is separated into different groups, then the groups will turn into subgroups, and subgroups will eventually turn into smaller sub subgroups. These groups are extremely hostile to each other. Ideological difference or self-seeking motivation—what is the main cause of such conflicts among leftist groups?"

Conflicts between leftist groups cost many lives in Bangladesh in the post-independence period. The left-wing parties could never convince large numbers of people to support them, and they failed to organize a socialist revolution. Exploitation by the ruling few continues to exist. In the 1960s, Kabir was known as a Maoist (Atikuzzaman and Paul 2018, 217). At that time, he made contact with prominent far-left political leaders of East Pakistan. From 1966 on, Kabir worked as a journalist in Dhaka. So Kabir and the protagonist of *Rupali shoikat e* have a lot in common. During a conversation with the left-wing leader, Lenin's words reveal his discontent with the leaders of left-wing parties: "These leaders have been active in politics for many years, yet the general people of the country hardly know the essence of socialist politics. Please let these leaders know that they will never be able to organize a revolution against the existing social and economic structure if they remain submissive to people in authority for personal gain."

Several sequences of *Rupali shoikat e* include documentary footage of the armed struggle against political oppression in Lebanon, Vietnam, and Angola. The use of real footage of political struggle, a device rarely used in Bangladeshi films, indicates the director's intention to dispense with traditional filmic techniques. Conversations in a newspaper office, political party meetings, and a police interrogation room include criticisms of the autocratic government, demonstrating that the film is political both in form and content. Certain real events, such as the government's attempt to ban Zahir Raihan's *Jibon thekey neya* and the attack on a Dhaka University professor by progovernment students, are included in the narrative.

One day in the newspaper office, Lenin finds out that the government intends to ban *Jibon thekey neya* during shooting. He quickly goes to the studio with a movie camera in order to keep some footage of the film in case it is really banned. As he starts recording the shooting scenes, the spectator sees real footage showing Zahir Raihan and other actors in the film. In another sequence, Lenin is again seen using his camera to film an interview with Professor Mahmud of Dhaka University, who was injured by activists in a progovernment student group. Because Professor Mahmud was critical of government policies, the progovernment students assaulted him. These scenes foreground the filmmaking process, thereby breaking the illusion of a fictional story line. The insertion of real events into the narrative lends an air of reality to the film, which is considered one of the important attributes of a politically critical film aiming to raise radical consciousness.

In 1966, during politically turbulent days marked by antigovernment agitation in East Pakistan, Alamgir Kabir was arrested and sent to prison. In the film, Lenin is arrested for his antigovernment stance. At one point he is taken to the office of a Special Branch officer for interrogation. During interrogation, Lenin comments about Field Marshal Ayub Khan, the despotic ruler of Pakistan, "President Ayub reminds me of the Roman king Nero. Having read the books written by the president, I have a feeling that he habitually looks down on people and despises Bengalis from the heart. But Bengalis constitute the majority of the population in Pakistan. And it could be dangerous to despise those who form the majority." In response to a question from the Pakistani Special Branch officer, Lenin boldly says, "You want fawning flatterers who would always say 'yes sir' to your decisions whether they are just or unjust. But I would like to have my right to say 'no sir.' I want to have my democratic right to live with my self-esteem along with others in the society."

The following shot shows Lenin's face in a big close-up. He says, "I don't want dictatorship, because dictatorship is an affront to humanity." A subsequent sequence shows documentary scenes of the people's plight and political protests in different countries. A famous Bengali song is heard on the soundtrack—*Bicharpati tomar bichar korbe jaara aaj jegeche shei janata* (Today the mass of people have risen up against the ruler to put him on trial). It becomes clear that the director is encouraging the spectators to protest unjust and oppressive political rule. Expressing disdain for dictatorship becomes the main political message of the film.

Bangladesh won independence through a people's war, yet the social, political, and economic structures of the society did not undergo total change after 1971. Military rule returned within a few years because the new society failed to fulfill the fundamental requirements of decolonization suggested by Frantz Fanon: a complete change in colonial social and political institutions and a change of consciousness (Hansen 1977, 119). For Fanon, a psychic change that helps one to perceive reality differently is essential in order to ensure authentic decolonization: "Decolonization is quite simply the replacing of a certain 'species' of men by another 'species' of men. Without any period of transition, there is a total, complete and absolute substitution" (quoted in Hansen 1977, 120). Under Pakistani rule, Bengalis struggled against a military establishment. But the return of military rule in independent Bangladesh and people's lack of protest indicate that the majority failed to turn themselves into a new species of men.

Rupali shoikat e, set in the 1960s, is a political allegory that strongly criticizes authoritarian rule. Robert Stam describes a variant of allegory, where the allegory "serves as a form of protective camouflage against censorious regimes, where the film uses the past to speak of the present, or treats a microcosmic power situation to evoke a macrocosmic structure" (Stam 2000, 288–89). By showing the political domination experienced by the Bengalis under Pakistani rule, Kabir provokes spectators to think critically about democracy, freedom of expression, political consciousness, and protest in the contemporary society of Bangladesh. By denying spectators the usual entertainment available in mainstream cinema and prioritizing direct political statements, *Rupali shoikat e* becomes a rare Bangladeshi film, which resembles a political pamphlet. The director's particular interest in pamphleteering makes his fourth feature different from other politically aware films made in this country to date.

In the realm of Bangladeshi cinema, both Zahir Raihan and Alamgir Kabir made important politically oriented films. Unfortunately, both of them died untimely deaths. Zahir Raihan disappeared after an attack on Bangladeshi soldiers and police personnel by pro-Pakistani elements just after the Liberation War. Alamgir Kabir died in a car accident. They tried to raise sociopolitical consciousness by dealing with important social and political issues in their films. To avoid the restrictions of censors, they made their politically alert films allegorical. The chapter discusses these particular films because they differ significantly from most other Bangladeshi films made to date that tend to address social issues. Numerous social and political problems continue to exist in Bangladesh, but in Bangladeshi alternative films we do not see attempts to confront such problems using unorthodox filmic techniques. Overt political statements are not made in Bangladeshi films. We may think that the directors are apprehensive about making political statements, assuming that their films will be subjected to ban or censor.

In recent years, we haven't seen many films in Bangladesh where the filmmakers provide scathing criticisms of burning political problems, unjust political circumstances, or social ills using a metaphorical narrative. Lack of formal experimentation in the majority of alternative films produced in Bangladesh makes us think that filmmakers are unwilling to create an opportunity for spectators to think critically about cinematic language. This is disappointing, because the use of unorthodox methods on a regular basis would have helped spectators attain a critical understanding of the language of cinema. Only a handful of Bangladeshi films are politically oriented in form and content. *Jibon thekey neya*, *Dhirey bohe Meghna*, *Surjokannya*, and *Rupali shoikat e* depart thematically and stylistically from most other Bangladeshi films.

Alamgir Kabir once said that in any country the filmmaker can shape the taste of the audience (Atikuzzaman and Paul 2018, 93). It is not logical to think that only the intellectual elite would understand the messages provided by films that use unorthodox film techniques. Important Bangla films made in West Bengal, India, and Bangladesh, such as Satyajit Ray's *Pather panchali* (Song of the little road, 1955), Ritwik Ghatak's *Meghe dhaka taara* (The cloud-capped star, 1960), Mrinal Sen's *Calcutta 71* (1972), Sheikh Niamat Ali and Masihuddin Shaker's *Surjo dighal bari* (The ominous house, 1979), and Tareque Masud's *Matir moina* (The clay bird, 2002), use innovative cinematic means. But these films show the problems that torment the lives of common people in towns and villages. Ordinary people living in towns and villages can relate the situations shown in these films to the circumstances they experience in their own lives or see in the lives of their neighbors and relatives. Therefore, it is not difficult for people who are not very educated to comprehend the messages conveyed by these films, even though they do not use a conventional storytelling pattern or stereotypical film strategies. If filmmakers make realistic, politically conscious, aesthetically innovative films and the state makes sure that such films reach the general public, people will become accustomed to thought-provoking films. Then, even the general public will acquire a taste for artistically innovative and socially meaningful films that do not resemble glitzy and showy profit-driven cinema.

In Bangladeshi films, we continue to witness a reluctance to experiment with cinematic language. We may suspect that because of such reluctance the auteur films of Bangladesh barely managed to attract worldwide attention. In Bangladesh, films made by Alamgir Kabir remain exceptional because they deploy innovative cinematic means, and they also come to terms with social and political issues in order to raise radical and critical consciousness. Many Bangladeshi films do not possess such attributes. Kabir's films are effective as a cinema of resistance because instead of prioritizing entertainment to secure financial benefit, his films are critical of social and political problems and attempt to raise people's sociopolitical consciousness. We can hope that new Bangladeshi filmmakers draw inspiration from the films of Alamgir Kabir, and that by making politically aware, stylistically innovative films, they will bring much-needed change to Bangladeshi cinema.

REFERENCES

Atikuzzaman, Abul Khaer Mohammad, and Priyam Pritim Paul, eds. 2018. *Chalatchitra o jatiya mukti* (Cinema and national liberation), vol. 1 of *Collected Works of Alamgir Kabir*. Dhaka: Agami Prokashoni, Modhupok.

Campbell, Leon G., and Carlos E. Cortés. 1979. "Film as a Revolutionary Weapon: A Jorge Sanjinés Retrospective." *History Teacher* 12, no. 3: 383–402.

Hansen, Emmanuel. 1977. *Frantz Fanon: Social and Political Thought*. Columbus: Ohio State University Press.

Hayat, Anupam. 2007. *Zahir Raihaner chalatchitra: Patabhumi, Bishoy O Boishistaya*. Dhaka: Dibyaprokash.

Kabir, Alamgir. 1979. *Film in Bangladesh*. Dhaka: Bangla Academy.

Manik, Julfiqar Ali. 2002. *Muktijuddher shesh ranangan Mirpur: Zahir Raihan ontordhan rahashshaybhed*. Dhaka: Subarna.

Nichols, Bill, ed. 1993. *Movies and Methods*, vol. 1. Calcutta: Seagull Books.

Pearson, Lyle. 1977. "Alamgir Kabir: Bangladesh's International Film-Maker." *Sequence* 3, no. 1 (Winter): 27–34.

Rushton, Richard, and Gary Bettinson. 2010. *What Is Film Theory? An Introduction to Contemporary Debates*. Berkshire, NY: Open University Press.

Stam, Robert. 2000. *Film Theory: An Introduction*. Oxford: Blackwell Publishing.

15 ETHICAL ENCOUNTERS

Friendship and Healing in Contemporary Films about the Bangladesh Liberation War

ELORA HALIM CHOWDHURY

BANGLADESHI FILMS ABOUT THE MUKTIJUDDHO (BANGLADESH Liberation War of 1971) occupy critical significance within the genre of national cinema. Many of these films show the struggle for independence through a gendered and sexualized lens of male valor and female shame, representing this defining event through genocidal violence, the heroism of the freedom fighters, and the sacrifices of women. The Muktijuddho has not been adequately recognized globally, or even regionally, and state-level negotiations involving India, Pakistan, and Bangladesh have failed to bring closure to the crimes against humanity. Instead, national governments have used "the inspiration of 1971" (*shadhinotar chetona*) to promote their varied political agendas. In this context, film and literature have been the mediums through which a collective memory and national solidarity have been shaped and maintained. Three contemporary films, *Shongram 71*, *Itihaash konna*, and *Meherjaan*, grapple with contested and intractable questions surrounding the war that are still very much relegated to the margins of historical memory. These films engage with the multifaceted narratives of the birth of a nation, the foundational struggle over identity, the intimate relation among gender, nation, and sexuality, the legacy of war, and the ethical reckoning with trauma. All three films narrate these stories through the lens of intimate, affective, interpersonal relationships as opposed to state or juridical negotiations, thereby emphasizing the personal at times over collective transformation or justice. In this chapter, I want to build on the idea of national cinema to explore how it may document and engender a conversation about nation, history, identity, healing, and reconciliation. Arguably, healing and reconciliation have not figured prominently in national conversations about the war and its tragic aftermath, where loss and suffering still prevail as an open wound in the national psyche. The chapter has two sections: the first provides historical context for Muktijuddho films, and the second analyzes war themes in more recent and divergent films that reveal the national silences about identity, gender, and healing. Finally, I conclude with comments about national cinema as a medium to generate a conversation about history and memory, politics and aesthetics, social as well as legal recognition of justice, and human rights—within an increasingly transnational space.

The Muktijuddho has figured prominently in films produced both in the commercial industry and outside of it. The films I draw attention to here represent a shift away from the binaries of oppression and resistance, and victimhood and agency, especially with regard to the depiction of women's experiences in the Muktijuddho. Instead of primarily focusing on state-level negotiations or masculine combat, each film equally highlights the intimate, domestic, or "feminine" sphere as a site of struggle and meaning. By a "feminine" sphere, I mean those spaces that are defined as feminized in dominant patriarchal ideology; these can also be read as a source and portrayal of nonconformity, mutuality, and solidarity. By allowing the viewer to remember, imagine, and work through traumatic events such as war and conflict by way of a feminine aesthetic, cinema can help us appreciate the moral choices and interpretive acts of women often cast as passive victims or witnesses. As viewers we learn to appreciate cinema as a site where diverse women's stories are memorialized, just as the state erects memorials and museums to commemorate martyrs.

Prominent film historian Zakir Hossain Raju (2015) argues that national cinema in Third World contexts is a vehicle to engage with the predicaments of nationhood and identity within colonial and postcolonial conditions. In Bangladesh, cinema as an institution has grown during a period of contestation about nationhood, modernity, and cultural identity. Categories such as Bengalis, Bengali-Muslims, and Bangladeshis have been shaped over the last century in different social, economic, and political circumstances and have interacted "with and upon the roles and functions of the cinema." Raju continues, "So this cinema, by constructing 'Bangladeshi' identity as the one-size-fits-all umbrella for all Bengali Muslims as well as non-Muslims and non-Bengalis living in Bangladesh, worked towards imagining the sense of a Bangladeshi modernity" (3). Historical events such as the Partition of the Indian subcontinent and the Muktijuddho have become points of reference in the region as touchstones against which the magnitude of postcolonial suffering and loss of human life is measured. Literature, memoir, and film in Bangladesh are essential accoutrements to the project of nation building; therefore, it is incumbent to question how national cinema about the liberation struggle—arguably the quintessential theme of national cinema in Bangladesh—has captured and evolved in representations of gender and identity. In turning to films about 1971, a close reading highlights the instability of paternalist postwar nationalism that lies at the heart of nationalist cinema and how in remembering the war and serving as memorials to it, films also retain the ambiguity of the nationalist project.

In a study mapping a comprehensive log of twenty-six full-length films and seven telefilms about the Liberation War set over several decades, Kaberi Gayen (2013) draws on alternative filmmaker Catherine Masud's definition of *national cinema* and its quality as an authentic reflection of a country's tradition, society, history, and culture in all its diversity and richness. Gayen studies these films in both world cinema and Bangladesh national cinema contexts and shows that in most prewar films women appear in marginal, fragmented, and supporting roles. Even though post-independence films have featured women more centrally, the roles in which they are represented are limited. In broad strokes, the abject sexual victimization of women, leading to loss of life (suicide or otherwise) and harm to mental stability, appear to set the stage for most mainstream and even some alternative war cinema.

Nayanika Mookherjee (2015) argues that women's wartime experiences have been memorialized in the public discourse in Bangladesh in certain elite class-coded ways. For instance, while secular Bengali resistance such as women's participation in nationalist song and theater troupes wearing sari and *teep*—a particular aesthetic that was coded as ethnically Bengali yet Muslim—is a source of pride, women's sexual suffering is either instrumentally evoked or metaphorized as the plundering of the motherland. Women speaking about sexual violence in Bangladesh challenges both the aesthetic and political memorializations of the war. Mookherjee documents how the narrative of the *birangona*'s[1] horrific history of rape is told, not forgotten or silenced, even as the complexities of her life story and trauma are occluded from the prevalent discourse of the war. It is not the knowledge of rape that brings social sanction and stigma against women but speaking of it in public. Thus, she calls the suffering of *birangona* women a "public secret."

Although scholarship about film and gender in Bangladesh remains quite thin, most comprehensive studies, Gayen's included, draw on Zahir Raihan's 1970 film *Jibon thekey neya*, one of the first and most critical representations in national cinema. The film is a political satire based on the Bengali Language Movement under the rule of West Pakistan, where an autocratic female lead symbolizes the political dictatorship of Ayub Khan in East Pakistan (now Bangladesh) within a familial setting. A domineering and calculating head of the household, she controls family members—her husband, two brothers, and the servants—reflecting the dynamic of Ayub Khan's rule. The two stories run in parallel. Outside, the people of East Pakistan rise in political protest, and inside, the family members raise their voices against the tyrannical woman. The film is critical in representing the myriad struggles leading up to the Liberation War—labor and language, to name only two. Despite several substantial roles, women appear as either autocratic and conniving or docile and self-sacrificing. Men's and women's roles are also starkly aligned along domestic and public space, and the struggle for power between women is largely over control of the domestic space. Ultimately, the film sets up a negative relationship between women and power where the head of the household—the tyrannical woman—is finally brought to justice in a public court by the oppressed men in the family.

Also in the genre of national cinema, one of the first noteworthy films in the 1970s about the Muktijuddho is *Ora egaro jon* (1972), directed by Chashi Nazrul Islam. This highly successful film is set apart because of its multiple and diverse female characters. The five most significant female characters have a range of roles. Keya is a freedom fighter and the daughter of the leader of the Peace Committee, who kills her father to protect freedom fighters from Pakistani soldiers. She is eventually captured, raped, and killed. Mita is a medical student who cares for wounded freedom fighters. She too is raped and attempts suicide. Sheela is a student who is captured for information and tortured. Shabur Ma is an elderly widow who lost a son in the war. There is also an unnamed village woman who provides care and food to freedom fighters. Even though the film highlights multiple female roles, sexual victimization and suicide in the face of shame remain the prominent themes. In addition, protection of women's honor as well as their rehabilitation are viewed as squarely male responsibilities, and women's suffering and shame are recognized only through validation by men. Even Mita, who is a medical student, deems her contributions to the freedom struggle meaningless by contrast with her romantic partner, a freedom fighter who is seen as the worthy hero. The film raises the question of social recognition and acceptance of *birangona* women at a time when the Bangladesh government was bestowing this title as a recognition of women's suffering and calling for their social integration.

Referring to critical films in the early years after the war, such as *Shongram* (dir. Chashi Nazrul Islam, 1974); *Roktakto Bangla* (dir. Momtaz Ali,

1972); *Joy Bangla* (dir. Fakhrul Alam, 1972); and *Orunodoyer ognishakkhi* (dir. Shubhash Dotto, 1972), Kaberi Gayen (2013) argues that sexual violence against women in film has become a trope. Women's roles are inevitably tied to sacrifice or loss of innocence leading to a loss of respectable place in society. Muktijuddho films were fewer in number in the post-1975 era, during the period of military dictatorships, a time period that Gayen claims produced films less critical of the liberation movement as the ruling regimes tried to alter the nationalist narrative. In the eighties, the influence of Bombay cinema became more pervasive, as dancing and singing sequences featuring women in provocative dress in Pakistani camps added to the sexualization of women. At the same time, Pakistani officers in these films are caricatured as drunk and lascivious. In *Orunodoyer Ognishakkhi*, for instance, Gayen points out that one-third of the film involves rape scenes. This is also one of a handful of films that take up the issue of the war child, as the male protagonist, Anwar Hossain, appeals to the nation to accept the child of rape. Harun ur Rashid's *Megher Onek rong* (1976) again raises the issue of the war child who is returned to his father when his mother commits suicide. Other noteworthy postwar films of this era are Khan Ataur Rahman's *Abaar tora manush ho* (1973) and Narayan Ghosh Mita's *Alor michil* (1974), both depicting the devastation, disappointment, and chaos of the times. In these films as well as the alternative films *Aguner poroshmoni* (dir. Humayun Ahmed, 1994) and *Shorot 71* (dir. Morshedul Islam, 2000), women are squarely returned to the domestic space.

A more recent film, *Guerilla* (dir. Nasiruddin Yusuf Bacchhu, 2011), is the first to center around a woman as a freedom fighter. Winner of the national award, *Guerilla* traces the story of Bilkis Banu, a middle-class Bengali woman through whose increasing involvement and awakening we see the freedom struggle unfolding. The film ends, however, with Bilkis taking her life after she avenges the death of her brother and prevents her own sexual assault by a Pakistani army officer. She succeeds in doing so by igniting a hand grenade and killing both herself and the Pakistani officer. Here the annihilation of woman is seen as preferable to rape, which is perceived as surrender to the oppressor. Throughout the film, we see a play on the title *Guerilla*, where an innocent and docile Bengali woman is capable of acting as an insurgent in the face of personal, community, and national threat. The motif of agency in death and sacrifice is ultimately embraced, while the question of women's place and integration in the independent nation remains unclear.

Feminist scholar Cynthia Enloe (2004, 104) alerts us to the tendency of masculinist discourses of war to generalize women as victims (and men as the militia), which diverts the gaze from exactly the "conditions and decisions" that turned them into casualties in the service of nationalist mobilization. In contrast to Enloe's critique, which posits war as necessarily gendered in its constitution and legacy, Bangladesh film criticism has centered around the portrayal of women as always already victims of war. To focus on the constitution and legacy of war as gendered shows the human agency in such mass atrocities and the frequent failure to fully integrate women in nation building in their aftermath. Ananya Jahanara Kabir (2005, 178) has argued that as a genre, film functions as "testimonial narratives for survivors." In her work on films based on the Partition of the Indian subcontinent, she suggests that films provide a means for narrative integration of traumatic memory and thereby open up possibilities for mourning and reconciliation. To that we might add, drawing on Enloe's analysis, that films can also reconstitute the process by which women are made victims. Kaberi Gayen's (2013) study of representations of women in Muktijuddho films is one such attempt to investigate the role of national films in recuperating, creating, and engendering a sense of national history, as well as the diverse and important roles women have played in it. She posits, in a book commissioned by the Bangladesh Film Archive, that in order to assess whether films about the Muktijuddho present a *shothik dharona* (correct understanding), specifically around women's diverse roles and contributions, one has to ask three critical questions: What social roles do women occupy in Liberation War films? What do these cinematic representations imply about women's place in society? What modes of participation in the liberation struggle are available to women? To this list, I add a fourth question: What are the terms through which subjects can become visible as victims/survivors of violence and agents of the nation?

In the last two decades, key texts and films have appeared that disrupt earlier narratives of suffering and bereavement and have begun to lay out a response to these questions surrounding Bangladeshi women's varied experiences of the 1971 War of Liberation.[2] Tahmima Anam's novels *A Golden Age* (2007) and its sequel, *The Good Muslim* (2011), Shaheen Akhtar's novel *The Search* (2011), Bina D'Costa's *Nationbuilding, Gender and War Crimes in South Asia* (2010), Nayanika Mookherjee's *The Spectral Wound: Sexual Violence, Public Memories, and the Bangladesh War of 1971* (2015), Yasmin Saikia's *Women, War, and the Making of Bangladesh: Remembering 1971* (2011), Tareque and Catherine Masud's films, Nasiruddin Yusuf's film *Guerilla* (2011), Shameem Akhtar's *Itihaash konna* (1999), Munsur Ali's *Shongram 71* (2014), and Rubaiyat Hossain's *Meherjaan* (2011) are contributing to a newer genre of cultural production. They challenge a number of cherished and inherited "truths" regarding the Bangladesh War of Liberation in 1971 while illuminating this history from a Bangladeshi point of view, particularly in a transnational frame.[3] Many of these texts debunk a number of national myths that have shaped the consciousness of the post-1971 nation of Bangladesh. The abundance of literature generated in Bangladesh about the war has remembered it as a triumphant narrative of masculinist liberation, by and large through stories of male valor and female victimization. Female characters are depicted as sacrificing mothers or rape victims who are often silent about their experiences and commit suicide or are otherwise killed off. Thus, women's wartime experiences and struggles in these narratives have not only been invisibilized but also reduced to sexual victimization, relegated to "the private sphere and . . . dealt with as private matters by the victims' families often solely by the victim who hides in shame" (Saikia 2011, 54).[4] In contrast, the texts mentioned above prioritize women's narratives as the primary vehicle for reconstructing this forgotten history. The female characters in these films are agentic and project what Janelle Hobson (2008, 232) calls "embodied resistance." In challenging women's representations, these films push against masculinist visions of national cinema and open the door to a more diverse scope for the genre as part of a larger movement—beyond the national, even regional and into the global—for human rights advocacy and political justice.

SHAMEEM AKHTAR'S *ITIHAASH KONNA* (1999)

Shameem Akhtar's 1999 art film *Itahaash konna* provides a counternarrative to more traditional masculine and nationalist-centric representations of the Muktijuddho by emphasizing a "reckoning" with the "Other," not necessarily at the state or juridical level but through interpersonal relationships. Notably, Akthar is one of the few women directors in Bangladeshi cinema, and the film's activist impulse is clear in its choice of prominent cultural activists as actors. Moreover, the explicit intent of the film as showcased through an interview with a woman survivor of war is to frame itself as a tool for mobilizing a campaign to address the atrocities of the 1971 genocide, bringing perpetrators to justice and offering healing and closure to victims. In calling for justice, Akhtar's film deploys an affective lens that underpins the notions of intimate histories, empathy, and friendship with the Other, namely a Pakistani citizen with ties to Bangladesh and a war child. The film opens up a conversation about a different self-Other relationship between the divided people of South Asia by bypassing recognizable visual representation of mass atrocities committed by the Pakistani army—often routine in the Muktujuddho cinema genre, which habituates audiences to such recognizable cues—and averting the arc of retributive violence. It is more interested in a human encounter where the self-Other relation generates not hostility but an obligation of care and reconciliation. *Itihaash konna* consciously attempts to broaden the scope of reconstructing and remembering 1971 beyond the borders of Bangladesh and to reestablish the intertwined history of the region.

One of the few films about the Muktijuddho directed by a woman and foregrounding the standpoint of women of divergent sides in the war, *Itihaash konna* deals with genocide, rape, and war children through the lens of moral reckoning and responsibility on either side. This reckoning is explored through a long and beleaguered friendship between a Bengali woman and a Pakistani woman, Monika (Rahnuma Ahmed) and Lalarukh (Sara Zaker). The intertwined histories of the two nations are reflected in the intimate relationship, which is severed at the bloody birth of Bangladesh. Monika was born in Rawalpindi, West Pakistan, and Lalarukh in Dhaka, East Pakistan. They studied together in Dhaka until Lalarukh's family left for West Pakistan in March of 1971, days prior to Operation Searchlight, the first massive and brutal strike by the West Pakistan Army against Bengali civilians. The campus of the largest public university in Bangladesh was especially affected by these strikes, which targeted academics and students, particularly from the Hindu minority.

Many years after the independence of Bangladesh, the two friends reacquaint as adults and activists in a seminar on genocide in London. Thereafter, Lalarukh comes to Dhaka twenty-eight years after leaving to conduct research and is hosted by Monika—who is archiving an Oral History Project about the women survivors of the war—and Monika's father (Abul Khair) and niece Ananya (Nasrin Siraj). Lalarukh expresses her noble objective to a stoic Monika: "I intend to work for an apology [at the state level]." Monika is skeptical of Lalarukh's intention to learn about war-affected families in a brief one-week visit and is hesitant to rekindle their friendship. One scene depicts the two seated on Monika's bed. Monika looks fatigued, bearing the weight of the war's devastation. Lalarukh probes, "I want to know everything. I have a personal stake in this." Earlier, Lalarukh insisted that she had a right to return to this land because her mother was Bengali. A stubborn Monika responded, "Two people can have totally different experiences of a war. These distinct experiences can change a relationship forever." Monika presses her friend about the silence from Pakistanis at the atrocities committed during 1971. Lalarukh tries to defend her position by touting propaganda from the government in that period about Bengalis dancing to the tune of India and acting as separatists. Her family was in the dark, claims Lalarukh, given the news blackout about what was happening in East Pakistan. Monika reminds her of the international movement on behalf of Bangladesh liberation as she admonishes Lalarukh about her silence and complicity.

Lalarukh is further confounded by an unspoken coldness from her friend's family members. The once lively house she used to visit in her childhood seems to be shrouded in gloom. Monika's father, Nanu (an affectionate term for a maternal grandfather), refuses to meet Lalarukh face to face even though he ensures proper hospitality for the guest. The silence is finally broken when the family sits down together for a feast on the day of Lalarukh's departure for Pakistan. Once again, Monika and Lalarukh are debating the merit of an apology from the Pakistan state and acknowledgment of war crimes, when Nanu directly confronts Lalarukh. He asks whether she would forgive the rape of her own sixteen-year-old daughter. "If she is raped, would you be able to forgive [the rapist]?" Lalarukh lowers her eyes and admits, "No." She adds, "But I would want a trial and punishment for the perpetrator." Nanu responds, "What about the victim? How would justice be served for them?" The confrontation leads to Nanu's revelation that Ananya, the daughter of his younger daughter Konika, is a child of rape. During the war thousands of women and girls were tortured in rape camps and army barracks. Rape was deployed as a weapon of war to subdue the Bengali-speaking Muslim majority and the Hindu minority of Bangladesh. Konika committed suicide months after Ananya's birth. Konok Khala (Bonna Lohani), who raised Ananya was held captive in the same rape camp set up by the Pakistani army. A member of the Hindu community, Konok's entire family was massacred in 1971.

As the other characters debate whether a national apology for war crimes would be meaningful, Konok quietly exits the room. By accepting the child that the state rejects, the family unit provides a challenge to the state's nationalist emphasis on "purity" and rejection of what it considers the Other. An irreconcilable conflict was institutionalized as a founding violence of the nation, an original trauma, when "war babies" were declared tainted and ejected from the nation (the womb) by state-sponsored postwar policies of abortion or foreign adoption. Unlike the state, however, the family unquestioningly accepts Ananya as their own. In the scene where this reckoning takes place, Konok nevertheless quietly leaves the room. Thus at the moment of reckoning this film poses an impasse: while the war child grapples with her belonging to the family and nation, the *birangona* exits the frame. The exit from the gathering and the frame of the *birangona* at this critical scene reemphasize the question of acceptance and justice for the victims of sexual violence, a question that remains largely unresolved and ignored in postwar social and political discourses.

Rather than assigning Ananya to the periphery, the film simultaneously develops the conflicted relationships between the three women as representative of the historical conflict between woman and nation. At their first meeting, when Lalarukh introduces herself as a foreigner (*bideshi*), Ananya corrects her by saying, "Not a foreigner, a Pakistani"—hinting at the intimacy to her identity, as the two nations were once one. Ananya becomes Lalarukh's guide and research assistant during her stay, taking her on a tour of the various war memorials and museums in the city. Lalarukh is left overwhelmed by the intensity and enormity of the atrocities and consequent losses. Ananya comforts her, and in turn Lalarukh urges her to address her as *tumi*—the less formal version of the pronoun *you* reserved for friends. Ananya ponders the request and says, "It will take time."

Ananya's brief association with Lalarukh leads to a different kind of reckoning between the younger woman and her older aunt, Monika. It is as though Monika comes to see Ananya in a new light, transformed into her own person. "You've grown up; I've never heard you speak like this," says Monika when Ananya raises the question of the somber household and the lack of festivities there. She asks her aunt about her childhood friendship with Lalarukh, when everything was different and more exuberant—the house, Nanu, Monika. Lalarukh's arrival leads to the opening of a pandora's box of memories, breaking the silence in the house and taking steps toward healing. The hatred of the Other was institutionalized through state-led policies of abortion and foreign adoption of war babies in order to erase the "enemy." But the intimate domestic sphere through which this film is framed rejects those masculinist war narratives and offers us a feminine revisioning of the relationships between three women, opening new possibilities for how we understand the complex histories they represent.

Lalarukh's return to Bangladesh stirs up repressed emotions, opens old wounds, and instigates an intimate as well as political reckoning across time, space, and history. Nanu confronts Lalarukh about her quest for "justice" and asks whether the victims of 1971 will be appeased by it. Following this encounter, he takes out a dusty old picture of his daughter and places it on the bureau. He is finally able to display the photo of his dead daughter and face that painful history. Ananya comes to terms with the story of her birth and the realization that it is inextricably interwoven with the individual and collective journeys of Monika and Lalarukh. Following her departure from Bangladesh, Lalarukh writes a letter to Monika from Pakistan admitting her and her family's complicity by not speaking up against the atrocities of 1971. Ananya continues to work on the Oral History Project with Lalarukh and Monika, becoming the bridge between the women separated by the burden of historical conflict. Monika begins to look at Ananya in a new light, and both women come to a realization of their shared struggle. Lalarukh leaves with a heavy heart, asking Monika and her family to "take care of Ananya." The question of women survivors may remain incomplete, yet the healing begins with them. Akhtar's film provides an opportunity to read the complex machinations of gender, nation, and patriarchy, particularly as they operate between women of opposing national contexts, while exploring both the limits and possibilities of solidarity.

MUNSUR ALI'S *SHONGRAM 71* (2014)

British Bangladeshi filmmaker Munsur Ali's *Shongram 71* urges viewers to grapple with questions of identity, culture, and history from a retrospective postcolonial framework. Like *Itihaash konna*, *Shongram 71* situates the independence struggle of Bangladesh beyond its national borders and through intimate relationships between self and a perceived Other (Bengali Muslim and Hindu communities). The film is framed through the memories of Karim (Anupam Kher). Karim is the son of a freedom fighter who grew up in Bengal and fought in the anticolonial struggle in India. Karim is also a *muktijoddha* (freedom fighter) who fought for the liberation of Bangladesh and now lies in a London hospital reminiscing to a British journalist about a forgotten genocide. His adopted son, a war child, listens as his dying father relates the story of the violent birth of Bangladesh and the unresolved questions of loss, responsibility, and reckoning. The Muktijuddho, at the outset, is framed within the long trajectory of antinationalist struggle in a continuum with the first Partition of the Indian subcontinent in 1947. This helps situate the war not only as a national struggle for independence but with regional and global roots and consequences.

Karim (played as a young man by Amaan Reza) grew up in the village of Lalghat near the India-Bangladesh border. The relationship between Jalaluddin, Karim's father, and Suraj (Shubrodho), his friend and comrade in the nationalist struggle, epitomizes the pluralist culture of the community, where Hindu and Muslim communities live side by side and share the political dream of an independent Bangladesh. They quote Tagore's anti-colonial and nationalist poetry and sing Nazrul's revolutionary songs. Their children play together. Gradually, however, a wedge is driven into this harmonious coexistence. While Karim, an East Pakistani Muslim, believes that the West Pakistan Army will not harm them because they are of the same nation, Asha (Dilruba Yasmeen Ruhee), Karim's Hindu love interest, reminds him, "They are *your* brothers; we are Hindu." When Asha, wearing a sari and the dot on the forehead that marks both Bengali and Hindu culture, and Karim are stopped by the army officers, they are warned, "Kaffir jaise kapra, sir pe bindi—fir na dekhu" (Do not dress like the infidel).

"You are a Bengali, not a Pakistani," says Major Iftikhar (Arman Parvez Murad) of the West Pakistan Army to Jalaluddin, and the latter responds by reminding the major that Bengali and Pakistani should not be seen as mutually exclusive, that one is an ethnic identity and the other a national identity. "Governments can come and go, but they cannot change my history; I am Bengali and nothing can change that." In another scene, Iftikhar tells Nath, owner of the local tea shop, "If you had learned to speak Urdu, we could have lived together." He asserts Urdu as the authentic language of the Muslims in the subcontinent. Nath responds in indignation, "Does everyone speak Urdu in Pakistan? The Qur'an is written in Arabic, not Urdu. Bengali is the language of this land."

The revolutionary struggle of the village community is brutally suppressed by the Pakistani army aided by Bengali Muslim *razakar*s (collaborators with the Pakistani army). Asha's family tries to cross the border to India but is captured on the way. Asha is raped by Major Iftikhar and manages to escape with the help of a sympathetic Pakistani soldier. She and her father find shelter in a refugee camp across the Indian border. Karim joins the guerrilla resistance and promises to avenge the deaths of his parents and brother Altaf (Ananta Hira) at the hands of the Pakistanis. His transformation into a freedom fighter is complete when he realizes, "You have to fight for the right to call it [Bangladesh] your country," thereby taking on the struggle of his father, Jalaluddin, and his surrogate uncle Suraj and martyred brother. Finally, with the help of the Indian Army, Bengalis win the war. The film uses historical footage from NBC News of Sheikh Mujibur Rahman's historic declaration of the freedom struggle on March 7, Ziaur Rahman's declaration of independence on March 26, and the Pakistani army's submission to joint Indian-Bangladeshi forces on December 16.

"The war is over, but are we free? How do you win what is your own right to begin with?" ponders Karim as he boards a bus to India in search of his beloved Asha. He finally locates her, but his dream is shattered when he sees the *sindoor* on Asha's forehead signifying her marriage to Rohit. Karim's premonition of the ambiguity of freedom is reflected in the scene where he and Asha stand side by side, hand in hand behind the iron bars of an open terrace. Asha recounts her painful story of crossing over to India, finding herself pregnant with Iftikhar's child, and giving birth to a son who only brought her sadness and hurt. She leaves the child at an orphanage. When they hear the news that everyone in their village has been killed, Suraj arranges her marriage to Rohit. "No one is to blame," she tells Karim tearfully.

The final scenes of the film show Karim bidding goodbye to Asha and embracing her son at the orphanage. Taking responsibility means sacrificing his love for Asha and raising the child whose biological father he killed. His story finally recorded by the journalist Sarah Myles (Asia Argento) in London, Karim breathes his last breath. Sarah, however, is unsuccessful in convincing her editor to publish the story of this forgotten genocide. Her report is tossed in the wastebasket by her cynical editor, who concludes, "No one gives a shit."

Munsur Ali's *Shongram 71* is an important contemporary film to consider for a number of reasons. First, it locates the struggle for Bangladeshi independence within the long trajectory of British and West Pakistani colonization, as opposed to continuing the more conventional understanding of it as a civil war in the region. Second, it draws attention to a forgotten struggle for self-determination through its setting in the international arena as opposed to a strictly national one in Bangladesh. Third, it contributes to the growing and critical genre of Bangladesh national cinema within a world cinema context. Fourth, it fosters critical understanding of war's impact through interpersonal and intimate relationships as opposed to presenting the conflict as a collective uprising—which of course it was, but a singular focus on collective resistance can obscure moments of interpersonal healing and transformation. The latter clearly is important, but less attention is frequently given to questions of trauma, healing, and responsibility alongside political justice in postconflict situations. The story has appeal for postwar generations, as it addresses the unresolved questions of identity, gender, culture, and healing. It pushes our thinking beyond nationalistic binaries through its emphasis on the ambiguities of survival, as well as the ongoing legacies and consequences of historical events such as Partition and the Muktijuddho on everyday human relationships.

RUBAIYAT HOSSAIN'S *MEHERJAAN* (2011)

Intimacy with the Other, transnationalism, and women-centered narratives are perhaps nowhere more centrally represented than in Rubaiyat Hossain's controversial film, *Meherjaan*. Hossain describes her debut feature film, *Meherjaan*, as a "women's 'feminine' re-visiting of the Bangladesh national liberation" and as a story of "loving the Other that advocates an aesthetic solution to violence" (*Meherjaan* press kit 2011). The film narrates the intertwined stories of four women: Sarah (Nasima Selim), a war child searching for the truth about her past and her mother; Neela (Reetu Sattar), who was captured, raped, and tortured by the Pakistani army in 1971; Meher (Jaya Bachchan), Neela's cousin, who was only seventeen during the war, when she fell in love with Wasim Khan (Omar Rahim), a renegade Pakistani soldier; and Salma (performed by the director, Rubaiyat Hossain), another war child born during the first Partition of the Indian subcontinent. Sarah comes to Bangladesh to search for Meher, and the adolescent Meher (Shaina Amin) becomes the lens through which the story is unraveled in flashbacks.

The film *Meherjaan* was deliberately promoted as a three-nation film featuring Bangladeshi, Indian, and Pakistani actors and musicians. The film is shot in Bangladesh, the ghazal of Urdu poet Faiz Ahmed Faiz is sung by Pakistani veteran singer Nayyara Noor, the background music is composed by Indian music director Neil Mukherjee, and it features Lalon Shah's mystic songs from Bangladesh. The actors were selected from the three countries of the subcontinent and contribute to what the press kit for the film called a "symbolic gesture to initiate a process of creative collaboration across the South Asia region."

Like Shameem Akhtar, Hossain emphasizes a reckoning with the Other, again not at the state or juridical level but through interpersonal relationships. In *Meherjaan*, the war baby—given up to adoption—returns to find her place in the nation, whereas in *Shongram 71* the baby is embraced by a freedom fighter. At the end of *Shongram 71*, however, we see the child, now a grown man, sitting at the foot of his father's hospital bed in London—a scene which hints that the freedom fighter emigrated from Bangladesh with his adopted son, perhaps because they were not welcome as citizens of independent Bangladesh. In *Meherjaan*, it is noteworthy that the arrival of the war child Sarah leads to Meher, her aunt, reminiscing, revisiting the trauma, and taking steps toward mutual healing. "If she had not come, this story would never have been told," says Meher. Unlike the state that rejected the war children, Meher unquestioningly accepts Sarah as family, inviting her to stay at her home without hesitation. The two then reckon with the past, begin to heal, even as they forge a kind of bonding.

Both *Meherjaan* and *Itihaash konna* reimagine the "feminine sphere" or domestic space as a place that facilitates the relationships necessary for coming to grips with the past. Most of the scenes depicting the encounter between Meher and Sarah are staged in Meher's present-day home, as they face each other in dialogue. The films use everyday domestic objects, books, newspapers, and art to facilitate the connections between the characters. Meher's healing is intertwined with Sarah's, as Meher finally faces her pain and her past and gives them expression in the form of a wood sculpture she chisels: "Two human forms encircling into each other's body. Their forms mingling, embracing each other. Creating a new form. Loving the Other." The sculpture reflects pieces of all of the women—Sarah, Meher, Neela, and Salma. While Meher and Wasim Khan's union is considered impossible by the family, community, and nation, the second (im)possible union in the film is still possible, but fleetingly. Sarah, "the passionate nomad," having found answers to her past, leaves again, but not before securing a familial bond. Similarly, after Lalarukh's departure in *Itihaash konna*, Nanu takes out his deceased daughter's photograph from the back of a bureau, wipes it clean, and puts it on display. Additionally, In *Shongram 71*, Karim, devasted by the loss to the war of his family, his beloved, and his innocence, learns a just responsibility in choosing to embrace the war baby born to Asha. This too is a reckoning with the legacy of war and the inextricable histories of the region: the baby raised by a freedom fighter who happened to take the life of his biological father, a soldier from the opposing side. In all three films, the body is a site of intervention. The photograph invoking the physical body of Konika, and the sculpture displayed in the home, as well as the physical body of Karim's adopted son at the foot of his bed, all serve to transform domestic spaces into a healing place of acceptance of the humanity of the Other.

CONCLUSION

Essential to the project of nation building, national cinema historically has deployed a particular gender ideology of male honor and female shame; however, key films in this genre also attempted to probe and pry open these difficult questions. In addition to creating an alternative archive of 1971 with complex and diverse gender representation, together these newer genre films explore the possibility of healing and reconciliation within the realm of intimate and interpersonal relations. Returning to the three questions about women's roles in war films, what these films together urge is a revisioning. In *Meherjaan* and *Itihaash konna* the directors enable a woman-centered vision of healing and reconciliation. *Meherjaan* and *Itihaash Konna* prioritize women's narratives as the primary vehicle for reconstructing this normalized circulation of women's history. In *Shongram 71*, a Hindu woman is the *birangona* whose progeny, a child of war, symbolizes the hope of rehabilitating a devastated *muktijoddha* (freedom fighter). Nevertheless, this same *birangona* of *Shongram 71* cannot return to her village in an independent Bangladesh with Karim. A woman's reintegration and location within the nation—outside of a heteropatriarchal union—is thus once again left ambiguous.

Jennifer Nash (2008) reminds us that Black feminism has functioned as a "critical social theory" in its engagement with visual culture, with the (re) production of what Patricia Hill Collins terms "controlling images," which Nash defines as "dominant representations that produce and entrench racial-sexual mythologies." The social purpose served by controlling images is "to provide a justification for the state's continued disciplining of the black female body." It is a useful term to deploy in the case of *birangonas*, where arguably controlling images of the *birangonas* illustrate the ideological power of these images in securing conceptions of their sexual subjugation and erasure from full citizenship. Like the regulation of the Black female body by the state, ultimately, the regulation of the *birangonas* has also rendered them to a public site of struggle, "a space onto which social debates and collective anxieties about morality, religion, policy and the state are inscribed" (Nash 2008, 97). This representation becomes normative rather than analytical and comes at the expense of women's sexual agency, heterogeneity, multiplicity, and diversity. Against such normative production, Nash urges feminist scholars to ask how objectification is mobilized in specific historical contexts and what could be alternative reading practices—a representational space for women to view themselves and each other as sexual subjects, as citizens.

Finally, I return again to the question, What are the terms through which subjects can become legible/visible as victims/survivors of violence and agents of nation? At the very least, the films under discussion in this chapter attempt in small ways to redirect our conversation from paternalist nationalism to fragmented but layered understanding of healing, the intricate and intimate relations within nations, communities, and individuals in the subcontinent torn asunder by colonial violence and nationalist upheavals. These films also gesture toward a critical aspiration toward healing and reconciliation even if within the interpersonal realm. To borrow a term from Rubaiyat Hossain, these are attempts at "feminine revisioning" of or ethical reckoning with masculinist narrations of war, nationalism, and agency.

NOTES

1 The word *birangona* means "brave woman" or "war heroine." Following independence, the honorific *birangona* was bestowed on the survivors of sexual violence by the government of Bangladesh to honor the women for their role in the freedom struggle. The label frequently served to further ostracize the women, as reintegration into society remained incomplete.

2 The Partition of British India in 1947 created the two new nation-states of India and Pakistan. Pakistan was formed along religious lines, as the two most populous Muslim regions of the subcontinent became its western and eastern wings. The eastern wing of the new Islamic state of Pakistan suffered under the political, cultural, and economic domination of West Pakistan until March 1971, when political discontent and cultural nationalism led to a military assault by the West Pakistan Army and the declaration of East Pakistan's independence and renaming as Bangladesh. The independence war of Bangladesh was ultimately supported by India. In December 1971 Bangladesh became an independent nation after a nine-month-long war. The lesser known history of the second Partition of the subcontinent can be found in D'Costa (2010).

3 In Pakistan, the Bangladesh Liberation War is often erased as a shameful past. In India, it is subsumed under the better known "Indo-Pak" war, in which India plays the heroic role in bringing liberation to the Bengalis. In the fields of genocide and trauma studies, very few know or discuss this history from the Bangladeshi point of view.

4 Numbers are contested with regard to the genocide in East Pakistan in 1971. Reportedly, 1–3 million lives were lost, 200,000–400,000 women were victims of sexual violence, and 25,000 forced pregnancies occurred during the war. Women were kept and tortured in army barracks for extended periods of time.

REFERENCES

Akhtar, Shameem, dir. 1999. *Itihaash Konna*. Dhaka, Bangladesh: Mrittika Productions.

Ali, Munsr, dir. 2014. *Shongram 71*. United Kingdom: Spotlight UK.

Chowdhury, Elora Halim. 2012. "Debunking 'Truths' Claiming Justice: Reflections on Yasmin Saikia's Women War and the Making of Bangladesh: Remembering 1971." *Human Rights Quarterly* 34, no. 4: 1201–11.

Daiya, Kavita. 2008. *Violent Belongings: Partition, Gender, and National Culture in Postcolonial India*. Philadelphia: Temple University Press.

D'Costa, Bina. 2010. *Nationbuilding Gender and War Crimes in South Asia*. New York: Routledge.

Enloe, Cynthia. 2004. *The Curious Feminist: Searching for Women in a New Age of Empire*. Berkeley: University of California Press.

Gayen, Kaberi. 2013. *Construction of Women in the War Films of Bangladesh (Muktijuddher Cholochchitre Naree Nirman)*. Dhaka: Bengal Publications.

Hobson, Janelle. 2008. "Militarizing Women in Film: Toward a Cinematic Framing of War and Terror." In *Security Disarmed: Perspectives on Gender, Race, and Militarization*, edited by Barbara Sutton, Sandra Morgen, and Julie Novkov, 231–43. New Brunswick, NJ: Rutgers University Press.

Hossain, Rubaiyat, dir. 2011. *Meherjaan*. Dhaka, Bangladesh: Era Motion Picture.

Kabir, Ananya Jahanara. 2005. "Gender, Memory, Trauma: Women's Novels on the Partition of India." *Comparative Studies of South Asia, Africa and the Middle East* 25: 177–90.

Meherjaan press kit. 2011. http://rubaiyat-hossain.com/meherjaan/.

Mookherjee, Nayanika. 2015. *The Spectral Wound: Sexual Violence, Public Memories, and the Bangladesh War of 1971*. Durham: Duke University Press.

Nash, Jennifer. 2008. "Strange Bedfellows: Black Feminism and Antipornography Feminism." *Social Text* 97, no. 25: 51–77.

Raju, Zakir Hossain. 2015. *Bangladesh Cinema and National Identity: In Search of the Modern?* London: Routledge.

Saikia, Yasmin. 2011. *Women, War, and the Making of Bangladesh: Remembering 1971*. Durham: Duke University Press.

CONTRIBUTORS

FAHMIDA AKHTER is an associate professor in the Department of Drama and Dramatics at Jahangirnagar University, Bangladesh. She holds a PhD in film studies from the University of Essex, having received a Commonwealth Scholarship. Her main research and teaching area is film studies, with particular interests in Bangladeshi cinema and women and war in Bangladeshi films. Her articles on Bangladeshi cinema have been published in *South Asian Popular Culture Journal* (2015), *Bangladesh Film Archive Journal* (2015, 2014, 2013, 2012), *Journals of the Asiatic Society of Bangladesh* (2014), and *Shilpakala* (2014). Besides teaching, Fahmida works as a documentary film director.

KAMRAN ASDAR ALI is professor of anthropology at the University of Texas, Austin. He is author of *Planning the Family in Egypt: New Bodies, New Selves* (University of Texas Press, 2002) and coeditor of *Gendering Urban Space in the Middle East, South Asia and Africa* (Palgrave, 2008), *Comparing Cities: Middle East and South Asia* (Oxford University Press, 2009), and *Gender, Politics, and Performance in South Asia* (Oxford University Press, 2015). He has published several articles on issues of health and gender in Egypt and on ethnicity, class politics, sexuality, and popular culture in Pakistan. His most recent book is *Communism in Pakistan: Politics and Class Activism, 1947–1972* (I. B. Tauris, 2015). On leave from University of Texas, he is currently dean of the School of Humanities and Social Sciences at Lahore University of Management Sciences (LUMS), Pakistan.

HARIPRASAD ATHANICKAL teaches in the Department of Film Studies at the English and Foreign Languages University, Hyderabad, India. His main interest is South Asian film history, and he has carried out research on South Indian cinemas, in particular Malayalam and Tamil film industries. He works on popular cinema and its political manifestations. He has published in journals in both Malayalam and English, and he has contributed to various edited collections in English, most recently *Salaam Bollywood: Representations and Interpretations* (Routledge, 2019) and the *Journal of Literature and Aesthetics*. He is the recipient of a University Grants Commission (UGC) Research Award (2014), to study the topic of searching for an authentic space in South Indian cinema, and a German Academic Exchange Programme (DAAD) fellowship (2011) to teach at the Technical University, Dresden

KABITA CHAKMA is an architect and independent researcher. Involved in community work, Kabita is also a coordinator of the Chittagong Hill Tracts Indigenous Jumma Association Australia (CHTIJAA) and a community adviser to the Benevolent Organisation for Development, Health and Insight (BODHI), a charity organization in Australia. Kabita's research interests include the history, literature, art, architecture, and cinema of disadvantaged communities, particularly indigenous peoples of the CHT, and environmental sustainability.

ELORA HALIM CHOWDHURY is professor of women's, gender, and sexuality studies at the University of Massachusetts, Boston. Her teaching and research interests include transnational feminisms, critical development studies, gender violence and human rights advocacy, narrative, and film with an emphasis on South Asia. She is the author of *Transnationalism Reversed: Women Organizing against Gendered Violence in Bangladesh* (SUNY Press, 2011), which was awarded the National Women's Studies Association Gloria E. Anzaldúa book prize in 2012; and coeditor of *Dissident Friendships: Feminism, Imperialism and Transnational Solidarity* (with Liz Philipose; University of Illinois Press, 2016) and *Interdisciplinary Approaches to Human Rights: History, Politics, Practice* (with Rajini Srikanth; Routledge, 2018). She is currently writing a book titled *Ethical Reckoning: Gender, Vulnerability, and Agency in Bangladeshi Muktijuddho Cinema*. Elora serves as a series editor for the Dissident Feminisms book series at the University of Illinois Press.

ESHA NIYOGI DE's current research interests lie in cross-border studies of South Asia. Based on research funded by the Fulbright Foundation and the UCLA School of Humanities, she is currently writing a book titled *Women's Transborder Cinema: Female Authors and Familial Modes across South Asia*, which studies gender politics in the roles taken by women directors and producers in the film industries of Pakistan, India, and Bangladesh. Her previous publications include *Empire, Media, and the Autonomous Woman* (Oxford University Press, 2011) and the coedited volume *Trans-status Subjects: Gender in the Globalization of South and Southeast Asia* (Duke University Press, 2002). Her research has appeared in leading international journals such as *Screen*, *diacritics*, and *Feminist Media Studies* and in many scholarly volumes. She serves on the Fulbright Senior Scholars Review Committee for South and Central Asia and the International Scientific Advisory Board of the Freiburg Institute for Advanced Studies, University of Freiburg, Germany (Pakistan studies referee). She teaches at the University of California, Los Angeles.

ZEBUNNISA HAMID is an assistant professor of film studies in the Department of Humanities and Social Sciences at Lahore University of Management Sciences (LUMS), Pakistan. She completed her PhD in film studies at SOAS, University of London, in 2017. She has a master's in journalism from Goldsmiths, University of London, and a bachelor's from New York University. In her dissertation, Zebunnisa focused on the developing industry, imaginaries, and transnational characteristics of New Pakistani Cinema. Her research interests lie in gender and the crisis of masculinity, the transnational city and urban spaces on screen, and the industries of small cinemas, which she brings together in her concept of the transnational cinematic city. She is currently working on a book on New Pakistani Cinema and is also on the Screen Worlds Advisory Board, an ERC-funded project led by Dr. Lindiwe Dovey at SOAS. Zebunnisa trained as a film editor at the Edit Center in New York and worked as a production consultant on Mira Nair's film *The Reluctant Fundamentalist* (2012). She has also served on Pakistan's Oscar committee to select the country's official submission for the International Feature Film Award category at the Academy Awards.

FAHMIDUL HAQ is visiting research professor of film and television at the University of Notre Dame. He has authored and edited ten books, mostly in Bengali. His international titles are being published by Routledge, Intellect, and Lapland University Press. His current book project, forthcoming from Intellect, deals with identity politics in cinema. He has taught in the Department of Mass Communication and Journalism, University of Dhaka, Bangladesh, for nearly two decades.

GLEN HILL is associate professor of architecture, design, and planning at the University of Sydney. He is the past head of the Architecture Discipline and past director of the Master of Architecture Program. His research interests include philosophical and design-related aspects of social and environmental sustainability. He is particularly interested in architectural design as an expanded practice, including its implications and potential benefits for indigenous and disadvantaged communities.

LOTTE HOEK is a media anthropologist based at the University of Edinburgh. Her ethnographic research explores the nature of the cinema at the end and edges of film in South Asia. She is author of *Cut-Pieces: Celluloid Obscenity and Popular Cinema in Bangladesh* (Columbia University Press, 2014; winner of the Bernard S. Cohn book prize) and coeditor of the journal *BioScope: South Asian Screen Studies.*

NAADIR JUNAID is professor of mass communication and journalism at the University of Dhaka, Bangladesh, where he teaches media studies and film. He has a PhD in film studies from the University of New South Wales, Sydney, and a master's in film studies from King's College, University of London. He has published articles and book chapters in Bangla and English on film theory, art cinema, and socially conscious films. He is author of four Bangla books on global political cinema, Bangladeshi unconventional films, and politically committed films of the famous Bengali directors Satyajit Ray, Ritwik Ghatak, and Mrinal Sen.

GWENDOLYN S. KIRK is an assistant professor in the Gurmani Centre for Languages and Literature at Lahore University of Management Sciences (LUMS), Pakistan. A linguistic anthropologist by training, she is interested in the intersection of language, performance, aesthetics, and visual culture. She is currently working on a book detailing her ethnographic research in the Punjabi cinema industry in Pakistan, and her other published works deal with a variety of topics in Pakistani film, television, and visual culture. Her other scholarly interests include language pedagogy, Punjabi dialectology, and language shift.

ALKA KURIAN is a senior lecturer at the University of Washington, Bothell, where she teaches postcolonial film and literature, gender studies, and human rights. Alka is author of *Narratives of Gendered Dissent in South Asian Cinemas* (Routledge, 2012) and coeditor of *New Feminisms in South Asia: Disrupting the Discourse through Social Media, Film and Literature* (Routledge, 2017). Alka has published book chapters on South Asian film and was the founder and coeditor of the peer-reviewed journal *Studies in South Asian Film and Media*. She is a board member of Tasveer (https://tasveerseattle.org), a South Asian film and art nonprofit, for which she has been volunteering since 2007.

MADHUJA MUKHERJEE is associate professor of film studies at Jadavpur University, Kolkata, India. Her primary research is on the history of the Indian film industry and historiography; she focuses on public cultures, technological transformations, techniques, authors, genre, and gender. She is author of *New Theatres Ltd.* (NFAI, 2009) and editor of *Aural Films, Oral Cultures* (JU Press, 2012) and *Voices of the Talking Stars* (Sage/Stree, 2017), which received the award for Excellence in Writing at the 19th Mumbai Film Festival (2017). Currently, she is coediting two anthologies, *Popular Cinema in Bengal* and *Networks of Cinemas of India*.

AMIT RANJAN is a visiting research fellow at the Institute of South Asian Studies, National University of Singapore. He is author of numerous articles in journals on South Asia. His forthcoming books include *India-Bangladesh Boundary Disputes: History and Post-LBA Dynamics* (Springer) and an edited volume, *Partition of India: Postcolonial Legacies* (Routledge). He holds a PhD from Jawaharlal Nehru University, India.

NASREEN REHMAN, an award-winning screenplay writer, has worked with directors Yash Chopra, Mehreen Jabbar, and Deepa Mehta. Her book, based on her PhD dissertation "A History of the Cinema in Lahore, c. 1919–1947: An Exploration of the Political Economy of Love," supervised by C. A. Bayly at the University of Cambridge, is in press. Her translation of Shaukat Kaifi's memoir, *Kaifi and I* (Zubaan Books, 2010), remains a best seller. Nasreen's translations of Saadat Hasan Manto's short stories from Bombay and Poona were published in 2019 by Aleph. She teaches at the School of Visual Arts and Aesthetics at Beaconhouse University Lahore.

INDEX

B

G

N

O

P

Q

R

T

U

CPSIA information can be obtained
at www.ICGtesting.com
Printed in the USA
BVHW081554291120
594241BV00002B/4

9 780295 747859